D0982188

Tokyo

"All you've got to do is decide to go
and the hardest part is over.

So go!"

TONY WHEELER, COFOUNDER – LONELY PLANET

THIS EDITION WRITTEN AND RESEARCHED BY

**Timothy Hornyak,
Rebecca Milner**

Contents

Plan Your Trip 4

Explore Tokyo 54

Understand Tokyo 217

Survival Guide 251

Tokyo Maps 284

Left: Gusokku-style armour at Tokyo National Museum (p158)
Above: The Nijū-bashi bridge at the Imperial Palace (p60)
Right: Dining in Yūrakuchō Yakitori Alley (p72)

Welcome to Tokyo

Yoking past and future, Tokyo dazzles with its traditional culture and passion for everything new.

You've Never Had Sushi Like This

Tokyo brims with astonishing cuisine. It out-Michelins every city in the world, and for good reason: Tokyoites take fresh ingredients, dining and service very seriously. Whether you're inhaling a thick bowl of miso *rāmen* noodles, sinking your teeth into some creamy tuna from the Tsukiji Central Fish Market or splashing out with a multi-course *kaiseki* meal of seasonal delicacies, you'll often be struck by the care that goes into the humble art of eating here.

Kampai!

The Japanese workaholic stereotype is very true, but stroll through a neon-lined row of Shinjuku *yakitori* joints on a Friday or any cherry grove in spring, and you'll see that people take pleasure very seriously here. There is ever-flowing sake, deep respect for heartfelt karaoke, and constant curiosity about how outsiders view this archipelago at the end of the world. From picnics to shot bars, Tokyo's nightlife is a drinker's delight. *Kampai!*

Blade Runner City

This ever-changing metropolis of over 12 million is perhaps the most gorgeous ugly city in the world. It's a superdense riot of mismatched buildings, overhead wiring and garish neon. Yet it has the moxie to build the tallest tower in the world on a foundation of reclaimed land and several bucking tectonic plates. Add one of the planet's best mass transit sytems and you have the perfect sci-fi cityscape.

Shop Till You Drop

From the superdeluxe shops of Ginza to the electronics stores of Akihabara to Harajuku hipster boutiques, Tokyo is a universe of beautifully designed clothing, antique prints and bizarre only-in-Japan gems like Pocari Sweat (a soft drink). Craftsmen, meanwhile, continue to produce finely wrought treasures such as kimono-clad dolls and samurai swords that make excellent souvenirs.

歌舞伎町一番街

Why I Love Tokyo

By Timothy Hornyak

I've spent over 10 years in Tokyo, but this capital of the shōgun always renews its spell. I love walking in a random direction and finding something unusual like a museum of musical boxes or an eye-popping glimpse of Mt Fuji over Shinjuku at sunset.

In a way, Tokyo has an infinite quality. It's always under construction, always crackling with new fads, and always swirling with people who are passionate about everything from anime to Zen. As Dr Johnson said of London, to be tired of Tokyo is to be tired of life.

For more about our authors, see p304.

Above: Kabukichō entertainment district (p129)

Tokyo's
Top 16

Shinjuku Nightlife (p136)

1 Shinjuku pulls you in and impresses with its scale and sheer variety. Where else in the world can you stand so completely enveloped by neon, flashing lights and the jangling soundtrack of *pachinko* (vertical pinball game) parlours and then, just a few blocks away, be among creaky wooden watering holes lit by the glow of just a few street lights? In Shinjuku you can sing karaoke to your heart's content, catch the city's best jazz musicians or dance the night away with drag queens.

🍷 *Shinjuku & West Tokyo*

Tokyo Sky Tree (p170)

2 Opened in 2012, the Tokyo Sky Tree is the world's tallest tower at 634m. This digital broadcasting monolith was built with a special antiquake structure borrowed from Japanese pagodas. Two observation decks present a stunning panorama of the greater Tokyo area. The views are best at sunset and in the colder months when Mt Fuji's peak pokes out above the distant mountains. It's the closest thing to a helicopter ride over the city, but far more affordable.

👁 *Asakusa & Sumida River*

FRANK DEIM / LONELY PLANET IMAGES ©

3

5

ASHLEY ST JOHN / GETTY IMAGES ©

Shopping (p50)

3 Where to begin? With the eye-popping, highly covetable fashions, the cutting-edge electronics or maybe with the traditional artisan crafts? Whichever way you look at it, Tokyo is full of dangerously tempting shops. There's literally something for everyone and even if it's crafted in the wilds of Oita prefecture, odds are you can get it here in the capital. You don't have to spend a fortune though to come away with an only-in-Tokyo treasure. And window-shopping alone provides a fascinating look into Japanese pop culture, craftsmanship and design.

🛍 *Shopping*

Tsukiji Central Fish Market (p68)

4 You've never seen so many fish in your life, no matter how many aquariums you've notched. The world's largest fish market sells billions of yen worth of seafood every year, from mountains of octopus to pallets of giant bluefin tuna. If you get up early enough and get one of the few spots, you can watch the auction action as these prized fish are bought, cut up and distributed to myriad buyers and consumers. Just don't forget to have the world's freshest sushi for breakfast.

👁 *Ginza & Tsukiji*

Meiji-jingū (p116)

5 This Shintō shrine, Tokyo's largest and most famous, feels a world away from the city. It's reached via a long, rambling forest path marked by towering *torii* (gates). The grounds are vast, enveloping the classic wooden shrine buildings and a landscaped garden in a thick coat of forested green. Meiji-jingū is a place of worship and a memorial to the Emperor Meiji, but it's also a place for traditional festivals and rituals. If you're lucky you may even catch a wedding procession, with the bride and groom in traditional dress.

👁 *Harajuku & Aoyama*

Roppongi Art & Design (p81)

6 Legendary for its nightlife and foreign drinkers, Roppongi also has a sophisticated art scene. Art Triangle Roppongi is a group of three outstanding museums in the district – the Suntory Museum of Art, the National Art Center, Tokyo, and the Mori Art Museum, perched atop the Roppongi Hills city-within-a-city. This is where Murakami Takashi, Yayoi Kusama and Yoshitomo Nara exhibit. The Andō Tadao–wrought 21_21 Design Sight, also in the area, showcases the best of Japanese contemporary design and artists. MORI TOWER, ROPPONGI HILLS

⊙ *Roppongi*

Sushi & Rāmen (p34)

7 Tokyo's food obsession knows no boundaries and two of the city's most beloved dishes couldn't be more different. On one hand there's sushi, the essential Japanese dish of delicate raw fish. The best seasonal catch is prepared by master chefs in the exclusive haunts of the rich and famous in Ginza. On the other hand is the wonderfully rich, stick-to-your-ribs Chinese import that is *rāmen,* for which Tokyoites will queue up around the block. Join them, and delight in the sheer variety of flavours that Tokyo has to offer.

✗ *Eating*

WIBOWO RUSLI / LONELY PLANET IMAGES ©

Onsen *(p247)*

8 Don't let Tokyo's slick surface and countless, beguiling diversions fool you; underneath the city it's pure, bubbling primordial pleasure. The natural wonder that is onsen exists even in the hyperdeveloped capital, rising from amazing depths into the tubs of tiny traditional bathhouses and lavish, modern bathing complexes. Travel an hour outside the city and you'll be rewarded with rustic *rotenburo* (outdoor baths) – the perfect foil to a packed itinerary of sightseeing. A day spent going from tub to glorious tub is the quintessential Japanese form of escape. ŌEDO ONSEN MONOGATARI (P181)

⊙ *Onsen*

Sensō-ji *(p168)*

9 The spiritual home of Tokyoites' ancestors, the great Sensō-ji was founded over one thousand years before Tokyo got its start. Today this temple retains an alluring, lively atmosphere redolent of Edo (old Tokyo) and the merchant quarters of yesteryear. The colourful Nakamise-dōri arcade approaching the Buddhist sanctuary overflows with sweet treats and tacky souvenirs in a heady mix of secular and sacred. The surrounding shops hawk everything from rice crackers to kitchen knives and elegantly patterned *fundoshi* (loincloths).

◉ *Asakusa & Sumida River*

Hanami *(p159)*

10 If Tokyoites have one moment to let their hair down en masse, this is it. The ugly riot of Tokyo's built environment becomes significantly more appealing when thousands of cherry trees burst into white and pink flower in springtime. Japanese poets have extolled their beauty and samurai have admired the noble, short lives of the blossoms, but modern residents of the capital are happy to drink, eat and party under the boughs. Is it all a pretext to get wild? As a popular saying goes, *hana yori dango* (forget the blossoms and dig into the dumplings). UENO-KŌEN (UENO PARK)

◉ *Ueno & Around*

Sumō in Ryōgoku *(p170)*

11 The purifying salt sails into the air. The two giants leap up and crash into each other. A flurry of slapping and heaving ensues. Who will shove the other out of the sacred ring and move up in the ranks? From the spectacle of its ancient ceremonies to the thrill of the quick bouts, sumō is a feast for the eyes. Even better is the feast nearby: the Kokugikan stadium in Ryōgoku is close to several restaurants serving wrestler chow: *chankonabe* stew.

◉ *Asakusa & Sumida River*

9

FRANK DEIM / LONELY PLANET IMAGES ©

Kabuki (p236)

12 Japan's iconic performing arts form belongs among the world's greatest. It's sensual, highly nuanced and intensely visual. The costumes and make-up are fantastic and the storylines deal with some of the most important themes in Japanese literature, such as the conflict between love and loyalty. Kabuki developed in Tokyo, then Edo, during the 18th and 19th centuries and an afternoon at the theatre has been a favourite local pastime ever since. Descendants of the great actors of the day still grace Tokyo stages, drawing devoted fans.

☆ *Arts*

YURIKO NAKAO / CORBIS ©

ADINA TOVY AMSEL / LONELY PLANET IMAGES ©

Mt Fuji *(p198)*

13 On a clear day, the perfect, snow-capped cone of Japan's national symbol, Mt Fuji, is visible in the distance – putting all of Tokyo's man-made monuments to shame. You can hunt for views from the observatories and restaurants that top many of the city's highest buildings. Or head to the mountains west of Tokyo for a better look. Or even better yet, join the thousands of pilgrims who climb the sacred peak each summer. The sunrise from the top is a profound, once-in-a-lifetime experience.

◉ *Day Trips*

Shibuya Crossing *(p105)*

14 This is the Tokyo you've dreamed about and seen in movies: the frenetic pace, the mind-boggling crowds, the twinkling neon lights and the giant video screens beaming larger-than-life celebrities over the streets. At Shibuya's famous scramble crossing, all of this comes together every time the light changes. It's an awesome sight. Come on a Friday or Saturday night and you'll find the whole scene turned up to 11, when fleets of fashionable young things embark for a night out on the town.

◉ *Shibuya & Around*

Baseball at Tokyo Dome City

(p143)

15 Even if you don't know anything about Japanese baseball, it's a thrill to visit this stadium (dubbed the 'Big Egg') and watch the Yomiuri Giants in action. The nation's oldest and most popular baseball organisation has legions of devoted fans who support them with sophisticated, coordinated cheers. Beyond their home field is a baseball museum, an amusement park and one of the most luxurious spas in the capital, La Qua, which pipes in water from nearly 2km underground. A fine way to unwind after the game!

◉ *Iidabashi & Northwest Tokyo*

GREG ELMS / LONELY PLANET IMAGES ©

JOCHEN TACK / ALAMY ©

Traditional Festivals *(p25)*

16 You might think you've stepped back in time if you see a parade of revellers in loincloths and *hachimaki* (headbands) jostling under the weight of a portable Shintō shrine. Tokyo's many local festivals, such as May's Sanja Matsuri (which draws over a million partiers), are primarily intended to celebrate Shintō deities but they also renew age-old community bonds. On the secular side, the Sumida River *hanabi* (fireworks) spectacle in July is a chance to don *yukata* (light summer kimono) and drink while the night sky explodes above. REVELLERS CARRY A SHINTŌ SHRINE DURING A *MATSURI* (FESTIVAL)

🎏 *Month by Month*

What's New

Tokyo Sky Tree

This 643m broadcasting tower reset the Tokyo skyline when it opened in spring 2012, pulling all eyes eastward. Located near Asakusa, Tokyo Sky Tree has two observation decks (the highest at 450m), shops and restaurants. It's the tallest tower in the world, though not the tallest structure. Expect a lot more to be going on (and up) in this older part of town, east of the Sumida-gawa. (p170)

Haneda International Terminal

Tokyo's other airport, Haneda – the one actually in the city – now has a slick new international terminal. Getting to Tokyo just got significantly easier. (p253)

Energy Awareness

Since the shutdown of the Fukushima nuclear power plant threatened Tokyo's power supply, *setsuden* (saving electricity) has become a big priority; some shops now keep their lights dimmer than before.

Tokyo Station Makeover

After nine years under a cloak of scaffolding, Tokyo Station will finally emerge fully transformed in 2013; one side evokes the historic old building, the other will be totally modern. (p61)

Shibuya Hikarie

Shibuya, too, got a new station building: the glittering 34-floor Hikarie shopping and entertainment complex, which aims to bring sophistication back to Shibuya. (p106)

Kabuki's New Home

Though many are still mourning the historic old building, after three years of construction, kabuki fans look forward to the reopening of Ginza's Kabuki-za, scheduled for 2013.

Tuna Auction Open

Tsukiji Central Fish Market has lifted its ban on tourists at the tuna auction, though still imposes some limits; the market itself is slated for a controversial move in 2014. (p68)

Artisan Movement

The east side of town has housed traditional craft makers for centuries and now the newest generation is bringing their own style to the table at artisan mall 2k540 Aki-Oka Artisan. (p154)

Kōenji Rising

Kōenji has risen to notoriety as a neighbourhood for inspired new looks and as the site of the first antinuclear protests following the March 2011 disaster. (p130)

Recession Chic

Standing bars, which do away with chairs in favour of cheap drinks and more people around the counter, are huge hits. The inexpensive clothing chain Uniqlo has never been so fashionable – or successful.

For more recommendations and reviews, see **lonelyplanet.com/tokyo**

Need to Know

Currency
Japanese yen (¥)

Language
Japanese

Visas
Generally not required for stays of up to 90 days.

Money
Post offices and some convenience stores have international ATMs. Credit cards are accepted at major establishments, though it's best to keep cash on hand.

Mobile Phones
Local SIM cards cannot be used in overseas phones and only 3G phones will work in Japan; prepaid phones and rentals are available.

Time
Japan Standard Time (GMT/UTC plus nine hours)

Tourist Information
Japan National Tourism Organization (Map p286; ☑3201-3331; www.jnto.go.jp; 1st Fl, Shin-Tokyo Bldg, 3-3-1 Marunouchi, Chiyoda-ku; ⊙9am-5pm ⊠Yūrakuchō, exit D3) English-language information and publications.

Your Daily Budget

Budget less than ¥8000
➡ Dorm bed ¥3000
➡ Garden entry ¥300
➡ Bowl of noodles ¥1000
➡ Back-row seats for kabuki ¥1500

Midrange ¥15,000–20,000
➡ Business hotel room ¥8000
➡ Museum entry ¥1000
➡ Dinner at an *izakaya* (Japanese-style pub) ¥3500
➡ Mezzanine seats for kabuki ¥5000

Top end over ¥25,000
➡ Luxury hotel ¥20,000
➡ Ginza sushi dinner ¥20,000
➡ Box seats for kabuki ¥17,000
➡ Taxi ride back to the hotel ¥3000

Advance Planning

Two months before Book tickets for major shows and the Ghibli Museum; make reservations for any exclusive restaurants.

Three weeks before Scan web listings for festivals and events; print out flyers and maps from venue websites.

As soon as you arrive Buy tickets that need to be purchased from convenience-store ticket machines; pick up a copy of *Metropolis* magazine for the week's event listings.

Useful Websites

➡ **Lonely Planet** (lonelyplanet.com/tokyo) Destination information, hotel booking, traveller forum and more.

➡ **Tokyo Tourism Info** (www.tourism.metro.tokyo.jp) The city's official website covers sights, events and tours.

➡ **Metropolis** (http://metropolis.co.jp) Arts and entertainment listings.

➡ **Tokyo Food Page** (www.bento.com) City-wide restaurant coverage.

➡ **Japan Trends** (www.japantrends.com) What's new in Tokyo.

WHEN TO GO

Spring and autumn are the best times to be in Tokyo. June or July are the rainy season, while August is hot and humid, but is also the month for summer festivals.

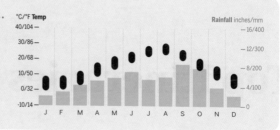

Arriving in Tokyo

Narita Airport Express train or highway bus to central Tokyo ¥3000, 6am to 10.30pm (1 to 2 hours); pick up tickets at the booths inside the terminal. Taxis cost at least ¥25,000.

Haneda Airport Train or bus to central Tokyo ¥400–1200, 5.30am to midnight (30 to 45 minutes). Taxis, your only option for before-dawn arrivals, cost between ¥4000–10,000 depending on the destination.

Tokyo Station Connect from the *shinkansen* (bullet train) terminal here to the JR Yamanote Line or the subway to destinations around central Tokyo.

For much more on **arrival** see p252.

Getting Around

➡ **Subway** The quickest and easiest way to get around central Tokyo. Runs 5am to midnight.

➡ **Train** JR Yamanote and Chūō Lines hit major stations; private-line trains head out of the city centre like spokes. Trains run from around 5am to midnight.

➡ **Taxi** The only transportation option that runs all night; unless you're stuck, taxis only make economical sense for groups of four.

➡ **Walking** Subway stations are close in the city centre; save a little cash by walking if you only need to go one stop.

For more on **getting around** see p254.

Sleeping

Tokyo accommodation runs the gamut from luxury hotels to cheap dorm rooms. Business hotels, though rather institutional, fall squarely in between. While boutique hotels haven't really taken off here, *ryokan* (traditional inns with Japanese-style bedding) fill the need for small, well-tended sleeping spaces; you can find these at any point on the price scale.

Even for hostels, it's wise to book in advance – even if it's just the day before – as walk-ins can fluster staff. Or, in the case of small establishments, staff might not be present at all.

Useful Websites

➡ **Japanican** (www.japanican. com) Comprehensive list of hotels in all price ranges, sometimes with discounted rates.

➡ **Japanese Inn Group** (http://japaneseinngroup. com) A nationwide association of inexpensive *ryokan*.

➡ **Economy Hotels in Tokyo** (www.e-conomyhotels.jp) Info and photos for budget rooms in northeast Tokyo.

For more on **sleeping** see p203.

WHAT TO PACK

Tokyo hotels can be tiny, so it's wise to bring as small a suitcase as possible. Remember that you'll be taking your shoes on and off a lot, so it helps to have ones that don't need lacing up. Casual clothes are fine, but you'll feel out of place if you're dressed as if you're heading to the gym. Tokyoites themselves are notoriously fashion conscious, though generally forgiving towards foreign tourists. It's useful to pack a handkerchief or two, as public restrooms often lack towels or dryers.

Top Itineraries

Day One

Harajuku & Aoyama (p114)

Start the day in Harajuku with a visit to **Meiji-jingū**, Tokyo's most famous Shintō shrine. If you get there by 8am you can catch the morning ritual, complete with *taiko* drumming. Next stroll down **Takeshita-dōri**, notorious for its wild teen fashions. If you skipped breakfast, treat yourself to a gooey, sweet crêpe – Harajuku's official street food.

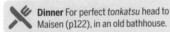
Lunch Honoji (p118) is a local favourite for its *sakana teishoku* (fish set) lunch.

Take a detour to the **Ukiyo-e Ōta Memorial Art Museum** for a look at works by some of the masters of the medium. Then head down Omote-sandō to gawk at the architectural wonders of some of Japan's leading contemporary designers. Allow yourself an hour to explore the antiquities galleries and woodsy grounds of the **Nezu Museum**.

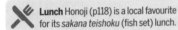
Dinner For perfect *tonkatsu* head to Maisen (p122), in an old bathhouse.

If the timing's right, you can catch a game at **Jingū Baseball Stadium** or a performance of traditional *nō* at the **Kokuritsu Nō-gakudō**. Otherwise make a beeline for swanky expat hangout **Two Rooms** in Aoyama to drink up the night views from the terrace.

Day Two

Asakusa & Sumida River (p166)

Take the subway to the old-world district of Asakusa. Stroll through up **Nakamise-dōri** to the great temple of **Sensō-ji**. Wander the streets and shopping arcades around the temple and browse traditional crafts shops.

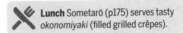
Lunch Sometarō (p175) serves tasty *okonomiyaki* (filled grilled crêpes).

Hop on a train to the **Tokyo Sky Tree**, the tallest tower in the world at 634m (see if you can stomach the top-deck glass corridor). Get on the subway to Ryōgoku to catch a bout of sumō wrestling (check bouts are being held beforehand). If not, take in the **Edo-Tokyo Museum**, and lean about the rich past of the shōgun's city.

Dinner Tomoegata (p177) dishes out hearty, sumō-sized *chankonabe* stew.

If you have the slightest liking for beer, hot-foot it to nearby **Popeye**. This delightful bar has the world's largest selection of Japanese beers, as well as a great happy-hour deal with free plates of food (if you can stomach more eating). If it's before 5pm, return to Asakusa and catch a Tokyo Cruise ferry down the Sumida River to Hinode pier, and the nearby Hamamatsuchō station on the JR Yamanote Line.

Day Three

Shinjuku & West Tokyo (p127)

 Head west to Mitaka to visit the fantastical **Ghibli Museum** (book your tickets early!). Instead of returning to Mitaka Station, stroll through **Inokashira-kōen** to Kichijōji Station. Don't miss the shrine in the park to Benzaiten, the jealous sea goddess.

> **Lunch** Pepa Cafe Forest (p136) has toothsome Thai and park views.

 Back in Shinjuku, check out the futuristic **Tokyo Metropolitan Government Offices**, including the view from the 202m-high observatories (free!). Wander among the skyscrapers all the way down to **Tokyo Opera City**, to visit the galleries there. Or head to the east side, to the beautifully landscaped **Shinjuku-gyoen**, stopping at a *depachika* (department store food floor) for picnic goodies along the way.

> **Dinner** Queue up for divine *rāmen* at Nagi (p134) in Golden Gai.

Stop by for a few skewers of *yakitori* and old-time ambiance in **Omoide-yokochō**, then plunge yourself into the neon flashing lights of **Kabukichō**. Make your way to the narrow lanes and wooden shanties of **Golden Gai**, a late-night drinking haunt for artists and writers. If you're looking for something more upbeat, head to **Shinjuku-nichōme**, the country's largest gay and lesbian neighbourhood, with hundreds of tiny bars and dance clubs.

Day Four

Ginza & Tsukiji (p66)

 Drag yourself out of bed at 4am and cab it to **Tsukiji Central Fish Market**. If you're lucky, you'll be one of the 120 people admitted to the tuna auctions from 5am, but if not the rest of the market is still worthwhile, especially the kitchenware shops in the Outer Market. Don't forget to have a sushi breakfast right on the premises. The unique shops and galleries of Ginza can keep you going until midday.

> **Lunch** Yabaton (p72) rewards with *miso-katsu* (pork cutlets in miso).

Marunouchi (Tokyo Station; p58)

Take the subway to Ōtemachi and walk to the **Imperial Palace East Garden**, where you can see the remains of the old castle of the shōgun. If you have the energy, walk through Kitanomaru-kōen on the north side of the Imperial Palace to **Yasukuni-jinja** shrine. Explore its controversial **Yūshūkan war museum** and fantastic military hardware.

> **Dinner** You won't find a better bowl of *rāmen* than at Kururi (p146).

Roppongi (p78)

 Complete your visit to Tokyo by jumping on the subway and raising a glass (or a couple of dozen) in Roppongi. There are bars for every budget, but you could do worse than cocktails at the swanky **R2 Supperclub** or bookish **These**. Don't forget to say *kampai!* (cheers!) to Tokyo Tower in the distance when you call it a night.

If You Like...

Temples & Shrines

Sensō-ji The granddaddy of Tokyo's Buddhist temples and epicentre of its old-world Shita-machi neighbourhoods. (p168)

Meiji-jingū Ringed by forests and majestic *torii* (gates), this Shintō oasis feels like another world. (p116)

Yasukuni-jinja Paying homage to millions of Japan's war dead in grandiose and controversial style. (p142)

Tōshō-gu The incredibly ornate mausoleum complex for the shōgun Tokugawa Ieyasu. (p185)

Zōjō-ji View the very rare main gate of this Pure Land Buddhist temple dates to 1605. (p82)

Sengaku-ji A real piece of samurai history, the Sōtō Zen temple is the final resting place of the famous 47 *rōnin* (masterless samurai). (p98)

Daibutsu The 11.4m-tall Great Buddha of Kamakura has sat here for nearly 800 years, and it's still thrilling. (p193)

Onsen-ji This typical mixture of a Buddhist temple and a hot-springs bath (onsen) north of Tokyo is the perfect tonic for those weary in body and mind. (p188)

Tsurugaoka Hachiman-gū Dedicated to the god of war, this elegant Shintō shrine in Kamakura is a great spot to contemplate the sweep of Japanese history. (p194)

Ryōsen-ji & Chōraku-ji Set in the quiet seaside town of Shimoda, southwest of Tokyo, these two temples played a unique role in the opening of Japan to foreign trade in the 19th century. (p201)

Tsurugaoka Hachiman-gū (p194)

Galleries & Museums

Tokyo National Museum Set in tranquil Ueno-kōen park, and home to the world's largest collection of Japanese art. (p158)

Mori Art Museum Sky-high and soaring with work by contemporary Japanese and foreign artists. (p80)

Edo-Tokyo Museum Telling the story of how a fishing village evolved into a metropolitan area of over 30 million. (p171)

Meguro Parasitological Museum The gallery for ultragross, unwanted bugs including an 8.8m tapeworm. (p95)

Nezu Museum Showing exquisite Japanese pottery and calligraphy, set by a large traditional garden. (p118)

Kite Museum Traditional kites loom large and small, often adorned with fierce samurai faces. (p64)

Daimyō Clock Museum Eccentric feudal timepieces created when Japan had little contact with other countries. (p160)

Hakone Open-Air Museum Located in the hills of Hakone, southwest of Tokyo, this museum has an impressive collection of 20th-century sculpture by Henry Moore and others. (p191)

Nihon Mingei-kan Also known as the Japan Folk Crafts Museum, this repository of ceramics and other practical art dazzles with its craftsmanship. (p107)

Bridgestone Museum of Art Recently marking its 60th anniversary, this fine museum near Tokyo Station houses an impressive collection centring on 19th-century French paintings. (p64)

Onsen

Rokuryu Kōsen This locals' favourite bathhouse near Ueno-kōen is said to bubble with curative minerals and the occasional leaf. (p165)

Kappa Tengoku Nestled on a hill above Hakone-Yumoto Station, southwest of Tokyo, this outdoor bath soothes after a day of sightseeing. (p192)

Yumoto Onsen This secluded hamlet in the highlands of Nikko is a lakeside gem that's perfect for relaxing. (p188)

Komparu-yu Onsen Tucked away on the fringes of Ginza, Komparu-yu invites weary travellers to soak in what feels like a bygone age. (p77)

Ōedo Onsen Monogatari You'll hardly believe you're soaking in a hot spring by the cargo cranes on Tokyo Bay, but it's the real thing. (p181)

Sawada Kōen Rotemburo Overlooking the sea at Dōgashima, this al fresco bath is blissfully off the beaten path, and especially delicious when the sun sets. (p200)

La Qua This deluxe spa bubbles over with ways to relax you with its spring water from 1700m underground – it's especially effective after taking in a baseball game at Tokyo Dome next door. (p149)

Asakusa Kannon Onsen There's zero pretension at this Shitamachi bathhouse, where locals immerse themselves under wonderfully retro tile murals. (p178)

Jakotsu-yu Amid the tumult of Asakusa, Jakotsu shimmers with serene Mt Fuji artwork and a tranquil outdoor rock bath. (p178)

For more top Tokyo spots, see
➡ Eating (p34)
➡ Drinking & Nightlife (p44)
➡ Entertainment (p48)
➡ Shopping (p50)

PLAN YOUR TRIP IF YOU LIKE...

Modern Architecture

Tokyo Station A massive, marvellous retrofit brings skyscrapers to this 1914 landmark. (p61)

Park Hyatt Tokyo Tange Kenzō-designed, futuristic skyscraper has some of the best views in town. (p210)

Tokyo International Forum This stunning multipurpose structure looks like a giant ship from the inside. (p61)

Prada Aoyama Building This giant honeycomb seems to pulsate with light. (p119)

Tokyo Sky Tree If an earthquake strikes and you're hundreds of metres up, trust its construction technology, based on ancient pagoda structures. (p170)

Unusual Eats

Sushi breakfast Get the world's freshest *makizushi* at Tsukiji Central Fish Market. (p68)

Stick chicken Sit yourself under the tracks at Yūrakuchō to munch on *yakitori* (chicken skewers) and swill beer. (p72)

Ninja nights Magic and stealth are on the menu at the maze-like Ninja Akasaka. (p85)

Depachika Dive into department-store basements, like that at Mistukoshi, for a cornucopia of fish, cheese, cakes and sweets. (p65)

Spectacle & Sport

Kabuki The acting may be outlandish, but the spectacle at Shimbashi Embujō Theatre is undeniable. (p76)

Bunraku Puppets performing at Kokuritsu Gekijō have never portrayed a story of love suicides so poignantly. (p65)

Nō An ancient, authentic drama form that is all about masks and restless spirits mesmerises audiences at Kokuritsu Nō-gakudō. (p123)

Sumō See the big boys slapping each other silly at the Ryōgoku Kokugikan stadium. (p170)

Baseball Home field of the uberpopular Yomiuri Giants, Tokyo Dome City also houses an amusement park and luxury spa. (p143)

Martial arts See jūdō and karate practitioners duelling at Kōdōkan and Budōkan. (p142; p165)

Pop Culture

AKB48 See if you can escape this omnipresent girl pop band with 60 members, one of whom is virtual. (p235)

Manga Comics are so culturally ingrained that nearly all appliance instructions come with cartoons. Get your fix at Mandarake. (p154)

Anime Spirit yourself away to the Ghibli Museum and enter the fantasy world of Totoro and Ponyo. (p130)

Robots Meet ASIMO, the world's most advanced humanoid robot, at Honda's showroom. (p81)

Fashion fairs See them strut their stuff on the catwalks of Tokyo Fashion Week. (p233)

Parks & Gardens

Ueno-kōen Tokyo's oldest park has oodles of temples, plus museums and a zoo. (p159)

Hama Rikyū Onshi-teien An ancient shōgunal hunting ground, now a vast garden with skyscraper views. (p71)

Shinjuku-gyoen Home to 1500 cherry trees and tens of thousands of other species, as well as a vast greenhouse. (p130)

Imperial Palace East Garden Right by the home of Japan's emperor, the garden still has the ruins of Edo Castle. (p60)

Chinzan-sō An old samurai garden now embraced by a luxury hotel and home to a wonderful soba restaurant. (p146)

Koishikawa Kōrakuen Built by the Tokugawa clan, this garden is one of Tokyo's finest. (p143)

Kitanomaru-kōen This park by the Imperial Palace explodes with cherry blossoms as well as museums. (p142)

Breathtaking Views

Tokyo Sky Tree You'd have to fly to get a better view than that from the lookouts on this 634m tower, the world's tallest. (p170)

Tokyo Metropolitan Government Offices The 45th-floor observation decks in this marvel by Tange Kenzō are free. (p129)

Tokyo Tower Only 333m tall and long in the tooth, but still lovable for its retro kitsch. (p82)

Luxury hotels Tokyo's finest beds, like those at Park Hyatt Tokyo, often have heavenly views of the city and Mt Fuji. (p210)

Mt Fuji Instead of trying to spot this icon from Tokyo, get a close-up in Hakone. (p189)

Markets

Tsukiji Central Fish Market Feast your eyes on the bounty of the sea and then tuck into the world's best sushi at this pantheon of fishmongers. (p68)

Nippori Nuno No Machi (Nippori Fabric Town) This collection of decidedly frumpy fabric shops in an unfashionable part of eastern Tokyo is perfect for those with patchwork passions. (p165)

Ōedo Antique Market Hunt for undiscovered antique treasures in this monthly gathering set in the streamlined Tokyo International Forum. (p61)

Hanazono-jinja Flea Market Set in riotous Shinjuku, the grounds of this quiet Shintō shrine come alive with merchants, knick-knacks and antiques. (p130)

Isetan You can come for the fashion, but you'll probably return for the cornucopia of food tucked away in dozens of stalls in this department store basement. (p138)

Month by Month

January

Tokyo comes to a virtual halt on the first few days of the year; most places close and many residents return to their hometowns. The city picks up again by mid-month.

✴ New Year's Day (O-shōgatsu)

Tokyoites flock to Shintō shrines and Buddhist temples to celebrate the New Year from 1 to 3 January. Meiji-jingū (p116) and Sensō-ji (p168) are popular destinations; both can get very crowded, but that's part of the experience.

◉ Greeting the Emperor

On the morning of 2 January, the emperor and imperial family make a brief – and rare – public appearance in one of the inner courtyards of the Imperial Palace (p60).

✴ Coming of Age Day

The second Monday of January is *seijin-no-hi*, the collective birthday for all who have turned 20 (the age of majority) in the past year. You'll spot young women in gorgeous kimono.

February

February is the coldest month, though it rarely snows here. Winter days are crisp and sunny – the best time of year to spot Mt Fuji in the distance.

✴ Setsubun

The first day of spring is 3 February in the traditional lunar calendar, a shift once believed to bode evil. As a precaution, people toss tiny sacks of roasted beans while shouting, *'Oni wa soto! Fuku wa uchi!'* ('Devil out! Fortune in!').

◉ Plum Blossoms

Plum (*ume*) blossoms, which appear towards the end of the month, are the first sign that winter is ending. Popular viewing spots include Inokashira-kōen (p130) and Koishikawa Kōrakuen (p143).

March

With spring on the horizon, all eyes are glued to the cherry blossom forecast that shows the tide of pink – and warmer days – moving up from southern Kyūshū.

✴ Hina Matsuri

On and around 3 March (also known as Girls' Day), public spaces and homes are decorated with dolls in the traditional dress of the *hina* (princess).

☆ Tokyo International Anime Fair

In late March, this major industry event draws everyone from big screen voice actors to teenage fans. (www.tokyoanime.jp/en)

April

Warmer weather and blooming cherry trees make this quite simply the best month to be in Tokyo. You'll never see Tokyoites let loose as they do during *hanami* season.

◉ Cherry Blossoms

From the end of March through the beginning of April, the city's parks and riversides turn utterly pink and Tokyoites toast spring in spirited parties, called *hanami*, beneath the blossoms. Ueno-kōen (p159) is the most famous spot; Shinjuku-gyoen (p130) and Yoyogi-kōen (p117) are good, too.

🎎 Buddha's Birthday

Buddha's birthday is 8 April and you'll find Hana Matsuri (flower festival) celebrations at temples all over the city. Look for the parade of children in Asakusa, pulling a white papier-mâché elephant.

May

There's a string of national holidays at the beginning of May. Known as Golden Week, this is when much of the country makes travel plans. Festivals and warm days make this an excellent time to visit.

🎎 Meiji-jingū Spring Festival

Traditional arts, such *nō* and *bugaku* (ancient imperial court music) are performed around noon on 2 May and 3 May at Harajuku shrine. (www.meijijingu.or.jp/english)

🎎 Boys' Day

On 5 May, homes with sons fly *koinobori* (colourful banners in the shape of a carp), a symbol of strength and other masculine virtues for *otoko-no-hi* (Boys' Day).

🎎 Kanda Matsuri

Held over a weekend in early May, this festival is one of the city's biggest, with a parade of *mikoshi* (portable shrines) around Kanda Myōjin (p153). It takes place every other year; the next one will be in 2013.

🎎 Sanja Matsuri

Arguably the grandest Tokyo *matsuri* of all, this three-day festival, held over the 3rd weekend of May, attracts around 1.5 million spectators to Asakusa-jinja (p170). The highlight is the rowdy parade of *mikoshi* carried by men and women in traditional dress.

June

Early June is lovely; though by the end of the month *tsuyu* (the rainy season) sets in. Japan doesn't see southeast Asia–style monsoons, just a steady rain that lasts for weeks.

🎎 Sannō Matsuri

Tokyoites turn out to Hie-jinja (p82) in mid-June for this major festival, with music, dancing and a procession of *mikoshi,* at the former protector shrine for Edo Castle. The parade takes place only every other year, next in 2014.

July

When the rainy season passes in mid to late-July, suddenly it's summer. Tokyo summers are hot and sticky, but make up for it with lively street fairs and *hanabi taikai* (firework shows).

🎎 Tanabata

On 7 July, the stars Vega and Altar (stand-ins for a princess and cowherd who are in love) meet across the Milky Way. Children tie strips of coloured paper bearing wishes around bamboo branches; look for decorations at youthful hangouts like Harajuku and Shibuya.

🎎 Mitama Matsuri

Yasukuni-jinja (p141) celebrates O-bon (see p26) early: from 13 to 16 July, the shrine holds a festival of remembrance for the dead with 30,000 illuminated *bonbori* (paper lanterns).

🎎 Sumida-gawa Fireworks

The grandest of the summer firework shows, held the last Saturday in July, features 20,000 pyrotechnic wonders. Head to Asakusa early in the day to score a good seat. Check events listings for other firework displays around town.

August

This is the height of summer; expect sights to be crowded with domestic tourists and students on holiday. For a week in mid-August, many Tokyoites head to the countryside for O-bon; some shops may close too.

🎎 O-bon

Three days in mid-August are set aside to honour the dead, when their spirits are said to return to the earth. Graves are swept, offerings are made and *bon-odori* (folk dances) take place throughout the country.

Top: Geisha at Jidai Matsuri (Festival of the Ages; p28)
Bottom: Cherry blossom trees, Shinjuku-Gyoen (p130)

PRISMA BILDAGENTUR AG / ALAMY ©

JOHN BANAGAN / LONELY PLANET IMAGES ©

🎏 Fukagawa Hachiman

This festival, at Tomioka Hachiman-gū (p174) in mid-August, is famous for its chant of *'Wasshoi! Wasshoi!'* as spectators pour sacred water over the *mikoshi* carriers along the route. It's held in a big way only every few years; next up in 2014 or 2015.

🎏 Tokyo Pride

In mid-August, Japan's LGBT community converges on Yoyogi-kōen for the country's biggest pride event, sometimes followed by a parade through Harajuku. It's not London or Sydney, but a spirited affair just the same. (www.tokyo-pride.org, in Japanese)

🎏 Kōenji Awa Odori

Some 12,000 participants do a spirited folk dance along a 2km stretch on the last weekend in August. If you happen to find yourself along the parade route at Kōenji Station, you're welcome to break into your own rendition. (www.koenji-awaodori.com)

🎏 Samba Carnival

On the last Saturday in August, Tokyo's Nikkei Brazilians stage an excellent show down Kaminarimon-dōri in Asakusa. The dancing is top-notch and the judged competition is fierce, drawing dancers all the way from Rio.

September

With the summer holidays over, sights are less crowded; days are warm, hot even – though the odd typhoon rolls through this time of year.

☆ Tokyo Game Show

Get your geek on when the Computer Entertainment Suppliers Association hosts this massive expo at Makuhari Messe in late September. (http://tgs.cesa.or.jp)

October

Pleasantly warm days and cool evenings make this one of the best times to be in Tokyo.

☆ Takigi Noh

Evening performances of *nō* backlit by bonfires are held year round, though particularly in October. Check event listings and look for performances at Shinjuku-gyoen (p130) and Kichijōji Geso-ji.

🎎 Chrysanthemum Festivals

Chrysanthemums are the flower of the season (and the royal family), and dazzling displays are put on from late October to mid-November in Hibiya-kōen (p71) and at shrines including Meiji-jingū (p116) and Yasukuni-jinja (p141).

November

Late autumn days are cool and clear; Tokyoites head to the countryside to view the autumn leaves, known as *kōyō*.

🎎 Meiji-jingū Autumn Festival

Taking place 1 to 3 November, this festival is similar to the shrine's spring festival held in May, but with the addition of martial arts exhibitions on the 3rd. (www.meijijingu.or.jp/english)

🎎 Jidai Matsuri (Festival of the Ages)

On National Culture Day, 3 November, locals dressed in splendid costumes representing figures from Japanese history parade around Sensō-ji (p168) in Asakusa.

🎎 Shichi-go-san

This adorable festival in mid-November sees parents dress girls aged seven (*shichi*) and three (*san*) and boys aged five (*go*) in wee kimono and head to Shintō shrines for blessings.

◉ International Robot Exhibition

The world's largest robot expo takes place every other year at Tokyo Big Sight (p182); next up in 2013. (www.nikkan.co.jp/eve/irex/english)

◉ Autumn Leaves

The city's trees undergo magnificent seasonal transformations during *kōyō* (autumn foliage season); the fiery maple is the most beloved of all. Koishikawa Kōrakuen (p143) is good this time of year, but even better are Takao-san (p134) and Nikkō (p185), outside the city.

December

Nen-matsu (year-end) is the busiest season in Tokyo with preparations for O-shōgatsu (p25) and numerous bōnenkai (end-of-the-year parties) to attend; you'll find restaurants and bars particularly crowded.

🎎 Gishi-sai

On 14 December, Sengaku-ji (p98) is a memorial service that honours the 47 *rōnin* (masterless samurai) who famously avenged their fallen master. Even better is the parade of locals dressed as the loyal retainers.

◉ Christmas Eve

Christmas Eve is refashioned as a romantic occasion in Japan. Couples dressed in their finest head out to admire the seasonal illuminations in places like Roppongi and Marunouchi.

✕ Toshikoshi Soba

Eating buckwheat noodles on New Year's Eve, a tradition called *toshikoshi soba*, is said to bring luck and longevity – the latter symbolised by the length of the noodles.

🎎 New Year's Eve

Temple bells around Japan ring 108 times at midnight and Tokyoites begin lining up at Shintō shrines shortly after for *hatsumōde*, the first shrine visit of the year.

For more arts events, see the timeline p236.

With Kids

In many ways, Tokyo is a parent's dream: hyperclean, safe and with every mod-con. The downside is that many of the top attractions aren't as appealing to younger ones. Older kids and teens, however, should get a kick out of Tokyo's pop culture and neon streetscapes.

Ghibli Museum

This museum will please fans young and old of animator Miyazaki Hayao (*Ponyo, Spirited Away*). There's a mini-theatre and a life-sized stuffed model of the cat bus from *My Neighbor Totoro*. Bonus: it's part of a larger park. (p130)

Odaiba

Odaiba is a popular destination for local families. The National Museum of Emerging Science & Innovation, where kids can meet ASIMO the humanoid robot, catch a planetarium show and interact with hands-on exhibits, is here; there's also the virtual-reality arcade Tokyo Joypolis and one of the world's tallest Ferris wheels. (p179)

Ueno

The sprawling park Ueno-kōen has a zoo (complete with pandas) and the excellent National Science Museum. Look for swords and armour at the Tokyo National Museum here, too. (p156)

Trains

Japanese kids are crazy about trains, chances are yours will be too. A platform ticket to see the *shinkansen* (bullet train) come and go costs just ¥130. Another popular train-spotting location is the southern terrace at Shinjuku Station, which overlooks the multiple tracks that feed the world's busiest train station.

Play

Tokyo Dome City

There's a day's worth of activity here, from thrill rides to play areas to baseball games. (p143)

Hanayashiki

Part fun, part history lesson, Japan's oldest amusement park has creaky classic rides. (p176)

Namco Namjatown

This 'food theme park' inside Sunshine City includes an attraction called Ice Cream City – enough said. (p143)

KiddyLand

Shop for only-in-Japan character goods, action figures and model kits at this multi-storey toy emporium. (p124)

Useful Resources

➡ **Chez Vous** (www.chezvous.co.jp/english) English-speaking babysitting services, from ¥2600 per hour.

➡ **Tokyo Mothers Group** (www.tokyo mothersgroup.com) Resources and an active discussion board.

➡ **Tokyo with Kids** (http://tokyowithkids. blogspot.jp) Info and ideas for parents in Tokyo.

Like a Local

Tokyo is far more liveable than you may think. Get beyond the skyscrapers, the omnipresent neon and the crowds and you'll find a city that's more like a patchwork of towns, each with its own character and characters.

Singing at a karaoke parlour

Local Hangouts

Shimo-Kitazawa

This tangle of alleys, shops and restaurants is a favourite place to *bura-bura suru* (to kick around), especially for students. Come evening the *izakaya* (Japanese-style pubs) and basement live music houses fill up with young revellers. (p106)

Yanaka

Yanaka is one of the few places in the city where prewar wooden buildings remain in abundance. Artists and artisans make this their home too, and there's a growing cafe scene that draws people here from across the city. (p164)

Naka-Meguro

The leafy canal here, lined with cafes and boutiques, feels light years from the hectic streets just a few stations away – and locals like it that way. (p94)

Shitamachi

Literally the 'low city,' Shitamachi was the area below Edo-jō (now the site of the Imperial Palace) where the merchants and artisans lived. Today the term applies to those neighbourhoods that come closest to approximating the spirit of old Edo – neighbourhoods like Kanda and Ueno and many that lie east of the Sumida-gawa. Those who've lived here for generations can call themselves Edokko, or 'children of Edo'. You'll find them down to earth, warm, curious and with a droll sense of humour.

Tradition

Hanami

Nothing gets Tokyoites worked up – or outside – quite like *hanami*, the annual cherry blossom viewing parties. Make like a local and get there early to claim a prime spot under the pillowy trees with a plastic tarp and a cooler of beer. Don't be surprised if your neighbours have a brought a grill, a stereo – or maybe even turntables. You'll want to stick around for *yozakura* (cherry blossoms at night) lit by the moon or electric lanterns strung up for the occasion.

Summer Festivals

During the warmer months Shintō shrines host raucous festivals, with participants dressed in traditional dress parading *mikoshi* (portable shrines) down the city streets. There are also street fairs and *hanabi taikai* (firework displays) that draw crowds dressed in colourful *yukata* (light summer kimono).

Sentō

Public bathhouses have a centuries' old tradition in Tokyo. Though their numbers are dwindling, most communities still have one. They're places to soak undisturbed and gossip with neighbours. (p249)

Eat Like a Local

Think seasonally

They may live in concrete boxes but Tokyoites are still attuned to the rhythms of nature – at least when it comes to food. Share their excitement over the first *takenoko* (young bamboo shoots) in spring or *sanma* (mackerel pike) in autumn. Restaurants advertise seasonal dishes, luring customers in for the taste of the month.

Get in line

Queuing for food is a daily ritual for some, intent on eating at their favourite *rāmenya* (which just so happens to be a lot of people's favourite). Always hungry for novelty, Tokyoites will queue for hours for a new restaurant or one recently featured on TV.

Look up

If you're accustomed to scanning the street at ground level, you stand to miss out on a lot in Tokyo. In downtown areas restaurants are stacked on top of each other, creating multiple storeys of competing vertical neon signs. Most department stores, and even some office buildings, have food courts on the top floors with restaurants that are often surprisingly good, and surprisingly popular.

Party Like a Local

Nomikai

With small apartments and thin walls, most Tokyoites do their entertaining outside the home. A *nomikai* is literally a 'meet up to drink,' and they typically take place in the *koshitsu* (private rooms) of restaurants. A 'party plan' is arranged, consisting of a course of food and a couple of hours of all-you-can-drink booze. Whatever you may have thought about Japanese people being quiet and reserved will change should you stumble upon a *nomikai*: they're loud and animated. There's no worry about disturbing the neighbours – or cleaning up.

Out all night

The trains might stop after midnight but the bars and club certainly don't – many stay open until 5am when the trains pick up again. There are also all-night karaoke parlours and manga *kissa* (manga cafes) where you can while away the early morning hours. In nightlife districts like Shibuya and Roppongi you'll find people on the streets at all hours.

Dress up

Tokyoites take their style seriously. It's not so much the clothes, as the act of wearing them that sets the capital's fashion mavens apart. Dressing up is part allegiance to a tribe and part personal expression. There's a meticulous devotion to a look that never fails to awe, from the expertly coiffed hair to just the right shoes. Whether it's lunch in downtown Marunouchi or drinks in Ebisu, Tokyoites always look the part – the perfect personification of place and time.

Bike around

Tokyo may not have many bike lanes but that doesn't stop a lot of locals from taking to the streets on two wheels. Young salarymen commute to the office on racing bikes, pocketing the money their companies give them for train passes. Housewives shuttle toddlers to preschool on *denki-jitensha*, hybrid electric bicycles. For running errands, the humble *mama-chari* (literally 'mum-bike'), a heavy-framed, upright bicycle with basket and bell, does the trick. Cycling is also an attractive alternative to waiting out the first train or an expensive taxi ride home, and you'll also see young people out on bikes in the evening, high heels and all.

For Free

Tokyo consistently lands near the top of the list of the world's most expensive cities. Yet many of the city's top sights cost nothing. Free festivals and events take place year round too, especially during the warmer months.

Kōkyo Higashi-gyōen (Imperial Palace East Garden; p60)

Shrines & Temples

Shintō shrines are almost always free in Tokyo and most Buddhist temples charge only to enter their *honden* (main hall). This means that two of the city's most famous sights, Sensō-ji (p168) and Meiji-jingū (p116), won't cost you a thing. Throughout the year festivals and rites of passage take place at Shintō shrines, allowing visitors a peek into Tokyo's traditional side.

Shrines and temples are tucked away everywhere in Tokyo. One of the pleasures of walking here is discovering shrines wedged between buildings, or ducking off the street into the calm grounds of a local temple. Yanaka (p164) has a particularly high concentration of temples.

Parks & Gardens

Many of Tokyo's parks and gardens are free; Shinjuku-gyōen is the big exception, though it only costs a few hundred yen to enter. These leafy escapes are a welcome respite from the omnipresent concrete; they can be great for people watching, too. Just grab a *bentō* (boxed lunch) from the convenience store and you have yourself an easy picnic.

Markets

You could spend hours wandering the lanes of Tsukiji (p68), the world's biggest fish market, while there are weekend farmers markets (p34) and flea markets (p50) year-round. In the summer, festivals and markets hosted by ethnic communities set up across from Yoyogi-kōen (p117), and often include free performances.

Views

Several skyscrapers have free observation floors, including the Tokyo Metropolitan Government Offices (p129) and the Sumitomo Building on the west side of Shinjuku. Tokyo Big Sight (p182) offers views of the bay from the roof (whenever there isn't a conference going on).

Shopping Streets

For 'just looking' nothing beats a classic shopping street. Tokyo has several of these, including Ameyoko-chō (p160) in Ueno, one of Tokyo's only remaining old-fashioned, open-air pedestrian markets. There's also Kappabashi-dōri (p170), where the makers of plastic food models have their shops; Nippori Nuno no Machi (p165), where seamstresses, tailors and designers buy their fabrics; and Nakamise-dōri (p170), the pedestrian lane leading up to Sensō-ji lined with trinket stalls.

Free Museums

Tokyo has many niche museums that are free. Often no bigger than a room, they nonetheless offer a succinct look at some of the more plebeian aspects of life. Learn about Shitamachi artisans at the Traditional Crafts Museum (p170), the history of beer in Japan at the Beer Museum Yebisu (p94) or the threat of parasites at the Meguro Parasitological Museum (p95). Some museums also offer free admission on International Museum Day (18 May), though naturally this attracts crowds.

Bookshops

Enter any bookshop or convenience store and you'll spot people flipping through books and magazines they have no intention of buying. This is so common a practice there's even a word for it: *tachiyomi* (literally 'standing read'). The expat community's favourite destination for *tachiyomi* is the Tsutaya bookstore in Roppongi Hills. You don't even have to stand – there's a coffee shop in the store.

Art Galleries

Tokyo galleries welcome visitors, even of the 'just-looking' sort. The city has no cohesive art district; instead you'll find galleries all over town, though Ginza (see p66) is a good bet. At Design Festa (p117) in Harajuku, the artists themselves are often hanging around in front of their work.

NEED TO KNOW

For more information on free events taking place during your visit, see the following websites:

➡ Japan National Tourism Organization (JNTO; www.jnto.go.jp)

➡ Tokyo Tourism Info (www.tourism.metro.tokyo.jp)

➡ Metropolis Magazine (http://metropolis.co.jp/listings)

Company Showrooms

Yes, these exist for marketing purposes, but you'll feel little pressure to buy. Instead, you'll find museum-like exhibitions and displays featuring the latest products. There is something for everyone: the Sony Building (p71) for electronics, Toyota Mega Web (p181) for cars and the Toto Tokyo Centre Showroom, in the Shinjuku L Tower for, uh, anyone interested in toilets.

On The Cheap

Museum Discounts

Check out the Mupon iPhone app, which offers a year's worth of discounted admission to Tokyo museums. The GRUTT Pass (see p259) offers free or discounted admissions to over 70 attractions.

Lunch

Many of Tokyo's more expensive restaurants are comparatively reasonable at lunch; you'll get better value if you splurge at midday.

¥100 Stores

Stock up on sundries (and even food and souvenirs) at these emporiums of cheap. Look for colourful signs proclaiming '¥100'.

After 5pm

In the evening, grocery stores, bakeries and even department store food halls slash prices on *bentō*, baked goods and sushi.

Before 6pm

Get your karaoke in during the afternoon and you'll pay less than half of what you would during peak evening hours.

The ever-popular *bentō* (boxed lunch)

 # Eating

As visitors to Tokyo quickly discover, the people here are absolutely obsessed with food. It's an obsession that includes not just the obviously divine, like the finest cuts of sashimi, but also everyday items, like a bowl of noodles with the toppings arranged just so.

An *izakaya* bar (p40)

Tokyo Dining Scene

We're hard pressed to think of something you can't get to eat in Tokyo. There are traditional restaurants that have been serving the same dishes, in the same way, for generations. There are also internationally acclaimed chefs reimaging just what is possible on a plate. Naturally all varieties of Japanese food are covered here, but you'll also find a truly cosmopolitan dining scene. There are whole neighbourhoods known for just one cuisine, like Kagurazaka (French) and Shin-Okubo (Korean).

You can get superlative meals on any budget, from a simple bowl of noodles to the multicourse procession of edible art that is *kaiseki*, Japan's classic haute cuisine. The biggest restaurant buzzword these days however is 'reasonable'. Diners want solid, good meals at a price that will allow them to come back again and again – and we can't blame them. Never mind the record number of Michelin stars, this is the best thing that could happen to the Tokyo dining scene.

What's Hot Now

Tokyoites have an unapologetic enthusiasm for novelty. There always seems to be a new ingredient or dish that everyone's talking about, be it the wonders of *tokoroten* (agar jelly) or collagen-rich stews said to improve one's complexion. Some dining trends come and go with lighting speed; others have a way of creeping into the mainstream and altering the fabric of the city. Following are two of the latter that you should know about.

NEED TO KNOW

Price Range

In our listings we've used the following price codes to represent the cost of a meal (not including drinks or dessert):

➡ ¥   less than ¥2000
➡ ¥¥¥   2000 to ¥5000
➡ ¥¥¥   over ¥5000

Opening Hours

➡ Most restaurants open 11.30am–2.30pm for lunch and 6pm–10pm for dinner. Chains and restaurants in high traffic areas often stay open all afternoon. *Izakaya* (traditional pubs) usually open around 5pm and stay open until 11pm or later.

Reservations

➡ Reservations are recommended for higher-end places or for bigger groups; we've noted in the reviews if a place is popular and likely to fill up on weekends.

➡ If you show up without a reservation and no table is available, give your name and the number in your party to the host or hostess.

Paying

➡ If a bill hasn't already been placed on your table, ask for it by catching your server's eye and making a cross in the air with your index fingers.

➡ Payment is usually settled at the counter.

➡ To ask to split the bill, say '*Betsubetsu de onegaishimas[u].*'

➡ Traditional or smaller restaurants may not accept credit cards.

Tipping

➡ Tipping is not customary, though many high-end restaurants will add a 10% service charge.

Websites

➡ Tokyo Food Page (www.bento.com)
➡ Tabelog (http://tabelog.com, in Japanese)
➡ Gurunavi (www.gnavi.co.jp/en)

FANTASTICJAPAN / ALAMY ©

36

Top: A chef at work at an *oden* restaurant, Shinjuku

Bottom: Tempura (p39)

B-KYŪ GURUME

Literally 'b-grade gourmet', *b-kyū gurume* is a dining trend for the prolonged recession and a celebration of humble, common fare. The popular movement has diners scouring the city for the best *yaki-soba* (pan-fried buckwheat noodles) or *buta-don* (grilled pork over rice), chronicling their findings extensively on the web and elevating weathered mom-and-pop eateries to celebrity status. Pretty much anything cheap, greasy and salty – just about the opposite of what you think about when you think about Japanese food – can count as *b-kyū gurume*, but it has to be done well – no limp cabbage or soggy breading. Many dishes have regional origins, too. You can find *b-kyū* joints pretty much anywhere, though Shitamachi and university neighbourhoods and under and along train tracks are all good bets.

FARM TO TABLE

Farmer's markets are springing up all over the city, catering to a population that has become increasingly sensitive about food safety. And for a generation of Tokyoites who have no hometown in the country, there's something attractive about gaining this connectivity to rural Japan through eating. You'll also see restaurants boasting of where their produce comes from, sometimes even including photos of the farmers on the menu. For a schedule of upcoming markets see www.marche-japon.org (in Japanese).

The Japanese Restaurant

Never mind if the food on the menu is Italian, if the restaurant is in Japan, you'll likely be treated to the Japanese restaurant experience – even in cosmopolitan Tokyo. The experience starts as soon as you enter and the staff all great you with a hearty *'Irasshai!'* (Welcome!). In all but the most casual places, where you seat yourself, the waiter or waitress will next ask you *'Nan-mei sama?'* (How many people?). Indicate the answer with your fingers, which is what the Japanese do. You may also be asked if you would like to sit at a *zashiki* (low table on the tatami), at a *tēburu* (table) or the *kauntā* (counter). Once seated you will be given an *o-shibori* (hot towel), a cup of tea or water (this is free) and a menu. The *o-shibori* is for wiping your hands and face; keep it to use as a napkin.

WORDS TO KNOW

Osusume If you're not sure what to have, say *'Osusume de onegaishimas[u]'* (I'll have what you recommend).

Ōmori Add more to your meal by ordering *ōmori* (an extra large serving of rice or noodles that usually costs only a hundred yen more). On the other hand, if you hardly ever finish your rice, order *gohan sukuname de* (a smaller portion of rice).

ETIQUETTE

Before digging in, it's customary to say *'Itadakimas[u]'* (literally 'I will receive' but closer to 'bon appétit' in meaning).

Don't stick your chopsticks upright in your rice or pass food from one pair of chopsticks to another – both are reminiscent of funereal rites.

When serving yourself from a shared dish, use the back end of your chopsticks to put the food on your own *torizara* (small plate).

At the end of the meal it's polite to say *'Gochisō-sama deshita'* (literally 'it was a feast'; a respectful way of saying that the meal was good) to the staff on your way out.

Rice, Soya Beans & Pickles

For millennia Japanese people survived on just three staple crops: rice; soya beans, which became miso (味噌), *shōyu* (soy sauce (醤油; soy sauce) and tofu (豆腐); and *tsukemono* (漬物; vegetables that were preserved as pickles). Rice is so central to the idea of eating that the word for it, *gohan* (ご飯), is also the word for a meal. It's also central to Japanese cultural identity: historically communities were founded and maintained through rice farming, and throughout the feudal period a fiefdom's wealth was measured in *koku*, the amount of rice needed to feed one person for a year (roughly 150 kilograms). Even with today's options, rice, miso soup and pickles continue to play a key role. They're eaten daily for breakfast, accompany every *teishoku* (set meal) at a *shokudō* (see p39), and make up the final course of Japan's ceremonial haute cuisine, *kaiseki*.

Sushi

The tonnes of fish that pass through the fish market in Tsukiji (p68) reflect what locals are eating. Sushi in Tokyo was once *edo-mae* – literally 'in front of Edo', meaning that the fish came directly from Tokyo Bay. Today the choicest catches from around the globe are flown in to fuel a never-diminishing appetite for unadulterated fish. Sushi (すし or 寿司) is raw fish served with sweetened, vinegared rice; sashimi (刺身) is slices of raw fish only. Sushi can be eaten with your hands. Both are flavoured with soy sauce and wasabi – lightly; if the fish is preseasoned with something else the chef will tell you. The slices of *gari* (pickled ginger) are to cleanse the palate in between bites.

At its best, sushi is prepared from seasonal fish. This is what you'll get if you splurge on a chef's tasting menu at one of the city's top restaurants. Staples like tuna and squid, meanwhile, can be found year-round at any local sushi counter or *kaiten-sushi* (回転寿司; conveyor-belt sushi restaurant). Sushi is straightforward: you generally get what you pay for. Still, you don't need to eat at the highest of the high-end to get fish that tastes better than anything back home.

Noodles

It's hard to imagine how Tokyo could function without noodles. You'll see the work force slurping away at *tachigui* (立ち食い; stand-and-eat) noodle bars in and around train stations. And yes, slurping is key: noodles are to be eaten at whip-speed and the slurping helps cool your mouth while you eat. At most *tachigui* and corner shops you buy a ticket for your meal from a vending machine, and hand it to the chef. Of course there are upscale noodle restaurants, too.

SOBA

Soba are thin buckwheat-based noodles, associated with the Kantō area; thicker white udon noodles are more reminiscent of Kansai (around Osaka). With that said, the vast majority of restaurants throughout the country serve both. The best noodles are *te-uchi* (手打ち; handmade).

Soba are served hot, in a large bowl of light, bonito-flavoured broth, or cold, often indicated on menus as *seiro-soba* (せいろそば), with broth on the side. At a standing noodle joint, you're likely to get them hot; if you eat at a fancier establishment, you'll impress the staff by ordering the cold ones (since hot soup quickly turns al dente noodles to mush, *soba* devotees prefer to savour them cold). One classic dish to try is *zaru soba* (ざるそば), cold noodles served on a bamboo mat topped with slivers of dried *nori* (海苔; seaweed). Along with it comes a small plate of wasabi and sliced

Nori soba (buckwheat noodles with seaweed)

spring onions, which you add, as you like, to a cup of broth. Eat the noodles by dipping them bite by bite into the broth. You may also be given a pitcher of *soba-yu* (そば湯; the water used to boil the noodles) to add to the remaining broth when you're finished with the noodles – so you get your hot soup after all!

RĀMEN

Rāmen originated in China, but its popularity in Japan is epic. Your basic *rāmen* is a big bowl of noodles in broth, served with toppings such as *chāshū* (sliced roast pork), *moyashi* (bean sprouts) and *negi* (leeks), though you can expect to see anything from Hokkaidō butter corn and fresh seafood to wontons and Chinese vegetables. In fact, *rāmen* impresses with its sheer variety of flavours, starting with the broth. There are four basic categories of soup: rich *tonkotsu* (pork bone), mild *shio* (salt), savoury *shōyu* (soy sauce) and hearty miso. Given the option, most diners get their noodles *katame* (literally 'hard' but more like al dente). If you're really hungry, ask for *kaedama* (another serving of noodles), usually only a couple of hundred yen more.

Yakitori

Putting away skewers of *yakitori* (焼き鳥; grilled chicken), which goes hand in hand with beer, is a popular after work ritual. Most *yakitori-ya* are convivial counter joints where the chicken is grilled over hot coals right in front of you. *Momo* (もも; thigh) and *sasami* (ささみ; breast) meat are just the beginning of it; yakitori also includes every edible part of the chicken, like *rebā* (レバー; liver) and *motsu* (もつ; giblets). It's customary to order skewers in twos; you can use your fingers to indicate. The chef will ask you if you want *shio* (salt) or *tare* (sauce) as seasoning. Most *yakitori-ya* also serve other *kushiyaki* (串焼き; skewers), including vegetables.

Japanese Classics

All of these classic Japanese dishes are best eaten in a restaurant that specialises in them.

Tempura (天ぷら) Seafood and vegetables deep-fried in a fluffy, light batter, flavoured with salt or a light sauce mixed with grated daikon (radish).

Sukiyaki (すき焼き) Thin slices of beef cooked piece by piece in a broth of soy sauce, sugar and sake at your table, then dipped in raw egg before eating.

Shabu-shabu (しゃぶしゃぶ) Thin slices of beef or pork swished briefly in a light, boiling broth then seasoned with *goma* (sesame-seed) or *ponzu* (citrus-based) sauce.

Tonkatsu (豚カツ) Tender pork cutlets breaded and deep-fried, served with a side of grated cabbage.

Unagi (うなぎ) Freshwater eel grilled over coals and lacquered with a rich, slightly sweet sauce.

Fugu (フグ) Poisonous globefish prepared by highly-trained chefs; a tasting menu usually consists of the fish prepared several different ways.

Okonomiyaki (お好み焼き) Savoury pancake stuffed with cabbage plus meat or seafood (or cheese or kimchi...), which you grill at the table and top with *katsuo bashi* (bonito flakes), *nori* (seaweed), mayonnaise and Worcestershire sauce.

Shokudō

Dining trends may come and go but *shokudō* (食堂; inexpensive, all-around eateries) remain. The city's workers take

Dining beneath the railway lines in Yūrakuchō Yakitori Alley (p72), Ginza

a significant number of their meals at these casual joints; you'll find them around every train station and in tourist areas. Most serve *teishoku* (定食; set-course meal), which includes a main dish of meat or fish, a bowl of rice, miso soup, a small salad and some *tsukemono*. There's also usually a variety of *washoku* (和食; Japanese) and *yōshoku* (洋食; Western) staples. *Kare-raisu* (カレーライス), a sweet and not at all spicy Japanese curry served over sticky rice, is a *shokudō* staple. Many will have a *kyo-no-ranchi* (daily lunch special), which is a safe bet if you're at a loss for what to order. Also good are *donburi*, bowls of rice with various toppings.

Izakaya

Izakaya (居酒屋) translates as 'drinking house' – the Japanese equivalent of a pub. Here food is ordered for the table a few dishes at a time and washed down with plenty of beer, sake or *shōchū* (strong distilled alcohol often made from potatoes). Menus at *izakaya* vary from almost illegible hand scrawls to tableside touch screens, but you can expect most to offer a wide selection of Japanese classics like *yakitori*, sashimi and grilled fish, as well as Western foods like French fries and beef stew. Classic *izakaya* have rustic facades and red lanterns outside their doors, though there are modern ones with fashionable interiors, too. Either way, you'll find a lively, casual atmosphere. Depending on how much you drink, you can expect to spend just ¥2000 to ¥5000 per person.

Yatai

Tokyo doesn't have much street food, but you will find the odd cluster of *yatai* (屋台; food stand) in alleyways of Shitamachi neighbourhoods or under train tracks. Festivals always have rows of *yatai*, too. Look for treats like *tako-yaki* (たこ焼き), grilled dough balls stuffed with octopus, and *taikyaki* (たい焼き), hotcakes shaped like sea bream and filled with *anko* (あんこ; red bean paste) or some other sweet filling. And keep an eye out for Tokyo's original food trucks: the *yaki-imo* (roasted whole sweet potatoes) carts that rove the city from October to March crooning '*yaki-imohhhhh…!*'. On a cold day, these stone-roasted treats warm your hands and your insides.

Top: Diners at an *izakaya* in Asakusa
Middle: Plastic food models in a restaurant window, Ginza
Bottom: A winter variety of *rāmen* (noodles in broth; p38)

Chain Restaurants

Some Tokyo chains actually have consistently good food and reasonable prices, not to mention convenient citywide locations. These are recommended in a pinch:

Ippūdō (一風堂; 291; www.ippudo.com, in Japanese; noodles from ¥750; ⊙11am-late) One of Japan's favourite Kyūshū-style *rāmen* shops is actually a chain.

Mos Burger (モスバーガー; 296, 292 & 294; www.mos.jp, in Japanese; burgers from ¥320; ⊙7am-late; 🅿) A step-up from fast food, this burger chain makes your food to order.

Za Watami (坐・和民; 292, 294 & 299; www.watamifoodservice.jp, in Japanese; dishes from ¥299; ⊙5pm-late; 🅿) This omnipresent chain of *izakaya* covers all the bases and is surprisingly good for the price.

Food to Go

The Japanese frown upon eating in public places (on the subway for example); picnics in parks and ice cream eaten on the street are two big exceptions. Yet they've managed to turn packaged food into an art form and made an efficient science of delivering it – no country in the world has more vending machines than Japan.

KONBINI

Konbini (convenience stores; コンビニ) are a way of life for many Tokyoites. Indeed, there seems to be a Sunkus, AM-PM, Lawson, 7-Eleven or Family Mart on just about every corner. In addition to *bentō* (boxed meals) and sandwiches, other *konbini* stables include: *onigiri* (おにぎり), a triangle of rice and *nori* (seaweed) enveloping something savoury (tuna salad or marinated kelp, for example); *niku-man* (肉まん), steamed buns filled with pork, curry and more; and *oden* (おでん), a hot wintertime dish of fish cakes, hard-boiled egg and vegetables in *dashi* (fish stock) broth that can be found stewing by the register.

DEPACHIKA

Depachika (デパ地下; department store basements) often take up several floors, housing a staggering array of foodstuffs of the highest order, freshly prepared and often gorgeously packaged for presentation as gifts (excellent if you find yourself dining at a Japanese person's house). Look for museum-quality cakes, flower-shaped *okashi* (sweets) and *bentō* that look too good to eat. Two *depachika* to try are Isetan (p138) in Shinjuku and Mitsukoshi (Map p286) in Ginza.

SUPERMARKETS

The following are expat favourites:

Kinokuniya International Supermarket (Map p293; 3-11-7 Kita-Aoyama, Minato-ku; ⊙9.30am-8pm; 🚇Ginza Line to Omote-sandō, exit B2) Rather pricey, but stocked with fresh bread, flawless fruits, cheeses and chocolates galore.

Natural House (Map p293; 3-6-18 Kita-Aoyama, Minato-ku; ⊙10am-10pm; 🚇Ginza Line to Omote-sandō, exit B4) Organic produce, hearty brown bread and vegetarian *bentō*.

Word of Mouth

With just a basic knowledge of Japanese characters (or deft cutting and pasting skills) you can navigate Tabelog (http://tabelog.com/), Japan's biggest word-of-mouth restaurant website. To use the search function, put a train station name in the first box and a type of food in the second, click the magnifying glass and there you have the top user-ranked restaurants in the vicinity.

PAUL DYMOND / LONELY PLANET IMAGES ©

PLAN YOUR TRIP EATING

Bean-filled pastries, a popular Japanese sweet

SOZAIJITEN/DATACRAFT GETTY IMAGES ©

Okonomiyaki (filled savoury crêpes; p39)

Vegetarian

Vegetarians, and especially vegans, generally have it hard in Japan. Even dishes with no visible meat or fish are often seasoned with *dashi* (fish stock). However, vegetarianism is on the rise in Tokyo and you'll find more and more restaurants able to accommodate the request: *'Bejitarian dekimas[u] ka'* (Can you do vegetarian?). The vegetarian symbol ( ) in eating listings indicates places that have a good selection of vegetarian options.

Cooking Classes

Cookbook author and long-time Japan resident Elizabeth Andoh offers private and small group lessons on both the basics and finer points of Japanese cooking (www.tasteofculture.com).

Eating by Neighbourhood

➡ **Marunouchi (Tokyo Station)** (p64) Midrange options for the local office crowd.

➡ **Roppongi** (p83) Both break-the-bank and midrange options, with a good selection of international cuisines.

➡ **Ginza & Tsukiji** (p72) Upscale restaurants and the best sushi in the city.

➡ **Ebisu, Meguro & Around** (p98) Cosmopolitan and hip, with excellent dining options in all price ranges.

➡ **Shibuya & Around** (p106) Lively restaurants that cater to a young crowd; good budget options and *izakaya*.

➡ **Harajuku & Aoyama** (p118) Fashionable midrange restaurants and excellent lunch options aimed at shoppers.

➡ **Shinjuku & West Tokyo** (p134) Gorgeous high-end restaurants, under-the-tracks dives and everything in between.

➡ **Iidabashi & Northwest Tokyo** (p146) Cheap student joints, tiny gems and good ethnic food.

➡ **Akihabara & Around** (p153) Famous for historic eateries in Kanda, noodles in Akihabara.

➡ **Ueno & Around** (p161) Classic Japanese restaurants, mostly midrange and budget.

➡ **Asakusa & Sumida River** (p175) Unpretentious Japanese fare, old-school charm and modest prices.

➡ **Odaiba & Tokyo Bay** (p182) Restaurants popular with teens and families; lots of big chains.

Lonely Planet's Top Choices

Kyūbey (p72) Rarefied Ginza sushi at its finest.

Agaru Sagaru Nishi Iru Higashi Iru (p118) Creative, affordable *kaiseki* served in a hip subterranean cave.

Higashi-Yama (p99) Modern cuisine in a stunning setting.

Kururi (p146) *Miso-rāmen* that draws lines down the street.

Tofuya-Ukai (p85) Handmade tofu becomes haute cuisine.

Tonki (p99) *Tonkatsu* (fried pork cutlets) raised to an art form.

Best by Budget

¥
Yabaton (p72)
Gonpachi (p85)
Nanbantei (p110)
Nabezō (p107)

¥¥
Nodaiwa (p107)
Kaikaya (p106)
Tsunahachi (p135)
Daiwa Sushi (p73)

¥¥¥
L'Osier (p72)
Ten-ichi (p72)
Asakusa Imahan (p175)
Shabu-zen Roppongi (p43)

Best by Cuisine

Japanese Traditional
Sasa-no-Yuki (p161)
Komagata Dojō (p175)
Kado (p147)
Tomoegata (p177)
Otafuku (p175)

Sushi
Fukuzushi (p83)
Edogin (p73)
Sushi-no-Midori (p107)
Sushi Take (p202)

Noodles
Nagi (p134)
Afuri (p98)
Honmura-An (p84)
Rāmen Jirō (p100)
MIMIU (p65)

Yakitori
Bird Land (p73)
Shimonya (p136)
Omoide-yokochō (p135)
Akiyoshi (p147)

Asian
Moti (p84)
Malaychan (p147)
San La Kyo (p84)
Lotus Palace (p85)
Hainan Jeefan Shokudō (p84)

European
Da Isa (p99)
Canal Café (p147)
Taverna (p148)
Le Bretagne (p147)

Best for Old Tokyo Atmosphere

Hantei (p161)
Botan (p153)
Isegen (p153)
Kanda Yabu Soba (p154)
Mucha-an (p148)

Best Izakaya

Hayashi (p85)
Shirube (p107)

Inakaya (p84)
Ippo (p98)
Dachibin (p135)
Sakana-tei (p107)

Best for a Special Occasion

New York Grill (p135)
R2 Supperclub (p83)
TY Harbor Brewing Company (p182)
Ninja Akasaka (p85)

Best for Brunch

Suji's (p84)
Las Chicas (p122)
Bills (p182)
Pariya (p122)

Best for Lunch

Nakajima (p134)
Honoji (p118)
Nirvana New York (p84)
Maisen (p122)
Chano-ma (p99)

Best For Late Night Dining

Harajuku Gyōza Rō (p118)
Ebisu Yokochō (p98)
Kyūsyū Jangara (p122)
Ganko Dako (p100)

Best for Vegetarians

Mominoki House (p122)
Nataraj (p73)
Magokoro (p198)
Nagi Shokudō (p107)
Kobachi-ya (p85)

Drinking & Nightlife

Slice into an ice cream-topped loaf of crispy bread while belting out your fave Queen tunes in a karaoke palace, quaff thimbles of sake with an increasingly rosy salaryman in a tiny postwar bar, or dance under the rays of the rising sun at an enormous bayside club. That's nightlife, Tokyo-style.

Tokyo Nightlife

Behind the conservative public face of Tokyoites lurks a party animal extraordinaire. You only have to stumble over a salaryman collapsed from drink in the subway or walk into any screaming high-rise karaoke parlour to realise that this city is passionate about having fun after dark. Tokyo will rock you 'til you drop in its clubs and live music houses, and drink you under the table in its bars and *izakaya* (Japanese pubs). Even its cafes can dazzle with everything from super-slick gems of design to proudly retro homages to barista culture. This city has something for everyone, and there's enough of it to spend months or even years exploring.

Crazes

Spurred by market deregulation, Japan has jumped on the global microbrew fad, with nearly 200 microbreweries opening in the archipelago, and some, like foreign-owned Baird Brewing, launching their own beer bars in Tokyo. The emphasis is on quality and unique offerings, sometimes in a smoke-free environment.

Retro is also on the menu in Tokyo, and highballs are a new favourite. The easy-drinking whisky and soda cocktail, once popular in the 1950s, has seen a resurgence thanks to a marketing campaign for Suntory's old-school Kakubin whisky.

Hoppy, a cheap, low-alcohol mix of carbonated malt and hops that debuted in 1948 is also finding new drinkers as Japanese raise a glass or two to the golden days of yore.

Social Lubricant

Drinking plays a big role in Japanese society, and there are few social occasions where beer or sake is not served. Alcohol (in this case sake) also plays a ceremonial role in various Shintō festivals and rites, including marriage ceremonies.

As a visitor to Japan, you'll probably find yourself in situations where you are invited to imbibe, but if you don't drink alcohol, simply order *oolong cha* (oolong tea). You can diffuse any pressure by saying '*Sake onomimasen*' (I don't drink alcohol).

What you pay depends on where you drink, so if you're not sure about a place, ask about prices and cover charges before sitting down. As a rule, if you are served a small snack (*o-tsumami*) with your first round, you'll be paying a cover charge (usually a few hundred yen, but sometimes much more).

Izakaya and *yakitori-ya* are cheap places for beer, sake and food in a casual atmosphere resembling that of a pub. In summer, some department stores and hotels in Tokyo open up beer gardens on the roof. Many of these places offer all-you-can-eat/drink specials for around ¥3000 per person.

Bars

Tokyo is blessed with more bars than there are stars in the sky and a drinking culture that values group bonding, great food and fun. Alcohol is very much a social lubricant in Japan, and a lot of heavy drinking goes on in the capital, something you'll soon realise if you happen to hop on any train after 10pm; violence, though, is quite rare.

Blissfully, there's a poison for every budget. Drinking establishments run the gamut from cheap shot bars and *tachinomi-ya* (standing-only bars) to high-end *izakaya* and ritzy hotel cocktail lounges. A staple is the humble *nomiya,* often a small, older establishment patronised by businessmen and regular customers. Some won't be as comfortable serving foreigners who don't speak or read Japanese, but often a smile will win the day.

Less accessible than *nomiya* and not recommended are *sunakku* (snack bars), cheap hostess bars that charge hefty sums, and *kyabakura* (cabaret clubs), exorbitant hostess clubs that are often fronts for prostitution. These are concentrated in Shinjuku's Kabukichō district.

Roppongi, long the *gaijin* (foreigners; literally 'outside people') bar capital of Tokyo, has the lion's share of bars per square metre, though Shinjuku itself is no slouch. Other favourite neighbourhoods to raise a glass are Shibuya, Ebisu, Shimbashi and Yūrakuchō. Shibuya is youth-heavy, while Shimbashi and Yurakuchō teem with salarymen. Ebisu and nearby Daikanyama have some excellent bars that cater to a mixed clientele; as do some neighbourhoods west of Shinjuku (p136).

Izakaya

A venerable eating and drinking institution that's catching on overseas, *izakaya* (p40) are Japanese-style pubs that often expertly marry food and drink. The focus here is on food – appetisers like *yakitori, tsukune* (chicken balls) or *hiyayakko* (fresh tofu) – served in a casual, sometimes downright raucous, atmosphere. But *izakaya* are also wonderful places to sample premium sake, *shōchū* (liquor distilled from grains or sweet potato, for example; 焼酎) and craft beer.

Karaoke

Karaoke may have been born in western Japan, but Tokyo has refined the art of singing with a machine in unique ways. If you've never tried a karaoke box (a small room for you and a few of your friends), it's definitely less embarrassing than singing in a bar in front of strangers. With free-flowing booze and eats brought directly to your room, it can easily become a guilty pleasure; rooms generally cost about ¥600 per person per hour.

NEED TO KNOW

Cheers

Don't forget to say (or yell, depending on the venue) *'Kampai!'* when toasting your drinking buddies.

Prices

Draft beer can be had for as little as ¥500, while cocktails generally cost from ¥900 to thousands of yen. Guys can expect to pay at least ¥2000 for entry into clubs, less for gals.

Smoking

The majority of Tokyo's night spots allow smoking, but there's a small but growing number of nonsmoking bars such as Popeye in Ryogoku.

Etiquette & Tipping

When drinking in a group, it's customary to pour for others and wait for them to refill your glass. At smaller bars, male bartenders are often called 'master' and their female counterparts are 'mama-san'. There's no need to tip in bars, but there may be an entrance fee and/or *otōshi*, a small dish that's automatically added to the bill; think of it as a tip substitute.

Opening hours

Tokyo's night spots stay open from 5pm well into the wee hours. Many patrons head for the nearest station around midnight to catch the last train home, while others hit the after-hours clubs until the early trains start.

Websites & Books

➡ Tokyo Journal (www.tokyo.to/city/index.html)

➡ Metropolis (http://metropolis.co.jp/arts)

➡ Beer in Japan (http://beerinjapan.com/bij/)

➡ Nonjatta (http://nonjatta.blogspot.com/)

➡ *Drinking Japan* by Chris Bunting

➡ *The Sake Handbook* by John Gauntner

Clubs

As a clubbing mecca, Tokyo holds its own with London and New York. You'll find tons of techno, disco and house in the city, as well as top international DJs and domestic artists who do regular sets at venues with top-notch sound systems. Most of the music starts when doors open, usually around 8pm – but you won't want to arrive until 10pm or so, when the volume increases and the floor fills. At most places, you can dance until dawn or later. The biggest concern is when the trains stop and start.

Cafes & Tea Rooms

Forget the bland chains like Doutor, Tully's, Excelsior and Starbucks (although the latter is a non-smoking oasis). Tokyo has some uniquely atmospheric cafes and tea rooms that range from homey old mom-and-pop shops to uberdesigned hipster hang-outs to French maid cafes for the anime geek set. They may not have a huge brew variety, but they make for a great spot to rest while sightseeing.

Japan's Spirits

When it comes to alcohol, the Japanese are avid consumers of *birru* (beer; ビール), which tend to be light and easy-drinking lagers. *Wain* (wine; ワイン) and *uisukī* (whisky; ウイスキー) are also fairly common tipples, though their high status means that they're often significantly more expensive than in the West.

SAKE & SHŌCHŪ

Sake, aka *nihonshū* (rice wine; 酒 or 日本酒), is Japan's national beverage, and the variety of grades, flavours and regions of origin can be astounding. Not surprisingly, sake makes the perfect accompaniment to traditional Japanese food, and sake pubs generally also serve excellent seasonal fish and other foods to go with the booze. Sake is drunk chilled (*reishu*), at room temperature (*jō-on*), warmed (*nuru-kan*) or piping hot (*atsu-kan*), according to the season and personal preference. The top-drawer stuff is normally served well chilled. Sake is traditionally served in a ceramic jug known as a *tokkuri*, and poured into tiny cups known as *o-choko* or *sakazuki*.

The website www.sake-world.com has a concise yet comprehensive guide to different types of sake.

Interestingly, sake is falling out of favour with the younger generation, while the potent *shōchū* is becoming ever more popular. Taste testing *shōchū onzarokku* (on the rocks) is a great way to sample the different flavours.

BEER

Introduced at the end of the 1800s, *biiru* (beer) is now the favourite tipple of the Japanese. The quality is generally excellent and the most popular type is light lager, although more recently some breweries have been experimenting with darker brews. The major breweries are Kirin, Asahi, Sapporo and Suntory, but a growing number of microbreweries is chipping away at the market. Beer is dispensed everywhere, from vending machines to beer halls and even in some temple lodgings.

A standard can of beer from a vending machine is about ¥250, although some of the gigantic cans cost more than ¥1000. At bars, a beer starts at ¥500 and the price climbs depending on the establishment. *Nama biiru* (draught beer) is widely available, as are imported beers. *Happōshu* (発泡酒) is a low-malt, beer-like beverage found in supermarkets and *kombini* (convenience stores) that's cheaper than beer because it's taxed less. Generally, the taste isn't worth the savings.

Tokyo has some fantastic annual beer festivals including the following.

Great Japan Beer Festival (www.craftbeer association.jp/beerfest.html) June

Nippon Craft Beer Festival (www.craftbeer festival.org/en/index.html) Spring and autumn

Asahi Beer Oktoberfest (www.oktoberfest.jp) September

WHISKY

Once pooh-poohed by foreign drinkers, Japanese whisky is now recognised as some of the finest in the world, able to stand up to the best from Scotland and elsewhere. A watershed event was when a bottle of 10-year-old Yōichi from Hokkaidō took home the top prize at a Whisky Magazine competition in 2001. Tokyo now has a growing number of dedicated whisky and scotch bars where travellers can sample the best of the major makers Suntory and Nikka, as well as products from the seven active single-malt distilleries in Japan.

Lonely Planet's Top Choices

Agave (p85) Premium tequilas in a cavern-like basement bar.

Ageha (p182) One of Asia's largest clubs, set on Tokyo Bay.

Golden Gai (p136) Travel back in time and wander this postwar maze of intimate bars.

Popeye (p177) Boasting the most beers on tap in Japan, Popeye is a nonsmoking, suds-lover's dream.

These (p88) Get bookish in this library-like, nook-ridden bar in Nishi-Azabu.

Zoetrope (p136) Try hundreds of different whiskies at this Shinjuku hole in the wall.

Best Bars with a View

New York Bar (p137)

Two Rooms (p122)

Bello Visto (p110)

Sky Bar (p89)

Best Nonsmoking Bars

Aldgate (p110)

Craft Beer Market (p88)

Harajuku Taproom (p122)

La Jetée (p136)

Best Clubs

Womb (p111)

Eleven (p88)

Club Asia (p112)

New Lex Tokyo (p88)

Best Cafes & Tea rooms

Nakajima no Ochaya (p76)

Benisica (p76)

Attic Room (p110)

Cha Ginza (p76)

PLAN YOUR TRIP DRINKING & NIGHTLIFE

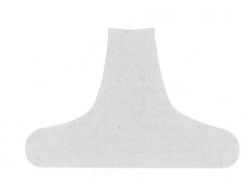

Entertainment

Tokyoites' intense passion for entertainment embraces world-class orchestras to sidewalk cos-players (costume players) and everything in between. The capital's smoky jazz bars, grand theatres and rockin' music festivals brim with home-grown and imported talent, both cutting edge and traditional. If your taste is new wave or nō (stylised Japanese dance-drama), there's a show on for you.

Live Music

Though the live-music scene keeps geriatric hours (shows often end around 10pm), rock, house, blues, jazz, classical and electronica are thriving in Tokyo. Big international acts often appear at large venues such as the National Stadium (p126) in Yoyogi or Budōkan (p142). But Tokyo also has many good small live houses, especially in Shibuya.

Some of the Tokyo area's most well supported musical events are festivals that draw thousands:

Fuji Rock Festival (rock; www.fujirockfestival.com)

Summer Sonic (rock; www.summersonic.com)

Tokyo Jazz Festival (jazz; www.tokyo-jazz.com)

La Folle Journee au Japon (classical; www.lfj.jp)

Traditional Theatre

If you've never seen fake snow falling on wildly made-up actors who have just dispatched their samurai foes in *The Tale of the Forty-Seven Rōnin,* a beloved Japanese epic of revenge, then you're in for a treat if you catch this classic of kabuki (p236). Along with the slower dance-drama of nō (p237), and bunraku, traditional puppetry involving large puppets manipulated by up to three black-robed puppeteers, kabuki can be a very worthwhile entertainment option for an afternoon.

Happily, if you want to see these three traditional dramas, Shimbashi Embujō, Kokuritsu Gekijō and Kokuritsu Nō-gakudō have earphones or subtitles with English translation of the dramatic dialogue.

Contemporary Theatre

Tokyo has a lively contemporary theatre scene. Language can be a barrier, as most of the productions are in Japanese, but the visual spectacle will more than make up for gaps in understanding.

Roppongi's SuperDeluxe (p89) often stages performance art pieces created by or involving foreign talent. The venerable Tokyo International Players troupe (www.tokyoplayers.org) also puts on English-language shows. Meanwhile, Festival/Tokyo (http://festival-tokyo.jp) shows avant-garde performing arts in autumn in Ikebukuro and elsewhere.

Dance

Tokyo's dance scene mixes international and indigenous styles. At venues around the city you will find ballet, modern, jazz and experimental. You may also see home-grown *butō,* an avant-garde genre in which dancers use their naked or seminaked bodies to express the most elemental human emotions. Check out these troupes for dance performances:

Sankai Juku (www.sankaijuku.com)

Tokyo Ballet (http://thetokyoballet.com)

Die Pratze (www.geocities.jp/kagurara2000)

Session House (p148)

Cinemas

Tokyo cinemas show blockbuster foreign movies in small spaces, though some Hollywood flicks take a while to open here. Other theatres show films you might not see anywhere else. See www.japantimes.co.jp for listings.

Lonely Planet's Top Choices

Kokuritsu Gekijō (p65) Top-notch *nō*, bunraku and other drama in a grand setting.

Shimbashi Embujō Theatre (p76) Best for kabuki while the Kabuki-za is being rebuilt.

Setagaya Public Theatre (p111) Renowned for contemporary drama and dance.

New National Theatre (p137) State-of-the-art venue for opera, ballet, dance and theatre.

Best Jazz Clubs

Shinjuku Pit Inn (p137)

Blue Note Tokyo (p90)

Jazz Spot Intro (p148)

Cotton Club (p65)

Best for Traditional Arts

Kokuritsu Nō Gakudō (p123)

Asakusa Engei Hall (p177)

Bunkamaru (p112)

Suehirotei (p137)

Best for Japanese Music

Unit (p101)

Loft (p138)

Club Quattro (p111)

Shibuya O-East (p112)

Best Cinemas

Toho Cinemas Roppongi Hills (p89)

Eurospace (p112)

Bunkamura (p112)

Uplink (p111)

Best Contemporary Theatre

Setagaya Public Theatre (p111)

Bunkamaru (p112)

Za Koenji (p138)

Honda Theatre (p112)

Best Clubs

Ageha (p182)

Womb (p111)

Unit (p101)

Eleven (p88)

Best for Spectator Sports

Ryōgoku Kokugikan (p170)

Tokyo Dome (p143)

National Stadium (p126)

Jingu Gaien (p126)

NEED TO KNOW

Tickets

Tickets for live music shows can start at around ¥5000 and climb way up depending on the artist and venue. Seats for kabuki performances generally start at ¥3000, not including the earphone rental fee.

Language

Music is a universal language, but theatre and comedy can be a big barrier. Fortunately, traditional drama such as kabuki and bunraku often provide English translation via rental headphones or captions.

Websites

➡ Metropolis (http://metropolis.co.jp/listings/)

➡ Kabuki Web (www.kabuki-bito.jp/)

➡ Japan Times (www.japantimes.co.jp/entertainment/advanced_booking.html)

➡ Creativeman (http://creativeman.co.jp)

A Hello Kitty–themed shop, Shinjuku

Shopping

Since the Edo–era, when courtesans set the day's trends in towering geta (traditional wooden sandals), Tokyoites have lusted after both the novel and the outstanding. The city remains the trendsetter for the rest of Japan, and its residents shop – economy be damned – with an infectious enthusiasm. Join them in the hunt for the best new camera, the latest fashions or the perfect teacup.

Fashion

A generation ago, Ginza *depāto* (department stores) were the supreme arbiters of style, but today they're seen as purveyors of more conservative tastes. Tokyo's fashion scene is now centred on the western side of town, in neighbourhoods like Shibuya, Harajuku, Aoyama and Daikanyama. You'll recognise many of the international brand names, but you'll also encounter a lot of Japanese labels, too. Young shoppers in particular prefer cheaper domestic brands that can turn out *kawaii* (cute) renditions of the latest global trends in a way that appeals to Japanese sensibilities.

While no recent homegrown designers have managed the kind of game-changing success that brands like Comme des Garçons achieved in the '80s, they continue to affect a series of quieter microrevolutions. Trawl the back streets of fashionable neighbourhoods to discover tiny boutiques with eccentric visions - Tokyo is definitely a city that rewards those who head off the main drag.

Secondhand shops also have a following among young Tokyoites; you'll find merchandise to be expensive but of excellent quality. Shimo-Kitazawa and Kōenji have lots of these shops and an irreverent attitude to go with them.

Contemporary Artisans

Trendy Tokyo still, fortunately, has a strong artisan tradition. Older neighbourhoods on the east side of town, like Asakusa and Ningyochō have shops that sell woven bamboo boxes, make-up brushes for kabuki actors and indigo-dyed *noren* (cloth hung as a sunshade, typically carrying the name of the shop or premises) – much like they did a hundred or more years ago. There's also a new generation of craftsmen and women who are no less devoted to *monozukuri* (the art of making things), but who are channelling more contemporary needs and tastes. Look to the creators who have set up in the newly developed 2k540 Aki-Oka Artisan mall (p154) under the elevated tracks between Akihabara and Okachi-machi. This is the place to get *tabi* (split-toed Japanese socks) in cool geometric prints and mobile phone cases carved from wood.

Collector Culture

Akihabara's *otaku* (geeks) are the greatest ambassadors of Japan's collector culture. But they're hardly an isolated example, and anime (Japanese animation) and computers aren't the only obsessions. You don't have to go further than famous *otaku* haunts like Akihabara and Nakano to find stores that specialise in model trains, radio parts, vintage cameras and nostalgic toys. Go further afield and you'll find vintage clothing stores that have painstakingly assembled everything you need to recreate the '80s (or the '20s) through to record stores and shops selling blue jeans hand-woven on age-old Levi's looms. Given the appetite for such collectors' items, a lot of fascinating and obscure things wind up in Tokyo, regardless of where they originated from.

Antique Fairs & Flea Markets

Tokyo has heaps of flea markets and antique fairs, many held on shrine grounds. Popular finds include vintage kimono and

NEED TO KNOW

Opening hours

➡ Department stores: 10am-8pm

➡ Electronic stores: 10am-10pm

➡ Boutiques: noon-8pm

Service

Service is attentive, increasingly so at more expensive stores, where sales staff will carry your purchase to the door and send you off with a bow. If you're feeling a little claustrophobic, you can put both yourself and the clerk at ease with '*Mitteiru dake desu*' ('I'm just looking').

Paying

Traditional and smaller stores may not accept credit cards.

Duty Free

Most major department stores and well-known tourist shops offer tax-exempt shopping for foreign tourists making purchases of more than ¥10,000. These should have tax-exemption counters where staff will speak some English (or at the very least have information that you can read). Otherwise, sales tax is 5%, which is included in the advertised price.

Sizes

Clothing sizes tend to run smaller than in Western countries. All sorts of sizing systems are used and often you'll find only a 'medium' that's meant to fit everyone. To ask if you can try something on say: '*Kore wo shichaku dekimasu ka?*'

Sales

Clothing sales happen, sadly, just twice a year in Japan: at the beginning of January (after the New Year's holiday, usually January 1st–3rd) and again in the beginning of July.

Websites

Tokyo Fashion (http://tokyofashion.com)

Spoon & Tamago (http://www.spoon-tamago.com)

Shopping by Neighbourhood

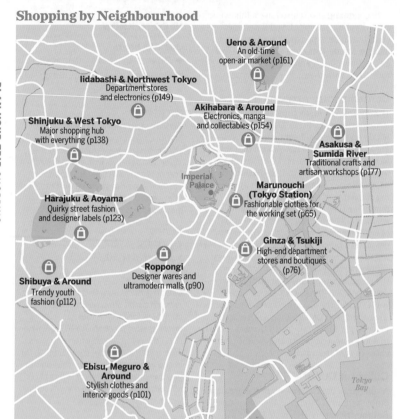

Ueno & Around
An old-time
open-air market (p161)

Iidabashi & Northwest Tokyo
Department stores
and electronics (p149)

Akihabara & Around
Electronics, manga
and collectables (p154)

Shinjuku & West Tokyo
Major shopping hub
with everything (p138)

**Asakusa &
Sumida River**
Traditional crafts and
artisan workshops (p177)

Imperial
Palace

**Marunouchi
(Tokyo Station)**
Fashionable clothes for
the working set (p65)

Harajuku & Aoyama
Quirky street fashion
and designer labels (p123)

Ginza & Tsukiji
High-end department
stores and boutiques
(p76)

Roppongi
Designer wares and
ultramodern malls (p90)

Shibuya & Around
Trendy youth
fashion (p112)

**Ebisu, Meguro &
Around**
Stylish clothes and
interior goods (p101)

Tokyo
Bay

yukata (light cotton kimono), pottery, old postcards and costume jewellery. Don't get your hopes up too much: gone are the days when astute buyers could cart off antique *tansu* (wooden chests). Though bargaining is permitted, remember that it is considered bad form to drive too hard a bargain. Note that sometimes shrine events (or weather) interfere with markets. For information on additional markets, see www. frma.jp (in Japanese).

Ōedo Antique Market (Map p286; www. antique-market.jp; ◷9am-4pm 1st & 3rd Sun of month) Japan's largest outdoor antique market is held in front of Tokyo International Forum.

Hanazono-jinja Flea Market (Map p294; http://kottou-ichi.jp, in Japanese; ◷dawn-dusk Sun)

Nogi-jinja Flea Market (Map p288; www. nogijinja.or.jp/news/main.html, in Japanese; ◷8am-3pm 2nd Sun of month, closed Nov)

O-miyage

O-miyage (souvenirs) needn't just be the obvious things, like chopsticks. The gift shops at contemporary art museums are stocked with covetable goods created in collaboration with local artists. And, in a pinch, you can stock up on only-in-Japan treats, like wasabi-flavoured Kit-Kats, at convenience stores. Also keep an eye out for *zakka* (miscellaneous goods) stores. Tokyoites love them – and visitors do to – for their offbeat selection of beauty goods, kitchen gadgets and other quirky sundries in clever, colourful packaging.

Lonely Planet's Top Choices

Tōkyū Hands (p112) Fascinating emporium of miscellaneous oddities.

2k540 Aki-Oka Artisan (p154) Modern artisan bazaar under the train tracks.

Mandarake Complex (p154) Home sweet home for anime and manga fans.

RanKing RanQueen (p112) The hottest, quirkiest consumer products ranked by sales.

MISC (p101) Tokyo's interior design district.

Okura (p101) Beautiful indigo everything.

Best for Traditional Crafts

Bingoya (p138)

Takumi (p77)

Japan Traditional Craft Center (p149)

Yoshitoku (p177)

Blue & White (p90)

Best Speciality Shops

Kamawanu (p101)

Tolman Collection (p90)

Musubi (p124)

Kyūkyodō (p77)

Isetatsu (p165)

Bengara (p178)

Best for Souvenirs

Itōya (p76)

Rin (p126)

Hara Museum of Contemporary Art gift shop (p94)

Oriental Bazaar (p124)

Mitsukoshi (p65)

Takashimaya (p65)

Best for Japanese Designers

Sister (p112)

Unlimited by Limi Feu (p101)

Isetan (p138)

Comme des Garçons (p125)

Issey Miyake (p125)

Best for Trendy Fashion & Accessories

Shibuya 109 (p112)

Laforet (p124)

Takeshita-dōri (p123)

Parco (p113)

Best for Only-in-Tokyo Fashion

Tsukikageya (p113)

Trunks-ya (p177)

Kita-Kore Building (p130)

6% Doki Doki (p123)

Closet Child (p123)

Dog (p123)

Best for Homewares

Axis (p90)

Natsuno (p77)

Kanesō (p178)

Spiral Market (p125)

Loft (p113)

Best for Antiques & Vintage

Japan Sword (p90)

Fuji-Torii (p124)

Ohya Shobō (p155)

Pass the Baton (p125)

Gallery Kawano (p125)

Chicago Thrift Store (p125)

Best for Gadgets & Electronics

Technologia (p155)

Yodobashi Akiba (p155)

Akihabara Radio Center (p152)

AssistOn (p124)

Best for Toys & Character Goods

Nakano Broadway (p130)

Akihabara Radio Kaikan (p155)

KiddyLand (p124)

Hakuhinkan (p77)

Tokyo Character Street (p65)

Puppet House (p149)

Best on a Budget

Daiso (p124)

Uniqlo (p76)

RagTag (p113)

Don Quijote (p90)

Muji (p77)

Best Shopping Streets

Nakamise-dōri (p170)

Kappabashi-dōri (p170)

Ameya Yokochō (p160)

Nippori Nuno no Machi (p165)

Explore Tokyo

Neighbourhoods at a Glance

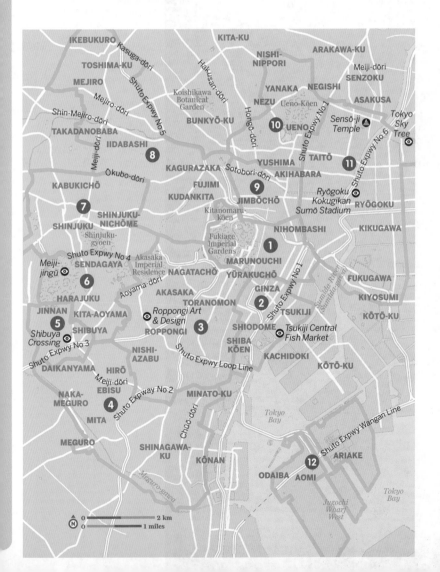

❶ Marunouchi (Tokyo Station) (p58)

Home to the headquarters of many large Japanese companies, Marunouchi (Tokyo Station) faces the Imperial Palace, the spiritual heart of Japan.

❷ Ginza & Tsukiji (p66)

Street upon street of luxury shops and boutiques only a few minutes' walk from the workmanlike Tsukiji Central Fish Market, home to the world's freshest sushi. Wake up early enough and you might catch the tuna auction.

❸ Roppongi (p78)

Legendary for its night spots and foreign party people, this is also the place to come if you want to see cutting-edge art and design (Mori Art Museum). You can even shop for samurai swords here if inspiration strikes.

❹ Ebisu, Meguro & Around (p92)

This broad collection of funky neighbourhoods (such as Naka-Meguro), interior design shops and unexpected museums (think beer and parasites) has something for just about everyone.

❺ Shibuya & Around (p103)

The superdense intersection at Shibuya Crossing, with its neon and giant TV screens, feels like the inspiration for *Blade Runner*, and nowhere will bring you closer to Tokyo's most current youth fashions.

❻ Harajuku & Aoyama (p114)

Home to one of Tokyo's grandest Shintō shrines, this nexus of tradition and trends swarms with young shoppers and some bold luxury brand architecture. The great boulevard of Omote-sandō is Tokyo's answer to the Champs-Élysées.

❼ Shinjuku & West Tokyo (p127)

The world's busiest train station (Shinjuku), a monumental city hall, and some of Japan's best drinking and nightlife spots (Golden Gai) make this a must-see. It's also the gateway to the Ghibli Museum and western hiking trails.

❽ Iidabashi & Northwest Tokyo (p139)

Encompassing the great Yasukuni-jinja shrine, the controversial tribute to Japan's war dead, this area also has an atmospheric hill (Kagurazaka) with old-world alleys. Baseball's Yomiuri Giants and traditional gardens are nearby.

❾ Akihabara & Around (p150)

Otaku (geeks) flock to this electronics mecca to snatch up the latest plastic figurines or sip tea in cafes staffed by French maids. It's bizarro-Tokyo but perfect for gadget and craft shopping.

❿ Ueno & Around (p156)

Tokyo's oldest park boasts giant pandas, the world's largest collection of Japanese art, cherry trees and some quaint residential neighbourhoods (Yanaka) where time seems to have stopped several decades ago.

⓫ Asakusa & Sumida River (p166)

The traditional heart of Tokyo, this riverside area includes the great temple of Sensō-ji, the sumō wrestling arena at Ryōgoku, and the new Tokyo Sky Tree.

⓬ Odaiba & Tokyo Bay (p179)

These artificial islands on Tokyo Bay are very much a new outgrowth of Tokyo as well as an amusement zone, with onsen (hot springs), arcades and a museum devoted to futuristic technologies.

Marunouchi (Tokyo Station)

MARUNOUCHI | IMPERIAL PALACE AREA | NIHOMBASHI

Neighbourhood Top Five

1 Strolling the perfectly manicured gardens of the **Imperial Palace** (p60), home of Japan's emperor, and watching for VIP visitors in horse-drawn carriages.

2 Admiring the century-old glory of **Tokyo Station** (p61), which is undergoing a massive refit.

3 Taking in the antiques market and sweeping architecture of the **Tokyo International Forum** (p61).

4 Browsing the impressionist works at the **Bridgestone Museum of Art** (p64), one of several fine galleries in the area.

5 Crossing **Nihombashi Bridge** (p64) and hitting the food floor at **Mitsukoshi** department store(p65).

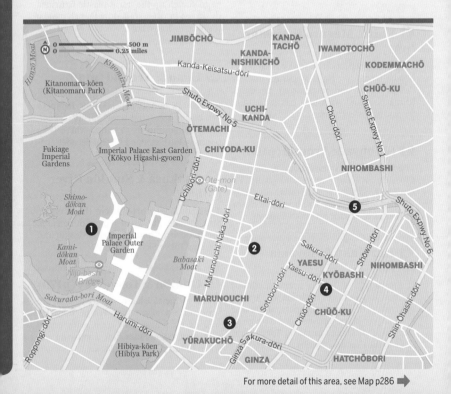

For more detail of this area, see Map p286 ➡

Explore Marunouchi

The Imperial Palace is the geographical and spiritual heart of Tokyo, and has been the centre of national affairs since 1600, when Tokyo was a small bayside city called Edo. From Tokyo Station, the western or Marunouchi exit will take you out towards the Imperial Palace after a 5-minute walk. The entire station is going through a massive ¥50 billion ($651 million) renovation. If all goes well, you'll be able admire the restored facade in time for its centenary in 2014.

In the Imperial Palace East Garden, admire some of the stones that once constituted the largest fortress in the world, Edo Castle. Save for two days a year, the Imperial Palace proper is off limits to the public, but part of it, a graceful bridge and a few buildings, is always visible. Kitanomaru-kōen, north of the palace, is renowned for the springtime cherry blossoms by its northern gate.

Once a drab business stronghold, the Marunouchi area has been reinvigorated in recent years with a slew of new buildings and high-end hotels, shops and restaurants. You could easily walk from here to Yūrakuchō, taking in the Tokyo International Forum, before hitting some museums in Kyōbashi and Nihombashi on the other side of the tracks; take the subway to save your energy. With a stroll in the Imperial Palace East Garden, you could easily spend an afternoon exploring this area. Visits to local museums may take up the better part of a day.

Local Life

→ **Eating** Tokyo Ramen Street (p64), in Tokyo Station, is where salarymen line up for their daily noodle fix.

→ **Cycling** Every Sunday from 10am to 3pm, a 3km stretch of Uchibori-dōri street by the Imperial Palace is roped off to create the Palace Cycling Course. Borrow one of 250 free bikes beside the *kōban* (police box) by exit 2 of Nijubashi Station. Not held on rainy days.

→ **Jogging** A popular jogging route is the 5km loop of the Imperial Palace, which has views of landmarks like the National Diet Building, as well as lots of greenery.

Getting There & Away

→ **Train** The Yamanote and other JR lines stop at Tokyo Station, as does the Narita Express service for Narita Airport. Tokyo Station is also a hub for *shinkansen* services north and south, including Kyoto and Osaka. Yūrakuchō Station, one stop south on the Yamanote Line, may be more convenient to some destinations.

→ **Subway** The Marunouchi Line connects with Tokyo Station. The Mita, Chiyoda and Hanzōmon Lines also have stops nearby.

 Best Places to Eat

→ MIMIU (p65)
→ Tokyo Ramen Street (p64)
→ Numazu Uogashi (p65)

For reviews, see p64 →

 Best Museums

→ Bridgestone Museum of Art (p64)
→ Kite Museum (p64)
→ Idemitsu Museum of Arts (p64)

For reviews, see p61 →

 Best Architecture

→ Tokyo International Forum (p61)
→ Tokyo Station (p61)
→ Imperial Palace (p60)

For reviews, see p61 →

MARUNOUCHI (TOKYO STATION)

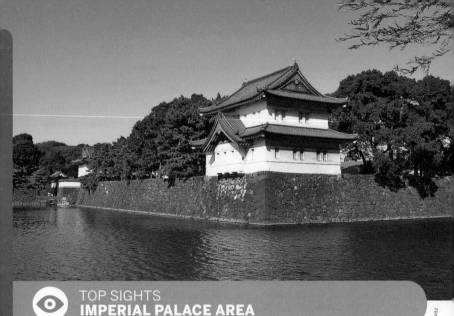

TOP SIGHTS
IMPERIAL PALACE AREA

The residence of Japan's emperor, the Imperial Palace occupies pride of place in the symbolic centre of the nation. Though the palace is usually closed to the public, its beautiful, extensive and free garden offers a respite from the city bustle.

Kōkyo (Imperial Palace)

The Imperial Palace (皇居) is the permanent residence of Japan's emperor and imperial family.

Completed in 1968, the palace itself is a contemporary reconstruction of the Meiji Imperial Palace, which was targeted by aerial bombers during WWII. However, on these grounds once stood Edo Castle, which in its time was the largest castle in the world. In 1590 Tokugawa Ieyasu chose the grounds as the site for an unassailable fortress from which the shōgun was to rule all Japan until the Meiji Restoration, though much was lost to fires. The Emperor Meiji took up power in Edo, and much of the remaining castle was torn down to make way for the new Imperial Palace.

If you don't enter the palace in one of these ways, you can wander round the perimeter and visit the gardens, from where you can catch a glimpse of the palace's most famous landmark, the double-barrelled bridge, **Nijū-bashi**.

DON'T MISS
➡ East Garden

PRACTICALITIES
➡ Map p286
➡ East Garden
☎ 3213-2050
➡ Admission free
➡ ⊗9am-4.30pm Mar–mid-Apr, Sep & Oct; 9am-5pm mid-Apr–Aug; 9am-4pm Nov-Feb, closed Mon & Fri year-round & for imperial functions
➡ Ⓡ Marunouchi Line to Ōtemachi (exits C13b or C8b)

Kōkyo Higashi-gyōen (Imperial Palace East Garden)

The East Garden of the Imperial Palace (東御苑) is the only corner of the grounds that is regularly open to the public, and it makes for a pleasant retreat from the grinding bustle of Tokyo. Here you can see the massive stones used to build the castle walls, and even climb the ruins of one of the keeps (fortified tower), off the upper lawn. Although entry is free, the number of visitors at any one time is limited, so it never feels crowded.

◉ SIGHTS

◉ Imperial Palace Area

IMPERIAL PALACE AREA   PALACE, GARDENS

The Imperial Palace Area includes Kōkyo (Imperial Palace; p60) and Kōkyo Higashi-gyōen (Imperial Palace East Garden; p60).

◉ Marunouchi Area

TOKYO STATION   BUILDING

Map p286 (東京駅; 1-9 Marunouchi, Chiyoda-ku) Tokyo Station, now in the final stages of a grand renovation and expansion (p228), will turn 100 in 2014. Behind its elegant brick facade on the Marunouchi side lies one of the busiest railway hubs in Japan, hosting over a dozen lines and launching *shinkansen* (bullet trains) to points north and south. You'll find people arriving from everywhere in Tokyo and Japan and even from overseas, but the shopping and dining options here present a microcosm of Japan's capital. Tokyo Station City, the name for the general nontransport complex, has various 'streets' on the Yaesu side such as Tokyo Ramen Street and Tokyo Character Street (p65), where you can find tasty noodles and *kawaii* (cute) toys respectively; the nearby Daimaru department store carries higher-end goods, while the underground GranSta arcade has shops specialising in *bentō* (boxed lunch) – perfect for long train rides.

TOKYO INTERNATIONAL FORUM   ARCHITECTURE

Map p286 (東京国際フォーラム; 3-5-1 Marunouchi, Chiyoda-ku; admission free; 🚇Yūrakuchō Line to Yūrakuchō, exit D5) Located between Tokyo and Yūrakuchō Stations, the Forum is one of Tokyo's architectural marvels. Architect Rafael Viñoly won Japan's first international architecture competition with his design, which is hemmed in by train tracks on the east side. It was completed in 1996.

The eastern wing looks like a glass ship plying the urban waters, while the west wing is a cavernous space of vaulted steel and glass. At night, the eastern glass hall is lit by hundreds of precisely placed beams, and takes on the appearance of a space colony. Although it's used mainly for its

DESIGN GEMS

The Imperial Hotel's Nacio 'Skip' Cronin, who runs an interior design office in Tokyo, recommends the following buildings for their standout architecture.

Tamasaka

(☑5485-6690;www.tamasaka.com, in Japanese; 2-21-11 Nishi-Azabu, Minato-ku) This building looks like a contemporary Japanese 'house' but done in traditional lines so it has a classical feeling – yet it's a Japanese restaurant and very subtle and understated .

Dior Building

My favourite big building is the diaphanous Dior building (p119) on Omotesandō – each floor shimmers in a slightly different hue of fluorescent white. The walls are mostly glass but insides are blocked off with curved plastic 'drapes'. Ingenious design.

meeting halls and live-music venues, many events are open to the public, and casual visitors are free to wander its courtyard-cum-sculpture garden and the glass eastern wing. Take the lift to the 7th floor of the eastern wing and look down on the tiny people below. There are restaurants, cafes and shops.

The Oedo Antique Market, held in the courtyard of the Forum on the first and third Sunday of every month (9am–4pm), is a colourful event and a good chance to bargain for retro and antique Japanese goods, from old ceramics to kitsch plastic figurines.

MITSUBISHI ICHIGŌKAN MUSEUM   MUSEUM

Map p286 (三菱一号館美術館; http://mimt.jp/english; 2-6-2 Marunouchi, Chūō-ku; admission varies; ◷10am-8pm Wed-Fri, to 6pm Tue, Sat & Sun; 🚇Chiyoda Line to Nijūbashimae, exit 1) This unique reproduction of the area's first office building (designed in 1894 by English architect Josiah Conder) was opened in 2010 to showcase European art from the late 19th to the mid-20th centuries, and has focused on its holdings of Toulouse-Lautrec works. Also on the premises are Café 1894, set in a reproduction of an old bank, and archive rooms (admission free) with period decor and furniture.

1. Imperial Palace (p60)
The palace's most famous landmark, the Nijū-bashi bridge, with the palace in the background.

2. Marunouchi (p58)
Window-shopping in Marunouchi's reinvigorated retail scene.

3. Kitanomaru-kōen (p142)
Boats ply the waters of Kitanomaru Park during cherry blossom season.

IDEMITSU MUSEUM OF ARTS   MUSEUM

Map p286 (出光美術館; www.idemitsu.co.jp/
museum, in Japanese; 9th fl, 3-1-1 Marunouchi,
Chiyoda-ku; adult/student/child ¥1000/700/free;
⊙10am-5pm Tue-Sun, to 7pm Fri; ⑭JR Yamanote
Line to Yūrakuchō) This excellent collection of
Japanese art, sprinkled with Chinese and
Korean pottery and a few stray Western pieces, is the result of the lifetime passion of pe-
troleum magnate Idemitsu Sazo. As there is
no permanent display, exhibits change every
few months, highlighting the complete depth
of Idemitsu's collection.

⊙ Nihombashi Area

NIHOMBASHI   BRIDGE

Map p286 (日本橋; ⑭Ginza Line to Mistukoshi-
mae, exits B5 or B6) Even with the bronze lions
guarding it, you could be forgiven for walking right past this granite bridge under an
expressway, where Chūō-dōri meets the river Nihombashi-gawa. Still, it bears mention
for its historic significance. Nihombashi
(Japan Bridge) was the point from which
all distances were measured during the
Edo period (p223), and the beginning of the
great trunk roads (the Tōkaidō, the Nikkō
Kaidō etc) that took *daimyō* (feudal lords)
between Edo and their home provinces. To
see a replica of the original wooden bridge,
visit the Edo-Tokyo Museum (p171).

BRIDGESTONE MUSEUM OF ART   MUSEUM

Map p286 (ブリヂストン美術館; www.bridge
stone-museum.gr.jp/en/; 1-10-1 Kyōbashi, Chūō-
ku; adult/student ¥800/500; ⊙10am-8pm Tue-
Sun; ⑭Ginza Line to Nihombashi, Takashimaya
exit) The Bridgestone Corporation's collection, which was previously kept as a private
collection by Bridgestone founder Ishibashi
Shōjiro, is one of the best French impressionist collections you will find in Asia.
Though European painting is undoubtedly
the main attraction (think Renoir, Ingres,
Monet, Corot, Matisse, Picasso, Kandinsky
et al), the museum also exhibits sculpture
and some works by Japanese impressionists
as well as European pieces that employ abstract or neoclassical aesthetics.

KITE MUSEUM   MUSEUM

Map p286 (凧の博物館; www.tako.gr.jp/eng/
museums_e/tokyo_e.html; 5th fl, 1-12-10 Nihombashi, Chūō-ku; adult/child ¥200/100; ⊙11am-
5pm Mon-Sat; ⑭Ginza Line to Nihombashi, exit C5)
In Japan, even the humble kite can be an art
form. There are 300 or so kites in this small
but fascinating museum, including bril-
liantly painted kites based on folk characters, wood-block prints or samurai armour.
None are particularly old (they're made of
paper, after all), but they're amazing to admire nonetheless. Ask for an English booklet at reception. The Kite Museum is located
above the restaurant Taimeiken (たいめいけ
ん), just beyond Finn McCool's Irish pub.

MITSUI MEMORIAL MUSEUM   MUSEUM

Map p286 (三井記念美術館; www.mitsui-mu
seum.jp; 7th fl, Mitsui Main Bldg, 2-1-1 Nihombashi-
Muromachi, Chūō-ku; adult/student ¥1000/500;
⊙10am-5pm Tue-Sun; ⑭Ginza Line to Mitsukoshimae, exit A7) Stately wood panelling surrounds
a small collection of traditional Japanese art
and artefacts, including ceramics, paintings,
and *nō* (stylised Japanese dance-drama)
masks, amassed over three centuries by the
families behind today's Mitsui conglomerate.

NATIONAL FILM CENTRE   MUSEUM

Map p286 (東京国立近代美術館フィルムセン
ター; www.momat.go.jp; 3-7-6 Kyōbashi, Chūō-ku;
screenings adult/student ¥500/300, exhibition
only ¥200/70; ⊙gallery 11am-6.30pm Tue-Sun,
check website for screening times; ⑭Ginza Line to
Kyōbashi, exit 1) The National Film Centre is
an archive of Japanese and foreign films, as
well as books, periodicals, posters and other materials. There are daily screenings of
classic films at bargain prices but few have
English subtitles. There are English captions, however, on the worthwhile 7th-floor
gallery, which has a fascinating collection
of projectors, props and scripts from the
golden age of Japanese cinema.

✕ EATING

There's no shortage of restaurants
in proximity to Tokyo Station and the
Imperial Palace, and many of the best
options are in Marubiru (Marunouchi
Building) and Shin-Marubiru, two recently
built high-rises on the Marunouchi side
of Tokyo Station. Within the station
itself, on the opposite side (Yaesu side),
is Tokyo Ramen Street, a collection of
eight *rāmen* shops including the popular
Mutsumi-ya (むつみ屋) from Hokkaidō (in
northern Japan) offering lip-smacking
soups such as *aka-miso rāmen* (red miso
rāmen; ¥850).

MIMIU
UDON ¥¥

Map p286 (美々卯; ☎3567-6571; 3-6-4 Kyōbashi, Chūō-ku; lunch ¥700-1400, side dishes ¥500-2200, dinner from ¥4800; ◯11.30am-8.30pm Mon-Sat, to 8pm Sun; 🅿; 📵Ginza Line to Kyōbashi, exit 1 or 2) Connoisseurs of udon say that Osaka-style broth is lighter in colour and more delicate in flavour than what Tokyoites favour. Try for yourself at this Osaka original that's said to have invented *udon-suki* (¥4070 per person), udon cooked sukiyaki-style in broth, with seafood, vegetables and meat. Look for the stately black building.

NUMAZU UOGASHI
SUSHI ¥¥

Map p286 (沼津魚がし; ☎5220-5550; 6th fl, Marunouchi Bldg, 2-4-1 Marunouchi, Chiyoda-ku; sets ¥980-3300; ◯11am-11pm Mon-Sat, to 10pm Sun; 📵; 🚇Marunouchi Line to Tokyo Station, exit 4b, JR Yamanote Line to Tokyo Station, Marunouchi centre exit) It may be in the lofty confines of Marubiru, but this friendly, workmanlike sushi shop feels like Tsukiji. Single serves are pretty expensive, but portions are generous and set lunches are a great deal.

TORAJI
YAKINIKU ¥

Map p286 (トラジ; 6th fl, Marunouchi Bldg, 2-4-1 Marunouchi, Chiyoda-ku; dishes ¥880-1600, sets ¥880-1880; ◯11am-11pm Mon-Sat, to 10pm Sun; 📵; 🚇JR Yamanote Line to Tokyo Station, Marunouchi centre exit) Although it originates from the humble Korean dish known as *bulgogi, yakiniku* at this Marubiru establishment is anything but ordinary. Choose from a variety of immaculate cuts of meat, grill them over charcoals set into your table, and dip into a variety of sauces before popping into your mouth – delicious!

 ENTERTAINMENT

KOKURITSU GEKIJŌ
TRADITIONAL THEATRE

Map p286 (国立劇場; National Theatre; ☎3230-3000; www.ntj.jac.go.jp/english/; 4-1 Hayabusachō, Chiyoda-ku; kabuki adult/student from ¥1500/1100, bunraku adult/student from ¥4500/discount varies; 🚇Hanzōmon Line to Hanzōmon, exit 1) The prestigious National Theatre is Japan's premier venue for traditional performing arts. Performances include kabuki, *gagaku* (music of the imperial court) and bunraku (classic puppet theatre). Earphones with English translation are available for hire (¥650 plus ¥1000 deposit). Check the website for performance schedules.

COTTON CLUB
JAZZ

Map p286 (コットンクラブ; ☎3215-1555; www.cottonclubjapan.co.jp; 2-7-3 Marunouchi, Chiyoda-ku; ◯shows begin 7pm, 9.30pm Mon-Sat, 5pm, 8pm Sun; 🚇JR Yamanote Line to Tokyo Station, Marunouchi south exit) You're more likely to hear Peter Cetera or Peabo Bryson here than musicians harkening back to the 1920s New York club it honours, but the Cotton Club does host a medley of interesting Japanese jazz artists such as saxophonist Itō Takeshi and the occasional great like Toots Thielemans. Check the website for schedules.

 SHOPPING

MITSUKOSHI
DEPARTMENT STORE

Map p286 (三越; 1-4-1 Nihombashi-Muromachi, Chūō-ku; 🚇Ginza Line to Mitsukoshimae, exit A2) Though there are branches of this department store in Ginza (Map p286) and Ebisu (Map p291), the Nihombashi branch has the cachet as Japan's first department store – it even has a subway station named after it. Check out the floor dedicated to the art of the kimono or peruse the morsels in the incredible *depachika* (department store food floor; p41). For the full effect, arrive at 10am for the bells and bows that accompany each day's opening.

TOKYO CHARACTER STREET
MISCELLANEOUS GOODS

Map p286 (東京キャラクターストリート; First Avenue, level B1, Tokyo Station; ◯10am-8.30pm; 🚇JR Yamanote Line to Tokyo Station, Yaesu exit) From Doraemon to Domo-kun, Hello Kitty to Ultraman, Japan knows *kawaii* (cute) and how to merchandise it. On the basement level of Tokyo Station, some 15 Japanese TV networks and toy manufacturers operate shop after shop selling official plush toys, sweets, accessories and the all-important miniature character to dangle from your mobile phone.

TAKASHIMAYA
DEPARTMENT STORE

Map p286 (高島屋; 2-4-1 Nihombashi, Chūō-ku; 🚇Ginza or Tōzai Line to Nihombashi, Takashimaya exit) Takashimaya's branch on New York's Fifth Ave is renowned for its cutting-edge Japanese-inspired interior, but the design of the Tokyo flagship store (1933) tips its pillbox hat to New York's Gilded Age. Uniformed female elevator operators still announce each floor in high-pitched sing-song voices.

Ginza & Tsukiji

GINZA | TSUKIJI | SHIODOME

Neighbourhood Top Five

1 Feasting your eyes on the denizens of the deep at **Tsukiji Central Fish Market** (p68) and then feasting on some for breakfast.

2 Browsing Japan's poshest shops along **Ginza Yonchōme Crossing** (p76) and the surrounding streets.

3 Witnessing the colourful traditional spectacle of kabuki drama at **Shimbashi Embujō Theatre** (p76).

4 Sipping green tea in a traditional teahouse with a skyscraper backdrop at **Hama Rikyū Onshi-teien** (p71).

5 Snacking on *yakitori* (chicken skewers) under the tracks at **Yūrakuchō Yakitori Alley** (p72).

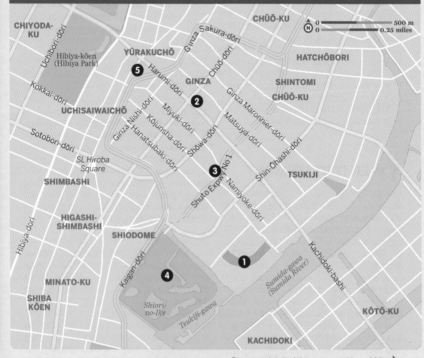

For more detail of this area, see Map p286 ➡

Explore Ginza & Tsukiji

Proudly reigning alongside Fifth Avenue, Beverly Hills and the Champs-Élysées, Ginza is one of the most famous shopping districts in the world. Ginza and the neighbouring district of Tsukiji, home to the world's largest fish market, make up a fairly compact area. Tsukiji Central Fish Market is best experienced in the wee hours for the tuna auction (visitor numbers are limited).

Starting outside Ginza Station, with Mitsukoshi department store behind you, you can explore the neat grid that draws Japan's best dressed by early afternoon. Window-shop till you drop at Mitsukoshi and the other department stores nearby, taking in the bustling basement *depachika* (department store food floor). Superstylish and uberpopular retailers Muji and Uniqlo are also worthwhile if you still have the energy, and don't forget the interesting art galleries in the area.

Refresh yourself at one of the area's cafes and consider a matinee kabuki performance at the Shimbashi Embujō Theatre or hop on the Ginza Line subway to Shimbashi, for the Shiodome skyscraper district and its advertising museum, as well as Hama Rikyū Onshi-teien, home to a beautiful traditional teahouse.

Local Life

→ **Eating** Treat yourself like a local executive with a deluxe sushi dinner (p72).

→ **On the rails** Sip beer with lower-ranking workers under the Yūrakuchō tracks (p72).

→ **People-watching** At night, Ginza's back streets swarm with high-class hostesses catering to salarymen.

Getting There & Away

Ginza

→ **Train** The JR Yamanote Line stops at Shimbashi Station and Yūrakuchō Station.

→ **Subway** The Ginza, Hibiya and Marunouchi Lines connect at Ginza Station, in the heart of Ginza.

Tsukiji & Shiodome

→ **Train** Shimbashi Station (JR and subway) is the hub for Shiodome. Shimbashi is also the terminus for the Yurikamome Line for Odaiba.

→ **Subway** For the fish market, take either the Hibiya Line to Tsukiji Station or the Ōedo Line to Tsukijishijō.

→ **Water bus** Tokyo Cruise ferries (p73) stop at Hama Rikyū Onshi-teien and go to Asakusa and Odaiba.

Best Places to Eat

→ Kyūbey (p72)
→ Daiwa Sushi (p73)
→ Yabaton (p72)

For reviews, see p72 →

Best Places to Drink

→ Benisica (p76)
→ Cha Ginza (p76)
→ Nakajima no Ochaya (p76)

For reviews, see p73 →

Best Shopping

→ Uniqlo (p76)
→ Muji (p77)
→ Natsuno (p77)

For reviews, see p76 →

GINZA & TSUKIJI

TOP SIGHTS
TSUKIJI CENTRAL FISH MARKET (TSUKIJI SHIJŌ)

The Central Fish Market is recovering from a bad 2011 but is busy as ever and open to visitors. Arguably Tokyo's top sight, everything at Tsukiji is allotted its own area, from mountains of octopus, rows of giant tuna, endless varieties of shellfish and tank upon tank of live exotic fish. Since the action takes place between 5am and 8am, you're either going to have to set the alarm clock for the wee hours of the morn or party all night long in Tokyo's bars.

The Market

If it lives in the sea, it's probably for sale at the Tsukiji Central Fish Market (築地市場), where acres of fish and fish products change hands in a lively, almost chaotic atmosphere. From squid to sardines, there seems to be everything under the waves here, all neatly iced in styrofoam containers and waiting for buyers and distributors to snatch them up.

But the undoubted king of the Tsukiji sea is the giant tuna. On the first auction day of 2012, a 269kg bluefin tuna sold for a record ¥56.49 million, some ¥210,000 per kilogram. Purchased by Kiyomura Co, which runs a chain of sushi restaurants, the fish inspired buyer Kimura Kiyoshi to remark, 'I wanted to liven up Japan, given that the country has been hit by the March disaster and economic stagnation'.

Tuna prices are usually inflated at the beginning of the year, and have actually been in decline for years. Indeed, Japan's fishing industry, and by extension Tsukiji, was clobbered in 2011 when the 11 March earthquake and tsu-

DON'T MISS

→ The tuna auction, when open to tourists
→ Sushi for breakfast

PRACTICALITIES

→ Map p286
→ ☎3261-8326
→ www.tsukiji-market. or.jp
→ 5-2-1 Tsukiji, Chūō-ku
→ Admission free; tuna auction limited to 120 people daily
→ ⏰tuna auction admissions from 5am, Seafood Intermediate Wholesalers' Area from 9am; market closed 2nd and 4th Wed most months, Sun and public holidays. Check the website before going.
→ Ⓗ Hibiya Line to Tsukiji (exit 1)

namis took a devastating toll on northern fishing communities and infrastructure. The Fukushima Daiichi nuclear plant crisis worsened the toll as operators continued to dump radioactive water in the surrounding sea to help bring the crippled reactors under control. Tsukiji itself was closed to tourists for four months following the quake to ensure the buildings were safe.

Even though 2011 was a bad year, Tsukiji managed to sell about 497,802 tonnes of seafood, down from 567,162 in 2008 but still worth a respectable ¥423 billion (US$5 billion).

The wholesale stalls are set up to sell directly to restaurants, retail shops and other commercial enterprises. In fact, some of the hundreds of merchants have been in business for more than 20 generations!

The hustle and bustle can be intoxicating, and as long as you're there before 8am, some kind of push and pull will doubtless be going on. Keep in mind, however, that the market shuts completely by 1pm for cleaning. Although the market is not as odoriferous as you might think, you still don't want to wear your nicest clothing (and especially not your best shoes).

Visiting the Auction

If you want to visit the tuna auction, you can watch from a visitors gallery between 5.25am and 6.15am. However, visitors are currently limited to 120 on a first come, first served basis. You'll have to line up first at the **Fish Information Centre** by the market's Kachidoki-mon gate; auction visits for the first 60 people then take place at 5.25am and the second 60 at 5.50am.

Afterwards, you are free to wander the market, but the Seafood Intermediate Wholesalers' Area only opens to visitors at 9am. For details, download the PDF on the market's website.

By late morning the action has pretty well wound down, but you can still visit the Outer Market. Tradition has it that you should finish your visit here with a sushi breakfast from one of the many restaurants in the area. Daiwa Sushi (p73) is within the market itself and gathers long, long queues.

Between the Central Fish Market and the Outer Market is **Namiyoke-jinja**, the Shintō shrine where wholesalers and middlemen come to pray before work. Highlights are the giant gold parade masks used for the lion dance and the dragon-shaped taps over the purification basins.

If you have arrived too late to see the fish auctions, or maybe you just can't stand the thought of dead sea creatures, we can almost guarantee you

TOURS & MEMENTOS

The **Tsukiji Market information centre** (☑3541-6521; www. tsukijitour.jp; 2nd fl, 4-7-5 Tsukiji, Chūō-ku; ◎8.30am-3pm market days; ℝHibiya Line to Tsukiji, exit 2) has historic images of the market including reproductions of *ukiyo-e* (wood-block prints), and conducts tours of the market by advance reservation (from ¥8000, including breakfast). It's in the Kyōei (aka KY) building, at the corner of Harumi-dōri and Shin-Ōhashi-dōri.

Tsukiji Fish Market may be a major attraction for visitors, but it is also very much a working market. Out of respect for the workers, make sure that your sightseeing doesn't get in of the way of commerce; groups in particular should not crowd around a stall. In addition, be very careful to stay out of the way of hand carts, and especially the hundreds of motorised carts which manoeuvre about the market at breakneck speed.

PLANS TO RELOCATE

Even before the 11 March 2011 earthquake, tsunami and nuclear crisis clobbered Japan's fishing industry, Tsukiji was struggling with its future direction. Under Governor Ishihara Shintarō, the Tokyo metropolitan government is pushing to spend ¥128 billion to move the fabled fish market 3km southeast to Toyosu, arguing that current facilities are decrepit, unsanitary and unsafe in a quake; some of the roughly 400 shops in the Tsukiji Outer Market would also move.

While the plan has support from some large seafood wholesalers, it has met with stiff opposition from Tsukiji workers, municipal politicians and environmentalists who argue that the relocation site in Kōtō-ku, a former Tokyo Gas refinery built on reclaimed land, is contaminated with arsenic and other toxins; benzene levels in the soil have been reported to be 43,000 times above the safe limit. When the quake hit, opponents said the site liquefied.

While opponents favour rebuilding the market on its current site, the government has held its ground and still plans to move the world's largest fish market by April 2015. Meanwhile, it wants to open a fresh seafood and vegetable market aimed at the public, tourists and people in the food industry.

The new market would be located on the site of a parking facility near the Outer Market and house about 100 shops. While the government says it would help to maintain the neighbourhood's food culture, opponents say it's simply an attempt to railroad the relocation through by creating a new attraction at Tsukiji. Whatever ultimately happens, this fish fight at the heart of Tokyo won't be resolved any time soon.

will find something of interest in the **Tsukiji Outer Market**. With that said, if you hate food in general – well, there is not much we can do to help you.

The Outer Market concentrates on fruits and vegetables and does a brisk business of its own, yet it's neither as famous nor as breathtakingly busy as its inner counterpart. That's usually a blessing, given that it allows you time to browse not just the produce but alley after alley of noodle shops, tiny cafes and cooking-supply shops, not to mention seafood and sushi counters. In addition, you'll also find boots, baubles, baskets, plates, picks (of the tooth variety) and pottery, all at reasonable prices.

In short, the Tsukiji Outer Market is a one-stop shop for anything you need to prepare and serve that next great Japanese meal. Be sure to first check your home country's import restrictions if you plan to take any food products home with you.

There has been much talk and several proposals over the last decade about the fish market moving eastward, but the 2011 quake caused parts of the proposed site to liquefy. For now, anyway, Tsukiji seems to be staying where it is.

◉ SIGHTS

◉ Ginza

TSUKIJI CENTRAL FISH MARKET (TSUKIJI SHIJŌ)   MARKET

See p68.

SONY BUILDING   SHOWROOM

Map p286 (ソニービル; www.sonybuilding.jp; 5-3-1 Ginza, Chūō-ku; admission free; ⊙11am-7pm; ⒭Marunouchi Line to Ginza, exit B9) Situated right on Sukiyabashi Crossing is the Sony Building, which attracts gadget hounds in search of gizmos that have yet to be released. On the first four floors of this mid-century international-style mini-skyscraper, kids will love the free Playstation games, while adults tend to lose an hour or so perusing all the latest audio and video accessories.

HIBIYA-KŌEN (HIBIYA PARK)   PARK

Map p286 (日比谷公園; admission free; ⒭Hibiya Line to Hibiya, exits A5 & A13) Built around the turn of the 20th century at the height of the Meiji era, this leafy park situated just west of Ginza was Tokyo's first Western-style park. At the time, Western design was the fashion, and it doesn't take long to notice the similarities to public spaces in London, Paris and New York. If you're in need of a break on a quiet afternoon, find your way to one of the two ponds for a nice cup of tea at a pavilion.

GALLERY KOYANAGI   ART GALLERY

Map p286 (ギャラリー小柳; www.gallerykoyanagi.com; 8th fl, 1-7-5 Ginza, Chūō-ku; ⊙11am-7pm Tue-Sat; ⒭Ginza Line to Ginza, exit A9) Exhibits include works from serious heavy hitters from Japan and abroad, like Sugimoto Hiroshi, Marlene Dumas and Olafur Eliasson. Enter from the alley behind Bank of Tokyo-Mitsubishi.

KABUKI-ZA THEATRE

Tokyo's Kabuki-za Theatre is the best place in town to view this signature Japanese art; however, it closed for renovation in April 2010 and was not due to reopen till spring 2013. Until then, look for kabuki performances at the Shimbashi Embujō Theatre (p76).

GINZA GRAPHIC GALLERY   ART GALLERY

Map p286 (ギンザ・グラフィック・ギャラリー; www.dnp.co.jp/gallery/ggg; 7-7-2 Ginza, Chūō-ku; ⊙11am-7pm Tue-Fri, to 6pm Sat; ⒭Ginza Line to Ginza, exit A2) Monthly changing exhibits of graphic arts from mostly Japanese but with the occasional Western artist, with a focus on advertising and poster art. The annual Tokyo Art Directors Conference exhibition takes place here in July.

SHISEIDO GALLERY   ART GALLERY

Map p286 (資生堂ギャラリー; www.shiseido.co.jp/e/gallery/html; 8-8-3 Ginza, Chūō-ku; admission free; ⊙11am-7pm Tue-Sat, to 6pm Sun; ⒭JR Yamanote Line to Shimbashi, Ginza exit) This gallery in the basement of the Shiseido Parlour Café is more experimental than the cosmetics company thereof. An ever-changing selection, particularly of installation pieces, lends itself well to the high-ceilinged space.

TOKYO GALLERY   ART GALLERY

Map p286 (東京画廊; www.tokyo-gallery.com; 7th fl, 8-10-5 Ginza, Chūō-ku; admission free; ⊙11am-7pm Tue-Fri, to 5pm Sat; ⒭Ginza Line to Shimbashi, exit 1) Tokyo Gallery collaborates with the Beijing–Tokyo Art Project, and shows challenging, often politically pointed works by Japanese and Chinese artists.

◉ Shiodome

HAMA RIKYŪ ONSHI-TEIEN (DETACHED PALACE GARDEN)   GARDENS

Map p286 (浜離宮恩賜庭園; adult/senior ¥300/150; ⊙9am-5pm; ⒭Ōedo Line to Shiodome, exits A2 or A3) Once a shōgunal palace extending into the area now occupied by the fish market, this sparse garden is one of Tokyo's finest. The Detached Palace Garden features a large duck pond with an island that's home to a charming tea pavilion, as well as some wonderfully manicured trees (black pine, Japanese apricot, hydrangeas etc), some of which are hundreds of years old. Besides visiting the park as a side trip from Ginza or Tsukiji, consider travelling by boat to or from Asakusa via the Sumida-gawa (Sumida River) aboard Tokyo Cruise (p73).

FREE ADVERTISING MUSEUM TOKYO   MUSEUM

Map p286 (アド・ミュージアム東京; www.admt.jp; B1 fl, 1-8-2 Higashi Shimbashi, Minato-ku; ⊙11am-6.30pm Tue-Fri, to 4.30pm Sat & public holidays; Ginza Line to Shimbashi, exit 4) Dentsu, Japan's largest advertising agency, operates this museum of Japanese ads in the basement of the Caretta building. The collection covers everything from wood-block printed handbills from the Edo period to sumptuous art nouveau and art deco Meiji- and Taisho-era works to the best of today. There's not a lot of English signage, but the strong graphics of many of the ads stand alone. If you see advertising as art, it's a spectacle, and there are video consoles to watch award-winning TV commercials from around the world.

EATING

Ginza has always been a stronghold of the city's finest restaurants, with excellent sushi, marvellous French haute cuisine and ethereal surroundings. It can be challenging to find a modestly priced meal in the evenings, but poking around the *resutoran-gai* (restaurant floors) of department stores can turn up good lunch deals. If all else fails, try the clutch of inexpensive stalls at Yūrakuchō Yakitori Alley under the tracks by Yūrakuchō Station, where chicken skewers and more mysterious kebabs are the food of choice and beer flows very freely. It's prudent to reserve when eating out in Ginza at night. Right on the waterfront of Tokyo Bay, the Tsukiji neighbourhood encircles the busiest fish market on earth and has the freshest sushi, a must-experience in Tokyo.

Ginza

TOP CHOICE KYŪBEY SUSHI, SASHIMI ¥¥¥
Map p286 (久兵衛; 3571-6523; 8-7-6 Ginza, Chūō-ku; sushi sets lunch ¥5000-8400, dinner from ¥10,500; 11.30am-2pm & 5-10pm Mon-Sat; ; Ginza Line to Shimbashi, exit 3) If you can splurge on only one Tokyo sushi experience, make it this one. Established in 1936, Kyūbey's quality and presentation have attracted a moneyed and celebrity clientele ever since, seeking incomparable quality and presentation. Go for broke with *kaiseki* (course menu, lunch/dinner from ¥10,500/15,750), or have it served on pottery by famed artisan Kitaoji Rosanjin for

¥31,500. Otherwise just peruse the Rosanjin exhibition on the restaurant's 4th floor. Kyūbey made headlines in 2009 when it bought at auction half of a single bluefin tuna that sold for a ¥9.63 million (and sold single cuts of toro from it for ¥2000).

YABATON TONKATSU ¥
Map p286 (矢場とん; 3546-8810; 4-10-14 Ginza, Chūō-ku; mains ¥1050-1890; 11am-10pm Tue-Sun; ; Hibiya or Toei-Asakusa Line to Higashi-Ginza, exit A2) Not everything in Ginza has to be chic and sleek. Yabaton sells *miso-katsu*, a very workmanlike take on *tonkatsu* (deep-fried, crumbed pork cutlet) that's slathered in miso sauce. *Waraji-tonkatsu* is a big-as-your-head flattened cutlet, or you can try *kani-korokke* (crab croquettes). *Yabaton-salada* (boiled pork with miso sesame sauce over vegetables) is kinda sorta good for you. Look for the pig wearing a sumō wrestler's apron, one block west of Shōwa-dōri.

L'OSIER FRENCH ¥¥¥
Map p286 (レストラン ロオジエ; 3571-6050; 7-5-5 Ginza, Chūō-ku; set meals lunch/dinner from ¥6800/19,000; noon-2pm & 6-9.30pm; JR Yamanote Line to Shimbashi, Ginza exit) In Tokyo, French restaurants are at the top of the culinary ladder, which is why it's no small accolade that local gourmets consider L'Osier to be the best around. But if you wish to analyse the foie gras yourself, you'll need to book as far as possible in advance since a table at L'Osier is a highly coveted commodity. However, once the wine hits your head and the food hits your lips, you'll key into the art-deco-inspired surroundings and realise that Paris isn't that far away after all.

TEN-ICHI TEMPURA ¥¥¥
Map p286 (天一; 3571-1949; 6-6-5 Ginza, Chūō-ku; set meals lunch/dinner from ¥8400/10,500; 11.30am-9.30pm; ; Ginza, Hibiya or Marunouchi Line to Ginza, exits A1, B3 & B6) Since 1930 Ten-Ichi has rightfully earned its reputation as Tokyo's go-to spot for tempura, which is supernaturally light and nongreasy here. The dignified dining area at the flagship Ginza restaurant has hosted royalty and corporate titans; if the set menus seem pricey, know that a single à la carte tempura prawn costs ¥1000. Book ahead. The entrance is on Namiki-dōri. Other locations include **Akasaka** (Map p302; 3581-2166; Akasaka Excel Tōkyū Hotel).

CRURISING THE SUMIDA RIVER

Though the heavily developed Sumida-gawa is no longer a quaint river, it is still famous for its 12 bridges, and a trip via *suijō bus* (water bus) is an excellent way to survey Tokyo's old geography and see the city from a different perspective.

Hinode Pier, the main pier for **Tokyo Cruise** (東京クルーズ; ☑0120-977-311; www.suijobus.co.jp) is in the Tsukiji/Shiodome area. There is a second pier by Hama Rikyū Onshi-teien (p71). The most popular destinations include upriver to Asakusa (p166; ¥760, 40 minutes from Hinode Pier and ¥720, 35 minutes from Hama Rikyū), and across Tokyo Bay to Odaiba (p179, ¥460, 20 minutes from Hinode Pier only). A special boat, the futuristic *Himiko*, designed by manga artist Matsumoto Reiji, makes the trip directly between Asakusa and Odaiba (¥1520, one hour).

Schedules vary by departure point, but most boats leave once or twice per hour between 9.45am and 5.10pm (with occasional extended departures during summer); the website has complete details. English leaflets describe the dozen or so bridges you'll pass under en route.

BIRD LAND
YAKITORI ¥¥

Map p286 (バードランド; ☑5250-1081; 4-2-15 Ginza, Chūō-ku; dishes ¥150-1200, set meals ¥6000-8000; ☺5.30-10pm Tue-Sat; ◙; ◪Ginza, Hibiya or Marunouchi Line to Ginza, exit C6) This kindly basement bar is a destination for gourmet grilled chicken. Chefs in whites behind a U-shaped counter dispense *yakitori* in all shapes, sizes, colours and organs – don't pass up the dainty serves of liver pâté or the tiny cup of chicken soup. Order a set menu for the most variety, and you can try *sansho-yaki* (like teriyaki) or *oyako-don* (chicken and egg on rice) as well. Enter beneath Suit Company.

NATARAJ
INDIAN ¥¥

Map p286 (ナタラジ; ☑5537-1515; 7th-9th fl, 6-9-4 Ginza, Chūō-ku; mains ¥1000-1450, sets ¥2100-3850; ☺11.30am-11pm; ☑◙; ◪Ginza, Hibiya or Marunouchi Line to Ginza, exit A2) Herbivores don't have it easy in Tokyo, though thankfully there is reason to rejoice at this Indian-influenced vegetarian spot. Nataraj brings its warm colours, low-key elegance and animal-friendly cuisine to this enormous three-storey branch shop in the heart of Ginza. Sizeable set meals include appealing choices such as pumpkin curry and chickpea pakora, which go down well with an extensive wine and beer list of domestic and international favourites.

✖ Tsukiji & Shiodome

DAIWA SUSHI
SUSHI, SASHIMI ¥¥

Map p286 (大和寿司; ☑3547-6807; Bldg 6, 5-2-1 Tsukiji, Chūō-ku; sushi set ¥3500; ☺5am-1.30pm Mon-Sat, closed occasional Wed; ◪Ōedo Line to Tsukijishijō, exit A2) Waits of over one hour are commonplace at Tsukiji's most famous sushi bar, but it's all worth it once you're past the *noren* (curtains) and your first piece of sushi hits the counter. Unless you're comfortable ordering in Japanese, the standard set (seven *nigiri*, plus *maki* and miso soup) is a good bet; there's a picture menu. Though the staff may be too polite to say so, you're expected to eat and run so others can partake in this quintessential Tsukiji experience.

EDOGIN
SUSHI, SASHIMI ¥

Map p286 (江戸銀; 4-5-1 Tsukiji, Chūō-ku; sushi sets ¥1000-4300; ☺11am-9.30pm Mon-Sat, to 8pm Sun; ◪Hibiya Line to Tsukiji, exit 2) Fat pieces of superfresh sashimi and sushi draw the crowds at this little hole-in-the-wall spot just up the way from Tsukiji Central Fish Market. The lunchtime *teishoku* (定食; set meal) is a steal at ¥1000, especially since the fish comes from up the street. Though there's nothing in the way of atmosphere, the locals who come here to eat provide the colour you need.

DRINKING & NIGHTLIFE

Ginza is a pricier drinking destination than Roppongi unless you stick to the *yakitori* joints under the *shinkansen* (ultra fast 'bullet' train) tracks. There are plenty of upscale *izakaya* (Japanese version of a pub/eatery) and European-style bars to clink glasses in here.

1. Ginza shopping (p76)
Shoppers bustle past Matsuya
Ginza department store.

**2. Yūrakuchō Yakitori
Alley (p72)**
Cheap and cheerful fast food
is on offer under the tracks by
Yūrakuchō Station.

**3. Hama Rikyū
Onshi-Teien (p71)**
A tea pavilion sits in the middle
of the lake in Detached Palace
Garden, one of Tokyo's most
beautiful.

BENISICA — CAFE

Map p286 (珈琲館紅鹿舎; 1-6-8 Yūrakuchō, Chiyoda-ku; ◎9.30am-11.45pm; ⛢Hibiya Line to Hibiya, exit A2) This charming cafe seems stuck in 1957 when it opened, with retro wooden furniture, mellow jazz on the stereo and an old black rotary phone that actually works. Benisica is known as the originator of 'pizza toast' (¥1200 drink set), which is exactly what it sounds like but surprisingly delicious.

CHA GINZA — TEAHOUSE

Map p286 (茶・銀座; 5-5-6 Ginza, Chūo-ku; ◎11am-7pm Tue-Sun; ⛢Ginza Line to Ginza, exit B3) In what must be one of the slickest tearooms in Tokyo, customers can plunk down ¥500 for a seat on one of the 2nd-floor benches, a cup of perfectly prepared *matcha* (green tea), and a small cake or two. A shop on the ground floor, where tokens for upstairs are sold, sells premium green tea from various growing regions in Japan.

NAKAJIMA NO OCHAYA — TEAHOUSE

Map p286 (中島の御茶屋; 1-1 Hama Rikyū-teien, Chūo-ku; park admission adult/senior ¥300/150; ◎9am-4.30pm; ⛢Ōedo Line to Shiodome, exits A2 & A3) This beautiful teahouse from 1704 stands elegantly by a pond and a long cedar bridge in the middle of Hama Rikyū Onshi-teien garden (p71). It's the ideal spot for a cup of *matcha* and a sweet (¥500) while contemplating the very faraway 21st century beyond the garden walls.

AUX AMIS DES VINS — WINE BAR

Map p286 (オザミデヴァン; 2-5-6 Ginza, Chūo-ku; ◎5.30pm-2am Mon-Fri, noon-midnight Sat; ⛢Yūrakuchō Line to Ginza-itchōme, exits 5 & 8) Even when it rains, the plastic tarp comes down and good wine is drunk alleyside. The enclosed upstairs seating area is warm and informal, and you can order snacks to go with your wine or full *prix-fixe* dinners. A solid selection of wine comes by the glass (¥800) or by the bottle.

⭐ ENTERTAINMENT

SHIMBASHI EMBUJŌ THEATRE — TRADITIONAL THEATRE

Map p286 (新橋演舞場; ☎3541-2600; www.shochiku.co.jp/play/enbujyo, in Japanese; 6-18-2 Ginza, Chūo-ku; tickets ¥3000-17,000; ⛢Hibiya Line to Higashi-Ginza, exit 6) While Ginza's storied Kabuki-za Theatre is being rebuilt until 2013, corporate owner Shōchiku will mainly stage the plays at its Embujō Theatre. A full performance of traditional kabuki (see p236) comprises three or four acts (usually from different plays) over an afternoon or an evening (typically 11am to 3.30pm or 4.30pm to 9pm), with long intervals between; English translation is available on rental earphones for ¥650. If four-plus hours sounds too long, you can always leave at the intermission. Since some acts tend to be more popular than others, enquire ahead as to which to catch, and arrive well in advance.

TAKARAZUKA GEKIJŌ — TRADITIONAL THEATRE

Map p286 (宝塚劇場; ☎5251-2001; http://kageki.hankyu.co.jp/english/index.html; 1-1-3 Yūra-kuchō, Chiyoda-ku; tickets ¥3500-11,000; ⛢Hibiya Line to Hibiya, exits A5 & A13) While not really traditional theatre, the all-female Takarazuka Gekijō revue, going back to 1914, exposes Tokyo's knack for complexity. These musicals are in Japanese, but English synopses are available. A mostly female audience swoons over actresses in drag. If you love camp, this is for you.

DENTSŪ SHIKI THEATRE UMI — CONTEMPORARY THEATRE

Map p286 (電通四季劇場[海]; ☎120-489-444; www.shiki.gr.jp; 1F Caretta Bldg, 1-8-2 Higashi-Shimbashi, Minato-ku; admission varies; ⛢Ōedo Line to Shiodome, Caretta Shiodome exit) Located in the Shio-Site complex beside the headquarters of the Dentsū advertising group, Shiki Theatre Sea stages Japanese versions of hit Western works such as *Mamma Mia!* and *Aida*.

SHOPPING

Start your power-shopping trip in the heart of Ginza at Ginza Y on-chōme Crossing, the intersection of Harumi-dōri and Chūo-dōri (aka Ginza-dōri) streets, right in front of Mitsukoshi Department Store and on top of Ginza Station on the Ginza Line.

UNIQLO — CLOTHING

Map p286 (ユニクロ; www.uniqlo.com; 5-7-7 Ginza, Chūo-ku; ◎11am-9pm; ⛢Ginza Line to Ginza, exit A2) Uniqlo has made its name by sticking to the basics and tweaking them with style –

designer Jil Sander participated in a recent new launch. Offering inexpensive, quality clothing, this chain has taken Tokyo by storm and is expanding overseas, too. The Ginza store was recently refurbished and expanded to a whopping 2300 sq metres. Other locations are citywide.

MUJI
CLOTHING

Map p286 (無印良品; www.mujiyurakucho. com, in Japanese; 3-8-3 Marunouchi, Chiyoda-ku; ⊙10am-9pm; ⋒JR Yamanoto to Yūrakuchō, Kyōbashi exit) Tokyo's famously understated no-name brand is one of the hippest in Paris. But Muji still sells simple, unadorned clothing and accessories for men and women. It also carries hard-to-find M and L sizes (though these, too, are small). This outlet in Yūrakuchō also has a great cafeteria.

NATSUNO
HOMEWARES

Map p286 (夏野; 6-7-4 Ginza, Chūo-ku; ⊙11am-8pm Mon-Sat, to 7pm Sun; ⋒Ginza Line to Ginza, exit B3) Shelf after shelf of *ohashi* (chopsticks) in wood, lacquer, even gold leaf line the walls of this intimate shop on a Ginza side street, alongside plenty of *hashi-oki* (chopstick rests) to match. Prices run from a few hundred yen to ¥10,000. On the 6th floor, its sister shop Konatsu sells adorable tableware for kids.

ITŌYA
ARTS & CRAFTS

Map p286 (伊東屋; 2-7-15 Ginza, Chūo-ku; ⊙10.30am-8pm Mon-Sat, to 7pm Sun; ⋒Ginza Line to Ginza, exit A13) Nine floors of stationery-shop love await visual-art professionals and seekers of office accessories from the everyday to luxury (fountain pens, Italian leather agendas). The 6th floor offers more traditional Japanese wares including *washi* (fine Japanese handmade paper), *tenugui* (beautifully hand-dyed thin cotton towels) and *furoshiki* (wrapping cloths).

TAKUMI
CRAFT

Map p286 (たくみ; www.ginza-takumi.co.jp, in Japanese; 8-4-2 Ginza, Chūo-ku; ⊙11am-7pm Mon-Sat; ⋒Ginza Line to Shimbashi, exit 5) Takumi has been around for more than 60 years and has acquired an elegant selection of toys, textiles, ceramics and other traditional folk crafts from around Japan. Ever thoughtful, the shop also encloses information detailing the origin and background of the pieces if you make a purchase.

KYŪKYODŌ
ARTS & CRAFTS

Map p286 (鳩居堂; 5-7-4 Ginza, Chūo-ku; ⊙10am-7pm Mon-Sat, 11am-7pm Sun; ⋒Ginza Line to Ginza, exit A2) Gorgeous traditional Japanese paper and note cards welcome you to the ground floor of this store in business since the early Edo period (the current building is 20th century). Upstairs, art is sold on *shikishi* (cardboard canvases), alongside hanging scrolls to display them. Should you want to try your own art, there are traditional brushes and ink stones, even incense for inspiration.

HAKUHINKAN
CHILDREN

Map p286 (博品館; www.hakuhinkan.co.jp; 8-8-11 Ginza, Chūo-ku; ⊙11am-8pm; ⋒JR Yamanote Line to Shimbashi, Ginza exit) This layer cake of a 'toy park' is crammed with this year's models of character toys, the hottest squawking video games, seas of colourful plastic, the softest plush toys ever invented and even a model racetrack (¥200 per five minutes, plus ¥100 car hire) on the 4th floor. If you arrive after hours, a few dozen top-selling toys are available from vending machines outside the store.

SPORTS & ACTIVITIES

KOMPARU-YU ONSEN
BATHHOUSE

Map p286 (金春湯; 8-7-5 Ginza, Chūo-ku; admission ¥450; ⊙2-11pm Mon-Sat; ⋒Ginza Line to Shimbashi, exit 1) The Meiji-era Komparu-yu is a refreshing slice of Shitamachi (low city) in the midst of posh Ginza. This is a simple bathhouse without a sauna or stand-up showers. Tile art includes old-school koi (carp) motifs. The matriarch here keeps a watchful eye over everyone from her perch on the old wooden *bandai* (counter).

Roppongi

ROPPONGI | NISHI-AZABU | SHIBA-KŌEN | AKASAKA | TORANOMON

Neighbourhood Top Five

❶ Soaking up the latest contemporary art at the sky-high **Mori Art Museum** (p80) in the ginormous Roppongi Hills.

❷ Imbibing, karaoke-ing and living it up in the best **watering holes** (p85) of Roppongi and Nishi-Azabu.

❸ Taking in the cutting-edge art and design ideas at 21_21 Design Sight in **Tokyo Midtown** (p80).

❹ Kitsching it up at the retro **Tokyo Tower** (p82) and then meeting a contemplative Buddha at **Zōjō-ji** (Zōjō Temple; p82).

❺ Digging some very curvy architecture and top-notch exhibitions at the **National Art Center, Tokyo** (p81).

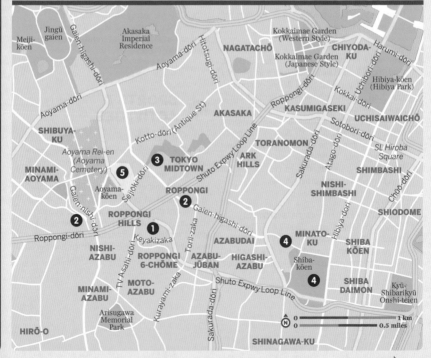

For more detail of this area, see Map p288 ➡

Explore Roppongi

One of Tokyo's prime nightlife districts, Roppongi (and its surrounding neighbourhoods) has a wealth of daytime culture-vulture attractions that can take up a day or two of touring.

Start at Roppongi Station and head west along Roppongi-dōri (topped by an expressway) to Roppongi Hills, taking in the lofty Mori Art Museum and its views of the city. Head back east to explore the area around Roppongi Crossing, which becomes an international crossroads of drinkers and touts at night, and hit the sights of Tokyo Midtown including the Suntory Museum of Art. When it's time to relax, the area north and south of the crossing has excellent dining and drinking options, but there are also some unique spots back down Roppongi-dōri in Nishi-Azabu, a 10- to 15-minute walk away.

Start day two by eyeballing the rather Stalinist architecture and taking a tour of Japan's parliament – the National Diet. Nearby Hie-jinja (Hie Shrine), an important Shintō sanctuary, is part of the Akasaka business district, which has its own share of nightlife, though it's decidedly tamer than Roppongi's. From Akasaka, a short ride on the Ginza Line subway takes you to Toranomon Station for the nearby Musee Tomo and, a 20-minute walk south, the Shiba-kōen (Shiba Park) area. Here you can climb the 1950s-vintage Tokyo Tower and take in the grand Buddhist temple of Zōjō-ji. Nearby, excellent Tofuya-Ukai tofu restaurant is superb at sunset.

Local Life

⟶ **Eating** Slurp some noodles after a long day off hitting the sights (p84).

⟶ **Crooning** You'll sing in the shower. Why not in the bath at Lovenet (p89)?

⟶ **Late nights** Miss the last train (p85) and party till the next morning.

Getting There & Away

Roppongi

⟶ **Subway** The Hibiya and Ōedo Lines run through Roppongi, though the latter is significantly deeper underground. The Hibiya Line is thus closer to Roppongi Crossing, Roppongi's main intersection.

Akasaka

⟶ **Subway** The Yūrakuchō, Hanzōmon, Namboku, Chiyoda, Marunouchi and Ginza Lines all converge in Akasaka. Akasaka-mitsuke is the most central station; nearby are Nagatachō, Akasaka and Tameike-sannō.

 Best Places to Eat

⟶ Tofuya-Ukai (p85)
⟶ Hayashi (p85)
⟶ Inakaya (p84)
⟶ Shabu-zen Roppongi (p84)

For reviews, see p83 ⟶

 Best Places to Drink

⟶ Agave (p85)
⟶ These (p88)
⟶ Mistral Bleu/Train Bar (p88)
⟶ Heartland (p88)

For reviews, see p85 ⟶

ROPPONGI

 Best Nightlife

⟶ Eleven (p88)
⟶ Superdeluxe (p89)
⟶ Muse (p88)
⟶ Bul-Let's (p88)

For reviews, see p85 ⟶

⊙ SIGHTS

⊙ Roppongi

ROPPONGI HILLS
LANDMARK

Map p288 (六本木ヒルズ; Roppongi 6-chōme; admission free; ⒭Hibiya Line to Roppongi, exit 1) Opened in 2003, Roppongi Hills was the dream of real-estate developer Mori Minoru, who long envisaged a transformation of Roppongi. The complex has received lofty praise, and is one of the more architecturally arresting sights in Tokyo. It's enhanced by public art such as Louise Bourgeois' giant, spiny alfresco **Maman spider sculpture**, and the benches-cum-sculptures along Keyakizaka-dōri.

With expertly drawn lines of steel and glass, expansive tree-lined public spaces and a healthy smattering of the city's top bars, restaurants and shops, Roppongi Hills stands as a testament to a new concept in urban planning. Although most Tokyoites can't even dream of owning a high-rise apartment at the city's most prestigious address, Roppongi Hills is a destination in its own right.

The centrepiece of the complex is the 54-storey **Mori Tower**, which is home to some of the world's leading companies, as well as the Mori Art Museum and Tokyo City View observatory. At the base of the tower is the marvellous Grand Hyatt Tokyo (p207) and some 200 shopping, drinking and dining establishments. On the plaza below, the TV Asahi network headquarters adjoin an ancient samurai garden and an arena where you can often catch outdoor performances. Just beyond, the brand-name shops ascending Keyakizaka are marvels of modern design.

MORI ART MUSEUM
MUSEUM

Map p288 (森美術館; www.mori.art.museum; Mori Tower, Roppongi 6-chōme; admission varies; ⊙10am-10pm Wed-Mon, to 5pm Tue; ⒭Hibiya Line to Roppongi, exit 1) Perched on the 52nd and 53rd floors of Mori Tower in the Roppongi Hills complex, the high ceilings, broad views and thematic programs of this museum have somehow managed to live up to all the hype. Contemporary exhibits are beautifully presented and run the gamut from Chinese artist-cum-rabble-rouser Ai Weiwei to the theme of medicine and art.

Upstaged by Tokyo Sky Tree (p170), **Tokyo City View** (東京シティビュー; ☑6406-6652; www.roppongihills.com/tcv/en; incl with admission to Mori Art Museum, observatory only adult/child ¥1500/500; ⊙11am-7.30pm) on the 52nd floor still has some of the best views in central Tokyo. Weather permitting, the rooftop **Sky Deck** (additional ¥300; ⊙10am-8pm) has open-air views, but lacks a 360-degree panorama due to ventilation systems, which fill the platform with restaurant odours from far below.

TOKYO MIDTOWN
LANDMARK

Map p288 (東京ミッドタウン; www.tokyo-midtown.com/en; Minato-ku; admission free; ⒭Hibiya Line to Roppongi, exit 8) Like Roppongi Hills, Tokyo Midtown (2007) is a composite urban district of ultramodern buildings surrounding a historic Japanese garden. Following the same design and urban planning lines that made Roppongi Hills so successful, the Tokyo Midtown complex brims with sophisticated bars, restaurants, shops, art galleries, a hotel and leafy public spaces. Escalators ascend alongside man-made waterfalls of rock and glass, bridges in the air are lined with backlit *washi* (Japanese handmade paper), and planters full of soaring bamboo draw your eyes through skylights to the lofty heights of the towers above.

LOCAL KNOWLEDGE

MORI MINORU

Japan's large redevelopment projects are nothing if not stories of determination despite overwhelming odds. Property mogul Mori Minoru, Japan's Donald Trump, had long eyed the western edge of Roppongi as a prime site for a large-scale complex. The land, however, was divided in typical Tokyo fashion into small lots and many owners. It took the tycoon 18 years of negotiations with over 500 landowners to secure the rights to raze the area and erect his $4 billion tower, which opened in 2003. Mori died in March 2012 at age 77. His dream of building 'vertical garden cities' became a reality in Tokyo, forever changing its traditionally low-slung skyline into a metropolis that reaches for the sky.

ART TRIANGLE ROPPONGI

A trio of world-class museums forms the backbone of Roppongi's art scene, all within several minutes' walk from each other. Start at the **Suntory Museum of Art** in Tokyo Midtown, then cross the street and walk about one block to the **National Art Center, Tokyo**. From there, follow your eyes to the Mori Tower in Roppongi Hills, crowned by the **Mori Art Museum**. Whether or not you're interested in the exhibits (check websites for details), the settings are worth a ramble. At any of these venues, pick up the *Art Triangle Roppongi* walking map, which lists dozens of additional options.

Behind the complex is **Hinokichō-kōen**. Formerly a private garden attached to an Edo-period villa, Hinokichō was reopened as a public park. The adjacent **Midtown Garden** is a cherry tree–lined grassy space that makes a perfect spot for a picnic. It's also home to a geometric clamshell of a building, **21_21 Design Sight** (21_21デザインサイト; www.2121designsight.jp; adult/child ¥1000/free; ⏱11am-8pm Wed-Mon), constructed by Pritzker Prize–winning architect Andō Tadao and featuring temporary exhibits of cutting-edge art and design.

Tokyo Midtown is also home to the Suntory Museum of Art (p81), as well as the glamorous Ritz-Carlton Tokyo (p207).

SUNTORY MUSEUM OF ART   MUSEUM
Map p288 (サントリー美術館; www.suntory.com/culture-sports/sma; Tokyo Midtown, 9-7-4 Akasaka, Minato-ku; admission varies; ⏱10am-6pm Sun-Thu, to 8pm Fri & Sat; ⓇHibiya Line to Roppongi, exit 8) Since its original 1961 opening, the Suntory Museum of Art has subscribed to an underlying philosophy of lifestyle art. Rotating exhibitions focus on the beauty of useful things: Japanese ceramics, lacquerware, glass, dyeing, weaving and such. Its new Midtown digs by architect Kuma Kengō are at turns understated and breathtaking. Admission is free for children and junior-high-school students.

FREE FUJIFILM SQUARE   MUSEUM
Map p288 (フジフイルム スクエア; http://fujifilmsquare.jp/en; Tokyo Midtown, 9-7-3 Akasaka, Minato-ku; ⏱11am-7pm; ⓇHibiya Line to Roppongi, exit 4A) This small gallery on the ground floor of the Tokyo Midtown West Tower is a fascinating look at the history of cameras (see also JCII Camera Museum, p142), from 18th-century camera obscuras to zoetropes to the latest Fujifilm DSLRs. There are two galleries of photography as well as a computer with a database of vintage Fujifilm TV ads starring Japanese celebs such as electronica group YMO.

NATIONAL ART CENTER, TOKYO   ARTS CENTRE
Map p288 (国立新美術館; NACT; www.nact.jp; 7-22-1 Roppongi, Minato-ku; building admission free, exhibition admission varies; ⏱10am-6pm Wed, Thu & Sat-Mon, to 8pm Fri; ⓇChiyoda Line to Nogizaka, exit 6) Designed by Kurokawa Kishō, this architectural marvel, which opened in 2007 as Japan's fifth national-class museum, has no permanent collection. However, it boasts the country's largest exhibition space for visiting shows, which have included Renoir, Modigliani and the Japan Media Arts Festival. The NACT is also worth visiting for its awesome undulating glass facade, its cafes atop giant inverted cones and the great gift shop.

NOGI-JINJA & GENERAL NOGI'S RESIDENCE   SHRINE, HISTORIC BUILDING
Map p288 (乃木神社と旧乃木邸; 8-11-32 Akasaka, Minato-ku; admission free; ⏱shrine 6am-5pm; ⓇChiyoda Line to Nogizaka, exit A1) Found a short walk from the urbanity that is Tokyo Midtown, this shrine makes for a relaxing break. This is where General Maresuke Nogi, a famed commander in the Russo-Japanese War, killed himself in an act of ritual suicide on the death of Emperor Meiji in 1912. Nogi's shiny black wooden residence is open to the public only on 12 and 13 September, but the rest of the year you can peek through its windows and notice the mash-up of Japanese and Western styles that defined the Meiji period (think a tatami room with a Western fireplace). Nogi himself is worshipped as a deity at the shrine.

HONDA WELCOME PLAZA AOYAMA   SHOWROOM
Map p288 (Honda ウエルカムプラザ青山; www.honda.co.jp/welcome-plaza, in Japanese; 2-1-1 Minami-Aoyama, Minato-ku; ⏱10am-6pm; ⓇGinza Line to Aoyama-itchōme, exit 5) The amazing, spacemanlike ASIMO, the world's most

advanced humanoid robot, does brief daily **demonstrations** (1.30pm & 3pm Mon-Fri, 11am, 1.30pm & 3pm Sat & Sun) on stage here, bowing, jogging and then posing for photos. Honda's latest cars and motorcycles are also on display.

◉ Shiba-kōen

TOKYO TOWER   TOWER
Map p288 (東京タワー; www.tokyotower.co.jp/english; 4-2-8 Shiba-kōen, Minato-ku; adult/child main observation deck ¥820/460, special observation deck ¥600/400; ⊙observation 9am-10pm; ⒭Ōedo Line to Akabanebashi, Akabanebashi exit) Built during the postwar boom of the 1950s when Japan was struggling to create a new list of monuments symbolising its modernity, Tokyo Tower resembles the Eiffel Tower, albeit 13m taller. The similarities stop there, however, as Tokyo Tower was painted bright orange and white in order to comply with international aviation safety regulations.

Tokyo Tower is something of a shameless tourist trap, though it's good fun if you go with the right attitude. Lifts whisk visitors up to the main observation deck at 150m (there's another 'special' deck at 250m), which provides some stunning views of the sprawling megalopolis that is Tokyo; there are loftier views at the new, taller and more expensive Tokyo Sky Tree (p170). The 1st floor of Tokyo Tower boasts an enormous **aquarium** (adult/child ¥1000/500), while the 3rd floor is home to a **wax museum** (adult/child ¥870/460) that has some degree of retro popularity.

ZŌJŌ-JI (ZŌJŌ TEMPLE)   TEMPLE
Map p288 (増上寺; Shiba-kōen; admission free; ⊙dawn-dusk; ⒭Ōedo Line to Akabanebashi, Akabanebashi exit) Behind Tokyo Tower is this former funerary temple of the Tokugawa regime, one of the most important temples of the Jōdō (Pure Land) sect of Buddhism. It dates from 1393, yet like many sights in Tokyo its original structures have been relocated and were subject to war, fire and other natural disasters. It has been rebuilt several times in recent history, the last time in 1974.

Nevertheless, Zōjō-ji remains one of the most monumental temples in town. The main gate, **Sanmon**, was constructed in 1605, and its three sections were designed to symbolise the three stages one must pass through to achieve nirvana. The giant **bell** (1673; 15 tonnes) is considered one of the great three bells of the Edo period. On the temple grounds there is a large collection of **statues** of the bodhisattva Jizō, said to be a guide during the transmigration of the soul, as well as a majestic **Himalayan cedar** planted by US president Ulysses S Grant in 1879.

◉ Toranomon

MUSÉE TOMO   MUSEUM
Map p288 (智美術館; www.musee-tomo.or.jp, in Japanese; 4-1-35 Toranomon, Minato-ku; admission varies; ⊙11am-6pm Tue-Sun; ⒭Hibiya Line to Kamiyachō, exit 4B) This marvellous museum may be one of Tokyo's most elegant and tasteful. It is named for Kikuchi Tomo, whose collection of contemporary Japanese ceramics wowed them in Washington and London before finally being exhibited in Tokyo. Exhibitions change every few months and might include highlights of the Kikuchi collection or a special study of raku pottery; you can bet that the displays will be atmospheric and beautiful. The museum is behind the Hotel Ōkura.

◉ Akasaka

HIE-JINJA (HIE SHRINE)   SHRINE
Map p288 (日枝神社; www.hiejinja.net; 2-10-5 Nagatachō, Chiyoda-ku; admission free; ⒭Ginza Line to Tameike-sannō, exits 5 & 7) This Shintō shrine traces its roots to the sacred Mt Hiei, northeast of Kyoto, and it has been the protector shrine of Edo Castle (what is now the Imperial Palace) since it was first built in 1478. The present site dates from 1659, though the shrine was destroyed in the 1945 bombings and later rebuilt in 1967.

These days, the shrine is chiefly known as the host of one of Tokyo's three liveliest *matsuri* (festivals), Sannō-sai. Given the shrine's protector status, the festival was regularly attended by the shōgun, and even now the route of the festival's *mikoshi* (portable shrines carried during the festival) terminates at the Imperial Palace.

If you're wondering about the carved monkey clutching one of her young, she is emblematic of the shrine's ability to offer protection against the threat of a miscarriage.

CARE FOR TISSUES?

Walk out of a busy station in Tokyo in the morning, and you may get a brochure thrust at you. Or, if you're lucky, a pack of tissues. Those handing them out will say '*Yoroshiku onegaishimasu*' (an untranslatable idiom akin to 'please treat me favourably'). They work for companies advertising everything from consumer loans to karaoke parlours. Tissues, however, are the most popular freebie because public bathrooms always lack paper towels (and sometimes even toilet paper).

NATIONAL DIET BUILDING   LANDMARK

Map p288 (国会議事堂; www.sangiin.go.jp; 1-7-1 Nagatachō, Chiyoda-ku; ⊘8am-5pm Mon-Fri, closed national holidays; ®Marunouchi Line to Kokkai-gijidōmae, exit 1) Built on a site once inhabited by feudal lords, the National Diet is Japan's legislature. It was completed in 1936 and features a pyramid-shaped dome. The chambers – the Shūgi-in (House of Representatives; the Lower House) and the Sangi-in (House of Councillors; the Upper House) – have witnessed fist fights and wrestling matches over the occasional hot-button issue. Recently things have been a bit more sedate.

Free one-hour **tours** (☑5521-7445; ⊘9am-4pm Mon-Fri) of the Sangi-in are available when the Diet is not in session (ring the day before to confirm); they take in the public gallery, the emperor's room (from where he addresses the Diet at the start of each session) and central hall, which features a floor mosaic of a million pieces of marble, and murals depicting the four seasons. Although an English pamphlet is available, there is no guarantee that an English-speaking guide will be available when you arrive. To avoid the largest tour groups it's best to arrive in the afternoon.

HOTEL NEW ŌTANI   GARDENS, MUSEUM

off map p288 (ホテルニューオータニ; www.newotani.co.jp/en/tokyo/index.html; 4-1 Kioi-chō, Chiyoda-ku; ®Ginza Line to Akasaka-mitsuke, exit D) The New Ōtani was a showplace when it opened in 1964 to coincide with the Tokyo Olympics. Even though the mantle of tippy-top hotel has since gone elsewhere, it remains worth visiting for its 400-year-old **garden** (admission free; ⊘6am-10pm), which once belonged to a Tokugawa regent, and for the **New Ōtani Art Museum** (☑3221-4111; guests/nonguests free/from ¥500; ⊘10am-6pm Tue-Sun), which displays a decent collection of modern Japanese and French paintings as well as wood-block prints. You can, of course, also stay at the hotel (p208).

SŌGETSU KAIKAN   CULTURAL BUILDING

Map p288 (草月会館; ☑3408-1151; www.sogetsu.or.jp/e/; 7-2-21 Akasaka, Minato-ku; ⊘9.30am-5.30pm Mon-Fri; ®Ginza Line to Aoyama-itchōme, exit 4) Sōgetsu is one of Japan's leading schools of avant-garde ikebana, offering classes in English (p240). Even if you have no interest in flower arranging, it's worth a peek in for the building (1977) designed by Tange Kenzō, and the giant, climbable piece of installation art by the revered Japanese-American sculptor Isamu Noguchi, which occupies the lobby.

✖ EATING

✖ Roppongi

INAKAYA   IZAKAYA ¥¥

Map p288 (田舎屋; www.roppongiinakaya.jp/en; ☑3408-5040; 5-3-4 Roppongi, Minato-ku; small dishes ¥650-1050, fish & seafood ¥1750-3600; ⊘5-11pm; ®Hibiya Line to Roppongi, exit 3) You're bombarded with greetings at the door, and the action doesn't stop at this old-guard *robatayaki* (a place that grills vegetables, fish and meat to go beautifully with booze). It's a party, it's joyous, it's boisterous – and that goes for the profusion of toothsome dishes as well as the attitude one must have when the bill arrives. Live large!

SHABU-ZEN ROPPONGI   SHABU-SHABU ¥¥¥

Map p288 (しゃぶ禅六本木; ☑3585-5600; Aoba Roppongi Bldg B1, 3-16-33 Roppongi, Minato-ku; meals from ¥3600; ⊘11am-11.30pm Mon-Sat, to 11pm Sun; 🄵; ®Hibiya Line to Roppongi, exit 5) This nationwide group of 20 *shabu-shabu* (sautéed beef) speciality restaurants started here in Roppongi. Single-order set menus start at ¥3600, but most guests plonk down an extra ¥600 for *tabe-hōdai* (all you can eat). Prices rise with the grade of beef and for extras, including *fugu* (poisonous blowfish; courses from ¥6100). Superclean rooms offer table or *zashiki* (tatami mat) seating and a nonsmoking section. Shabu-zen is downstairs from the Hobgoblin bar.

R2 SUPPERCLUB   CONTEMPORARY ¥¥

Map p288 (☑6447-0002; www.r2sc.jp; Centrum Bldg, 7-14-23 Roppongi, Minato-ku; mains ¥3300; ☺4pm-4am; 📶; 🚇Hibiya Line to Roppongi, Tokyo Midtown exit) This superslick offering from ECN Holdings (the group behind Minami-Aoyama's Two Rooms; p122) is themed on the speakeasies of the US Prohibition era. The stark interior highlights an enormous central bar where the beautiful people gravitate to dance grooves after midnight. However, dining early on the excellently executed seared swordfish, *wagyū* steaks and lamb chops, topped off with homemade chocolates and a caipirinha or Montecristo cigar, is the best part of the experience.

FUKUZUSHI   SUSHI, SASHIMI ¥¥¥

Map p288 (福寿司; 5-7-8 Roppongi, Minato-ku; lunch sets ¥2656-4725, dinner sets from ¥6300; ☺lunch & dinner Mon-Sat; 📶; 🚇Hibiya Line to Roppongi, exit 3) Arguably some of Tokyo's best sushi is served at Fukuzushi's lovely wooden counter, where the chefs can satisfy your palate with conventional favourites, but can just as easily piece together something more innovative, if you wish. Reservations aren't taken at this popular spot, so plan on a few minutes' wait – it's a small inconvenience for great sushi. Dress code for gents: no sleeveless shirts.

NIRVANA NEW YORK   INDIAN ¥¥

Map p288 (ニルヴァーナニューヨーク; Tokyo Midtown, Minato-ku; dishes ¥1200-2400, dinner courses ¥3000-8000; ☺11am-midnight Mon-Sat, to 11pm Sun; 📶; 🚇Hibiya Line to Roppongi, exit 8) Upmarket Tokyo Midtown's signature Indian eatery is shiny and sceney. Nirvana's butter-chicken curry has fans all over town. If dinner's a bit pricey for you, the lunch buffet (¥2000) is practically a steal; the half-dozen desserts alone would cost that much elsewhere.

MOTI   INDIAN ¥¥

Map p288 (モティ; ☑3479-1939; 6-2-35 Roppongi, Minato-ku; set lunches ¥950-1450, mains ¥1350-2310; ☺11.30am-10pm; 📶; 🚇Hibiya Line to Roppongi, exits 1C & 3) Loved by local expats, Moti maintains a loyal base of foodies who come for the set lunches and well-seasoned curries. Settle into one of the comfortable booths and watch as one embassy staffer, and then another, comes and goes. Moti can fill to the rafters around noon.

SUJI'S   AMERICAN ¥

Map p288 (スージーズ; www.sujis.net; 3-1-5 Azabudai, Minato-ku; sandwiches & brunches ¥900-1500, mains ¥1200-2500; ☺11am-11pm Mon-Fri, 9am-11pm Sat & Sun; 📶; 🚇Hibiya Line to Roppongi, exit 5) Suji's is a landmark for homesick Americans and Japanese craving a bite of the Big Apple. Yummy lunch items include *yakiniku* (grilled beef) wrap, turkey club sandwiches and chicken soup. Suji's house-cured meats (pastrami, corned beef, honey-cured ham etc) are a rarity in Tokyo.

SAN LA KYO   CHINESE ¥

Map p288 (三辣居; 5-10-19 Roppongi, Minato-ku; dishes ¥880-1980; ☺lunch daily, 5.30-10pm Sun-Thu, to 11pm Fri & Sat; 📶; 🚇Namboku or Ōedo Line to Azabu-Jūban, exit 7) Walking into this two-storey spot on a corner near Roppongi Hills is like walking across the Sea of Japan. There are whitewashed walls reminiscent of Shanghai, plus Peking duck, Sichuan-style dishes, renowned dumplings and service more typical of Beijing than snooty Edo. Dishes are typically meant for sharing.

HONMURA-AN   SOBA ¥

Map p288 (本むら庵; 7-14-18 Roppongi, Minato-ku; dishes ¥980-2625; ☺lunch & dinner Tue-Sun, closed 1st & 3rd Tue of month; 📶; 🚇Hibiya Line to Roppongi, exit 4B) The *soba* (buckwheat noodles) are made right here at this minimalist noodle shop on a Roppongi side street; try these delicately flavoured noodles served on a bamboo mat, with tempura or with dainty slices of *kamo* (duck). Honmura-An had legions of fans when it was a famed and fashionable shop in Lower Manhattan; the owner has since returned home and created legions of fans here, too.

HAINAN JEEFAN SHOKUDŌ   SINGAPOREAN ¥

Map p288 (海南鶏飯食堂; 6-11-16 Roppongi, Minato-ku; mains ¥850-1300; ☺lunch & dinner; 📶; 🚇Hibiya Line to Roppongi, exits 1C & 3) This cosy, white-walled 'hawker-style Asian canteen' is a small slice of Singapore near Roppongi Hills. Hainan-style chicken rice, Singapore's national dish, is the speciality; the steamed chicken and rice springs to life with the addition of accompanying sauces (detailed eating instructions are offered), alongside other sprightly dishes. It's located in the alley behind the main street.

✖ Nishi-Azabu

GONPACHI IZAKAYA ¥

Map p288 (権八; ☎5771-0170; 1-13-11 Nishi-Azabu, Minato-ku; dishes ¥290-1280, lunch sets ¥900-1050; ⊙11.30am-5am; 回; 園Hibiya Line to Roppongi, exit 1) Longtime expats deride this foreigner-friendly institution on the busy Nishi-Azabu crossing, but many of them probably had their first meal in Japan here. The first two storeys are a cavernous glam space where Quentin Tarantino shot *Kill Bill*, and now *soba* and *kushiyaki* (skewers) are served here. A separate 3rd floor specialises in sushi. There's also a branch in Odaiba (p182).

✖ Shiba-kōen

TOP CHOICE ✓**TOFUYA-UKAI** TOFU ¥¥¥

Map p288 (とうふ屋うかい; ☎3436-1028; www.ukai.co.jp; 4-4-13 Shiba-kōen, Minato-ku; lunch courses ¥5500-6500, dinner courses ¥8400-12,600; ⊙11am-10pm; 回; 園Toei Ōedo Line to Akabanebashi, exit 8) Make your reservations for this place when you book your flights. You'll be glad you did, for this is perhaps Tokyo's most gracious restaurant, located in a former sake brewery (moved from northern Japan) with an exquisite garden, in the shadow of Tokyo Tower. Seasonal preparations of tofu and accompanying dishes are served in many ways in *kaiseki* style (a Japanese cuisine that abides by very strict rules of etiquette).

✖ Akasaka

NINJA AKASAKA CONTEMPORARY ¥¥¥

Map p288 (忍者赤坂; www.ninjaakasaka.com; Akasaka Tōkyū Plaza, 2-14-3 Nagata-chō, Chiyoda-ku; set meals from ¥7777; ⊙5pm-1am Mon-Sat, 5-11pm Sun; 回; 園Ginza Line to Akasaka-mitsuke, Belle Vie exit) Staff dressed like ninja escort you via trapdoors to your table, take your order and might even perform special ninja magic tricks. Sure it's campy and even touristy, but dude, they're ninjas! Kids will love it, and grown-ups don't have to suffer through bad food. À la carte dishes with ninja-fied names ('transformation of tuna and *negi* (leek) sashimi') are creative but dainty for the price; go for the 10-dish set menus.

HAYASHI IZAKAYA ¥

Map p288 (林; 4th fl, 2-14-1 Akasaka, Minato-ku; dishes ¥200-800, yakitori sets ¥1000; ⊙dinner Mon-Sat; 回; 園Ginza Line to Akasaka-mitsuke, Belle Vie exit) Ensconce yourself in your *hori-kotatsu* (low table with hollowed-out space in the floor for your legs) or on a log bench, and drape a napkin made of kimono fabric over your lap. Kindly staff grill *yakitori* (chicken and other meats or vegetables, cooked on skewers) over *irori* (hearths) set into your table. It's a great place to observe local salarymen and the occasional actor from the theatre down the street. It's upstairs from Lotus Palace.

KOBACHI-YA VEGETARIAN ¥¥

Map p288 (小鉢や; www.kobachi-ya.com; 3-6-10 Akasaka, Minato-ku; lunch sets ¥940-3045; ⊙lunch & dinner Mon-Fri; ⊖✏回; 園Chiyoda Line to Akasaka, exit C6) This refreshingly down-to-earth cafe across from Hie-jinja serves up hearty macrobiotic lunch sets as well as tofu steak, keema (minced meat) curries and vegetable soups. There are a few counters or a large common table for seating.

LOTUS PALACE VIETNAMESE ¥

Map p288 (ロータスパレス; 2-14-1 Akasaka, Minato-ku; dishes ¥950-1600; ⊙11am-11pm; 回; 園Ginza Line to Akasaka-mitsuke, Belle Vie exit) Lunch and dinner are an absolute steal at this foreigner-friendly Vietnamese noodle shop, which serves up set meals that are centred on huge bowls of *pho* (rice-noodle soup) and rounded out with prawn spring rolls and mung-bean pudding. If you need to put an extra spring in your step, the syrupy Vietnamese coffee with condensed milk will no doubt get you where you want to be.

⬤ DRINKING & NIGHTLIFE

TOP CHOICE ✓**AGAVE** THEME BAR

Map p288 (アガヴェ; www.agave.jp; B1 fl, 7-15-10 Roppongi, Minato-ku; 園Hibiya Line to Roppongi, exit 2) Rawhide chairs, *cruzas de rosas* (crosses decorated with roses) and tequila shots for the willing make Agave a good place for a long night in search of the sacred worm. Luckily, this gem in the jungle that is Roppongi is more about savouring the subtleties of its 400-plus varieties of tequila than tossing back shots of Cuervo.

ROPPONGI DRINKING & NIGHTLIFE

1. Tokyo City View (p80)
The view of the city and Tokyo Tower from the Sky Deck, Roppongi.

2. National Art Center, Tokyo (p81)
The last great work by architect Kurokawa Kishō, this gallery is famed for its undulating facade.

3. *Maman* sculpture (p80)
Louise Bourgeois' spider looms outside the Mori Tower, Roppongi Hills.

4. Tokyo Midtown (p80)
Interior of the Tokyo Midtown building, Roppongi.

FAIR WARNING

Roppongi is quite innocent and even upmarket during the day, but at night the footpaths along Gaien-Higashi-dōri south of Tokyo Midtown become populated with hawkers trying to entice patrons into clubs, promising age-old entertainments such as women and liquor. Some of these touts can be aggressive, others just chatty. Use caution if you follow them, as instances of spiked drinks followed by theft, beatings and blackouts have been reported to the point where Western embassies have issued warnings. Exercise common sense and healthy scepticism. If someone offers you illegal drugs, leave.

TOP CHOICE THESE   LOUNGE
Map p288 (テーゼ; www.these-jp.com, in Japanese; 2-15-12 Nishi-Azabu, Minato-ku; ⓇHibiya Line to Roppongi, exit 3) 'These' (*tay*-zay), a delightfully quirky, nook-ridden space, calls itself a library lounge and overflows with armchairs, sofas, and books on the shelves and on the bar. Imbibe champagne by the glass, whiskies or seasonal fruit cocktails. Bites include escargot garlic toast, which goes down very nicely with a drink in the secret room on the 2nd floor. Look for the flaming torches outside.

BUL-LET'S   CLUB
Map p288 (ブレッツ; www.bul-lets.com; B1 fl, Kasumi Bldg, 1-7-11 Nishi-Azabu, Minato-ku; admission ¥2000; ⓇHibiya Line to Roppongi, exit 2) This mellow basement space plays worldwide trance and ambient sounds for barefoot patrons. Mattresses in the middle of the floor provide refuge from the madding crowd, but don't get the wrong idea – it's not always tranquillity.

ELEVEN   CLUB
Map p288 (イレブン; www.go-to-eleven.com; B1 fl, Thesaurus Nishiazabu, 1-10-11 Nishi-Azabu, Minato-ku; admission ¥3000-4000; ⓇHibiya Line to Roppongi, exit 2) This popular two-basement dance mecca in a residential corner of Nishi-Azabu used to be the famed Space Lab Yellow. It now has a collection of stylishly lit bars and lounge areas with wood accents, and plays a range of electro, dub and house music.

HEARTLAND   BAR
Map p288 (ハートランド; www.heartland.jp, in Japanese; 6-10-1 Roppongi, Minato-ku; ⓇHibiya Line to Roppongi, exit 3) Named for the house beer from Kirin, Heartland is a chic, easy-going watering hole at the base of Roppongi Hills' West Tower that caters to professional expats and Japanese.

MISTRAL BLEU/TRAIN BAR   BAR
Map p288 (ミストラルブルー; www.trainbar.com; 5-5-1 Roppongi, Minato-ku; ⓇHibiya Line to Roppongi, exit 3) This lovable hole in the wall is about as unpretentious as it gets in Roppongi. The many foreign customers who have drained cheap beers here have left their mark – every surface, even the light bulbs, is covered with signatures.

MUSE   CLUB
Map p288 (ミューズ; www.muse-web.com, in Japanese; B1 fl, 4-1-1 Nishi-Azabu, Minato-ku; admission Fri, Sat & Sun women/men incl 2 drinks free/ ¥3000; ⓇHibiya Line to Roppongi, exit 3) Muse, a catacomb-like underground space with intimate booths, dance floors and billiards, has an excellent mix of locals and foreigners. There's something for everyone here, whether you want to dance up a storm or just feel like playing darts or table tennis.

CRAFT BEER MARKET   BAR
Map p288 (クラフトビア マーケット; 1-23-3 Nishi-Shimbashi, Minato-ku; ◷Mon-Fri; ◷; ⓇGinza Line to Toranomon, exit 1) One of Tokyo's many new craft beer pubs, this convivial bar in the Toranomon business district has over 30 craft beers on tap (including obscure Japanese brews), as well as a small patio out the front.

NEW LEX TOKYO   CLUB
Map p288 (ニューレックストウキョウ; B1 fl, 3-13-14 Roppongi, Minato-ku; admission women/men from ¥3000/4000; ⓇHibiya Line to Roppongi, exit 3) The Lex was one of Roppongi's first discos and stakes its popularity on visiting celebrities and models. The cover here starts at around ¥3000 unless you've had your visage on the front of *Vogue* or *Rolling Stone*. But even noncelebrities get a free drink with admission.

SALSA SUDADA   DANCE
Map p288 (サルサスダーダ; www.salsasudada. org; 3rd fl, Fusion Bldg, 7-13-8 Roppongi, Minato-ku; admission Fri & Sat ¥1500; ⓇHibiya Line to

Roppongi, exit 4B) Tokyo's salsa fanatics both Japanese and foreign come here to mingle and merengue. If you don't know how to dance, they'll teach you (lessons held nightly).

SUPERDELUXE — LOUNGE
Map p288 (スーパー・デラックス; www.super-deluxe.com; B1 fl, 3-1-25 Nishi-Azabu, Minato-ku; admission varies; Hibiya Line to Roppongi, exit 1B) This groovy basement performance space, also a cocktail lounge and club of sorts, stages everything from hula-hoop gatherings to literary evenings. Check the website for event details. It's in an unmarked brown-brick building by a shoe-repair shop.

LOVENET — KARAOKE
Map p288 (ラブネット; www.lovenet-jp.com; 3rd fl, Hotel Ibis, 7-14-4 Roppongi, Minato-ku; suites per hr from ¥4000; Hibiya Line to Roppongi, exit 4A) Lovenet has 25 themed suites with a dizzying range of decor. There's an Arabian Suite, a Heaven Suite and an Aqua Suite, complete with large Jacuzzi for getting wet while yodelling. Just watch the microphones!

PASELA — KARAOKE
Map p288 (パセラ; www.pasela.co.jp, in Japanese; 5-16-3 Roppongi, Minato-ku; per hr per person Sun-Thu ¥525, Fri & Sat ¥630; Hibiya Line to Roppongi, exit 3) Pasela boasts decor that is a cut above the other yodelling parlours, as well as six floors of karaoke rooms (including swanky VIP suites). There's an extensive selection of Western songs, wine, champagne and sweets on the menu, and a decent Mexican bar-restaurant in the basement. From 5pm to 7pm it's karaoke happy hour – ¥400, including one drink.

SAKE PLAZA — SAKE
Map p288 (日本酒造会館; 1-1-21 Nishi-Shimbashi, Minato-ku; 10am-5.30pm Mon-Fri; Ginza Line to Toranomon, exit 9) Sake Plaza isn't a bar, but who cares when you can get five thimbles of regionally brewed sake for only ¥525. This showroom and tasting space is a perfect way to start the night while learning about the national drink. It's on the ground floor of the Japan Sake Brewers Association Building (日本酒造会館).

SKY BAR — COCKTAIL BAR
off map p288 (スカイ・バー; 17th fl, Hotel New Ōtani, 4-1 Kioi-chō, Chiyoda-ku; Ginza Line to Akasaka-mitsuke, exit D) Sip cocktails from ¥1300 on vine-print seats while diners revolve around you above a sublime cityscape. The rotating rim is a buffet restaurant with exquisite sushi, teppanyaki, Chinese and Western fare from ¥9240.

ROYAL GARDEN CAFÉ — CAFE
Map p288 (ローヤルガーデンカフェ; www.royal-gardencafe.com, in Japanese; 2-1-19 Kita-Aoyama, Minato-ku; 11am-11pm; Ginza Line to Gaienmae, exit 4A) This large airy bakery along the ginkgo-lined path to Jingū Gaien park has year-round outdoor seating and wi-fi, plus lunch sets from ¥950. The menu includes a limited selection of decent coffees and teas such as caramel latte and chamomile mint tea. To support sustainable lifestyles, it also hosts the occasional farmers market.

★ ENTERTAINMENT

BILLBOARD LIVE — LIVE MUSIC
Map p288 (ビルボードライブ東京; www.billboard-live.com; 4th fl, Tokyo Midtown, 9-7-4 Akasaka, Minato-ku; admission varies; 5.30-9.30pm Mon-Fri, 5-9pm Sat & Sun; Hibiya Line to Roppongi, Tokyo Midtown exit) This glitzy amphitheatre-like space in Tokyo Midtown plays host to major foreign talent such as Steely Dan, The Beach Boys and Arrested Development. Japanese jazz, soul and rock groups also come in to shake the rafters. Better still, the service is excellent and the drinks are reasonably priced.

TOHO CINEMAS ROPPONGI HILLS — CINEMA
Map p288 (TOHOシネマズ六本木ヒルズ; www.tohotheater.jp; 6-10-2 Roppongi, Minato-ku; adult ¥1800-3000, child ¥1000, 1st day of month & women on Wed ¥1000; 10am-midnight Sun-Wed, to 5am Thu-Sat; Hibiya Line to Roppongi, Roppongi Hills exit) Toho's nine-screen multiplex has the biggest screen in Japan, as well as luxurious reclining seats and internet booking up to two days in advance for reserved seats. This state-of-the-art theatre also holds all-night screenings on nights before holidays.

KINGYO — THEATRE
Map p288 (金魚; 3478-3000; www.kingyo.co.jp; 3-14-17 Roppongi, Minato-ku; admission from ¥3500; shows 7.30pm & 10pm daily, 1.30am Fri & Sat; Hibiya Line to Roppongi, exit 3) By a cemetery off Roppongi's main drag,

cheeky Kingyo puts on a glitzy, colourful cabaret of *nyū hāfu* (transsexual) and drag queen performers who revel in social critique. Look for the yellow sign showing a *kingyo* (goldfish) kissing a penis.

BLUE NOTE TOKYO   JAZZ

off Map p288 (ブルーノート東京; www.bluenote. co.jp; 6-3-16 Minami-Aoyama, Minato-ku; admission ¥6000-15,000; ☺5.30pm-1am Mon-Sat, 5pm-12.30am Sun; ®Ginza Line to Omote-sandō, exit B3) The serious cognoscenti roll up to this, Tokyo's prime jazz spot in Aoyama, to take in the likes of Maceo Parker, Herbie Hancock and Doctor John. Just like its sister acts in New York and Milan, the digs here are classily decorated with dark wood and deep velvet, making this the perfect spot for a slow night of cool sounds.

STB 139   JAZZ

Map p288 (ススイートベイジル; ☎5474-1395; http://stb139.co.jp; 6-7-11 Roppongi, Minato-ku; admission¥3000-7000; ☺6-11pm Mon-Sat; ®Hibiya Line to Roppongi, exit 3) STB has a large, lovely space that draws big-name domestic and international jazz acts. Performances run the gamut of the genre; check the website for the current line-up. This classy joint is also a good place to have an Italian dinner before a show; call for reservations between 11am and 8pm Monday to Saturday.

B-FLAT   JAZZ

Map p288 (ビーフラット; B1 fl, 6-6-4 Akasaka, Minato-ku; admission from ¥2500; ☺6.30-11pm; ®Chiyoda Line to Akasaka, exit 5A) Located in a part of Akasaka that empties and grows quiet at night, this hip jazz club often features local and European talent, as well as healthy doses of Latin jazz.

 # SHOPPING

JAPAN SWORD   ANTIQUES

Map p288 (日本刀劍; www.japansword.co.jp; 3-8-1 Toranomon, Minato-ku; ☺9.30am-6pm Mon-Fri, to 5pm Sat; ®Ginza Line to Toranomon, exit 2) One of Tokyo's most-famous sellers of samurai swords and weaponry, Japan Sword sells the genuine article – such as antique sword guards and samurai helmets dating from the Edo period – as well as convincing replicas crafted by hand. Make sure you enquire about export and transport restrictions.

TOLMAN COLLECTION   ARTS & CRAFTS

(トールマンコレクション; www.tolmantokyo.com; 2-2-18 Shiba-Daimon, Minato-ku; ☺11am-7pm Wed-Sun; ®Ōedo Line to Daimon, exit A3) American Norman Tolman has been collecting Japanese print art for 50 years and has authored many books on the subject. His gallery, located in a traditional building, represents some 48 leading Japanese artists of printing, lithography, etching, woodblock and more. Prices aren't cheap – prints start at around ¥12,000 – but neither is the quality. From exit A3 of Daimon Station on the Ōedo Line, walk west towards Zōjo-ji temple. Turn left at the Bank of Tokyo-Mitsubishi UFJ. You'll soon see the gallery on your left.

BLUE & WHITE   CRAFT

Map p288 (ブルー アンド ホワイト; http://blue andwhitetokyo.com; 2-9-2 Azabu-Jūban; ☺10am-6pm Mon-Sat, 11am-6pm Sun; ®Namboku Line to Azabu-Jūban, exit 4) Amy Katoh, the expat American behind this small crafts store, sells traditional and contemporary items such as *tenugui* (hand-dyed towels) indigo-dyed *yukata* (light cotton kimono), bolts of nubby cloth and painted chopsticks. Pick through tiny dishes of ceramic beads or collect bundled-up swatches of fabric for your own creations. Katoh's inspiration is the cherubic Japanese good-luck goddess Otafuku, who smiles from every corner of the shop.

AXIS   DESIGN

Map p288 (アクシスビル; www.axisinc.co.jp, in Japanese; 5-17-1 Roppongi, Minato-ku; ☺11am-7pm; ®Hibiya Line to Roppongi, exit 3) Salivate over some of Japan's most innovative interior design at this high-end design complex. Of the 16-odd galleries and shops selling art books, cutting-edge furniture and other objets d'art, highlights include **Nuno** (布; www.nuno.com; B1 fl; ☺closed Sun), whose innovative fabrics incorporating objects from feathers to *washi* appear in New York's Museum of Modern Art; **Living Motif** (リビング・モティーフ), with three floors of soothing, contemporary design (both Japanese and international) from cushions to candle holders; and **Le Garage** (ル・ガラージュ; 2nd fl), with gear and accessories for motor-racing enthusiasts.

DON QUIJOTE   DEPARTMENT STORE

Map p288 (ドン・キホーテ; www.donki.com/index.php; 3-14-10 Roppongi, Minato-ku; ☺24hr; ®Hibiya Line to Roppongi, exit 3) The Roppongi branch of this jam-packed bargain castle is where Japanese kids of all ages come to stock up for fun. Don Quijote sells everything from household goods and electronics to French-maid costumes, usually at cut-rate prices. You'll need to hack your way through cluttered aisles, but it's possible to find some really funky gifts here.

SPORTS & ACTIVITIES

AQUA FIELD SHIBA PARK   SWIMMING
off Map p288 (アクアフィールド芝公園; (2-7-2 Shibakōen, Minato-ku; admission up to 2hr adult/child ¥400/150; ☺9am-8pm Jul & Aug, to 5pm Sep; ☒Mita Line to Shiba-kōen, exit A3) Open from the beginning of July through till mid-September, this outdoor 50m x 18m pool near Tokyo Tower is a great spot to beat the heat (it's a sports field the rest of the year). There's also a kids' pool with a slide and a sauna.

BODY ARTS & SCIENCE
INTERNATIONAL   PILATES
Map p288 (BASI; BASIピラティス; www.basipil ates.jp, in Japanese; 7th fl, Fleg Roppongi Quarto, 7-19-9 Roppongi, Minato-ku; trial lessons from ¥3000; ☒Hibiya Line to Roppongi, exits 4B & 2) This Pilates studio near Roppongi Hills is small but modern and has upper-floor views of western Roppongi. Its hospitable staff are very comfortable with foreign clients.

Ebisu, Meguro & Around

EBISU | DAIKANYAMA | NAKA-MEGURO | MEGURO

Neighbourhood Top Five

1 Strolling along the Meguro-gawa in **Naka-Meguro** (p94). It's not so much the river – it's a canal, really – but the unhurried village vibe and artsy shops on either side that make this one of Tokyo's most cherished spots.

2 Seeing Japan's contribution to the world of photography at the **Tokyo Metropolitan Museum of Photography** (p94).

3 Squeezing into a space at one of Ebisu's popular standing bars, like **Buri** (p100).

4 Visiting **Meguro Fudōson** (p95), a spiritual centre since the days of Edo.

5 Browsing the design shops on Meguro-dōri, home of **MISC** (Meguro Interior Shops Community; p95).

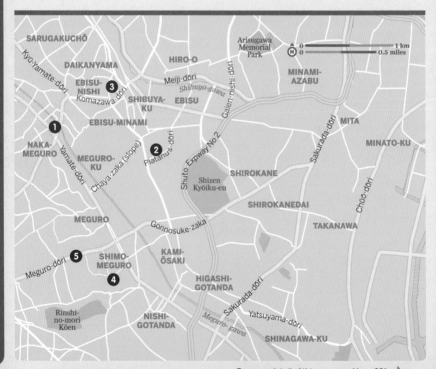

Explore Ebisu, Meguro & Around

Ebisu and Meguro are Tokyo on a more human scale, with low-rise buildings, shopping arcades and a smattering of down-to-earth eateries and bars. This conspires to create a bit of a retro Showa period (1926–89) vibe, which makes the area popular with the 30- and 40-somethings who came of age in the last throes of the era.

The residential districts of Daikanyama and Naka-Meguro, to the southwest, pair this low-key vibe with some serious style, evident in the high concentration of trendsetting shops, restaurants and cafes. Here, it's the neighbourhoods themselves that are the attraction and an afternoon wandering these quiet alleys is the perfect antidote to bouncing from sight to sight in central Tokyo.

None of the sights in this chapter are major, but they are rewarding nonetheless: you'll find the museums and temples here less crowded and less commercial, frequented primarily by those who live nearby. If you feel like stretching your legs, it's a pleasant walk down Komazawa-dōri from Ebisu to Daikanyama and Naka-Meguro, or alternatively down Meguro-dōri to the MISC design district. Foodies too will find much to ooh and ah over here, as these neighbourhoods are chock-a-block with small, but highly rated restaurants.

Local Life

→ **Eating** Foodies can't get enough of the pizzas at Da Isa (p99), and the Ebisu lunchtime crowd loves the *rāmen* (noodles in broth) at Afuri (p98).

→ **Hangouts** Ebisu is known for its lively *tachinomi-ya* (standing bars), Naka-Meguro for its riverside cafes and hard-to-find lounges.

→ **Shopping** Daikanyama style blends imported prêt-à-porter with local designs. Naka-Meguro style adds secondhand finds to the mix.

→ **Galleries** Ebisu, Daikanyama and Naka-Meguro have a dispersed scene; get maps and flyers at NADiff (p95).

Getting There & Away

→ **Train** The JR Yamanote Line stops at Ebisu and Meguro Stations. The Tōkyū Tōyoko Line runs from Shibuya to Daikanyama and Naka-Meguro.

→ **Subway** The Hibiya Line runs through Ebisu to Naka-Meguro; from Naka-Meguro, check if your train is going to Shibuya on the Tōkyū Tōyoko Line or to Ebisu on the Hibiya Line. The Namboku and Mita Lines stop at Meguro and Shirokanedai.

→ **Bus** Buses 2 and 7 run from Meguro Station along Meguro-dōri, stopping at Ōtori-jinja-mae.

Lonely Planet's Top Tip

You don't have to spend much time walking around Daikanyama or Naka-Meguro to discover that bicycles are the preferred mode of transportation for many locals. It's the best way to explore the nooks and crannies of these residential enclaves, where many shops, cafes and parks are hidden away from the main train-station areas. Get wheels at Tokyo Rent a Bike (p102).

Best Places to Eat

→ Higashi-Yama (p99)

→ Tonki (p99)

→ Da Isa (p99)

→ Ippo (p98)

→ Afuri (p98)

For reviews, see p98

Best Places to Drink

→ Nakame Takkyū Lounge (p100)

→ Buri (p100)

→ Kinfolk Lounge (p100)

→ What the Dickens! (p100)

For reviews, see p100

Best Places to Shop

→ MISC (p95)

→ Okura (p101)

→ Kamawanu (p101)

For reviews, see p101

EBISU, MEGURO & AROUND

⊙ SIGHTS

⊙ Ebisu & Around

NAKA-MEGURO
NEIGHBOURHOOD

Map p291 (中目黒; 🚇Hibiya Line to Naka-meguro)
Also known as 'Nakame', Naka-Meguro
doesn't look like much when you get out of
the station. Cross the street with the tracks
overhead, however, and in one block you'll
hit the Meguro-gawa, a tree-lined canal
flanked by stylish cafes, restaurants and
boutiques. You'll find more hip options in
the lanes behind. Nakame is a favourite
haunt (and home) of fashion, art and media
types, whose tastes are reflected here. This
is the kind of place that rewards exploring –
for Eating and Drinking recommendations,
see p98 and p100.

TOKYO METROPOLITAN MUSEUM OF PHOTOGRAPHY
MUSEUM

Map p291 (東京都写真美術館; www.syabi.com;
1-13-3 Mita, Meguro-ku; admission ¥500-1650;
⊙10am-6pm Tue-Thu & Sun, to 8pm Fri & Sat;
🚇JR Yamanote Line to Ebisu, east exit) This is
the city's top photography museum, with
excellent changing exhibitions of both international and Japanese photographers.
Ticket prices are based on how many exhibits you see (there are usually three going on
at once); there's also a research library here.
Take the Sky Walk from the station to **Yebisu Garden Place**; the five-storey museum is
on the right towards the back.

YAMATANE MUSEUM OF ART
MUSEUM

Map p291 (山種美術館; Yamatane Bijutsukan;
www.yamatane-museum.or.jp; 3-12-36 Hiroo,
Shibuya-ku; adult/student/child ¥1000/800/free,
special exhibits extra; ⊙10am-5pm Tue-Sun; 🚇JR
Yamanote Line to Ebisu, west exit) This excep-
tional collection of *nihonga* (Japanese-style

paintings) includes some 1800 works dating
from the Meiji Restoration and onwards,
of which a small selection is on display at
any one time. Two names to look for: Hay-
ami Gyoshū (1894–1935), whose *Dancing
Flames* is an important cultural property;
and Okumura Togyū (1889–1990), whose
Cherry Blossoms at Daigo-ji Temple is a
masterpiece in pastel colours.

HARA MUSEUM OF CONTEMPORARY ART
MUSEUM

(原美術館; www.haramuseum.or.jp; 4-7-25 Kita-
Shinagawa, Shinagawa-ku; adult ¥1000, student
¥500-700; ⊙11am-5pm Tue & Thu-Sun, to 8pm
Wed; 🚇JR Yamanote Line to Shinagawa, Takanawa
exit) Housed in a Bauhaus-style mansion
from the 1930s, this museum is one of Tokyo's more adventurous. In addition to cutting-edge exhibitions from Japanese and
international artists, there are fascinating
permanent installations designed especially for the house's nooks and crannies. The
garden-view cafe and excellent gift shop
will make you extra glad you made the trip.
It's 1.5km from Shinagawa Station; check
the website for a map.

FREE BEER MUSEUM YEBISU
MUSEUM

Map p291 (エビスビール記念館; www.sapporo
holdings.jp/english/guide/yebisu; 4-20-1 Ebisu,
Shibuya-ku; ⊙11am-7pm Tue-Sun; 🚇JR Yamanote
Line to Ebisu, east exit) Yes, this is the site of the
original Yebisu brewery (1889). Inside you'll
find a gallery of photographs and antique
signage that documents the rise of Yebisu,
and beer in general, in Japan. Skip the tour
(¥500), unless your Japanese language skills
can handle a guided tasting. Instead, head
for the 'tasting salon' where you can sample
four kinds of beer (¥400 each) at your own
pace. It's inside Yebisu Garden Place, behind
the Mitsukoshi department store.

DAIKANYAMA
NEIGHBOURHOOD

Map p291 (代官山; 🚇Tōkyū Tōyoko Line to
Daikanyama) Daikanyama is the anti-
Shibuya: a shopping district that favours
small boutiques, quiet streets and a
wealthy, impeccably dressed clientele (occasionally walking impeccably dressed
dogs). Not everything here is outrageously
priced, and it can be an excellent place
to discover Japanese designers, as many
have shops here (start at La Fuente Mall).
If shopping's not your thing, take a seat at
one of the neighbourhood's excellent people-watching cafes, like Sign (p99).

LOCAL KNOWLEDGE

MEGURO-GAWA HANAMI

Those trees along the Meguro-gawa
(Meguro River) are *sakura* (cherry)
trees, and during *hanami* (blossom-
viewing) season vendors line the canal
selling more upmarket treats than
you'll find anywhere else. Rather than
stake out a space to sit, visitors stroll
under the blossoms, hot wine in hand.

NADIFF A/P/A/R/T
ART GALLERY

Map p291 (ナディフアパート; www.nadiff.com; 1-18-4 Ebisu, Shibuya-ku; ⊘noon-8pm Tue-Sun; 🚃JR Yamanote Line to Ebisu, east exit) Part gallery, part bookstore, NADiff is a local art-scene hub. The bookstore is among the city's best for art books and there are a few other galleries in the same building, which makes it a worthy stop despite the tricky location. Walk towards Meiji-dōri then take a right just before the canal: follow the street and keep an eye out for directional signs on the telephone poles.

⊙ Meguro & Around

MEGURO FUDŌSON
TEMPLE

(目黒不動尊; http://park6.wakwak.com/~meguro fudou/top.htm, in Japanese; 3-20-26 Shimo-Meguro, Meguro-ku; 🚃JR Yamanote Line to Meguro, west exit, 🚌2 or 7 to Ōtori-jinja-mae) The third Tokugawa shōgun designated this Tendai-sect temple as one of the five protectors of Edo, which earned it a mention in Edo-era travel guides. The temple's official name is Taieizan Ryūsen-ji; its nickname comes from the *meguro* ('black-eyed') statue of Fudō Myō originally enshrined here. Though the statue isn't on display, many others are visible around the sprawling complex. In the *honden* (main hall), modest *goma* (fire rituals) are held several times a month; your best bet to catch one is at 3pm on a Sunday. To get here, walk downhill from the station and turn left onto Yamate-dōri; at the first traffic light, take the road heading diagonally to the right. When the road bends, you should see a large sign indicating the path to the temple.

MISC
DESIGN DISTRICT

(ミスク; Meguro Interior Shops Community; http://misc.co.jp, in Japanese; Meguro-dōri; 🚃JR Yamanote Line to Meguro, west exit) Meguro-dōri, the broad boulevard that runs southwest from Meguro Station, is Tokyo's de facto interior design district (MISC stands for Meguro Interior Shops Community). Design shops punctuate a 3km stretch of Meguro-dori, starting roughly around the Parasitological Museum. There is something for everyone here, whether your tastes run towards antiques or industrial. Even if you're not planning to shop, it's interesting to poke around and imagine what Tokyo's concrete box apartments might look like on the inside. For shopping recommendations,

FUDŌ FESTIVAL

Meguro Fudōson is very much an active temple. On the 28th day of every month it holds a festival to honour the principal deity, complete with food vendors, game stalls and a small market. Nearby shops set out tables and turn it into a block party.

see p101). Buses that run along Meguro-dōri can take you back to Meguro Station (¥210).

FREE MEGURO PARASITOLOGICAL MUSEUM
MUSEUM

(目黒寄生虫館; http://kiseichu.org; 4-1-1 Shimo-Meguro, Meguro-ku; ⊘10am-5pm Tue-Sun; 🚃JR Yamanote Line to Meguro, west exit; 🚌2 or 7 to Ōtori-jinja-mae) Here's one for fans of the grotesque: this small museum was established in 1953 by a local doctor concerned by the increasing number of parasites he was encountering due to unsanitary postwar conditions. The grisly centrepiece is an 8.8m-long tapeworm found in the body of a 40-year-old Yokohama man. There's not a lot of English signage, but little explanation is necessary because you can easily see how these nasties might set up house inside you. The museum is about a 1km walk from Meguro Station; the entrance is on the ground floor of a small apartment building, just uphill from the Ōtori-jinja-mae bus stop.

INSTITUTE FOR NATURE STUDY
PARK

(自然教育園; Shizen Kyōiku-en; www.ins.kahaku. go.jp; 5-21-5 Shirokanedai, Minato-ku; adult/concession ¥300/free; ⊘9am-4.30pm Tue-Sun Sep-Apr, to 5pm Tue-Sun May-Aug, last entry 4pm year-round; 🚃Namboku Line to Shirokanedai, exit 1) Although the 200,000 sq metres of this land was the estate of a *daimyō* (domain lord) some six centuries ago and was the site of gunpowder warehouses in the early Meiji period, you'd scarcely know it now. Since 1949 this garden has been part of the Tokyo National Museum (p158) and preserves the local flora in undisciplined profusion. There are wonderful walks through its forests, marshes and ponds, making this one of Tokyo's least known and most appealing getaways.

SIMON RICHMOND / LONELY PLANET IMAGES ©

1. *Hanami* (p94)
Cherry blossoms in bloom along Meguro-gawa (Meguro River).

2. Yebisu Garden Place
Home to Tokyo Metropolitan Museum of Photography (p94) and the Beer Museum Yebisu (p94).

3. Sengaku-ji (p98)
The graves of the 47 'masterless samurai' are visited daily by people paying their respects.

PHOTO JAPAN / ALAMY ©

 **EATING**

 Ebisu

IPPO IZAKAYA ¥

Map p291 (一歩; ☎3445-8418; 2nd fl, 1-22-10 Ebisu, Shibuya-ku; mains from ¥800-1500; ⏲6pm-3am; ❑JR Yamanote Line to Ebisu, east exit) This mellow little *izakaya* (Japanese version of a pub/eatery) specialises in simple pleasures: fish and sake (there's an English sign out front that says just that). The menu changes daily depending on what's in season; the friendly chefs help you decide what to have grilled, steamed, simmered or fried. There's only a counter and a few small tables, so groups should call ahead. Follow the wooden stairs under the sage ball.

AFURI RAMEN ¥

Map p291 (あふり; 1-1-7 Ebisu, Shibuya-ku; mains from ¥750; ⏲11am-5am; ⊖◐; ❑JR Yamanote Line to Ebisu, east exit) Hardly your typical, surly *rāmen-ya*, Afuri has upbeat young cooks and a hip industrial interior. The unorthodox menu might draw eye-rolls from purists, but house specials like *yuzu-shio* (a light, salty broth flavoured with the peel of *yuzu* – a type of citrus) are a perfect match for the trim, young professionals who live and work in the neighbourhood.

EBISU YOKOCHŌ STREET FOOD ¥

Map p291 (恵比寿横町; www.ebisu-yokocho; 1-7-4 Ebisu, Shibuya-ku; dishes from ¥500; ⏲dinner-late; ❑JR Yamanote Line to Ebisu, east exit) This retro arcade is chock-a-block with colourful counters dishing up everything from grilled scallops to *yaki soba* (fried buck-wheat noodles). Even if you don't stop to eat it's worth strolling through. If you do eat here, be warned that, this being Ebisu, the food is not as cheap as the decor might suggest.

TA-IM FELAFEL ¥

off Map p291 (タイーム; www.ta-imebisu.com; 1-29-16 Ebisu, Shibuya-ku; lunch set/dinner mains from ¥980/1200; ⏲11am-11pm Thu-Tue; ⊖🔑◐;

> **WORTH A DETOUR**
>
> **SENGAKU-JI & HATAKEYAMA COLLECTION**
>
> **Sengaku-ji** (泉岳寺; 2-11-1 Takanawa, Minato-ku; ⏲7am-6pm Apr-Sep, to 5pm Oct-Mar; ❑Asakusa Line to Sengaku-ji, exit A2), a Sōtō Zen temple, is famous for its role in the historical incident of the 47 *rōnin* (masterless samurai). These *rōnin* plotted for two years (1701–03) to wreak vengeance on the man who caused what they believed to be the unjust and humiliating death of their master, Lord Asano of Akō province. After having brought the head of his enemy to their master's grave at Sengaku-ji, 46 of the *rōnin* were condemned to commit *seppuku* (ritual suicide by self-disembowelment) in the samurai fashion – the 47th apparently escaped this communal fate on a technicality. Their graves are here along with their master's.
>
> With its theme of paying the supreme sacrifice in the name of loyalty, this story, also called *The Akō Incident*, has captured the Japanese imagination like no other, and has been adapted into countless films and plays (usually by the name *Chūshingura*).
>
> The **cemetery** here is quite atmospheric as there always seems to be incense burning; you can buy your own to add for ¥100. There is also a **museum** (adult/student child/¥500/400/250; ⏲9am-4pm) on the premises – there's not a lot of English explanation, but a video presentation in English is available.
>
> To get a sense of the more refined (and less violent) side of the feudal era, visit the **Hatakeyama Collection** (畠山記念館; www.ebara.co.jp/csr/hatakeyama; 2-20-12 Shirokanedai, Minato-ku; adult/student ¥500/300; ⏲10am-5pm Tue-Sun Apr-Sep, to 4.30pm Tue-Sun Oct-Mar; ❑Asakusa Line to Takanawadai, exit A2). This under-visited museum was created and designed by Hatakeyama Issei, an industrialist and devotee of the way of tea. Inside, you'll find seasonal displays of priceless works of teaware from the Muromachi, Momoyama and Edo periods, some of them with important cultural properties. It's all reached via a lovely garden.
>
> Both sights are on the Asakusa Line, which runs from Gotanda Station (on the JR Yamanote Line, one stop past Meguro).

AISUKURIIMU, YŪSUKURIIMU...

Although most Japanese had never tried dairy products until the Meiji period (1868–1912), they've taken a big licking to *aisukuriimu* (ice cream). And green tea isn't the only flavour they've contributed to the ice cream playbook; other delicious innovations include *kuro-goma* (black sesame) and *beni imo* (purple sweet potato). **Ouca** (Map p291; 1-6-6 Ebisu, Shibuya-ku; ice cream from ¥380; ⏱11am-11.30pm or until sold out; 🚉JR Yamanote Line to Ebisu, east exit) serves these and others along with only-in-Japan sundae toppings like *shio konbu* (salted kelp) and *yuzu-shiromiso mitsudare* (citrus and white miso syrup).

🚉JR Yamanote Line to Ebisu, east exit) Swing by this counter restaurant for authentic Israeli cooking from expat Dan Zuckerman. Ta-im just opened in 2011 but has already turned on a number of local diners to the wonders of homemade hummus.

✗ Daikanyama

BOMBAY BAZAR   INTERNATIONAL ¥

Map p291 (ボンベイバザー; www.bombaybazar.jp, in Japanese; 20-11 Sarugaku-chō, Shibuya-ku; mains from ¥900; ⏱11.30-7.30pm; 🚉Tōkyū Tōyoko Line to Daikanyama) Mismatched furniture and 'found' objects conspire to make this cafe look like a hippie camp (don't miss the birdsong in the bathroom). There's a spin-the-globe menu of pizza, pastas and curries made with organic vegies. Bombay Bazar is below Okura (p101) clothing shop.

SIGN   INTERNATIONAL ¥

Map p291 (サイン; 19-4 Daikanyama-chō, Shibuya-ku; mains ¥980-1680; ⏱11am-11pm; 🚉Tōkyū Tōyoko Line to Daikanyama) At this stylish cafe, sit yourself on the terrace or inside the glass jewel box of a room for some of the neighbourhood's best people-watching. Despite the hip decor, the menu is full of classic comfort foods like *omu raisu* (rice topped with a soupy omelette and demi-glace sauce).

✗ Naka-Meguro

TOP CHOICE HIGASHI-YAMA   JAPANESE ¥¥¥

(ヒガシヤマ; ☎5720-1300; http://higashiyama-tokyo.jp; 1-21-25 Higashiyama, Meguro-ku; courses ¥8000; ⏱dinner Mon-Sat; 🚉Hibiya Line to Naka-Meguro) Gorgeous modern Japanese cuisine paired with gorgeous crockery – this restaurant is run by the design firm that makes them. The tasting course is excel-

lent, from the homemade tofu starter all the way to the *matcha* (powdered green tea) panna cotta for dessert. The stark, dim basement lounge is perfect for an after-dinner drink. Higashi-Yama is tucked away on a side street with minimal signage; check the map on the website before heading out. Book ahead.

DA ISA   PIZZERIA ¥¥

off Map p291 (ダイーサ; www.da-isa.jp; 1-28-9 Aobadai, Meguro-ku; lunch ¥1000, dinner ¥1500-2500; ⏱lunch & dinner Tue-Sun; 🚉Hibiya Line to Naka-Meguro) We know you didn't come all the way to Tokyo for pizza, but Da Isa is world class – and has the trophies to prove it. There are over 30 varieties on the menu, all produced at whip-speed by the master *pizzaiolo* himself and cooked to perfection in a wood-fired oven. Tables, both indoors and on the pavement, are usually full, but with brisk service the wait usually isn't long.

CHANO-MA   JAPANESE ¥

Map p291 (チャノマ; 1-22-4 Kami-Meguro, Meguro-ku; lunch ¥880, mains from ¥850; ⏱noon-2am Sun-Thu, to 4am Fri & Sat; 🚉Hibiya Line to Naka-Meguro) By day, Chano-ma is a laid-back cafe with a popular 'deli lunch' special that includes a choice of three side dishes (like deep-fried lotus root and stuffed shiitake mushrooms). By night, it's a hip lounge where you can sip cocktails by candlelight on a row of raised mattresses. The dinner menu includes pastas, salads and rice dishes.

✗ Meguro

TOP CHOICE TONKI   TONKATSU ¥

(とんき; 1-2-1 Shimo-Meguro, Meguro-ku; meals ¥1800; ⏱4-11pm Wed-Mon (closed 3rd Mon); 🚉JR Yamanote Line to Meguro, west exit)

EBISU, MEGURO & AROUND EATING

LOCAL KNOWLEDGE

RĀMEN JIRŌ

The *rāmen* at Rāmen Jirō consists of a mound of pork and bean sprouts topping a bowl already crammed with heavy noodles and oily, thick-as-gravy soup. It's exactly this unapologetic excess that has earned it a cult following.

Journalist and *rāmen* fan Nakagawa Junichirō explains: 'There's a saying: *jirō* is not *rāmen*, *jirō* is a food called *jirō*.' Love it or hate it, there's nothing else quite like it.

While knock-offs abound, Rāmen Jirō is in Mita, near Keiō University. There's also a branch in **Meguro** (ラーメン二郎目黒店; 3-7-2 Meguro, Meguro-ku; ☺lunch & dinner Thu-Tue; ℝJR Yamanote Line to Meguro, west exit) on Yamate-dōri.

At this *tonkatsu* (crumbed pork cutlet) restaurant, there are only two things on the menu – *rosu-katsu* (fatty loin meat cutlets) and *hire-katsu* (lean fillet meat cutlets) – but Tonki's loyal customers never tire of it. Sit at the counter to watch the perfectly choreographed chefs breading, frying and garnishing the tender cutlets. From the station, walk down Meguro-dōri, take a left at the first alley and look for a white sign and *noren* (doorway curtains) across the sliding doors.

GANKO DAKO STREET FOOD ¥

(頑固蛸; 3-11-6 Meguro, Meguro-ku; takoyaki ¥500; ☺11am-1am; ℝJR Yamanote Line to Meguro, west exit) This street stall dishes out steaming hot *tako-yaki* (grilled octopus dumplings), topped with everything from kimchi to Worcestershire sauce. It's located, unfortunately, across from the Meguro Parasitological Museum; nonetheless, Ganko Dako draws them in – check out the celebrity signings on the wall.

🍷 DRINKING & NIGHTLIFE

NAKAME TAKKYŪ LOUNGE LOUNGE

Map p291 (中目卓球ラウンジ; 2nd fl, Lion House Naka-Meguro, 1-3-13 Kami-Meguro, Meguro-ku; admission ¥500; ☺7pm-2am Mon-Sat; ℝHibiya Line to Naka-Meguro) 'Takkyū' means table tennis and it's a serious sport in Japan. This hilarious bar looks like a university table-tennis clubhouse – right down to the tatty furniture and posters of star players on the wall. The clientele are local hipsters, and some of them are pretty good. It's in an apartment building (the one in back) to the right of a parking garage; ring the doorbell for entry.

BURI BAR

Map p291 (ぶり; www.buri-group.com; 1-14-1 Ebisu-Nishi, Shibuya-ku; 🅼; ℝJR Yamanote Line to Ebisu, west exit) The name means 'super' in Hiroshima dialect and the lively crowd that packs in on weekends certainly seems to agree. Generous quantities of sake (over 50 varieties; ¥750) are served semifrozen, like slushies in colourful jars. Although there are some stools around the horseshoe-shaped counter, Buri is a *tachinomi-ya* (standing bar) at heart.

KINFOLK LOUNGE LOUNGE

Map p291 (キンフォーク; http://wegotways. com/kinfolk; 2nd fl, 1-11-1 Kami-Meguro, Meguro-ku; ☺Tue-Sun; 🅼; ℝHibiya Line to Naka-Meguro) Sip mojitos under wooden rafters in this dim, moody lounge run by custom bicycle makers Kinfolk. From Naka-Meguro Station, cross Yamate-dōri and the river, then take the first left. It's a few minutes' walk on the left, up a rickety metal staircase above a restaurant.

WHAT THE DICKENS! PUB

Map p291 (ワット・ザ・ディッキンズ; www.what thedickens.jp; 4th fl, 1-13-3 Ebisu-Nishi, Shibuya-ku; ☺Tue-Sun; 🅼; ℝJR Yamanote Line to Ebisu, west exit) This British pub is a long-time favourite of down-to-earth expats and cosmopolitan Japanese alike. The beer and pub grub are well up to scratch, while there are local bands that play for free nightly. It has an unlikely location inside a building that looks like adobe decorated with a mosaic of a hummingbird.

BAJA BAR

(バハ; 1-16-12 Kami-Meguro, Meguro-ku; ☺5pm-5am Mon-Fri, noon-5am Sat & Sun; ℝHibiya Line to Naka-Meguro) Roll up to this tiny white taco shack off Yamate-dōri and knock back beers for ¥500, tacos for ¥330 and tequila for ¥300. It's operated by a friendly skateboarder, who's happy to dispense tips on hip local hangouts.

⭐ ENTERTAINMENT

LIQUID ROOM
LIVE MUSIC

Map p291 (リキッドルーム; ☑5464-0800; www. liquidroom.net; 3-16-6 Higashi, Shibuya-ku; 🚇JR Yamanote Line to Ebisu, west exit) Some of the world's greatest performers have graced the stage at Liquid Room, from the Flaming Lips and Sonic Youth to Linton Kwesi Johnson. This is an excellent place to see an old favourite or find a new one, but you'll have to buy tickets as soon as they go on sale. Tickets can be purchased from kiosks in Lawson convenience stores, but you'll need to enlist the help of a Japanese speaker.

UNIT
LIVE MUSIC

Map p291 (ユニット; ☑5459-8630; www. unit-tokyo.com; 1-34-17 Ebisu-nishi, Shibuya-ku; 🚇Tōkyū Tōyoko Line to Daikanyama) On weekends, this subterranean club has two shows: live music in the evening and a DJ-hosted event after hours. Acts range from Japanese indie bands to overseas artists making their Japanese debut. Unit is less grungy than other Tokyo live houses; it draws a stylish young crowd and, thanks to its high ceilings, it doesn't get too smoky.

STANDING BARS

Stylish reincarnations of those classic, cheap salarymen haunts, *tachinomi-ya*, are the latest big thing in Ebisu. A true *tachinomi-ya* is nothing more than a counter, but to accommodate a different clientele – women in heels, for example – newer, fashionable joints often have a handful of stools. The reasonable prices remain: drinks average around ¥500.

Two popular hangouts are Spanish-flavoured **Ebisu 18-ban** (恵比寿18番; Map p291; 2-3-13 Ebisu-minami, Shibuya-ku; 🚇JR Yamanote Line to Ebisu, west exit) and the more authentically old-school **Ebisu Tachinomiya** (恵比寿立呑屋; Map p291; 1-1-6 Ebisu-minami, Shibuya-ku; 🚇JR Yamanote Line to Ebisu, west exit), which serves inexpensive *yakitori* (charcoal-broiled chicken and other meats or vegetables, cooked on skewers) and *chūhai* (cocktails made with *shōchū* – a distilled grain liquor).

🛍 SHOPPING

ᵀᴼᴾ﹒CHOICE MISC
HOMEWARES, ANTIQUES

(ミスク; Meguro-dōri; 🚇JR Yamanote Line to Meguro, west exit) There are dozens of shops here, spread out over a 3km stretch of Meguro-dōri on both sides of the street. Some favourites include: **Meister** (マイスター; www. meister-mag.co.jp, in Japanese; 4-11-4 Meguro, Meguro-ku; ⏱Thu-Tue) for ultrastylish modern wares; **Do** (ドー; www.claska.com/gallery, in Japanese; 2nd fl, 1-3-18 Chūō-chō, Meguro-ku), on the 2nd floor of the Claska Hotel, for artisan crafts from around Japan; and **Otsu Furniture** (オツファニチュア; www.demode-furniture. net/otsu, in Japanese; 1-4-9 Takaban, Meguro-ku) for early-20th-century Japanese antiques. It's a pleasant 3.5km walk from Meguro Station all the way to Otsu Furniture, the furthest shop on this list. Buses (¥210) running up Meguro-dōri can take you back to the station at any point along the way. Note that many stores close on Wednesday.

ᵀᴼᴾ﹒CHOICE OKURA
FASHION, ACCESSORIES

Map p291 (オクラ; 20-11 Sarugaku-chō, Shibuya-ku; 🚇Tōkyū Tōyoko Line to Daikanyama) Almost everything in here is dyed indigo. While the classic dye has a long history in Japan, the styles here are totally modern – think jeans and T-shirts. There are some beautiful, original items, though most aren't cheap. The shop itself looks like a rural house, with worn wooden floorboards and whitewashed walls. Note: there's no sign out the front, but look for the traditional building facing the perpendicular street.

KAMAWANU
CRAFT

Map p291 (かまわぬ; www.kamawanu.co.jp, in Japanese; 23-1 Sarugaku-chō, Shibuya-ku; ⏱11am-7pm; 🚇Tōkyū Tōyoko Line to Daikanyama) Kamawanu specialises in *tenugui*: dyed rectangular cloths of thin cotton, which can be used as tea towels, kerchiefs or gift wrap (the list goes on; they're surprisingly versatile). There are over 200 different patterns available here, with motifs from traditional to modern. Turn down the little street to the right of the post office, and you'll find it in a traditional building. There's also a branch in the Ukiyo-e Ōta Museum of Art (p117).

UNLIMITED BY LIMI FEU
FASHION

Map p291 (アンリミテッド・バイ・リミフゥ; www. limifeu.com; 7-4 Daikanyama-chō, Shibuya-ku;

◷noon-9pm; ⊠Tōyoko Line to Daikanyama) Designed by Yohji Yamomoto's daughter, Limi Feu creations are voluminous, dark and street smart. This is the brand's outlet store, with items from past seasons at serious markdowns. They're not marked, but if you look like you might be falling for something, the sales clerk arrives with a calculator to show you what a bargain it would be. Merchandise changes weekly and fans stalk the place.

DAIKANYAMA T-SITE BOOKS

Map p291 (http://tsite.jp/daikanyama, in Japanese; 17-5 Sarugaku-chō, Shibuya-ku; ◷7am-2am; ⊠Tōkyū Tōyoko Line to Daikanyama) Locals have gone mad for this stylish shrine to the printed word. There's a decent selection of books on Japan in English, as well as international magazines, art tomes and a whole floor of music. It's as much a hangout as it is a bookshop.

GOOD DAY BOOKS BOOKS

(www.gooddaybooks.com; 3rd fl, 2-4-2 Nishi-Gotanda, Shinagawa-ku; ◷11am-8pm Mon-Sat, to 6pm Sun; ⊠JR Yamanote Line to Gotanda) Tokyo's best shop for secondhand English-language books has a good selection of books on Japanese culture and language. From Gotanda Station, head right from the ticket gates and then make another right turn, following the tracks until you see the Big Size Shoes store on the ground floor.

KOROMON FASHION

Map p291 (衣; 12-10 Sarugaku-chō, Shibuya-ku; ◷Fri-Wed; ⊠Tōkyū Tōyoko Line to Daikanyama) In the back of a shopping building, this little shop blends Japanese and Western sensibilities. Look for jeans painted with designs you might expect to see on scroll paintings, and for kimono fabric to put to creative use.

🏃 SPORTS & ACTIVITIES

TOKYO RENT A BIKE CYCLING

Map p291 (東京レンタル自転車; ☎080-3209-9996; www.tokyorentabike.com; 8th fl, 3-5-11 Naka-Meguro, Meguro-ku; per day ¥1000; ◷10am-1pm Sat & Sun, by appointment Mon-Fri; ⊠Hibiya Line to Naka-Meguro) Has multi- and single-gear bikes for touring Tokyo. Call to reserve on weekdays. Multiday rentals are available if your lodging has bicycle parking; otherwise, bikes have to be back by 8pm.

YOGAJAYA YOGA

Map p291 (ヨガジャヤ; www.yogajaya.com; 2nd fl, 1-25-11 Ebisu-nishi, Shibuya-ku; ⊠JR Yamanote Line to Ebisu, west exit) In addition to a daily line-up of bilingual classes (mostly Hatha yoga), Yogajaya holds workshops with teachers visiting from overseas. It's one of Tokyo's more established studios, with a roster of professional teachers and a dedicated, though sufficiently relaxed, vibe.

Shibuya & Around

SHIBUYA | SHIMO-KITAZAWA

Neighbourhood Top Five

1 Surrendering to the crowd at **Shibuya Crossing** (p105). Let yourself be swept along into the beating heart of desire, aspiration and materialism that is Shibuya.

2 Wandering the tiny alleys of **Shimo-Kitazawa** (p106), the neighbourhood that time forgot.

3 Living the teenage girl experience at fashion hive **Shibuya 109** (p112).

4 Singing your heart out at karaoke parlour **Shidax Village** (p111).

5 Scoping out the all-night club scene on Dōgenzaka, also known as **Love Hotel Hill** (p106).

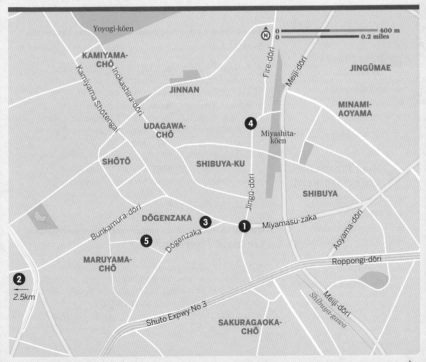

For more detail of this area, see Map p292

Lonely Planet's Top Tip

Missed the last train? You're not alone – or stuck for options. Shibuya has plenty for night crawlers who were lured out late by the neighbourhood's charms but who'd rather not fork over the yen for a taxi ride home. In addition to love hotels and *manga kissa* (cafes where you pay by the hour to read *manga*, Japanese comic books), consider waiting for the first train by heading to a karaoke parlour; most offer discounted all-night packages from midnight to 5am.

 ### Best Places to Eat

➡ Nodaiwa (p107)

➡ Kaikaya (p106)

➡ Sushi-no-Midori (p107)

➡ Shirube (p107)

For reviews, see p106 ➡

 ### Best Places to Drink

➡ Pink Cow (p110)

➡ Ushitora (p110)

➡ Aldgate (p110)

For reviews, see p110 ➡

 ### Best Places for Entertainment

➡ Shidax Village (p111)

➡ Womb (p111)

➡ Club Quattro (p111)

➡ Setagaya Public Theatre (p111)

➡ Shelter (p111)

For reviews, see p111 ➡

Explore Shibuya & Around

Shibuya has few sights, but makes up for it with sheer presence. As you exit the station you'll first hit Shibuya Crossing – a typical Tokyo scene of neon flashes and fashionable youth. From here, the pedestrian traffic carries onto Shibuya Sentā-gai (Shibuya Centre Street), the neighbourhood's main artery, lined with shops, cheap eateries and bars. Just shop and soak up the energy.

The area around Sentā-gai is primarily a teen hangout, but head out to the fringes and you'll find wealthy residential enclaves, shanty bars under the tracks and the headquarters of major IT industry companies (all the better to keep an eye on their future clientele). As a result, you'll find places to eat and drink for all budgets and tastes.

Further afield is the cosy neighbourhood of Shimo-Kitazawa, 3km southwest of central Shibuya, with small, quirky shops, good restaurants and hole-in-the-wall bars around every corner. It's popular with students, but also with an artsy and intellectual grown-up crowd; there's also an active underground music and theatre scene here.

Shibuya is, above all, an entertainment centre and it really comes alive at night. There are dance clubs, live music venues, theatres and cinemas galore. While weekends are the busiest, you'll find people from all over Tokyo here any night of the week. Bars and karaoke parlours stay open until dawn.

Local Life

➡ **Fashion** Shibuya 109 (p112) is ground zero for the 'real clothes' fashion movement, which favours affordable domestic brands over designer imports.

➡ **Record Stores** Shimo-Kitazawa (p106) and the Udagawa-chō neighbourhood of Shibuya are studded with tiny specialist record shops that are popular with local DJs.

➡ **Drinking** Ushitora (p110) and Aldgate (p110) are two key players in the growing local craft beer scene.

➡ **Theatre** Shimo-Kitazawa is known as the actors' neighbourhood, thanks to a number of theatres, such as Honda Theatre (p112).

Getting There & Away

➡ **Train** The JR Yamanote Line stops at Shibuya Station. You can also connect here to the private Tōkyū Toyoko Line (for Naka-Meguro) and the Keiō Inokashira Line (for Shimo-Kitazawa and Kichijōji).

➡ **Subway** The Ginza, Hanzōmon and Fukutoshin Lines stop in Shibuya.

TOP SIGHTS
SHIBUYA CROSSING

Step out of Shibuya Station after dark and you'll find yourself in the Tokyo of your dreams: an awesome spectacle of giant video screens and neon, streets radiating out like a starburst and an omnipresent flow of people. Rumoured to be the busiest intersection in the world (and definitely in Japan), Shibuya Crossing is an epic sight. Perhaps nowhere else says 'Welcome to Tokyo' better than this.

DON'T MISS

➡ The Scramble

PRACTICALITIES

➡ Map p292

➡ Ⓡ JR Yamanote Line to Shibuya, Hachikō exit

The Scramble

Hundreds of people – and at peak times said to be over 1000 people – cross here every time the light turns green. People come from all directions at once yet still manage to dodge each other with a practiced, nonchalant agility. Then, in the time that it takes for the light to go from red to green again, all corners have replenished their stock of people – like a video on loop. Shibuya Crossing (渋谷交差点) is a prime photo opportunity, but a still image doesn't do justice to the energy and the sense that this is indeed the beating heart of Shibuya. There's an excellent view from the Starbucks on the 2nd floor of the Q-front building across the street (though it's hard to get a seat).

The intersection is most impressive after dark on a Friday or Saturday night, when the crowds pouring out of the station are dressed in their finest and neon-lit by the signs above. Enter the thick of it and you'll brush by some of Shibuya's infamous characters: the fun-loving *gyaru* (teenage girls who prioritise shopping over studying) in colourful clothes and high-heel boots, her male counterpart (the tousle-haired *gyaru-o*) and the impetuous scouts looking to lure young women into working at dubious clubs. The rhythms here are, however, tied to the train station and after the last train pulls out for the night, the intersection becomes eerily quiet.

⊙ SIGHTS

SHIBUYA CROSSING
INTERSECTION

See p105.

HACHIKŌ STATUE
MONUMENT

Map p292 (ハチ公像; ℝJR Yamanote Line to Shibuya, Hachikō exit) In the early 1920s, a professor who lived near Shibuya Station kept Hachikō, a small akita dog, who came to the station every day to await the return of his master. The professor died in 1925, but the dog continued to show up and wait at the station until his own death 10 years later. The story became legend and a small statue was erected here in the dog's memory. Hachikō is perhaps Tokyo's most famous meeting spot, usually swarming with trendy teens.

LOVE HOTEL HILL
NEIGHBOURHOOD

Map p292 (ラヴホテルヒル; ℝJR Yamanote Line to Shibuya, Hachikō exit) *Rubuho* ('love hotels': places specifically for amorous encounters) aren't just for the sleazy. Sky-high residential rents means many young people live at home in cramped quarters until marriage. This cluster of love hotels in downtown Shibuya is one of Tokyo's largest and is a stone's throw from many nightclubs. In addition to hotels with castle and Arabian palace themes, you'll find many advertising in-room Wii consoles. If you're travelling as a couple, a night in a *rubuho* can be a cheap alternative to a business hotel (they average about ¥9000 per night).

SHIMO-KITAZAWA
NEIGHBOURHOOD

(下北沢; ℝKeiō Inokashira Line to Shimo-Kitazawa) The narrow streets of Shimo-Kitazawa (Shimokita to its friends) are barely passable by cars, meaning a streetscape like a dollhouse version of Tokyo. Although lacking big-name sights or landmarks, Shimokita has a lively street scene all afternoon and evening, especially on weekends.

There have long been plans to build a road through the centre of this neighbourhood, much to the dismay of local residents and business owners. In a city awash with skyscrapers and new developments, cosy, organic communities like Shimo-Kitazawa are a rare breed.

Restaurants, bars and entertainment venues are clustered on the south side; the more laid-back north side has many cafes and secondhand shops. See p107 and p110 to get you started – this is one neighbourhood where getting lost is more than half the fun.

TOGURI MUSEUM OF ART
MUSEUM

Map p292 (戸栗美術館; www.toguri-museum. or.jp; 1-11-3 Shōto, Shibuya-ku; adult/student/ child ¥1000/700/400; ⊙9.30am-5.30pm Tue-Sun; ℝJR Yamanote Line to Shibuya, Hachikō exit) In an upmarket residential neighbourhood northwest of Shibuya Crossing, this small museum has an excellent collection of Edo-era ceramics. Changing exhibits are designed as much to educate students of pottery as to impress connoisseurs. It's a 1km walk from Shibuya Station; you'll see blue signs on the utility poles (in Japanese) marking the way when you get close. The museum occasionally closes the last week of the month, in between exhibitions.

✕ EATING

✕ Shibuya

KAIKAYA
SEAFOOD ¥¥

Map p292 (開花屋; ☑3770-0878; www.kaikaya. com; 23-7 Maruyama-chō; dishes ¥700-2300; ⊕📖; ⊙lunch & dinner Mon-Sat; ℝJR Yamanote Line to Shibuya, Hachikō exit) The chef here demonstrates his love for the sea through thoughtfully prepared seasonal seafood dishes; some are seasoned with *shōyu* (soy sauce), others with rosemary. Everything on the menu is caught in nearby Sagami Bay. It's a boisterous place that fills up fast on the weekend; call ahead for a table. From Dōgenzaka, turn right after the police box and the restaurant, with a red awning, will be on your right.

SHIBUYA HIKARIE

The 34-floor **Shibuya Hikarie** (渋谷ヒカリエ; www.hikarie.jp; 2-21 Shibuya, Shibuya-ku) building next to Shibuya Station was set to open in 2012. Featuring shops, restaurants and a glass-walled theatre (Theatre Orb), the complex threatens to attract grown-up sophisticates to a neighbourhood ruled by irreverent teens. Also, take the time to see the underground station extension, designed by Andō Tadao and completed in 2008; it looks like a subterranean spaceship.

NIHON MINGEI-KAN

The *mingei* (folk crafts) movement was launched in the early 20th century to promote the works of ordinary craftspeople over cheaper, mass-produced goods. Central to the *mingei* philosophy is *yo no bi* (beauty through use), where everyday objects should bring pleasure through their aesthetics, touch and ease of use. The excellent **Nihon Mingei-kan** (日本民芸館; Japan Folk Crafts Museum; www.mingeikan. or.jp/english; 4-3-33 Komaba, Meguro-ku; adult ¥1000, student ¥200-500; ⊙10am-5pm Tue-Sun; ⓇKeiō Inokashira Line to Komaba-Tōdaimae, west exit), west of Shibuya, houses a collection of some 17,000 pieces in a farmhouse-like building designed by one of the movement's founders. From Komaba-Tōdaima Station, walk with the train tracks on your left; when the road turns right (after about five minutes), the museum will be on your right. Note that it closes between exhibitions.

SUSHI-NO-MIDORI   SUSHI ¥¥

Map p292 (寿司の美登利; Mark City, 4th fl, 1-12-3 Dōgenzaka, Shibuya-ku; sets from ¥2100; ⊙11am-10pm Mon-Fri, to 9pm Sat & Sun; ❤️🍴💻; ⓇJR Yamanote Line to Shibuya, Hachikō exit) A line in front of a restaurant usually means one of two things: it's recently been on TV or it has a solid reputation for being good value. Sushi-no-Midori is the latter. Don't let the wait put you off; service is quick and generous and sushi sets are worth it. From inside Shibuya Station (but outside the ticket gates) look for signs to the Mark City complex, near the entrance for the Inokashira line.

SAKANA-TEI   IZAKAYA ¥

Map p292 (酒菜亭; 📞3780-1313; www.sakanatei. net; 4th fl, 2-23-15 Dōgenzaka, Shibuya-ku; small dishes ¥500-1000; ⊙dinner Mon-Sat; ⓇJR Yamanote Line to Shibuya, Hachikō exit) This unpretentious, grown-up *izakaya* (Japanese version of a pub/eatery) serves home-style cooking from the chef's native Shizuoka prefecture, paired with excellent sake. Get started with one of the tasting sets. The service here is, uh, leisurely, but it's a good escape from the crowds outside. Call ahead on weekends, but turn your phone off once inside – house rules.

NAGI SHOKUDŌ   VEGAN ¥

off Map p292 (なぎ食堂; http://nagi-shokudo. jugem.jp; 15-10 Uguisudani-chō, Shibuya-ku; small dishes/lunch set ¥300/1000; ❤️🍴💻; ⊙lunch & dinner Mon-Sat; ⓇJR Yamanote Line to Shibuya, west exit) Tucked behind Shibuya Station, towards Daikanyama, this little neighbourhood joint serves up a tasty, healthy lunch. Your choice of three dishes (like falafel with sour tofu sauce) comes with miso soup, brown rice and pickles; at dinner the same dishes, and more, are served à la carte. It's at the intersection with the post office.

NABEZŌ   SHABU-SHABU ¥

Map p292 (鍋ぞう; www.nabe-zo.com; 6th fl, Beams Bldg, 31-2 Udagawa-chō; lunch/dinner from ¥1280/1980; ⊙lunch & dinner; 💻; ⓇJR Yamanote Line to Shibuya, Hachikō exit) Here's one for when you're really hungry: diners get a bubbling tabletop pot of broth and 90 minutes to dunk as much beef or pork as they like into it. Though it's a chain, Nabezō gets points for including a vegie bar with plenty of greens and mushrooms.

✖ Shimo-Kitazawa

NODAIWA   UNAGI ¥¥

(野田岩; 📞3413-0105; 2-19-15 Kitazawa, Setagaya-ku; meals ¥2100-4730; ⊙dinner Thu-Tue, lunch Sun; ⓇKeiō Inokashira Line to Shimo-Kitazawa, south exit) This 5th-generation shop has been serving up melt-in-your-mouth *unagi* (eel) in this location since the 1960s. There's normally a line stretching out the door, but once you take a seat beneath the country-style beams and tuck into your *ojū* (*unagi* over rice in a classic lacquer box) or *shirayaki-don* (grilled *unagi*) set lunch, you'll understand why. Walk down the hill with McDonald's on your left and make the first turn on your right; the restaurant is on the right at the end of the alley.

SHIRUBE   IZAKAYA ¥

(汁べゑ; 📞3413-3785; 2-18-2 Kitazawa, Setagaya-ku; dishes ¥580-880; ⊙5.30pm-midnight Mon-Thu & Sun, to 2am Fri & Sat; 🍴💻; ⓇKeiō Inokashira Line to Shimo-Kitazawa, south exit) Loud and lively, this popular *izakaya* has an open kitchen and friendly young chefs. The food (a mix of classic dishes and fusion) is good, too. An all-you-can drink tasting menu (¥4000) makes ordering easy. Make a right

省エネ規制を抜本的に見直す。電力不足

1. Shibuya Crossing (p105)
Crowds and neon at Tokyo's
nonstop intersection.

2. Shibuya girls (p103)
Girls pose on a street in Shibuya, a
popular haunt for young Tokyoites.

3. Hachikō Statue (p106)
Takeshi Ando's bronze statue of the
famously faithful dog is a popular
meeting place in Shibuya.

4. High fashion
Two well-heeled young women
pause at a Shibuya intersection.

in front of Mr Donuts and look for the white *noren* (doorway curtains) on your right. Call ahead on weekends.

NANBAN-TEI
OKONOMIYAKI ¥

(なんばん亭; 2nd fl, 2-12-3 Kitazawa, Setagaya-ku; mains ¥900-1100; ☺dinner daily, lunch Sat & Sun; 📶; 🚉Keiō Inokashira Line to Shimo-Kitazawa, south exit) Knock back a *shōchū* (strong distilled alcohol often made from potatoes) and groove out to the rock'n'roll while a skilled young chef prepares *okonomiyaki* (cabbage pancakes) so you don't have to. Recommended combos include *negi-pokkake* (piled high with green onion and beef) and *mikkusu* (a mix of everything). Turn left where you see Softbank and look for the staircase plastered with *shōchū* labels.

DRINKING & NIGHTLIFE

PINK COW
WINE BAR

Map p292 (ピンクカウ; www.thepinkcow.com; B1 fl, 1-3-18 Shibuya, Shibuya-ku; ☺Tue-Sun; 🚉Ginza Line to Omote-sandō, exit B2) With its animal-print decor, rotating display of local artwork and terrific all-you-can-eat buffet (¥2625) every Friday and Saturday, the Pink Cow is a funky, friendly place to hang out. Also host to stitch-and-bitch evenings, writers' salons and indie film screenings, it's a good bet if you're in the mood to mix with a creative crowd.

USHITORA
BAR

(うしとら; http://blog.ushitora.jp, in Japanese; 2nd fl, 2-9-3 Kitazawa, Shibuya-ku; 📶; 🚉Keiō Inokashira Line to Shimo-Kitazawa, south exit) Ushitora I is a classic counter bar with black-vested waiters and seats. Ushitora II, two doors down, is a small *tachinomi-ya* (standing bar) with vinyl sheets for a door and stacks of manga on the shelves. Be-

tween the two, there are over 30 domestic craft beers on tap. From the station, duck under the tracks, make a right when the road dead ends at a grocery store, followed by a quick left; the bars are at the end of the alley. Ushitora I serves food while Ushitora II is smoke free.

ALDGATE
PUB

Map p292 (ジ・オールゲイト; www.the-aldgate. com; 3rd fl, 30-4 Udagawa-chō, Shibuya-ku; ☺📶📶; 🚉JR Yamanote Line to Shibuya, Hachikō exit) This British pub hits the high notes (20 beers on tap, including several local craft brews) without hitting the lows (it's remarkably clean and smoke free). It's a cosy place that draws a laid-back international crowd. The TV is usually tuned to soccer and the Aldgate often stays open late when big tournaments are on.

HEAVEN'S DOOR
BAR

(ヘブンズドア; http://heavensdoortokyo.com; 2nd fl, 2-17-10 Kitazawa, Setagaya-ku; 📶; 🚉Keiō Inokashira Line to Shimo-Kitazawa, south exit) Run by an Englishman, this bar is a local expat institution. The seats are tatty and comfortable, the conversation lively and multilingual. It's across the street from Shirube (p107), with Christmas lights twinkling in the window year round.

ATTIC ROOM
CAFE

Map p292 (アティックルーム; 4th fl, 31-1 Udagawa-chō, Shibuya-ku; coffee from ¥600; ☺noon-midnight Tue-Sun, 5pm-midnight Mon; 🚉JR Yamanote Line to Shibuya, Hachikō exit) Take the stairs up to the 4th floor of this old corner building near Tōkyū Hands department store (p112) and you'll find a haven of dark wood and old leather recliners. Although the coffee isn't cheap, the price includes peace and quiet.

BELLO VISTO
BAR

Map p292 (ベロビスト; 40th fl, 26-1 Sakuragaoka-chō, Shibuya-ku; admission ¥1155, cocktails & wine

---

LOCAL KNOWLEDGE

KAMIYAMA SHŌTENGAI

Just past Bunkamura cultural centre (p112), this narrow one-way *shōtengai* (market street) is lined with tiny bistros, bars and corner shops. Some look as though they've been around for decades; others are part of a hip scene that defines itself in contrast with brash, commercial Shibuya. Check out what's going on at Uplink cinema or join the crowd of young creative professionals for a drink at the terrace bar **Stand S** (37-16 Udagawa-chō, Shibuya-ku; 🚉JR Yamanote Line to Shibuya, Hachikō exit).

from ¥1300; ⏰4pm-midnight Mon-Fri, 3pm-midnight Sat & Sun; 🚉JR Yamanote Line to Shibuya, south exit) This 40th-floor eyrie on the Cerulean Tower keeps the interior dim so that you can see the lights on the far horizon. You can duck the cover charge if you sit at the counter – not bad considering that you can gaze over the bar at the glowing nightscape through the large plate-glass windows.

ENTERTAINMENT

SHIDAX VILLAGE KARAOKE

Map p292 (シダックスビレッジ; www.shidax. co.jp/sc, in Japanese; 1-12-13 Jinnan, Shibuya-ku; per hr Fri-Sun ¥1180, Mon-Thu ¥1080, 2hr all you can drink package ¥4200; ⏰11am-5am; 🚉JR Yamanote Line to Shibuya, Hachikō exit) Topped by a massive red neon sign, Shidax Shibuya outshines all the other karaoke joints in the neighbourhood. Rooms are spacious and make a stab at being stylish; there are nonsmoking rooms available, too. There are several branches of **Karaoke-kan** (カラオケ館; www.karaokekan.jp; per hr Fri-Sun ¥1280, Mon-Thu ¥1040; ⏰11am-6am) around Shibuya, too. Like most karaoke parlours, Shidax and Karaoke-kan have cheaper rates on weekdays before 6pm.

WOMB DJ

Map p292 (ウーム; www.womb.co.jp; 2-16 Maruyama-chō, Shibuya-ku; admission ¥2000-4000; 🚉JR Yamanote Line to Shibuya, Hachikō exit) Womb has a state-of-the art sound system, an enormous mirror ball and frenetic laser lighting that goes perfectly with the house and techno music usually played here. Though it draws more diehard music fans than scene chasers, Womb's four floors still get jammed at weekends. Bring a flyer and they'll knock ¥500 to ¥1000 off the cover – check around Shibuya music shops beforehand, or print one from Womb's website. Photo ID is required at the door.

CLUB QUATTRO LIVE MUSIC

Map p292 (クラブクアトロ; www.club-quattro. com; 32-13-4 Udagawa-chō, Shibuya-ku; admission ¥3000-4000; 🚉JR Yamanote Line to Shibuya, Hachikō exit) This venue feels like a concert hall, but it's actually more along the lines of a slick club. It books local and international bands of generally high quality.

Though there's no explicit musical focus, emphasis is on rock and roll and world music. Expect a more varied, artsy crowd than the club's location – near Sentā-gai – might lead you to expect.

SETAGAYA PUBLIC THEATRE PERFORMING ARTS

(世田谷パブリックシアター; ⏰5432-1526; setagaya-pt.jp; 4-1-1 Taishidō, Setagaya-ku; admission ¥3500-7500; 🚉Tōkyū Den-en-toshi Line to Sangenjaya, Carrot Tower exit) This is the rare Tokyo theatre that is both commercially successful and consistently interesting, producing contemporary dramas along with modern *nō* (a stylised Japanese dance-drama, performed on a bare stage) and *kyōgen* (comic drama). It's not surprising that it's in Setagaya-ku, southeast of Shibuya, Tokyo wealthiest residential district. The smaller Theatre Tram here shows more experimental works.

SHELTER LIVE MUSIC

(シェルター; www.loft-prj.co.jp/SHELTER; 2-6-10 Kitazawa, Setagaya-ku; admission ¥2000-3500; 🚉Keiō Inokashira Line to Shimo-Kitazawa, south exit) Of all the venues on the Shimo-Kitazawa circuit, this small basement club, which just celebrated its 20th anniversary, has the most consistently solid line-up. It can be an excellent place to catch (and even meet) up-and-coming artists, usually of the rock persuasion.

UPLINK CINEMA

Map p292 (アップリンク; www.uplink.co.jp; 2nd fl, 37-18 Udagawa-cho, Shibuya-ku; 🚉JR Yamanote Line to Shibuya, Hachikō exit) Day and night Uplink screens quirky independent films (domestic and foreign) in a tiny art-house cinema with comfy chairs. There's also an event space that hosts equally quirky music and talk events on some evenings, and popular restaurant **Tabela** (meals from ¥1000; ⏰lunch & dinner) can be found on the ground floor.

RUBY ROOM LIVE MUSIC

Map p292 (ルビールーム; www.rubyroomtokyo. com; 2nd fl, Kasumi Bldg, 2-25-17 Dōgenzaka, Shibuya-ku; admission ¥1500; 🚉JR Yamanote Line to Shibuya, Hachikō exit) This tiny, sparkly gem of a cocktail lounge hosts both DJd and live-music events. It's an appealing spot for older kids hanging out in Shibuya; Tuesday's open mic night (free entry with two-drink minimum) draws a laid-back international crowd.

HONDA THEATRE THEATRE

off map p292 (本多劇場; www.honda-geki.com, in Japanese; 2-10-15 Kitazawa, Shibuya-ku; 圓Keiō Inokashira Line to Shimo-Kitazawa, south exit) This is the original – and the biggest – of a collection of *shōgekijō* (small theatres) that set up in Shimo-Kitazawa in the early '80s. You'll gain a fair amount of Japanese ability to get through the performances, but it's worth swinging by just to check out the bohemian atmosphere.

CLUB ASIA DJ

Map p292 (クラブエイジア; www.clubasia.co.jp, in Japanese; 1-8 Maruyama-chō, Shibuya-ku; admission around ¥2500; 圓JR Yamanote Line to Shibuya, Hachikō exit) This massive club is worth a visit if you're on the younger end of 20-something. Events here are usually jam-packed every night. Occasionally the club hosts some of Tokyo's bigger DJ events and hip-hop acts.

EUROSPACE CINEMA

Map p292 (ユーロスペース; www.eurospace. co.jp; Q-Ax Bldg, 1-5 Maruyama-chō, Shibuya-ku; 圓JR Yamanote Line to Shibuya, Hachikō exit) The focus at this fine theatre remains unwaveringly on lesser-known European and Asian films. Eurospace also occasionally hosts documentary or feature-film festivals, which are listed in the major English-language weeklies, and it sometimes screens late shows.

BUNKAMURA PERFORMING ARTS

Map p292 (文化村; ☎3477-9111; www.bunkamura. co.jp; 2-24-1 Dōgenzaka, Shibuya-ku; 圓JR Yamanote Line to Shibuya, Hachikō exit) *Bunkamura* means 'culture village', and this was Japan's first cross-cultural centre. Productions at Theatre Cocoon swing between commercial and fairly edgy. There's also a cinema and a concert hall (Orchard Hall) here.

SHIBUYA O-EAST LIVE MUSIC

Map p292 (渋谷オーイースト; www.shibuya-o. com; 2-14-8 Dōgenzaka, Shibuya-ku; 圓JR Yamanote Line to Shibuya, Hachikō exit) Shibuya O-East is the big mama of several related venues forming a compound of clubs up Love Hotel Hill. With its sheer size, this house draws bigger-name international and domestic acts. You'll encounter everything from J-Pop to indie here, plus mini-festivals that can introduce curious audiophiles to a whole slew of new bands and DJs (some better than others).

SHOPPING

TOP CHOICE TŌKYŪ HANDS DEPARTMENT STORE

Map p292 (東急ハンズ; http://shibuya.tokyu -hands.co.jp, in Japanese; 12-18 Udagawa-chō, Shibuya-ku; 圓JR Yamanote Line to Shibuya, Hachikō exit) This DIY and *zakka* (miscellaneous goods) store has eight fascinating floors of everything you didn't know you needed. It's perfect for souvenir hunting – surely someone you know needs reflexology slippers, right? There's another huge store in Shinjuku's Takashimaya Times Sq and a more upscale version, Ginza Hands, in Ginza.

TOP CHOICE RANKING RANQUEEN SPECIALITY STORE

Map p292 (ランキンランキン; 2nd fl, Shibuya Station, Shibuya-ku; ◷9am-11pm; 圓JR Yamanote Line to Shibuya, Hachikō exit) If it's trendy, it's here. This clever shop stocks only the top-selling products in any given category, from eyeliner and soft drinks to leg-slimming massage rollers. Given its location smack inside Shibuya Station, Ranking Ranqueen is always crowded with teens and 20-somethings.

SHIBUYA 109 FASHION

Map p292 (渋谷109; Ichimarukyū; 2-29-1 Dōgenzaka, Shibuya-ku; ◷10am-9pm; 圓JR Yamanote Line to Shibuya, Hachikō exit) See all those dolled-up teens walking around Shibuya? This is where they shop. Nicknamed *marukyū*, this cylindrical tower houses dozens of small boutiques, each with their own carefully styled look (and loud competing music). Even if you don't intend buying anything, you can't understand Shibuya without making a stop here. For guys, there's **109 Men's** (109 メンズ; 1-23-10 Jinnan, Shibuya-ku) to the right of Shibuya Crossing.

SISTER FASHION

Map p292 (シスター; www.faketokyo.com, 2nd fl, 18-4 Udagawa-cho, Shibuya-ku; ◷noon-10pm; 圓JR Yamanote to Shibuya, Hachikō exit) This is one of the best places in the city to discover hot new Japanese designers. The sales clerks are painfully stylish, but surprisingly nice; they'll happily help you put together an enviable outfit from the shop's collection of new and vintage (though it won't be cheap). Look for the 'Fake Tokyo' banners.

RECYCLE SHOPS

Take Tokyoites' love of fashion, pair it with impossibly small closets and what do you get? Possibly the world's best consignment shops. Called *risaikuru shoppu* (recycle shops), they're often stocked with local favourites like Comme Des Garçons and Vivienne Westwood. The items still may not be cheap (about half the retail price), but they look hardly worn. **RagTag** (www.ragtag.jp) is a reliable chain with clothes for men and women; there's a branch in **Shibuya** (Map p292 1-17-7 Jinnan, Shibuya-ku; ⊘noon-9pm; ℝJR Yamanote Line to Shibuya, Hachikō exit).

TSUKIKAGEYA   FASHION

(月影屋; www.tsukikageya.com; 1-9-19 Tomigaya, Shibuya-ku; ⊘noon-8pm Thu-Mon; ℝChiyoda Line to Yoyogi Kōen) If you're looking for a *yukata* (cotton kimono) that's more punk rock than Hello Kitty, this is your store. Natsuki Shigeta's designs come in a dozen different irreverent patterns and pair with snakeskin obi (sash) and wild accessories. It's a bit of a walk to get here – from Shibuya Station, head along Kamiyama Shōtengai way past Bunkamura, cross the big intersection with Inokashira-dōri and then look for the bright pink signboard on your right.

PARCO   DEPARTMENT STORE

Map p292 (パルコ; www.parco-shibuya.com; 15-1 Udagawa-chō, Shibuya-ku; ⊘10am-9pm; ℝJR Yamanote Line to Shibuya, Hachikō exit) Parco stretches over several buildings and includes restaurants, gallery space (Parco Factory), a theatre, cinema and Club Quattro. The Parco 1 building has the best shops, which get edgier as you ascend; look for fun Japanese labels like Hysteric Glamour and Merci Beaucoup on the 3rd and 4th floors. There's also an excellent bookshop in the basement.

LOFT   DEPARTMENT STORE

Map p292 (ロフト; 21-1 Udagawa-chō, Shibuya-ku; ℝJR Yamanote Line to Shibuya, Hachikō exit) This emporium of cute homewares and accessories generally attracts a younger crowd than Tōkyū Hands. Check out the candy-coloured stationary and travel goods on the first two floors.

Harajuku & Aoyama

HARAJUKU | AOYAMA

Neighbourhood Top Five

1 Making a wish at **Meiji-jingū** (p116). Leave the city behind as you pass through the towering *torii* (gate) and follow the wooded, gravel path to Tokyo's most famous Shintō shrine.

2 Scouting new looks on **Takeshita-dōri** (p117) and around the back streets of Harajuku.

3 Stretching out on the lawn of **Yoyogi-kōen** (p117), one of Tokyo's largest parks.

4 Gawking at the architectural wonders (and eyebrow-raising consumerism) along **Omote-sandō** (p119).

5 Retreating into the calm galleries and gardens of **Nezu Museum** (p118).

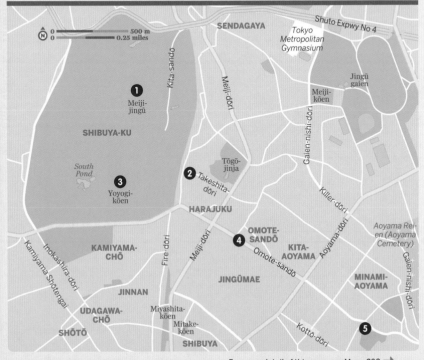

For more detail of this area, see Map p293 ➡

Explore Harajuku & Aoyama

Harajuku's colourful teen culture hits you as soon as you exit the station. Strolling down Takeshita-dōri is a rite of passage for anyone who has ever felt themselves outside the mainstream. Further down Omote-sandō, the boulevard that connects Harajuku and Aoyama, crowds become increasingly refined; moneyed Aoyama is where Japan's leading designers have their flagship shops. Somewhere in between are the style mavens of Ura-Hara, Harajuku's backstreets, where street trends are born.

On weekends in particular, this is the city's living catwalk. Harajuku and Aoyama have a powerful allure that draws shoppers from all over Japan, and increasingly from around Asia, too. Saturdays and Sundays can be incredibly crowded.

There's a lot more to do than just shop. There's Meiji-jingū, one of the city's top attractions, and a handful of excellent museums, both traditional and modern. The weekend scene in Yoyogi-kōen is worth checking out, too. Broad Omote-sandō, once the official road leading to the shrine, is now adorned with luxury brand boutiques designed by leading Japanese architects; for fans of contemporary architecture, this is a must-see. There's a healthy cafe culture and some good restaurants, too.

Once the shops close, Harajuku becomes a much quieter place. Aoyama too, though there are some high-end establishments here that fuel the well-heeled after hours. This may be no place to bar-hop, but after a long day you could do worse than making yourself at home in one of the many cafes here that stay open late.

Local Life

➡ **Street Snaps** Photographers for street fashion magazines line Omote-sandō looking for the next big thing. Teens and 20-somethings know it and dress for a shot at their 15 minutes of fame.

➡ **Festivals** On most weekends during summer, the plaza across the street from Yoyogi-kōen (p117) hosts festivals for Tokyo's ethnic communities.

➡ **Hangouts** Two Rooms (p122) is the place to see and be seen; Montoak (p123) is the place to escape to.

Getting There & Away

➡ **Train** The JR Yamanote Line stops at Harajuku Station.

➡ **Subway** The Chiyoda Line runs beneath Omote-sandō, stopping at Omote-sandō and Meiji-jingūmae Stations. The Fukutoshin Line also stops at Meiji-jingūmae Station. The Ginza and Hanzōmon Lines both stop at Omote-sandō Station.

Lonely Planet's Top Tip

The recent arrival of fast-fashion mega-chains (like H&M) hasn't pushed Harajuku fashion off the map; it's just pushed it further into the back streets. Ura-Hara (literally 'behind Harajuku') is the nickname for the maze of back streets behind Omote-sandō. Here you'll find the tiny, eccentric shops and secondhand stores from which Harajuku hipsters cobble together their head-turning looks. Whether your aim is acquisitive or more of the anthropological sort, it's worth spending a few hours exploring these streets.

 ## Best Places to Eat

➡ Agaru Sagaru Nishi Iru Higashi Iru (p118)

➡ Maisen (p122)

➡ Honoji (p118)

➡ Harajuku Gyōza Rō (p118)

For reviews, see p118 ➡

Best Places to Drink

➡ Two Rooms (p122)

➡ Harajuku Taproom (p122)

➡ A to Z Café (p123)

For reviews, see p122 ➡

Best Places to Shop

➡ Takeshita-dōri (p123)

➡ Laforet (p124)

➡ KiddyLand (p124)

➡ Pass the Baton (p125)

➡ Musubi (p124)

For reviews, see p123 ➡

TOP SIGHTS
MEIJI-JINGŪ (MEIJI SHRINE)

Tokyo's grandest Shintō shrine is dedicated to the Emperor Meiji and Empress Shōken. The reign of the Emperor Meiji (1868–1912) coincided with the country's transformation from isolationist, feudal state to modern nation. Constructed in 1920, the shrine was destroyed in WWII air raids and rebuilt in 1958; however, unlike so many of Japan's postwar reconstructions, Meiji-jingū has an authentic feel. The shrine itself occupies only a small fraction of the sprawling forested grounds.

Several wooden *torii* (gates) mark the entrance to Meiji-jingū (明治神宮). The largest, created from a 1500-year-old Taiwanese cypress, stands 12 metres high. Before approaching the main shrine, visitors purify themselves by pouring water over their hands at the *temizuya* (font). The main shrine is made of cypress from the Kiso region of Nagano. Every day at 8am and 2pm a priest strikes the large drum as part of a ritual offering of food to the deities enshrined here. Should you wish to make an offering too, toss a five-yen coin in the box, bow twice, clap your hands twice and then bow again.

The 70 hectares of forested grounds contain some 120,000 trees collected from all over Japan. On the left, along the path towards the main shrine, is the entrance to **Meiji-jingū Gyoen** (明治神宮御苑; Inner Garden; admission ¥500; ☺9am-4.30pm), a landscaped garden. It once belonged to a feudal estate; however, the emperor himself designed the iris garden to please the empress when the grounds passed into Imperial hands. The garden is most impressive in June when the irises bloom; the azaleas in April are pretty too. Recently an urban legend has turned a long-neglected well here into a good-luck spot; you'll see visitors queuing up to photograph it with their mobile phones.

DON'T MISS

➡ Main Shrine
➡ Inner Garden

PRACTICALITIES

➡ Map p293
➡ www.meijijingu.or.jp
➡ 1-1 Yoyogi Kamizono-chō, Shibuya-ku
➡ ☺dawn-dusk
➡ ℝJR Yamanote Line to Harajuku, Omote-sandō exit

◉ SIGHTS

◉ Harajuku

MEIJI-JINGŪ (MEIJI SHRINE)
SHRINE

See p116.

TAKESHITA-DŌRI
STREET

Map p293 (竹下通り; ⬛JR Yamanote Line to Harajuku, Takeshita exit) This is Tokyo's famous fashion subculture bazaar, where aspiring goths and Lolitas come to shop. The narrow alley is a pilgrimage site for teens from all over Japan and the pedestrian traffic is intense. There are some wild things on display, though most visitors are happy to shop for more wearable items. For a glimpse of Harajuku past, peek into **Takenoko** (竹の子; 1-6-15 Jingūmae, Shibuya-ku; ◷11am-8pm; JR Yamanote Line to Harajuku, Takeshita exit), the boutique that spawned a wacky movement of proto-rave dance tribes in 1979; the shop now mostly sells costumes to entertainers. See p123 for more shopping recommendations.

YOYOGI-KŌEN
PARK

Map p292 (代々木公園; ⬛JR Yamanote Line to Harajuku, Omote-sandō exit) If it's a sunny and warm weekend afternoon you can count on there being a crowd lazing around the large grassy expanse that is Yoyogi-kōen. You can also usually find revellers and noisemakers of all stripes, from hula-hoopers to African drum circles to a group of retro greasers dancing around a boom box. It's an excellent place for a picnic and probably the only place in the city where you can reasonably toss a frisbee without fear of hitting someone. While you're there, check out the nearby **Yoyogi National Stadium**, an early masterpiece by architect Tange Kenzō, built for the 1964 Olympics.

UKIYO-E ŌTA MEMORIAL ART MUSEUM
MUSEUM

Map p293 (浮世絵太田記念館; www.ukiyoe-ota-muse.jp; 1-10-10 Jingūmae, Shibuya-ku; adult ¥700-1000, student ¥500-700, child free; ◷10.30am-5.30pm Tue-Sun, closed 27th to end of month; ⬛JR Yamanote Line to Harajuku, Omote-sandō exit) Trade your shoes for slippers at the door to view the excellent *ukiyo-e* (wood-block prints) collection of Ōta Seizo, the former head of the Toho Life Insurance Company. The museum usually displays no more than a few dozen works at a time from its collection of over 10,000 prints, including those by masters of the art such as Hokusai and Hiroshige.

Downstairs from the museum is a branch of the shop Kamawanu (p101), which specialises in beautifully printed *tenugui* (traditional hand-dyed thin cotton towels).

DESIGN FESTA
ART GALLERY

Map p293 (デザインフェスタ; www.designfestagallery.com; 3-20-2 Jingūmae, Shibuya-ku; ◷11am-7pm; ⬛JR Yamanote Line to Harajuku, Takeshita exit) Design Festa has been a leader in Tokyo's DIY art scene for over a decade. The madhouse building itself is worth a visit; it's always evolving. Inside there are a dozen small galleries rented by the day. All proceeds from sales go directly to the artists. Design Festa also sponsors a twice-yearly exhibition, actually Asia's largest art fair, at Tokyo Big Sight (see p182).

JINGŪ-BASHI
BRIDGE

Map p293 (神宮橋; ⬛JR Yamanote Line to Harajuku, Omote-sandō exit) If you're hunting to take photos of Harajuku's legendary *cosplayers* (costume players), this is your best bet. Though the scene appears to be fading, on sunny weekends (especially Sundays) you might catch eccentrically dressed teens assembling here.

INTERNET HOT SPOTS

Terminal (Map p293; 3rd fl, Terminal, 3-22-12 Jingūmae, Shibuya-ku; per hr ¥380; ◷24hr; ⊖☏; ⬛JR Yamanote Line to Harajuku, Takeshita exit) This is everything your standard internet cafe isn't: airy and sunlit, with good coffee and big-screen Macs kitted out with Adobe Suite software. You'll have to sign up for a membership card (¥150).

Wired Café 360 (Map p293; 5th fl, 4-32-16 Jingūmae, Shibuya-ku; ◷10am-8pm; ⊖☏; ⬛JR Yamanote Line to Harajuku, Takeshita exit) On top of the KDDI Design Studio, Wired has five computers that you can use for an unlimited time so long as you buy a drink or a meal here (coffee costs ¥450).

◉ Aoyama

NEZU MUSEUM
MUSEUM

Map p293 (根津美術館; www.nezu-muse.or.jp; 6-5-1 Minami-Aoyama, Minato-ku; adult/student/child/¥1000/800/free, special exhibitions ¥200 extra; ⊙10am-5pm Tue-Sun; 🚇Ginza Line to Omote-sandō, exit A5) This recently renovated museum offers a striking blend of old and new: a renowned collection of Japanese, Chinese and Korean antiquities in a gallery space designed by contemporary architect Kuma Kengō. Select items from the extensive collection are displayed in manageable monthly collections.

The museum building is just the half of it. Behind the galleries is a woodsy strolling garden laced with stone paths and studded with teahouses and sculptures. There's a glass-walled cafe (also designed by Kuma), too.

WATARI MUSEUM OF CONTEMPORARY ART (WATARI-UM)
MUSEUM

Map p293 (ワタリウム美術館; www.watarium. co.jp, in Japanese; 3-7-6 Jingūmae, Shibuya-ku; adult/student ¥1000/800; ⊙11am-7pm Tue & Thu-Sun, to 9pm Wed; 🚇Ginza Line to Gaienmae, exit 3) This progressive and often provocative museum was built in 1990 to a design by Swiss architect Mario Botta. Exhibits range from retrospectives of established art-world figures (like Yayoi Kusama and Nam June Paik) to graffiti and landscape

---

LOCAL KNOWLEDGE

AOYAMA REI-EN

Aoyama Rei-en (青山霊園; off Map p293; 2-32-2 Minami-Aoyama, Minato-ku; 🚇Ginza Line to Gaienmae, exit 1B), Japan's first public cemetery, is very much a public place; locals use the tree-lined paths between the graves as short cuts through the neighbourhood. It's a peaceful place for a stroll and the elaborate stone-carved tombs are rather impressive. A number of important Meiji-era figures are buried here; so is Professor Ueno, owner of Hachikō the dog (see p106). There are many *sakura* (cherry blossoms) and Aoyama Rei-en is a pretty, if not unusual, *hanami* (blossom viewing) spot. Why should the living have all the fun?

---

artists – with some exhibitions spilling onto the surrounding streets. There's an excellent art bookshop in the basement called **On Sundays** where you can browse through an enormous collection of obscure postcards.

✖ EATING

✖ Harajuku

TOP CHOICE AGARU SAGARU NISHI IRU HIGASHI IRU
KAISEKI ¥¥

Map p293 (上ル下ル西入ル東入ル; 🕿3403-6968; Basement fl, 3-25-8 Jingūmae, Shibuya-ku; lunch/dinner course ¥2680/3990; ⊙lunch & dinner; 🚇JR Yamanote Line to Harajuku, Takeshita exit) Good, affordable *kaiseki* (Japanese formal haute cuisine) is as unconventional as anything else you're likely to find in Harajuku, which makes this restaurant a real gem. The young, friendly chefs serve up a procession of artful dishes that are Kyoto-inspired but tweaked for Tokyoites' been-there-done-that tastes. Also, it looks like a cave. There's only a counter and a few tables, so call ahead on weekends; sitting at the counter is more fun.

HONOJI
TRADITIONAL ¥

Map p293 (ほの字; 4th fl, 5-10-1 Jingūmae, Shibuya-ku; lunch set ¥900, small dishes ¥350-1000; ⊙lunch & dinner; 🚇JR Yamanote Line to Harajuku, Omote-sandō exit) The lunchtime *sakana teishoku* (fish set meal) here has a loyal following; it's fresh, filling and a steal – especially considering the location on top of Chanel. There are several options that change daily. The dinner menu expands to include sashimi, small dishes and skewers of grilled meat and vegetables. Look for the white *noren* (curtains).

HARAJUKU GYŌZA RŌ
GYŌZA ¥

Map p293 (原宿餃子楼; 6-4-2 Jingūmae, Shibuya-ku; 6 gyōza ¥290; ⊙11.30am-4.30am; 🚇JR Yamanote Line to Harajuku, Omote-sandō exit) *Gyōza* (dumplings) are the only thing on the menu here, but you won't hear any complaints from the regulars who queue up to get their fix. Have them *sui* (boiled) or *yaki* (pan-fried), with or without *niniku* (garlic) or *nira* (chives) – they're all delicious. Expect to wait on weekends.

START **OMOTESANDŌ HILLS**
END **NEZU MUSEUM**
DISTANCE **1.5KM**
DURATION **1½ HOURS**

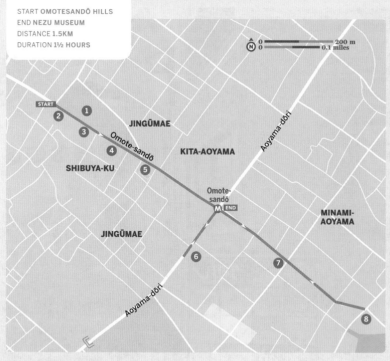

Neighbourhood Walk
Omote-sandō Architecture

➡ Omote-sandō is a walk-through show-room for the who's who of contemporary Japanese architects.

Andō Tadao's deceptively deep ❶ **Omotesandō Hills** (表参道ヒルズ; 2003) is a high-end shopping mall that spirals around a sunken central atrium. It replaced an ivy-covered pre-WWII apartment building (to considerable protest); the low horizontal design pays homage to the original structure.

Across the street, the ❷ **Dior Building** (ディオールビル; 2003), designed by recent Pritzker Prize winner SANAA (Sejima Kazuyo and Nishizawa Ryūe), has a filmy exterior that seems to hang like a dress.

Nearby, a glass cone marks the unlikely location of the ❸ **Japan Nursing Association** (日本看護協会; 2004), designed by Kurokawa Kishō.

Next up is Aoki Jun's ❹ **Louis Vuitton Building** (ルイヴィトンビル; 2002), meant to evoke a stack of trunks. There's a gallery on the 7th floor.

Climb onto the elevated crosswalk to better admire Itō Toyō's construction for ❺ **Tod's** (トッズ; 2004). The criss-crossing strips of concrete take their inspiration from the zelkova trees below; they're also structural.

Maki Fumihiko's ❻ **Spiral Building** (スパイラルビル; 1985) is worth a detour down Aoyama-dōri. The patchwork, uncentred design is a nod to Tokyo's own incongruous landscape. Inside, a spiralling passage doubles as an art gallery.

You can't miss the convex glass fishbowl that is the ❼ **Prada Aoyama Building** (プラダ青山ビル; 2003), designed by Herzog and de Meuron.

A thicket of bamboo marks the entrance to the traditional-meets-modern Kuma Kengō building that houses the excellent ❽ **Nezu Museum** (根津美術館; 2009).

1. Takeshita-dōri (p117)
Shoppers throng Tokyo's famous subculture bazaar.

2. Prada Aoyama Building (p119)
Shoppers pass the signature bubbled windows of this Jacques Herzog and Pierre de Meuron creation.

3. Yoyogi-kōen (p117)
Rockabilly dancers strut their stuff in Harajuku's popular park.

4. Cosplay
A teenager poses in a *cosplay* (costume play) outfit on Takeshita-dōri, Harajuku.

MOMINOKI HOUSE ORGANIC ¥

Map p293 (もみの木ハウス; www2.odn.ne.jp/mominoki_house/index.htm; 2-18-5 Jingūmae, Shibuya-ku; lunch/dinner set from ¥800/3200; ⏰11.30am-11pm; ✆✏🅿; 🚇JR Yamanote Line to Harajuku, Takeshita exit) Boho Tokyoites have been coming here for tasty and nourishing macrobiotic fare since 1976. The casual, cosy dining room has seen some famous visitors too, like Paul McCartney. Chef Yamada's menu is heavily vegetarian, but also includes free-range chicken and *Ezo shika* (Hokkaidō venison; ¥4800).

KYŪSYŪ JANGARA RAMEN ¥

Map p293 (九州じゃんがら; 1-13-21 Jingūmae, Shibuya-ku; dishes ¥600-1050; ⏰10.45am-2am Mon-Fri, to 2am Sat & Sun; 🅿; 🚇JR Yamanote Line to Harajuku, Omote-sandō exit) There always seems to be a line for seats outside this Kyūshū-style *rāmen* (noodles in broth) shop near Harajuku Station, and with good reason: elegantly thin noodles, your choice of a half-dozen broths, silky *chāshū* (roast pork) and righteous *karashi takana* (hot pickled greens). Go for the popular *zembu-iri* (everything in).

🍴 Aoyama

MAISEN TONKATSU ¥

Map p293 (まい泉; http://mai-sen.com; 4-8-5 Jingūmae, Shibuya-ku; lunch/dinner from ¥995/1680; ⏰11am-10pm; ✆🅿; 🚇Ginza Line to Omote-sandō, exit A2) You could order something else (fried shrimp, for example), but pretty much everyone else will be ordering the famous *tonkatsu* (breaded, deep-fried pork cutlets). There are different grades of pork on the menu, including prized *kurobuta* (black pig), but even the cheapest is melt-in-your-mouth divine. The restaurant is housed in an old public bathhouse. There's also a takeaway window that serves delicious *tonkatsu sando* (sandwich).

PARIYA INTERNATIONAL ¥

Map p293 (パリヤ; 3-12-14 Kita-Aoyama, Minato-ku; meals from ¥1000; ⏰11.30am-11pm; ✆; 🚇Ginza Line to Omote-sandō, exit B2) Food is served cafeteria-style here: grab a tray and choose one main, one salad and one side dish. It's not cheap slop though; typical dishes include avocado and *hijiki* (seaweed) with sesame dressing and curried potato salad with chorizo and egg. There

are colourful cupcakes and gelato for dessert. Pariya is a favourite lunchtime spot for the local fashion crowd.

LAS CHICAS INTERNATIONAL, CAFE ¥

Map p293 (ラスチカス; www.vision.co.jp; 5-47-6 Jingūmae, Shibuya-ku; dishes around ¥1500; ⏰11.30am-11pm; ✆✏🅿📶; 🚇Ginza Line to Omote-sandō, exit A2) Urbane and relaxed, Las Chicas draws an international crowd with its inviting terrace, comfort food and friendly foreign staff. The all-day menu is expansive, covering light bites, big salads, sandwiches and pastas. It's popular day and night, with evening events like swing dance workshops and masquerade parties taking place in the basement lounge.

DRINKING & NIGHTLIFE

TWO ROOMS BAR

Map p293 (トゥールームス; ☎3498-0002; www.tworooms.jp; 5th fl, 3-11-7 Kita-Aoyama, Minato-ku; ⏰11.30am-2am Mon-Sat, to 10pm Sun; 🅿; 🚇Ginza Line to Omote-sandō, exit B2) With its sleek contemporary design, this new restaurant and bar, popular with expats, could be anywhere – save for the sweeping view towards the Shinjuku skyline from the terrace. Expect a crowd dressed like they don't care that wine by the glass starts at ¥1400. You can eat here too, but the real scene is at night by the bar. Call ahead on Friday or Saturday night to reserve a table on the terrace.

HARAJUKU TAPROOM BREWERY

Map p293 (原宿タップルーム; http://bairdbeer.com/en/bairdbeer; 2nd fl, 1-20-13 Jingūmae, Shibuya-ku; ✆🅿; 🚇JR Yamanote Line to Harajuku, Takeshita exit) Baird's Brewery is one of Japan's most successful and consistently good craft breweries. This is one of their two Tokyo outposts, where you can sample over a dozen of their beers on tap; try the top-selling Rising Sun Pale Ale. The crowd here, which includes suited salarymen and English teachers, are way out of their comfort zone on Takeshita-dōri, which speaks volumes for Baird's popularity. Take a left after Cafe Solare; the bar is at the end of the lane on the right.

A TO Z CAFÉ CAFE, BAR

Map p293 (エートゥーゼットカフェ; 5th fl 5-8-3 Minami-Aoyama, Minato-ku; ⏰noon-11.30pm; 🚻; 🚇Ginza Line to Omote-sandō, exit B3) Artist Yoshitomo Nara teamed up with design firm Graf to create this spacious and only slightly off-kilter cafe. Along with wooden schoolhouse chairs, whitewashed walls and a small cottage, you can find a few scattered examples of Nara's work. The Japanese-style diner food – think fried chicken with *yuzu* (citrus sauce) – is delicious, too.

MONTOAK CAFE, BAR

Map p293 (モントーク; 6-1-9 Jingūmae, Shibuya-ku; ⏰11am-3am; 🚻🚻; 🚇JR Yamanote Line to Harajuku, Omote-sandō exit) This smoky glass cube is a calm, dimly lit retreat from the busy streets. It's perfect for holing up with a pot of tea or carafe of wine and watching the crowds go by. Or, if the weather is nice, score a seat on the terrace. It's right next door to the giant toy emporium KiddyLand.

ENTERTAINMENT

KOKURITSU NŌ-GAKUDŌ
(NATIONAL NŌ THEATRE) TRADITIONAL THEATRE

(国立能楽堂; ☎3423-1331; www.ntj.jac.go.jp/english; 4-18-1 Sendagaya, Shibuya-ku; tickets from ¥2600; 🚇JR Sōbu Line to Sendagaya) This theatre stages the traditional music, poetry and dances that *nō* (stylised Japanese dance-drama; performed on a bare stage) is famous for, as well as the interludes of *kyōgen* (short, lively comic farces) that serve as cathartic comic relief. The stark legends and historical dramas unfold on an elegant cypress stage. Each seat has a small screen that can display an English translation of the dialogue. Shows take place only a few times a month and tickets can sell out quickly. The theatre is 400m from Sendagaya Station; from the exit, walk right along the main road and take the third left (if you reach a traffic light you've gone too far).

CROCODILE LIVE MUSIC, COMEDY

Map p293 (クロコダイル; www.crocodile-live.jp; Basement fl, 6-18-8 Jingūmae, Shibuya-ku; 🚇Chiyoda Line to Meiji-jingūmae, exit 1) This casual, if not slightly grungy, subterranean venue hosts all sorts of music acts as well as a popular English comedy night, with stand-up, sketch and improv from the Tokyo Comedy Store (last Friday of the month; admission ¥2000).

SHOPPING

Harajuku

Harajuku favours young, adventurous shoppers. Long a star on Tokyo's tourist map, the neighbourhood is also a good place to pick up souvenirs.

TAKESHITA-DŌRI FASHION STRIP

Map p293 (竹下通り; 🚇JR Yamanote Line to Harajuku, Takeshita exit) Even if you're not in the market for a Victorian-era dress, there is still plenty to pull out your wal-

---

SHOPPING IN URA-HARA

The side streets of Harajuku known as **Ura-Hara** (Map p293; 🚇JR Yamanote Line to Harajuku) draw shoppers who prefer to dress firmly outside the mainstream. Along with Kōenji (p130) and Shimo-Kitazawa (p106), it's an excellent place for trawling second-hand shops and gleaning inspiration from fellow browsers.

There are a few landmark boutiques, too. Club kids and stylists love the showpiece items at **Dog** (ドッグ; Map p293; Basement fl, 3-23-3 Jingūmae, Shibuya-ku), which stocks bold and brash vintage and remake items. Followers of *fairy-kei* – a light and fluffy '80s throwback look – stock up on candy-coloured accessories at **6% Doki Doki** (ロクパーセントドキドキ; Map p293; 2nd fl, 4-28-16 Jingūmae, Shibuya-ku). And those thick-soled shoes you've seen on all over? The chances are they're from **Tokyo Bopper** (トーキョーボッパー; 4-25-7 Jingūmae, Shibuya-ku).

let for here, like funky tights and mobile-phone charms. If you are on the hunt for a Victorian-era dress, head to **Closet Child** (クローゼットチャイルド; 2nd-4th fl, 1-6-11 Jingūmae, Shibuya-ku), which stocks second-hand items from gothic and Lolita brands for way below their original retail prices. You'll also find a three-storey branch of ¥100 store **Daiso** (ダイソー; 1-19-24 Jingūmae, Shibuya-ku) here, where you can stock up on everything from toilet slippers to fake eyelashes.

LAFORET
FASHION

Map p293 (ラフォーレ; 1-11-6 Jingūmae, Shibuya-ku; www.laforet.ne.jp; ℝJR Yamanote Line to Harajuku, Omote-sandō exit) Laforet has been a beacon of cutting-edge Harajuku style for decades. It's been looking a little mainstream lately (see the Topshop on the ground floor) but you can still find plenty inside to turn your head. Look for cult favourite brands like Fur Fur and Nozomi Ishiguro (at Wall). There's also a gallery, **Laforet Museum Harajuku**, on the 6th floor that holds exhibitions with a pop culture slant.

KIDDYLAND
CHILDREN

Map p293 (キデイランド; www.kiddyland.co.jp/en/index.html; 6-1-9 Jingūmae, Shibuya-ku; ⊙10am-9pm; ℝJR Yamanote Line to Harajuku, Omote-sandō exit) This multistorey toy emporium is packed to the rafters with character goods, including nostalgia inducers like Hello Kitty and Ultraman. It's not just for kids either; you'll spot plenty of teens and even adults indulging their love of *kawaii* (cute). KiddyLand moved up the street while its building was renovated, but it should be back in this location, its original spot on Omote-sandō-dōri, by the time you read this.

MUSUBI
SPECIALITY SHOP

Map p293 (むす美; http://kyoto-musubi.com, in Japanese; 2-31-8 Jingūmae, Shibuya-ku; ⊙11am-7pm Thu-Tue; ℝJR Yamanote Line to Harajuku, Takeshita exit) Before shopping bags, Japanese carried their *bentō* (boxed lunch) and packages in elegant wrapping cloths called *furoshiki*. This shop sells the cloths and gives lessons in how to use them (email info@kyoto-musubi.com for information about lessons).

UT STORE HARAJUKU
CLOTHING

Map p293 (ユーティーストア原宿; http://store.uniqlo.com/jp/store/feature/ut/top; 6-10-8 Jingūmae, Shibuya-ku; ⊙11am-9pm; ℝJR Yamanote Line to Harajuku, Omote-sandō exit) This spin-off of Uniqlo (p76) may be a triumph of marketing over substance, but the design is fun just the same. Scrolling red LEDs signs announce the specials both outside and in; T-shirts with catchy designs are sold in clear canisters.

ASSISTON
SOUVENIRS

Map p293 (アシストオン; www.assiston.co.jp; 6-9-13 Jingūmae, Shibuya-ku; ℝJR Yamanote Line to Harajuku, Omote-sandō exit) If you're hunting for made-in-Japan souvenirs that won't just look pretty sitting on the shelf, this is your shop. AssistOn carries quirky and fun lifestyle gadgets, many of which have earned the Good Design Award, Japan's top honours for design.

BEAMS
FASHION

Map p293 (ビームス; www.beams.co.jp/en/index.html; 3-24-7 Jingūmae, Shibuya-ku; ℝJR Yamanote Line to Harajuku, Takeshita exit) Beams, a chain of trend-setting multi-brand boutiques, is a national institution. This cluster of stores is its headquarters. Check out the gallery space **Beams Cultuart** on the 3rd floor of the men's shop and **Beams T** (entrance on Harajuku-dōri). There's another Beams T outpost, Mangart Beams T, in Daikanyama.

FUJI-TORII
ANTIQUES

Map p293 (富士鳥居; www.fuji-torii.com; 6-1-10 Jingūmae, Shibuya-ku; ⊙11am-6pm Wed-Mon, closed 3rd Mon of month; ℝJR Yamanote Line to Harajuku, Omote-sandō exit) For more than half a century, this dealer has specialised in both antique and modern lacquerware, ceramics, scrolls and *ukiyo-e*. Authenticity is guaranteed and the helpful staff speak English well.

ORIENTAL BAZAAR
SOUVENIRS

Map p293 (オリエンタルバザー; www.orientalbazaar.co.jp; 5-9-13 Jingūmae, Shibuya-ku; ⊙10am-6pm Mon-Wed & Fri, to 7pm Sat & Sun; ℝJR Yamanote Line to Harajuku, Omote-sandō exit) Stocking a wide selection of souvenirs at very reasonable prices, Oriental Bazaar is an easy one-stop destination for holiday keepsakes or gifts. Items to be found here include fans, pottery, *yukata* (light summer kimono) and, uh, T-shirts, some made in Japan, but others not (read the labels). The branch at Narita Airport opens at 8am for last-chance purchases.

CONDOMANIA
SPECIALITY SHOP

Map p293 (コンドマニア; 6-30-1 Jingūmae, Shibuya-ku; ⊙10.30am-10.30pm Mon-Thu, 10am-11pm Fri-Sun; ⊠JR Yamanote Line to Harajuku, Omote-sandō exit) This irreverent outpost may be Tokyo's cheekiest rendezvous point. Popular items include *omamori* (traditional good-luck charms) with condoms tucked inside.

🅰 Aoyama

Aoyama draws high-end shoppers and this is where the big names in Japanese fashion design have their flagship boutiques. The neighbourhood is also known for interior-design shops.

PASS THE BATON
VINTAGE

Map p293 (パスザバトン; www.pass-the-baton. com, in Japanese; 4-12-10 Jingūmae, Shibuya-ku; ⊙11am-9pm Mon-Sat, to 8pm Sun; ⊠Ginza Line to Omote-sandō, exit A3) This clever concept store bills itself as a 'curated' consignment shop. From personal castaways to dead stock from long defunct retailers, everything here comes tagged with a profile of its previous owner. It's in the basement of the Omotesandō Hills West Wing, but you'll need to enter from a separate street entrance on Omote-sandō.

ISSEY MIYAKE
FASHION

Map p293 (イッセイミヤケ; www.isseymiyake. com; 3-18-11 Minami-Aoyama, Minato-ku; ⊠Ginza Line to Omote-sandō, exit A4) Japan's most famous fashion designer displays his virtuosity not by engineering the latest it-bag, but by developing innovative new techniques that allow him to realise his conceptual, and ultimately wearable, designs. Check out the A-POC garments – each made from a single piece of fabric – and his signature Pleats Please collection.

COMME DES GARÇONS
FASHION

Map p293 (コム・デ・ギャルソン; www.comme -des-garcons.com; 5-2-1 Minami-Aoyama, Minato-ku; ⊠Ginza Line to Omote-sandō, exit A5) Designer Kawakubo Rei threw a wrench in the fashion machine in the early '80s with her dark, austere designs. That her work doesn't appear as shocking today as it once did speaks volumes for her far-reaching success. This eccentric, vaguely disorienting architectural creation is her brand's flagship store.

YOHJI YAMAMOTO
FASHION

Map p293 (ヨウジヤマモト; www.yohjiyamamoto. co.jp; 5-3-6 Minami-Aoyama, Minato-ku; ⊠Ginza Line to Omote-sandō, exit A5) Yamamoto Yohji was right next to Kawakubo Rei in the '80s putting Tokyo on the world fashion map. His designs are still bold and often romantic; his flagship store is stark and industrial.

SPIRAL MARKET
GIFTS

Map p293 (スパイラル・マーケット; 5-6-23 Minami-Aoyama, Minato-ku; ⊠Ginza Line to Omote-sandō, exit B1) On the second floor of the Spiral Building (see p119), this shop carries covetable, modern Japanese homewares,

---

SHOPPING FOR KIMONO

Gorgeous as they are, new kimono are prohibitively expensive – a full set can easily cost a million yen. Used kimono, on the other hand, can be found for as little as ¥3000, though one in good shape will cost more like ¥10,000. Another affordable option is the *yukata* (light cotton kimono). During summer you can pick up a new one at most department stores and even Uniqlo for as little as ¥10,000.

Note that ready-made kimono and *yukata* are generally one-size-fits-all. They're also tricky to put on by yourself; **Hakubi Gakuen** (www.hakubi.net/en), a school with branches all over Tokyo, offers lessons in English on how to wear kimono.

For vintage kimono, here are few places to start:

Gallery Kawano (ギャラリー川野; Map p293; 4-4-9 Jingūmae, Shibuya-ku; ⊙11am-6pm; ⊠Ginza Line to Omote-sandō, exit A2) Has a good selection of secondhand kimono in decent shape; the staff will help you try one on and pick out a matching obi (sash).

Chicago Thrift Store (シカゴ; Map p293; 6-31-21 Jingūmae, Shibuya-ku; ⊠JR Yamanote Line to Harajuku, Omote-sandō exit) Has several racks of cheap used kimono and *yukata* of varying quality; you're on your own in the dressing room here.

Flea markets (蚤の市; see p51) Usually have a handful of vintage kimono vendors.

plus artsy jewellery and stationery goods. Don't miss **Spiral Records** in the back corner, which carries quirky and experimental music, some of which is produced by the shop's in-house label.

RIN
SOUVENIRS

Map p293 (リン; 3-6-26 Kita-Aoyama; Ⓡ Ginza Line to Omote-sandō, exit B2) Rin sells high-quality ceramics, accessories and beauty products all made in different regions of Japan. There are some beautiful things here and some, like the smaller cups and dishes, are not prohibitively expensive.

BAPE EXCLUSIVE
FASHION

Map p293 (ベイプ・エクスクルーシブ; www. bape.com; 5-5-8 Minami-Aoyama, Minato-ku; Ⓡ Ginza Line to Omote-sandō, exit A4) Streetwear label A Bathing Ape (called 'Bape' for short) doesn't have the cachet that it once did. Still, the brand's collaboration with design unit Wonderwall produced some of the city's more outrageous interiors. This is one of them; come see what all the fuss was about.

SPORTS & ACTIVITIES

Jingū Gaien (www.meijijingugaien.jp/english), literally the 'outer garden' of the shrine, is now a sprawling sports and recreation complex. In addition to the facilities described, there's a batting cage, cycling course, driving range, playground and culture centre.

JINGŪ BASEBALL STADIUM
BASEBALL

Map p293 (神宮球場; Jingū Kyūjō; ☎3404-8999; www.jingu-stadium.com; 3-1 Kasumigaoka, Shinjuku-ku; tickets adult/child from ¥1500/500; Ⓡ Ginza Line to Gaienmae, north exit) Home to the Yakult Swallows, Tokyo's number two team, Jingū Baseball Stadium was originally built in 1926. You can buy tickets from the booth in front of the stadium; same-day outfield tickets (¥1500) are available at the booth by gate 17. Night games start at 6pm; Saturdays and Sunday games start at 2pm or 3pm.

MEIJI-JINGŪ GAIEN ICE SKATING RINK
SKATING

off Map p293 (明治神宮アイススケート場; 11-1 Kasumigaoka, Shinjuku-ku; adult/child ¥1300/900; ⏰ noon-6pm Mon-Fri, 10am-6pm Sat & Sun; Ⓡ Toei Ōedo Line to Kokuritsu-Kyōgijō, exit A2) This indoor NHL-sized rink is open year-round. You can chose between figure skates and hockey skates (sizes run to 31cm; rentals cost ¥500). Discounts on admission are offered after 3pm (adult/child ¥1000/700).

TOKYO METROPOLITAN GYMNASIUM INDOOR POOL
SWIMMING

off Map p293 (東京体育館; ☎5474-2114; 1-17-1 Sendagaya, Shibuya-ku; admission up to 2½hr adult/child ¥600/260; ⏰9am-11pm Mon-Fri, to 10pm Sat, to 9pm Sun & holidays; Ⓡ JR Sōbu Line to Sendagaya) If all that movement on land has made you crave a few laps, head here. There's a 250m pool and a 50m one, plus a weight room. Walk straight from the station and you'll reach the gymnasium in a few minutes; it closes irregularly so call ahead before heading there.

NATIONAL STADIUM
SOCCER

Map p293 (国立競技場; Kokuritsu Kyōgijō; ☎3403-1151; 10-2 Kasumigaoka-machi, Shinjuku-ku; admission from ¥2000; Ⓡ Ōedo Line to Kokuritsu Kyōgijō, exit A2) Completed in 1958 and used as one of the primary venues for the 1964 Olympics, National Stadium now hosts the annual Toyota Cup (November or December) and other international soccer events.

Shinjuku & West Tokyo

SHINJUKU | WEST TOKYO

Neighbourhood Top Five

1 Exploring the crackling neon canyons of **East Shinjuku** (p129). From the narrow lanes of seedy Kabukichō to the main boulevards, the light show here and the sheer volume of dining, drinking and entertainment options is something to behold.

2 Looking out over the city from the observatory atop the **Tokyo Metropolitan Government Offices** (p129).

3 Laying on the lawn at **Shinjuku Gyoen** (p130) and gazing up at the skyscrapers.

4 Immersing yourself in the imagination of animator Hayao Miyazaki at the **Ghibli Museum** (p130) in Mitaka.

5 Getting cosy in the bars of **Golden Gai** (p129), Shinjuku's literary and artistic hangout.

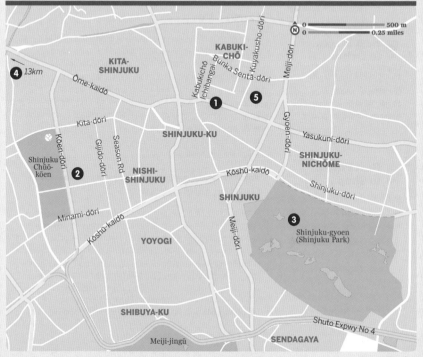

For more detail of this area, see Map p294 ➡

Lonely Planet's Top Tip

Shinjuku is nothing if not intimidating. Should you want to grab a quick bite to eat – without having to brave the crowded streets – head to one of the food courts on the top floors of the shopping centres inside Shinjuku Station, such as Lumine or Mylord. Both have over a dozen reasonably priced options with plastic food models out front. Takashimaya Times Sq has good restaurants too, though they can be rather pricey.

Best Places to Eat

→ Nakajima (p134)
→ Nagi (p134)
→ Tsunahachi (p135)
→ Dachibin (p135)

For reviews, see p134

Best Places to Drink

→ La Jetée (p136)
→ Zoetrope (p136)
→ Advocates Café (p136)
→ New York Bar (p137)

For reviews, see p136 →

Best Places to Shop

→ Disk Union (p138)
→ Bingoya (p138)
→ Nakano Broadway (p130)

For reviews, see p138 →

Explore Shinjuku & West Tokyo

Shinjuku is a whole city within the city. Its breadth and scale are simply awesome – over three million people a day pass through the station alone. It's a good idea to pay attention to the signs in the station to orient yourself.

To the west of the station are the skyscrapers that make up the prefectural government and the largest business district on the west side of Tokyo. Some of the buildings themselves are impressive. The unusual, elliptical Mode Gakuen Cocoon Tower can also be handy for navigating. There are some good museums on this side, too.

To the east is the lively entertainment district, where many will stop off for something to eat and drink on their way home. Tipplers are spoiled for choice here: you could hang out on a different block each night of the week and have a completely different experience. Shinjuku is that rare Tokyo neighbourhood that truly has something for everyone: young or old, rich or poor. It's also home to the nation's largest gay district, Shinjuku-nichōme.

The JR Chūō Line heads west of Shinjuku, where the neighbourhoods become gradually more suburban. None of these are major sightseeing destinations, yet they are dear to the Tokyoites who live and hang out there, and each has its own personality. You could spend a leisurely day working your way stop by stop from Mitaka to Kōenji.

Local Life

→ **Parks** Shinjuku-gyoen (p130) is a popular picnic spot; Inokashira-kōen (p130) has a lively weekend scene. Both are excellent for *hanami* (blossom viewing).

→ **Nightlife** Golden Gai (p136) draws late-night drinkers from the arts, media and entertainment industries.

→ **Romance** The sky-high New York Grill (p135) is famous as a date spot, and also for marriage proposals.

→ **Shopping** Kōenji (p130) is known for its high concentration of thrift stores; Nakano Broadway (p130) is a collector's paradise.

Getting There & Away

→ **Train** The JR Yamanote and Chūō-Sōbu Lines stop at Shinjuku Station; Chūō-Sōbu continues west, stopping at Nakano, Kōenji, Kichijōji and Mitaka. The private Keio New Line stops at Hatsudai, west of Shinjuku.

→ **Subway** The Marunouchi, Shinjuku and Ōedo Lines run through Shinjuku. The Marunouchi, Fukutoshin and Shinjuku Lines stop at Shinjuku-sanchōme, convenient for east Shinjuku. For west Shinjuku, Tochōmae Station on the Ōedo Line is more convenient.

◉ SIGHTS

◉ West of Shinjuku Station (Nishi-Shinjuku)

FREE **TOKYO METROPOLITAN GOVERNMENT OFFICES**　BUILDING

Map p294 (東京都庁; www.metro.tokyo.jp; 2-8-1 Nishi-Shinjuku, Shinjuku-ku; ◉Ōedo Line to Tochōmae, exit A4) Known as Tokyo Tochō, this grey granite complex designed by Tange Kenzō has stunning, distinctive architecture and great views from the 202m-high **observatories** (◉9.30am-11pm) on the 45th floors of the twin towers of Building 1 (the views are virtually the same from either tower). On a clear day, look west for a glimpse of Mt Fuji.

Back on the ground, look up at Building 1 and see if it doesn't look like a cathedral fashioned out of computer chips. There's even a 'rose window', only this being Tokyo the rose is replaced by a gingko leaf, the city's official tree.

While you're here, it's worth heading over to nearby **Shinjuku I-Land** (Map p294; 新宿アイランド; 6-5 Nishi-Shinjuku, Shinjuku-ku) to see Robert Indiana's *Love* sculpture and two *Tokyo Brushstroke* sculptures by Roy Liechtenstein.

TOKYO OPERA CITY　ARTS CENTRE

off map p294 (東京オペラシティ; www.operacity.jp; 3-20-2 Nishi-Shinjuku, Shinjuku-ku; ◉Keio New Line to Hatsudai, north exit) In addition to housing one of the world's most acoustically perfect concert halls, this complex also has two of Tokyo's more consistently interesting art spaces. **Tokyo Opera City Art Gallery** (www.operacity.jp/ag; 3rd fl; admission varies; ◉11am-7pm Tue-Thu & Sun, to 8pm Fri & Sat) features changing exhibits from contemporary Japanese artists and designers, plus the occasional international show.

The **NTT Intercommunication Centre** (ICC; www.ntticc.or.jp; 4th fl; admission varies; ◉11am-6pm Tue-Sun) focuses on cutting-edge works and installations that examine the intersection of art and technology. The centre's 'open space' exhibition hall is free to enter; its superlative video library includes important works by artists such as Idemitsu Mako, Bill Viola and Nam June Paik. The 'project space' features conceptual, interactive works by artists like Mikami Seiko. If you've already visited the art gallery, show your ticket here for a discount on admission.

JAPANESE SWORD MUSEUM　MUSEUM

(刀剣博物館; www.touken.or.jp; 4-25-10 Yoyogi, Shibuya-ku; adult/student ¥600/300; ◉9am-4.30pm Tue-Sun; ◉Keio New Line to Hatsudai, east exit) In 1948, after American forces returned the *katana* (Japanese swords) they'd confiscated during the post-war occupation, the national Ministry of Education established a society to preserve the feudal art of Japanese sword-making. There are about 120 swords with their fittings in the collection, of which about one-third are on exhibition at any one time. The museum's location, in a residential neighbourhood, is not obvious. Head down Kōshū-kaidō to the Park Hyatt and make a left, then the second right under the highway, followed by another quick right and left in succession. There's also a map on the website.

◉ East Shinjuku

KABUKICHŌ　NEIGHBOURHOOD

Map p294 (歌舞伎町; ◉JR Yamanote Line to Shinjuku, east exit) Tokyo's most notorious red-light district was famously named for a kabuki theatre that was never built; instead you'll find an urban theatre of a different sort playing out in the neighbourhood's soaplands (bathhouses just shy of anti-prostitution laws), peep shows, cabarets, love hotels and fetish bars.

The neighbourhood covers an area of several blocks north of Yasukuni-dōri. Remarkably, the area is generally safe (and much more interesting) to walk through at night (see East Shinjuku walking tour p131), though it's wise to go with a friend or two or you may find yourself the object of unwanted, and irritating, attention (both for males and females). Most establishments don't welcome tourists, as their pricing schemes are complicated (and often extortionist).

GOLDEN GAI　NEIGHBOURHOOD

Map p294 (ゴールデン街; ◉JR Yamanote Line to Shinjuku, east exit) This warren of tiny alleys was first a post-WWII black market, then a licensed quarter until prostitution was outlawed in 1958. The narrow two-storey wooden buildings remain the same, though they're now filled with over a hundred closet-sized bars that seat no more than a dozen. Each is as unique and eccentric as the 'master' or 'mama' who runs it. That

Golden Gai – prime real estate – has so far resisted the kind of development seen elsewhere in Shinjuku is a credit to these stubbornly bohemian characters. For recommendations on where to eat and drink, see p134 and p136.

SHINJUKU-GYOEN
PARK

Map p294 (新宿御苑; www.env.go.jp/garden/shinjukugyoen; 11 Naito-chō, Shinjuku-ku; adult/6-15yr/under 6yr ¥200/50/free; ⊙9am-4.30pm Tue-Sun; ⊠Marunouchi Line to Shinjuku-gyoen-mae, exit 1) Though Shinjuku-gyoen was designed as an imperial retreat (completed 1906), it's now definitively a park for everyone. The wide lawns make it a favourite for urbanites in need of a quick escape from the hurly-burly of city life. It's perfect for picnics: pick up a *bentō* (boxed lunch) from a *depachika* (department store food floor) or convenience store on the way. There's also a **greenhouse** (set to reopen after renovation in autumn 2012) and a **traditional teahouse**.

HANAZONO-JINJA
SHRINE

Map p294 (花園神社; 5-17 Shinjuku, Shinjuku-ku; ⊙24hr; ⊠Marunouchi Line to Shinjuku-sanchōme, exits B10 & E2) During the day merchants from nearby Kabukichō come to this Shintō shrine to pray for the solvency of their business ventures. At night, despite signs asking revellers to refrain, drinking and merrymaking carries over from the nearby bars onto the stairs here. On Sunday the grounds become a **flea market** (⊙8am-4pm), where you'll find knick-knacks and, possibly, some antiques.

◉ West Tokyo

NAKANO
NEIGHBOURHOOD

(中野; ⊠JR Chūō Line to Nakano) If Shinjuku is ever looking to the future, Nakano is a shrine to the recent past. Step out of the station's north exit and you'll see the **Nakano Sun Mall** (中野サンモール), a classic 1960s covered shopping arcade. It leads to **Nakano Broadway** (中野ブロードウェイ), another retro shopping complex. This one's filled with small shops aimed at collectors of all sorts; many sell manga (Japanese comics) and vintage toys, but there are also those specialising in antique watches and darts. The original Mandarake (see p154) is here, too.

KŌENJI
NEIGHBOURHOOD

(高円寺; ⊠JR Chūō Line to Kōenji) For decades Kōenji has been the haunt of counterculture types. Wander the neighbourhood's narrow roads and you'll find scores of small bars, live-music venues and secondhand stores. Don't miss the **Kita-Kore Building** (キタコレビル; 3-4-11 Kōenji-kita, Suginami-ku; ⊙varies), where some of Tokyo's most irreverent young fashion designers have set up shop. To find it, head left from the north exit of the station, following the tracks to a narrow shopping street; walk straight past the 7-Eleven and you'll soon see a building on the left that looks like an abandoned funhouse. Restaurant Dachibin (p135) and Cocktail Shobō (p137) are on the same street.

KICHIJŌJI
NEIGHBOURHOOD

(吉祥寺; ⊠JR Chūō Line to Kichijōji) The area around the station here is full of cafes and shops and Kichijōji's small scale makes it an appealing alternative to Shinjuku or Shibuya.

The neighbourhood's primary attraction, however, is its large, leafy park, **Inokashira-kōen** (井の頭公園; 1-18-31 Gotenyama, Musashino-shi). At the centre is a pond with rowboats and swan-shaped pedal boats. There's also an ancient shrine to the sea goddess Benzaiten. Be warned though: Benzaiten is known to be a jealous goddess and urban legend has it that couples who flaunt their romance and row across the water break up soon afterwards.

On weekends, craft vendors and performance artists set up on the eastern end. To get to the park from Kichijōji Station, take the Kōen exit and walk straight, crossing at the light and veering to the right of the Marui ('0101') department store; you're on the right path if you see food trucks on your left.

GHIBLI MUSEUM
MUSEUM

(ジブリ美術館; www.ghibli-museum.jp; 1-1-83 Shimo-renjaku; adult ¥1000, child ¥400-700; ⊙10am-6pm Wed-Mon; ⊠JR Chūō Line to Mitaka, south exit) Master animator Hayao Miyazaki, whose Studio Ghibli produced *Princess Mononoke* and *Spirited Away*, designed this museum himself. Fans will enjoy the original sketches; kids, even if they're not familiar with the movies, will fall in love with the fairy-tale atmosphere. Don't miss the original 20-minute animated short playing on the 1st floor; it changes regularly to keep fans coming back.

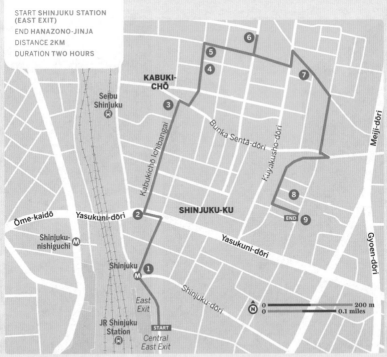

START **SHINJUKU STATION (EAST EXIT)**
END **HANAZONO-JINJA**
DISTANCE **2KM**
DURATION **TWO HOURS**

Neighbourhood Walk
East Shinjuku

It's best to start at dusk, when you'll observe the perceptible change of east Shinjuku's day life turn over to nightlife. From the station, head towards the big screen of **1** **Studio Alta** (スタジオアルタ), a popular Shinjuku meeting spot.

Then take the pedestrian street to Yasukuni-dōri, where the neon onslaught of Shinjuku begins. Cross the street and pass through the flashing red **2** **torii** (鳥居; gate) that marks the entrance to Kabukichō, Tokyo's biggest red light district (see p129). A few blocks ahead is a ghostly plaza surrounded by entertainment complexes; if you haven't yet primped for *purikura* (print club photos), pop into the arcade **3** **Humax** (ヒューマックス).

As you head deeper into Kabukichō, you'll see the backlit signs that advertise the neighbourhood's **4** **host bars**, where bleach-blond pretty boys wait to do for the gals what the hostess bars do for the guys.

There is more than one way to blow off steam in Kabukichō. On your right look for **5** **Oslo Batting Centre** (オスローバッティングセンター); it's ¥300 for 20 pitches if you feel like taking a swing. Take a slight detour up to **6** **Niban-kan** (二番館; 1970), postmodern architect Minoru Takeyama's stripy, multifaceted building.

From here, continue east past architecture of a different sort: **7** **love hotels** with fabulous kitschy facades suggesting European castles and tropical getaways. Then look for the stone-paved, tree-lined path that leads to **8** **Golden Gai** (ゴールデン街) and get yourself a drink (see p136). Before calling it a night, pay your respects at **9** **Hanazono-jinja** (花園神社).

CHRISTOPHER GROENHOUT / LONELY PLANET IMAGES ©

WILL ROBB / LONELY PLANET IMAGES ©

MICHAEL COYNE / LONELY PLANET IMAGES ©

1. Shinjuku skyscrapers (p128)
High-rise buildings reach for the sky in the Shinjuku business district.

2. Shinjuku-gyoen (p130)
Autumn foliage lights up this former imperial park.

3. Pinball wizards
Passing the time at a pinball parlour in Shinjuku.

4. Shinjuku Station (p129)
Commuters stream out of the southern exit of the station.

> ### WORTH A DETOUR
>
> #### HIKING TAKAO-SAN & OKUTAMA
>
> Less than an hour by train from Shinjuku, **Takao-san** (高尾山; 599m) is the mountain right on Tokyo's doorstep. The most popular trail (No 1) takes about 3¼ hours round-trip and passes a temple, **Yaku-ō-in** (薬王院). Alternatively, a cable car and a chairlift (adult/child one way ¥470/230, return ¥900/450) can take you part of the way up the mountain. It's a family-friendly hike, though it does get crowded on weekends.
>
> From Shinjuku Station, take the Keio Line to Takaosanguchi (*tokkyū*; ¥370, 47 minutes). The tourist village (with snack and souvenir shops), trail entrances, cable car and chairlift are a few minutes' walk away to the right.
>
> You can continue for another hour to **Okutama**. Here you'll find lofty cedars and more trail options. The **tourist information centre** (奥多摩観光案内所; ☎0428-83-2152; 210 Hikawa, Okutama-machi; ◎8.30am-5pm) near Okutama Station has English maps as well as information on trail conditions (note that many can get dangerously icy during the winter months). One moderate five-hour climb follows the Nokogiri Ridge to **Nokogiri-yama** (鋸山; 1109m) and continues to **Ōdake-san** (大岳山; 1267m), which has superb vistas, and **Mitake-san** (御岳山; 929m), a charming old-world hamlet with an ancient shrine. This is one trail that will get icy during winter.
>
> A funicular (¥570, five minutes) leads down from Mitake-san to Takimoto, where buses run to Mitake Station on the Ōme Line; otherwise it's a 30-minute walk. JR Ōme Line trains run from Shinjuku to Okutama (¥1050, 110 minutes); you may need to transfer at both Tachikawa and Ōme stations.
>
> For more information on area hikes, pick up a copy of Lonely Planet's *Hiking in Japan*. Tokyo's foreigner-friendly **International Adventure Club** (www.iac-tokyo.org) organises regular excursions for hikers of all abilities.

Getting to Ghibli (which is pronounced '*jiburi*') is all part of the adventure. Entry tickets must be purchased in advance, and you must also choose the exact time and date you plan to visit. You can do this online through a travel agent before you arrive in Japan (which is the easy option) or from a kiosk at any Lawson convenience store in Tokyo (which is the difficult option, as it will require some Japanese-language ability to navigate the ticket machine). Both options are explained in detail on the website, where you will also find a useful map.

A useful minibus (round trip/one way ¥300/200) leaves for the museum approximately every 20 minutes from Mitaka Station (bus stop no 9). Alternatively, you can walk there by following the canal and turning right when you reach Inokashira-kōen (which will take about 15 minutes). The museum is actually on the western edge of Inokashira-kōen and you can walk there through the park from Kichijōji Station. This option will take you about 30 minutes.

 EATING

✗ Shinjuku

TOP CHOICE **NAKAJIMA**   KAISEKI ¥

Map p294 (中嶋; ☎3356-7962; www.shinjyuku-nakajima.com; Basement fl, 3-32-5 Shinjuku, Shinjuku-ku; lunch/dinner from ¥800/8400; ◎lunch & dinner Mon-Sat; ◉; ◎Marunouchi Line to Shinjuku-sanchōme, exit A1) In the evening, this Michelin-starred restaurant serves exquisite *kaiseki* dinners. During the week it also serves a set lunch of humble *iwashi* (sardines) for one-tenth the price. In the hands of Nakajima's chefs they're divine; get yours sashimi or *yanagawa nabe* (stewed with egg). The line for lunch starts to form shortly before the restaurant opens at 11.30am; there is no cheap lunch special on Saturdays or national holidays. Reservations are necessary for dinner.

NAGI   RĀMEN ¥

Map p294 (凪; www.n-nagi.com; 1-1-10 Kabukichō, Shinjuku-ku (Golden Gai G2); mains from ¥750;

lunch & dinner, until 5am Mon-Sat; JR Yamanote Line to Shinjuku, east exit) Nagi has a handful of highly-rated shops around town, each dedicated to making a different style of noodles and broth. At this outpost in Golden Gai, up a treacherous flight of stairs and almost always with a wait, the speciality is thin flat noodles in a dark broth deeply flavoured with *niboshi* (dried sardines). There's another branch in **Nishi-Shinjuku** (1st & 2nd fl, 7-13-7 Nishi-Shinjuku, Shinjuku-ku; lunch & dinner; JR Yamanote Line to Shinjuku, west exit).

TSUNAHACHI TEMPURA ¥¥

Map p294 (つな八; www.tunahachi.co.jp; 3-21-8 Shinjuku, Shinjuku-ku; sets ¥1995-3990; 11am-10pm; JR Yamanote Line to Shinjuku, east exit) Tsunahachi has been expertly frying prawns and seasonal vegetables for nearly 90 years. The sets are served in courses so each dish comes piping hot. Sit at the counter for the added pleasure of watching the chefs at work. Indigo *noren* (curtains) mark the entrance.

NEW YORK GRILL STEAK HOUSE ¥¥¥

Map p294 (ニューヨークグリル; 5322-1234; http://tokyo.park.hyatt.com; 52nd fl, 3-7-1-2 Nishi-Shinjuku, Shinjuku-ku; dinner course from ¥11,000, mains from ¥4800; lunch & dinner; Ōedo Line to Tochōmae, exit A4) Perched on the 52nd floor of the Park Hyatt, this a date spot of the highest order. The food is perfectly executed and the views are divine, but the prices are commensurately steep. Lunch is more reasonably priced: the set course includes a gorgeous all-you-can-eat spread of entrees and desserts, plus a main dish. On weekends, a glass of sparkling wine is included (bringing the bill to ¥6600); book ahead.

OMOIDE-YOKOCHŌ YAKITORI ¥

Map p294 (思い出横丁; Nishi-Shinjuku 1-chōme, Shinjuku-ku; skewers from ¥100; dinner; JR Yamanote Line to Shinjuku, west exit) Since the postwar days, smoke has been billowing nightly from the *yakitori* stalls that line this alley by the train tracks. Literally translated as 'Memory Lane' (and less politely known as Shoben-yokochō, or 'Piss Alley'), Omoide-yokochō may actually be just a memory someday; there's been on-again, off-again talk of razing it to make way for new development. Be sure to stop by to indulge in a few skewers and some pre-emptive nostalgia.

NUMAZUKŌ SUSHI ¥

Map p294 (沼津港; Basement fl, My Bldg, 1-10-1 Nishi-Shinjuku, Shinjuku-ku; plates ¥180-550; 11am-10:30pm; JR Yamanote Line to Shinjuku, west exit) This is one of Tokyo's better *kaiten-sushi* (conveyor-belt sushi restaurant). The long, snaking counter is usually packed at meal times, meaning nothing makes it around the loop too many times without being scooped up. It's in an underground passage inside Shinjuku Station; follow signs to the highway bus stop and you should see the entrance to the My Building and the restaurant on your right.

✖ West Tokyo

DACHIBIN OKINAWAN ¥

(抱瓶; www.dachibin.com/dachibin.html, in Japanese; 3-2-13 Kōenji-kita, Suginami-ku; dishes ¥400-1000; 5pm-5am; JR Chūō Line to Kōenji, north exit) One of Tokyo's most popular destinations for Okinawan food, Dachibin is a raucous *izakaya* (Japanese version of a pub/eatery) where island folk songs play and strong *awamori* (local alcohol of

---

LOCAL KNOWLEDGE

THE WAY OF RĀMEN

Chef Ivan Orkin, owner of **Ivan's Ramen** (www.ivanramen.com; 3-24-7, Minami-karasuyama, Setagaya-ku; lunch & dinner Thu-Tue; Keio Line to Rokakōen), filled us in on the art of noodle slurping and some of his favourite ramen shops.

How to Eat It

Rāmen is like a brick-oven pizza – if you let it sit for a few minutes it becomes something different. So you need to start slurping right away, even if it burns a little. Keep slurping, make noise and don't chew.

Where to Eat It

Nagi is one of my favourites. The one in Golden Gai is a great place to go after drinking. I also like **Kikambo** (鬼金棒; 2-10-10 Kaji-chō, Chiyoda-ku; lunch & dinner Mon-Fri, lunch Sat; JR Yamanote Line to Kanda, north exit) in Kanda. It's sort of new wave. It serves very serious, delicious spicy miso *rāmen*.

Okinawa) is poured with a liberal hand. While there's no English menu, you can get a good sampling of the southern island cuisine by choosing the items marked 'おすすめ' (*osusume*; recommended). It's one block before the Kita-Kore Building (p130).

SHIMONYA
YAKITORI ¥

(四文屋; 3-69 Kōenji-minami, Suginami-ku; small plates from ¥200; ☺dinner; ⓇJR Chūō Line to Kōenji, south exit) Head right from the train station, duck back under the tracks and you'll find dozens of tiny *izakaya* and *yakitori* (chicken, meat or vegetable skewers) shops. Shimonya is famous for its low prices and 'waste not, want not' approach: the menu includes organ meats of the kind that don't always make it to the table. Safe bets include the *gyu suteki* (beef steak) and *gyu nikomi* (stewed cow guts); adventurous eaters can just close their eyes and point.

PEPA CAFE FOREST
THAI ¥

(ペパカフェフォレスト; www.peppermintcafe.com/forest/index.html; 4-1-5 Inokashira, Mitaka-shi; mains from ¥1000; ☺noon-10pm; ⊘⊝; ⓇJR Chūō Line to Kichijōji, Kōen exit) This funky terrace cafe sits inside Inokashira-kōen and serves authentic Thai food, plus coffee and sweets. It's across the pond, if you're coming through the park from Kichijōji Station.

DRINKING & NIGHTLIFE

TOP CHOICE GOLDEN GAI
BAR

Map p294 (ゴールデン街; ⓇJR Yamanote Line to Shinjuku, east exit) Bars here usually have a theme – from punk rock to photography – to draw customers with matching expertise and obsessions. Since regular customers are their bread and butter, most establishments are likely to give tourists a cool reception. Don't take it personally; Japanese visitors unaccompanied by a regular get the same treatment – this is Golden Gai's peculiar, invisible velvet rope.

Still, there are a handful of places where you can get your foot in the door. **La Jetée** (ラジェッティ; Akarui Hanazono 3-ban-gai; ☺Mon-Sat; ⊝) has been a hangout for filmmakers for decades, but won't turn away tourists if there are seats available.

Araku (亜楽; 2nd fl, G2-dōri) is also a welcoming place; managed by an Australian, it is part of the newer wave of bars with a more democratic door policy. Note that cover charges (varying from ¥300 to ¥2500) are standard in Golden Gai and many bars won't open until after 9pm.

One place with no hidden charges is **Champion** (チャンピオン; G2-dōri), at the entrance to the neighbourhood. Here drinks are just ¥500 and the karaoke is loud; it's not exactly representative of Golden Gai, but it's fun just the same.

TOP CHOICE ZOETROPE
BAR

Map p294 (ゾートロープ; http://homepage2. nifty.com/zoetrope; 3rd fl, Gaia Bldg, 7-10-14 Nishi-Shinjuku, Shinjuku-ku; ☺Mon-Sat; ⓇJR Yamanote Line to Shinjuku, west exit) Behind the small counter here are 300 varieties of Japanese whiskey – more than you'll find anywhere else. As if that weren't enough to set this place apart, silent movies are screened on the wall. The owner is happy to chat whiskey (or films) and if you tell him what you like, he'll help you narrow down some choices from the daunting menu. It's also a good idea to tell him your price range (some whiskies are pretty expensive).

SHINJUKU-NICHŌME
GAY, LESBIAN

Map p294 (新宿二丁目; ⓇMarunouchi Line to Shinjuku-sanchōme, exit C8) 'Nichōme,' named for a block in Shinjuku, has literally hundreds of small gay and lesbian bars; some are welcoming, others are cliquey. All the bars described here draw a good mix of Japanese and foreigners; none have cover charges except in the case of special events. You'll probably see many of the same faces all night, as the crowd hops from bar to bar.

Advocates Café (アドボケイツカフェ; http://advocates-cafe.com; 2-18-1 Shinjuku, Shinjuku-ku), a tiny corner bar, is a good place to start the evening, especially during the warmer months when the crowd spills out onto the street in block party style. There's also **Dragon Men** (ドラゴン; 2-11-4 Shinjuku, Shinjuku-ku), one of the largest gay bars in the neighbourhood and much-loved for its hot, underwear-clad waiters. Both Advocates and Dragon have popular happy hour specials.

Arty Farty (アーティファーティ; www.arty-farty.net; 2nd fl, 2-11-7 Shinjuku, Shinjuku-ku), open to men and women, has been a gateway to the community for many a moon.

LOCAL KNOWLEDGE

PARTIES

Goldfinger (www.goldfingerparty.com) is Tokyo's sexiest women-only party. **Fancy Him** (www.fancyhim.com) is the city's most fashion-forward; the mixed straight and gay crowd are known to arrive in stunning, handmade costumes. Both parties usually take place in Nichōme (check the websites for upcoming events and details). But for something totally 'only in Tokyo,' you'll need to head up the Yamanote Line to **Kinema Club** (キネマ倶楽部; www. kinema.jp; 6th fl, 1-1-14 Negishi, Taito-ku; ®JR Yamanote Line to Uguisudani, south exit) for monthly event **Dept H** (http:// ameblo.jp/department-h, in Japanese). Here, in an old prewar opera house, you'll find drag queens rubbing shoulders with *cos-players* (costume players) watching *shibari* (Japanese-style bondage) shows – it's Tokyo at its most out-there and open-minded.

This is the neighbourhood's most welcoming spot; there's a small dance floor here that gets packed on weekends.

GB (2-12-13 Shinjuku, Shinjuku-ku) favours a gay crowd who prefer chatting to dancing; the dimly lit counter bar has a friendly, if not somewhat cruisy, vibe. Ladies should head to **Kinswomyn** (キンズウィミン; 3rd fl, Dai-ichi Tenka Bldg, 2-15-10 Shinjuku, Shinjuku-ku; ⊙8pm-4am Wed-Mon), one of the few women-only bars in the neighbourhood. Both GB and Kinswomyn are places where solo, first-time visitors will be made to feel welcome.

Neighbourhood hub **Cocolo Cafe** (ココ ロカフェ; 2-14-6 Shinjuku, Shinjuku-ku; ⊙lunch-late; 📶) is a good place to take a break and browse flyers for parties and events.

NEW YORK BAR   BAR

Map p294 (ニューヨークバー; http://tokyo.park. hyatt.com; 52nd fl, 3-7-1-2 Nishi-Shinjuku, Shinjuku-ku; ®Ōedo Line to Tochōmae, exit A4) You may not be lodging at the Park Hyatt, but that doesn't mean you can't ascend to the 52nd floor to swoon over the sweeping nightscape. In a nod to the bar's *Lost in Translation* fame, you can sip the signature LIT cocktail or Suntory whisky. There's a cover charge of ¥2200 after 8pm (7pm Sunday) and live music nightly; cocktails start at ¥1800.

COCKTAIL SHOBŌ   BAR

(コクテイル書房; 2-24-13 Kōenji-kita, Suginami-ku; ⊙Wed-Mon; 📶; ®JR Chūō Line to Kōenji, north exit) The wooden counter here doubles as a bookshelf and the local crowd comes as much to sip cocktails (from ¥400) mixed with old-fashioned soda pop as they do to flip through the selection of used books. It's a cosy place and, like most bars in Kōenji, a labour of love. Look for the bar on the same street as the Kita-Kore Building (see p130), on the left-hand side.

ALBATROSS   BAR

Map p294 (アルバトロス; www.alba-s.com; 1-2-11 Nishi-Shinjuku, Shinjuku-ku; 📶; ®JR Yamanote Line to Shinjuku, west exit) Tucked away in aromatic Omoide-yokochō (Memory Lane), Albatross is a tiny wooden bar done up in red and gold. There's a cover charge of ¥300, but drinks are reasonable at ¥600; there's additional seating up the narrow stairs if the counter is full.

⭐ ENTERTAINMENT

SUEHIROTEI   COMEDY

Map p294 (末廣亭; http://suehirotei.com, in Japanese; 3-6-12 Shinjuku, Shinjuku-ku; adult/student ¥2800/2200; ⊙afternoon show noon-4.30pm, evening show 5-9pm; ®Marunouchi Line to Shinjuku-sanchōme, exit B2) This is one of the very few remaining *yose* (vaudeville) theatres in the city. Each show features 18 acts, of which more than half are *rakugo* (comedic monologue; see p237). You'll need pretty good Japanese to follow the shows, though there's something to be gained from just soaking up the atmosphere. You can arrive or leave mid-show, but you can't reenter.

NEW NATIONAL THEATRE   PERFORMING ARTS

off Map p294 (新国立劇場; Shin Kokuritsu Gekijō; ☎5351-3011; www.nntt.jac.go.jp/english/index. html; 1-1-1 Honmachi, Shibuya-ku; ®Keio New Line to Hatsudai, Theatre exit) Tokyo's premier public performing arts centre includes state-of-the-art venues for opera, dance and theatre. Many of the plays and dance productions are Japanese; the opera stage is usually given over to visiting international stars.

SHINJUKU PIT INN   JAZZ

Map p294 (新宿ピットイン; ☎3354-2024; www. pit-inn.com; Basement fl, 2-12-4 Shinjuku, Shinjuku-ku; ⊙daytime show from 2.30pm, evening show from 7.30pm; Marunouchi Line to Shinjuku-sanchōme, exit C5) This is not the kind of place you come to talk over the music. Aficionados have been coming here for over 40 years to listen to Japan's best jazz performers. Weekday matinees feature new artists and cost only ¥1300.

ZA KŌENJI
THEATRE

(座・高円寺; ☎3223-7300; http://za-koenji.jp; 2-1-2 Kōenji-kita, Suginami-ku; JR Chūō Line to Kōenji, north exit) This public theatre stages contemporary plays, dance (including *butō*), music and story-telling events. Since opening in 2009, Za Kōenji has emerged as one of Tokyo's best non-commercial theatre spaces. Exit the station to the right, head down the road next to the tracks and the theatre will be on the left. You can't miss it – the Itō Toyō–designed building is dark and dramatic.

LOFT
LIVE MUSIC

Map p294 (ロフト; www.loft-prj.co.jp, in Japanese; B2 fl, 1-12-9 Kabukichō, Shinjuku-ku; JR Yamanote Line to Shinjuku, east exit) The chequerboard stage here has hosted the feedback and reverb of many a Tokyo punk over the last 35 years. The music here is loud and usually good.

SHOPPING

Shinjuku is a major shopping hub. You can find branches of most major department stores and electronic stores.

DISK UNION
MUSIC

Map p294 (ディスクユニオン; 3-31-4 Shinjuku, Shinjuku-ku; 11am-9pm; JR Yamanote Line to Shinjuku, east exit) Scruffy Disk Union is known by local audiophiles as Tokyo's best used CD and vinyl store. Eight storeys carry a variety of musical styles; if you still can't find what you're looking for there are several other branches in Shinjuku that stock more obscure genres (pick up a map here).

BINGOYA
CRAFT

(備後屋; www.quasar.nu/bingoya; 10-6 Wakamatsu-chō, Shinjuku-ku; Tue-Sun, closed 3rd Sat & Sun; Toei Ōedo Line to Wakamatsu-Kawada) Here you'll find five floors of quality, unpretentious crafts sourced from all over Japan. There's a particularly good selection of folksy pottery and textiles. Since it's a little out of the way, Bingoya is better for buyers than browsers; the store can help arrange shipping overseas. It's just in front of the station; look across the main street, to the right.

ISETAN
DEPARTMENT STORE

Map p294 (伊勢丹; www.isetan.co.jp; 3-14-1 Shinjuku, Shinjuku-ku; Marunouchi Line to Shinjuku-sanchōme, exits B3, B4 & B5) Most department stores play to conservative tastes, but this one doesn't. Women should head to the Re-Style section on the 4th floor for an always changing line-up of up-and-coming Japanese designers. Men get a whole building of their own (connected by a passageway). Don't miss the basement food hall, featuring some of the country's top purveyors of sweet and savoury goodies.

KINOKUNIYA
BOOKS

Map p294 (紀伊國屋書店; www.kinokuniya. co.jp; Takashimaya Times Sq, 5-24-2 Sendagaya, Shinjuku-ku; 10am-8pm; JR Yamanote Line to Shinjuku, south exit) The 6th floor here has a broad selection of foreign language books and magazines, including English-teaching texts.

YODOBASHI CAMERA
ELECTRONICS

Map p294 (ヨドバシカメラ; 1-11-1 Nishi-Shinjuku, Shinjuku-ku; JR Yamanote Line to Shinjuku, west exit) This branch of the electronics megastore has ten floors of the latest cameras, computers and household gadgets.

SPORTS & ACTIVITIES

AIKIKAI FOUNDATION
MARTIAL ARTS

(財団法人合気会; ☎3203-9236; www.aikikai.or. jp; 17-18 Wakamatsu-chō, Shinjuku-ku; 6am-8pm Mon-Sat, 8.30am-11.30am Sun; Toei Ōedo Line to Wakamatsu-Kawada) Practising aikidō at the Aikikai Foundation requires filling out an application form and paying a registration fee in addition to a monthly course fee. Shorter-term visitors should check the website for details about training at the headquarters. The five-storey *dōjō* (training centre) is a 500m walk from the station; head left down the main road and turn right after the post office.

Iidabashi & Northwest Tokyo

IIDABASHI | IKEBUKURO | TAKADANOBABA | KAGURAZAKA | KŌRAKUEN

Neighbourhood Top Five

1 Passing under the giant *torii* (gates) at the controversial **Yasukuni-jinja** (p141) and viewing the fascinating armaments at its war museum.

2 Wandering the old-world alleys of **Kagurazaka** (p142), an old geisha quarter with enticing shops and bars.

3 Relaxing in the splendour of a classic Japanese garden at **Koishikawa Kōrakuen** (p143).

4 Cheering on the Yomiuri Giants baseball team at **Tokyo Dome** (p143).

5 Slurping some of the best miso *rāmen* in Tokyo at **Kururi** (p146).

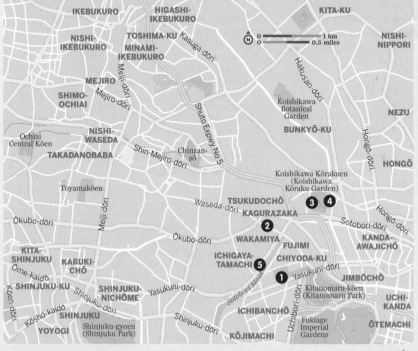

For more detail of this area, see Map p299

Lonely Planet's Top Tip

In spring, the Sotobori Moat west of Iidabashi Station and the groves in Yasukuni-jinja explode with cherry blossoms. These are prime spots for *hanami* (blossom viewing), afternoon and evening picnic parties where revellers drink until they're pinker than the petals.

 ### Best Places to Eat

➡ Kururi (p146)

➡ Kado (p147)

➡ Mucha-an (p148)

➡ Namco Namjatown (p143)

For reviews, see p146 ➡

 ### Best Places to Drink

➡ Beer Bar Bitter (p148)

➡ Canal Café (p147)

➡ Jazz Spot Intro (p148)

For reviews, see p148 ➡

 ### Best Gardens

➡ Koishikawa Kōrakuen (p143)

➡ Rikugi-en (p146)

➡ Chinzan-sō (p146)

For reviews, see p142 ➡

(side) IIDABASHI & NORTHWEST TOKYO

Explore Iidabashi & Northwest Tokyo

From gardens to spas, the mixed sights in this large swathe of Tokyo are scattered among smaller districts. Start at Kudanshita and walk through the grand *torii* of Yasukuni-jinja shrine, a controversial tribute to Japan's war dead. The history museum on the grounds is well worth an hour or two, especially for its vintage Mitsubishi Zero fighter planes and other armaments.

Next, make your way over the old outer moat for lunch in the Iidabashi and Kagurazaka area; Kururi is an excellent *rāmen* shop not too far away or you could try Canal Café on the moat itself. Kagurazaka makes for some atmospheric shopping and strolling, though the Koishikawa Kōrakuen gardens to the east are a better place to stretch your legs. You can relax at the grand La Qua spa near Tokyo Dome, or try to catch a baseball game if the Yomiuri Giants are playing.

From here, the subway can take you to the farther-flung sights in this chapter, such as the excellent Chinzan-sō and Rikugi-en gardens, the Takadanobaba student area with its myriad ethnic restaurants, or Ikebukuro's Namjatown, a theme park devoted in part to Chinese dumplings and ice cream. Don't bother counting those calories.

Local Life

➡ **Drinking** Beer Bar Bitter (p148) is one of many excellent watering holes off Kagurazaka hill where locals unwind with fine foreign brews.

➡ **Soaking** La Qua (p149) is a deluxe spa favoured by tired shoppers and others from all over Tokyo.

➡ **Eating** Takadanobaba (p148), near Waseda University, is a teeming student zone with new *izakaya* (Japanese version of a pub/eatery) and *yakitori* (chicken, meats or vegetables, cooked on skewers) joints opening all the time.

Getting There & Away

➡ **Train** The JR Sōbu Line stops at Iidabashi (rapid-service JR Chūō Line trains, which use the same track, skip it but stop at Suidōbashi). The Yamanote and other JR lines stops at Ikebukuro.

➡ **Subway** Useful stations include Iidabashi (Nanboku, Yūrakuchō, Tōzai and Ōedo lines), Kōrakuen (Nanboku and Marunouchi lines), Kagurazaka (Tōzai Line) and Kudanshita (Hanzōmon, Tōzai and Shinjuku lines). The Marunouchi, Yūrakuchō and Fukutoshin lines stop at Ikebukuro Station.

TOP SIGHTS
YASUKUNI-JINJA (YASUKUNI SHRINE)

One of Tokyo's grandest Shinto shrines is also one of the most controversial religious sites in East Asia. Yasukuni is an imposing sanctuary that honours millions of Japanese war dead, including men hanged as war criminals after World War Two. The shrine is especially beautiful when the cherry blossoms come out in spring.

Literally 'For the Peace of the Country Shrine', Yasukuni-jinja (靖国神社) is the memorial to Japan's war dead, around 2.5 million souls who died in WWII and other wars. Despite a postwar constitutional commitment to the separation of religion and politics, 14 class-A war criminals are enshrined here. Japanese politicians have also visited the shrine in recent years, angering Japan's wartime victims.

Nonetheless, Yasukuni is one of the most beautiful shrines in Tokyo. Its enormous *torii* (gate) at the entrance is made of steel, while the second, inner, set is made of bronze. The beautiful inner shrine is laid out in the style of Ise Shrine, the most important in Japan. The grounds are charmingly home to a flock of doves, which balances out all the war hawks, as well as cherry trees that bloom in spring.

The **Yūshūkan war museum**, Japan's oldest museum (1882), paints a controversial picture of WWII from a viewpoint that staunchly supports the actions of the Empire of Japan and its military forces.

Armaments on display, though, are fascinating and harrowing. Note the *kaiten* (human torpedo), essentially a submarine version of the kamikaze aeroplane. The walls of the last galleries are covered with endless photos of dead soldiers, enough to make one wonder about the value of any war.

DON'T MISS

➡ Yūshūkan war museum

PRACTICALITIES

➡ Map p299

➡ ☏3261-8326

➡ www.yasukuni.or.jp

➡ 3-1-1 Kudankita, Chiyoda-ku

➡ shrine free, war museum adult ¥800, student ¥300-500

➡ ⊗shrine 6am-5pm; museum 9am-4pm Oct-Mar, 9am-5pm Apr-Sep

➡ 🚇Hanzōmon Line to Kudanshita (exit 1)

◉ SIGHTS

⊙ Iidabashi & Kagurazaka

YASUKUNI-JINJA
(YASUKUNI SHRINE)   SHRINE
See p141.

YŪSHŪKAN WAR MUSEUM   MUSEUM
See p141.

KAGURAZAKA   NEIGHBOURHOOD
Map p299 (神楽坂; ℝJR Sōbu Line to Iidabashi, west exit) Kagurazaka is old geisha quarter that's worth a visit more for an atmospheric stroll than for any particular sights. Its quaint backstreet alleys are lined with *ryōtei* (upscale, traditional restaurants) and recall bygone days of Edo, or parts of modern Kyoto. They also have some great drinking spots (p148). From Sotobori-dōri, head up Kagurazaka Hill, turn right at Royal Host restaurant, and wander the lanes. If you're very lucky, in the evening you might catch a glimpse of one of the several dozen geisha who still work in the area.

SHŌWA-KAN   MUSEUM
Map p299 (昭和館; ☏3222-2577; 1-6-1 Kudan-Minami, Chiyoda-ku; adult/student/child ¥300/150/80; ☉10am-5pm; ℝHanzōmon Line to Kudanshita, exit 4) This museum of WWII-era Tokyo gives a sense of everyday life for the common people: how they ate, slept, dressed, studied, prepared for war and endured martial law, famine and loss of loved ones. Galleries on the 6th and 7th floors are filled with many hundreds of artefacts. The personal perspective of this museum makes it much more accessible than Yūshūkan. An English audio guide (free) explains the basics.

On the 5th floor are consoles where you can view ten videos about the war in English, mostly news footage from Western media. There are a great many more videos in Japanese.

KITANOMARU-KŌEN
(KITANOMARU PARK)   PARK
Map p299 (北の丸公園; ℝHanzōmon Line to Kudanshita, exit 2) This large park north of the Imperial Palace grounds is home to noteworthy museums as well as the **Nihon Budōkan** (2-3 Kitanomaru-kōen), a legendary concert hall that has hosted acts from The Beatles to Beck; it was originally built for martial arts championships (judō, karate, kendō and aikidō) for the 1964 Olympics. These arts are still practised and exhibited here today.

Southeast of the Budōkan is **Kagaku Gijitsukan** (Science Museum; www.jsf.or.jp/eng; 2-1 Kitanomaru-kōen, Chiyoda-ku; adult/child ¥700/250; ☉9.30am-4.50pm Thu-Tue), which features a good selection of exhibits aimed primarily at children and teenagers. There is little in the way of English explanations, but there is an excellent bilingual guidebook (¥200) available. Even without a guidebook or an understanding of Japanese, you can still stand inside a soap bubble and visit the 'methane boy' (he emits exactly what you think he emits).

In the south of the park, facing the Imperial Palace East Garden, is the **Kokuritsu Kindai Bijutsukan** (National Museum of Modern Art, Tokyo; MOMAT; www.momat.go.jp/english; 3-1 Kitanomaru-kōen, Chiyoda-ku; adult/student ¥420/130, 1st Sun of month free; ☉10am-5pm Tue-Thu, Sat & Sun, 10am-8pm Fri). The expansive collection here documents contemporary Japanese art from the Meiji period onward; there is a sense of a more modern Japan through portraits, photography and grim wartime landscapes. Its collection of more than 9000 works is arguably the best in the entire country.

The nearby **Bijutsukan Kōgeikan** (Crafts Gallery; www.momat.go.jp/english; 1 Kitanomaru-kōen, Chiyoda-ku; adult/student ¥200/70, 1st Sun of month free; ☉10am-5pm Tue-Sun), which stages excellent changing exhibitions of *mingei* crafts (see p107): ceramics, lacquerware, bamboo, textiles, dolls and much more.

The gate at the park's northern end, **Tayasu-mon**, dates from 1636, making it the oldest remaining gate in the park. The area surrounding it along the moat explodes with cherry blossoms (and flower photographers) in spring.

JCII CAMERA MUSEUM   MUSEUM
Map p299 (日本カメラ博物館; www.jcii-cameramuseum.jp; 25 Ichiban-cho, Chiyoda-ku; adult/child ¥300/free; ☉10am-5pm Tue-Sun; ℝHanzōmon Line to Hanzōmon, exit 4) This museum holds more than 10,000 cameras, of which some 600 may be on show at any one time. Highlights of the collection include the world's first camera, the 1839 Giroux daguerreotype, and Japan's first, the ornate Tsui-kin from 1854. There's an English booklet at the reception.

Behind the museum in an alley is the **JCII photo salon** (☎3261-0300; admission free; ☺10am-5pm Tue-Sun) with a changing roster of photography exhibits.

⊙ Kōrakuen

TOKYO DOME CITY
SPORTS

Map p299 (東京ドームシティ; www.tokyo-dome. co.jp/e/; 1-3 Kōraku, Bunkyō-ku; 🚇JR Chūō Line to Suidōbashi, west exit) Tokyo Dome (aka 'Big Egg') is home to the Yomiuri Giants, the most successful team in Japanese baseball. If you're looking to see the Giants in action, the baseball season runs from the end of March to the end of October. Baseball fans will not want to miss the **Japanese Baseball Hall of Fame & Museum** (野球体育博物館; 1-3-61 Kōraku, Bunkyō-ku; adult/child ¥500/200; ☺10am-6pm Tue-Sun Mar-Sep, 10am-5pm Tue-Sun Oct-Feb), which chronicles baseball's rise from a hobby imported by a US teacher in 1872 to the national obsession it's become. The entrance to the museum is adjacent to Gate 21 of the Tokyo Dome.

Tokyo Dome is surrounded by the amusement park **Tokyo Dome City Attractions** (東京ドームシティアトラクションズ; ☎5800-9999; www.tokyo-dome.co.jp/e; day pass adult/child ¥2900/2000; ☺10am-9pm) with the usual assortment of coasters and spinners, including Big-O, the world's largest hubless Ferris wheel. If you don't want to invest in an all-day pass offering access to all of the rides, tickets are available for individual rides (¥200 to ¥1000).

KOISHIKAWA KŌRAKUEN
(KOISHIKAWA KŌRAKU GARDEN)
GARDENS

Map p299 (小石川後楽園; 1-6-6 Kōraku, Bunkyō-ku; adult/senior & child ¥300/free; ☺9am-5pm; 🚇JR Sōbu Line to Iidabashi, exit C3) This 70,000-sq-metre formal Japanese garden is one of Tokyo's most beautiful and least visited by foreigners – if you have the slightest interest in gardens, you should make a beeline here.

Established in the mid-17th century as the property of the Tokugawa clan, the garden incorporates elements of Chinese and Japanese landscaping, although nowadays the *shakkei* (borrowed scenery) also includes the otherworldly Tokyo Dome. The garden is particularly well known for plum trees in February, irises in June and autumn colours. Of special note is the Engetsu-kyō (Full-Moon Bridge), which dates from the early Edo period.

⊙ Ikebukuro

SUNSHINE CITY
LANDMARK

Map p296 (サンシャインシティ; 3 Higashi-Ikebukuro, Toshima-ku; admission free;🚇JR Yamanote Line to Ikebukuro, east exit) A complex of four buildings east of the station, Sunshine City is visited by shoppers and for **Namco Namjatown** (ナムジャタウン; www.namja.jp; 2nd fl, World Import Mart bldg; adult/child admission ¥300/200, passport ¥3900/3300; ☺10am-10pm). The main activities are carnival-style rides and attractions. Foodies will prefer the food 'theme parks' dedicated to adventures in *gyoza* (pan-fried dumplings), ice cream and desserts. The passport gets you into Namjatown as well as most of the attractions, though some still cost extra, as do food and treatments. Check the website or the Namjatown map for attractions that don't require knowledge of Japanese.

Other Sunshine City highlights include the **observatory** (adult/child ¥620/310; ☺10am-9.30pm) an **aquarium** (adult/student/child ¥1800/900/600; ☺10am-8pm Apr-Oct, 10am-6pm Nov-Mar), and the quiet **Ancient Orient Museum** (古代オリエント博物館; Kodai Oriento Hakubutsukan; admission ¥500; ☺10am-5pm), which features art and antiquities from Iran, Iraq, Uzbekistan and especially Syria.

FREE IKEBUKURO EARTHQUAKE HALL
(IKEBUKURO BŌSAI-KAN)
MUSEUM

Map p296 (池袋防災館; 2-37-8 Nishi-Ikebukuro, Tōshima-ku; ☺9am-5pm Wed-Mon, closed 3rd Wed of month; 🚇JR Yamanote Line to Ikebukuro, Metropolitan exit) Quick: what should you do in case of an earthquake? What if your house is on fire? This facility operated by the Tokyo Fire Department prepares you for these and other disasters by means of videos (available in English) and incredibly realistic simulations; it's hard not to be rattled once the room starts a-shaking. A visit here is important preparation if you're planning on living in Japan. Even if you're not, it's an important insight into a possibility that's never far from the mind of any Japanese.

GOKOKU-JI
TEMPLE

off Map p296 (護国寺; admission free; ☺dawn-dusk; 🚇Yūrakuchō Line to Gokokuji, exit 1) Declared an important cultural property, Gokoku Temple gets surprisingly few visitors. One of the few surviving Edo temples, it dates from 1680 and was built by the fifth Tokugawa shōgun for his mother.

DIANE COOK AND LEN JENSHEL / LONELY PLANET IMAGES ©

NOBORU KOMINE / LONELY PLANET IMAGES ©

1. Rikugi-en (p146)
The formal garden at Rikugi-en is rich with literary associations.

2. Sunshine City (p143)
Atrium of Sunshine City Convention Center.

3. Aquarium (p143)
Visitors watch rays swoop and dive at the Sunshine City aquarium.

WORTH A DETOUR

CLANG-CLANG! CHIN-CHIN!

Given Tokyo's tangled streets, it's hard to imagine that streetcars were common here until the 1960s. The **Toden Arakawa Line** (都電荒川線) is the last remaining street-car within central Tokyo, arcing across the city's north side between Minowabashi in the east and Waseda, near Takadanobaba, in the west. It was due to be demolished along with the other streetcar lines, but public outcry preserved it, and it's been in municipal hands since the 1970s. Apart from being about the cheapest ride in Tokyo (one way ¥160, 50 min; day pass ¥400), it's also a great way to observe the city up close and personal.

Cheery, historical trams that look like they could be friends of Thomas the Tank Engine depart Minowabashi Station, about 275 metres to the north of Minowa Station on the Hibiya Line.

An interesting detour on that walk is the Buddhist temple **Jōkan-ji** (浄閑寺), where many of the souls who perished in the 21 fires that raged through the nearby Yoshi-wara pleasure quarters (see p223) are enshrined.

Once you've boarded the tram, the route is lined with cherry trees, homes with hanging laundry, pocket parks and plenty of the sort of everyday street life that most visitors miss. During cherry blossom season, it's worth getting off at Asukayama Station for *hanami* (blossom viewing) in the park, and train *otaku* (geeks) will want to alight at Arakawa Shako-mae, where a couple of antique streetcars can be inspected up close.

The train terminates at Waseda (早稲田), from where it is a lovely cherry-tree-lined walk of under 10 minutes to Chinzan-sō (p146).

RIKUGI-EN   GARDENS

(六義園; 6-16-3 Hon-Komagome; admission ¥300; ⏰9am-5pm; ▣JR Yamanote Line to Koma-gome, south exit) Rikugi Garden is a fine garden with landscaped views unfolding at every turn of the many pathways that criss-cross the grounds. The garden is rich in literary associations: its name is taken from the six principles of *waka* (31-syllable poems), and the landscaping evokes famous scenes from both Chinese and Japanese literature. The garden is about 100m south of the station; there are signs showing the way.

⦿ **Takadanobaba**

CHINZAN-SŌ   GARDENS

(椿山荘; www.chinzanso.com; 2-10-8 Sekiguchi, Bunkyō-ku; admission free; ⏰10am-9.30pm; ▣Yūrakuchō Line to Edogawa-bashi, exit 1a) This lovely, hilly 66,000-sq-metre strolling garden was part of the estate of a Meiji-era politician and statesman, and lining its many pathways are a number of antiquities transported from all over Japan. Most notable is a 16.7m three-storey pagoda, estimated at nearly a millennium old, which was transported from the Hiroshima area, as well as lanterns, monuments and *torii*. The con-

temporary construction of hotels and wedding halls around it are regrettable, but all that is forgotten in the garden's lovely soba shop **Mucha-an** (p148). From exit 1a, walk west for 10 minutes along the Kanda-gawa canal until the gate to Chinzan-sō appears on your right.

 EATING

✖️ **Iidabashi & Kagurazaka**

TOP CHOICE KURURI   RAMEN ¥

Map p299 (麺処くるり; 3-2 Ichigaya-Tamachi, Shinjuku-ku; dishes ¥700-950; ⏰11am-9pm; ▣JR Sōbu Line to Iidabashi, west exit) The line-up of ramen fanatics outside this cramped, anonymous noodle shop proves its street cred among connoisseurs of miso, the house seasoning. The *miso-rāmen* (みそらぁめん) broth is swamp-thick, incredibly rich and absolutely delicious. There's no sign, so look for the lineup next to a liquor shop with a striped awning; buy a ticket inside from the machine and wait for some perfection in a bowl.

KADO
TRADITIONAL ¥¥

Map p299 (カド; ☎3268-2410; 1-32 Akagi-Motomachi, Shinjuku-ku; lunch sets ¥800-1000, dinner sets ¥3150; ®Tōzai Line to Kagurazaka, exit 1) Set in a house built in 1950, Kado reveals a rare glimpse of old Tokyo. Lunch is simple, such as *korokke teishoku* (croquettes with seasonal veggies), while five-course dinners emphasise traditional Japanese recipes and seasonal produce, enhanced by the familial ambience. There is no English menu, though the staff do their best to accommodate. From Kagurazaka Station, turn left and left again into the jagged street across from Café Copain; Kado is at the first four-way corner. Call ahead on weekends.

CANAL CAFÉ
ITALIAN ¥¥

Map p299 (カナルカフェ; ☎3260-8068; 1-9 Kagurazaka, Shinjuku-ku; mains ¥1400-2800; ⊘closed Mon; ⓓ; ®JR Sōbu Line to Iidabashi, west exit) When summer evenings in the capital hang heavy with humidity, this is one of the rare spots in the city centre with breathing room, allowing you to enjoy a cold glass of white wine and a light meal by the water. The specialities are wood-fired thin-crust pizza, and pasta dishes such as prawns in a light cream sauce, though the real reason you're here is to savour a cocktail while soaking up the European atmosphere. Call ahead on weekends.

LE BRETAGNE
FRENCH ¥

Map p299 (ル ブルターニュ; 4-2 Kagurazaka, Shinjuku-ku; crêpes ¥550-1680; ⊘11.30am-11.30pm Tue-Sat, 11.30am-9pm Sun; ✏ⓓ; ®JR Sōbu Line to Iidabashi, west exit) This French-owned Kagurazaka cafe is credited with starting the Japanese rage for crêpes. Its stucco walls, beamed ceilings and front terrace make for a rustic setting to sample savoury crêpes with ingredients like ham, gruyère, artichokes and tomato, or sweet crêpes like Quimpéroise with caramelised butter, apple compote and vanilla ice cream.

✕ Ikebukuro

MALAYCHAN
MALAYSIAN ¥

Map p296 (マレーチャン; 3-22-6 Nishi-Ikebukuro, Toshima-ku; mains ¥740-1680, dinner ¥2100-2400; ⊘lunch & dinner; closed Mon lunch; ®JR Yamanote Line to Ikebukuro, west exit) If you've never tried Malaysian cooking, it's like a mix of Thai and Indonesian with a bit of Indian thrown in, redolent with chilli, lemon grass, garlic and dried prawns. At this cosy, corner halal eatery at the end of Ikebukuro's gourmet street, start off with spring rolls, chicken satay and *murtabak* (ground chicken crêpes) then move on to savoury curries and *nasi goreng* (fried rice).

AKIYOSHI
YAKITORI ¥

Map p296 (秋吉; 3-30-4 Nishi-Ikebukuro, Toshima-ku; dishes around ¥500; ⊘5-11pm; ®JR Yamanote Line to Ikebukuro, west exit) If you're in the mood for *yakitori,* Akiyoshi is an approachable, ebullient place to partake. The open grill at centre stage ignites a festive, sociable space. The chefs work quickly to help move traffic along, but that doesn't mean you can't sit comfortably through several small courses and at least one conversation. Look for the red lantern-like sign outside.

ANPUKU
UDON ¥

Map p296 (あんぷく; 1-37-8 Nishi-Ikebukuro, Toshima-ku; mains ¥680-1380; ⓓ; ®JR Yamanote Line to Ikebukuro, west exit) Udon goes international at this spiffy little white-walled cafe. Creative young chefs make the noodles right there and put them in *so* not Japanese dishes: carbonara, chicken with mushrooms in cream sauce or spicy

EVERYWHERE VENDORS

Japan has the largest number of vending machines in the world – 5 million (including coin lockers) and counting – and they suck in nearlyUS$65 billion yearly. They are remarkable for both their ubiquity – they can be found everywhere from bullet trains to desolate rural villages to the slopes of Mt Fuji – and their variety. They dispense almost every consumer product conceivable: from cigarettes to sake, canned drinks (cold *or* hot!), rice, popcorn, hamburgers, hot noodles, pornography, sex toys, bouquets, kerosene, toys, toilet paper, fishing tackles, horseracing bets, travel insurance and underwear. Where do they all come from? Probably the best answer was from a newspaper cartoonist who drew a giant Japanese vending machine dispensing – you guessed it – vending machines.

Sichuan eggplant. It's eaten with chopsticks, so staff supply you with a paper bib. There's also stellar traditional udon for purists, and side dishes including grills.

Takadanobaba

TAVERNA
ITALIAN ¥

Map p296 (タベルナ; 2nd fl, 2-5-10 Takadanobaba, Shinjuku-ku; dishes ¥1000, set meals ¥1980-3880; ◎5-11pm Mon-Sat; ☒JR Yamanote Line to Takadanobaba, main exit) Here are some reasons this cosy, Roman-inspired spot has been here forever: spaghetti *all'amatriciana* (with bacon and tomato sauce) or *vongole* (clams, olive oil and garlic), and pizza *mista* (with anchovy, tuna and prosciutto). Some people eat here every night, inspired by the authentic cuisine, the charm of the owner and reasonable prices.

MUCHA-AN
SOBA ¥

無茶庵; (☒3943-5489; 2-10-8 Sekiguchi, Bunkyō-ku; mains ¥1100-1890; ◎daily; ☒JR Yūrakuchō Line to Edogawa-bashi, exit 1a) Perched on a hill inside Chinzan-sō garden (p146), this shop in a wood-built former ryokan (transported from across town) makes its own noodles and serves them simply: on a *seiro* (bamboo mat on a wooden box) or with *kamo* (duck), hot or cold. Grab a seat by the window for the best views. Reserve on Saturdays and holidays.

KAO TAI
THAI ¥

Map p296 (カオタイ; 2-14-6 Takadanobaba, Shinjuku-ku; mains ¥840-1200; ◙; ☒JR Yamanote Line to Takadanobaba, main exit) From the bamboo-framed doorway to its snug dining room, Kao Tai feels like a warm slice of southeast Asia. Most dishes are small-plate affairs, allowing you to sample and share while swigging on a Singha. While it's not the most complicated Thai food around, the atmosphere more than makes up for it.

🍷 DRINKING & NIGHTLIFE

BEER BAR BITTER
BAR

Map p299 (ビアバービター; 2nd fl, 1-14 Tsukudochō, Shinjuku-ku; ◎Mon-Fri; ☒JR Sōbu Line to Iidabashi, west exit) This mellow Euro-bar in Kagurazaka has a super selection of Belgian beers from around ¥900, as well as snacks such as Iberico ham (¥1300). Going up Kagurazaka hill, look for the fourth lane on your right, called Honda-yokochō (本多横丁). Go down it until you see a pale, three-storey building on your right with a red *yakitori* lantern hanging outside. Take the stairs on the right.

☆ ENTERTAINMENT

JAZZ SPOT INTRO
JAZZ

Map p299 (イントロ; www.intro.co.jp; B1 fl, NT Bldg, 2-14-8 Takadanobaba, Shinjuku-ku; admission ¥1000; ◎closed Sun; ☒JR Yamanote Line to Takadanobaba, main exit) It's a good sign when a little club allows a quarter of its floor space to be monopolised by a grand piano. It also bodes well when the place is staffed by musicians who love to talk shop all night. At Jazz Spot Intro, all the omens are favourable.

HOT HOUSE
JAZZ

(ホットハウス; http://hothouse.cocolog-nifty.com/blog, in Japanese; 3-23-5 Takadanobaba, Shinjuku-ku; admission varies; ◎8.30pm-2am; ☒JR Yamanote Line to Takadanobaba, Waseda exit) This must be the smallest jazz dive in the world. Musicians play in twos and threes (there's no room for more). Audience members usually number about 10; get here early if you're set on sitting in for the evening. From the station, walk west along Waseda-dōri for about 10 minutes. You'll see Hot House on the right, across the street from the Citizen Plaza bowling and skating complex.

SESSION HOUSE
DANCE

Map p299 (セッションハウス; ☒3266-0461; www.session-house.net, in Japanese; 158 Yaraichō, Shinjuku-ku; about ¥3000; ☒Tōzai Line to Kagurazaka, exit 1) Session House, which celebrated its 20th year in 2011, is considered one of the best modern dance spaces in the city; it also hosts folk music concerts. The small theatre seats only 100 people, which means that all performances have an intimate feel to them. Exit right from the station, make a right into the first narrow alley, and turn left where it becomes a dead-end. Session House will be a few metres on your right. Performances start around 7pm.

SHOPPING

JAPAN TRADITIONAL CRAFT
CENTER   CRAFT

Map   p296   (全国伝統的工芸品センター;
📱5954-6066; www.kougei.or.jp/english/center.
html; 1st fl, Metropolitan Plaza Bldg, 1-11-1 Nishi
Ikebukuro, Toshima-ku; 🚉JR Yamanote Line to
Ikebukuro, Metropolitan exit) Supported by the
Japanese Ministry of Economy, Trade and
Industry, this showroom is a valuable re-
source for working artisans and crafts collectors. You'll find on display more than 130
different types of crafts, often with English
labels, ranging from lacquerwork boxes to
paper, textiles to earthy pottery.

PUPPET HOUSE   CRAFT

Map p299 (パペットハウス; www.puppet-house.
co.jp; 1-8 Shimomiyabi-chō, Shinjuku-ku; 🕐Tue-
Sat; 🚉JR Sōbu Line to Iidabashi, east exit) This
is a wondrous workshop of functional international marionettes, run by a super-
friendly couple who are happy to talk shop.
Look for the sign of Punch in an alley near
Mizuho Bank.

 SPORTS &
ACTIVITIES

LA QUA   ONSEN

Map p299 (スパ　ラクーア; www.laqua.jp; 1-3-
61 Kōraku, Bunkyō-ku; admission ¥2565, extra
charges can apply; 🕐11am-9am; 🚉Marunouchi
Line to Kōrakuen, exit 2) One of Tokyo's few
true onsen, this chic spa complex is where
serious bathing aficionados go for some
class and luxury. There are multiple floors
with a variety of baths, massage parlours,
restaurants and relaxation areas. Access to
the Healing Baden area is an extra ¥525.

Akihabara & Around

AKIHABARA | KANDA

Neighbourhood Top Five

1 Wandering the teeming streets of **Akihabara Electric Town** (p152). This is an experience in soaking up the *otaku* (geek) vibe – the blazing neon, the cafe maids, the ubiquitous electronics and anime (Japanese animation) and manga (Japanese comics) goods make a mighty cultural stew.

2 Marvelling at the vintage components stalls under the tracks at **Akihabara Radio Center** (p152) and the latest gadgets at **Yodobashi Akiba** (p155).

3 Browsing the wooden keyboards, guns and kaleidoscopes at eclectic arcade **2k540 Aki-Oka Artisan** (p154).

4 Taking the plunge and having a cuppa at a maid cafe like **@Home Café** (p154).

5 Chilling out at the quiet religious sanctuaries of **Kanda Myōjin shrine** and **Nikolai Cathedral** (p153).

For more detail of this area, see Map p298 ➡

Explore Akihabara & Around

Akihabara is synonymous with *otaku* (geeks) but you don't have to obsess about manga or anime (to enjoy this quirky neighbourhood that is at once sensory overload and cultural mindbender. From Akihabara Station, take in the old-school Akihabara Radio Center under the tracks, and figurine-filled Akihabara Radio Kaikan next door for a quick intro to what gets the *otaku* heart beating.

Along neon-lined Chūō-dōri, west of the station, you'll see touts hawking cheap goods, and perhaps a French maid enticing customers to a local cafe. Electric Town is across the street, and holds a huge concentration of electronics shops, DVD retailers and figurine sellers. You can expect squads of geeks on the lookout for the latest anime goods, but it also draws shoppers from across the world.

You can find respite in the recently opened 2k540 Aki-Oka Artisan arcade, with its serene atmosphere and eclectic, craft-oriented shops tucked beneath the tracks north of the station. From here walk north along the tracks toward Ueno-kōen (Ueno Park; p159) or go west along Kuramaebashi-dōri. You'll find the usually quiet Kanda Myōjin (Kanda shrine), home to Yushima Seidō, a rare Confucian shrine by the Kanda-gawa. If you want to stretch your legs further, Origami Kaikan has fine displays on the art of folding paper into exquisite shapes.

To the south, the Jimbōchō and Kanda quarters have a no-nonsense vibe and a plethora of shops selling used and antique books, sporting goods and musical instruments.

To the north of Kanda Station are some excellent traditional restaurants housed in vintage and traditional buildings. These are a great choice to cap an afternoon and early evening exploring this area.

Local Life

➡ **Shopping** Yodobashi Akiba (p155) is an excellent electronics shop on the east side of Akihabara station.

➡ **Wandering** The crowded streets of Akihabara Electric Town (p152) are great for exploring the maze of small electronics shops and maid cafes.

➡ **Eating** Kanda-sudachō (p153), south of Akihabara Station, is home to wonderful traditional restaurants.

Getting There & Away

➡ **Train** The JR Yamanote, Sōbu, and Keihin-Tōhoku lines stop at Akihabara. Ochanomizu on the JR Chūō and Sōbu lines is convenient for other sights.

➡ **Subway** The Hibiya Line stops near Akihabara, while the Ginza Line stops at Suehirochō. The Shinjuku and Hanzōmon lines stop at Jimbōchō.

Lonely Planet's Top Tip

Check electronics prices in your home country online before buying big-ticket items in Akihabara; they may or may not be a good deal. If you do buy, have your passport handy since travellers spending more than ¥10,001 in a single day at one shop can get a refund of the 5% consumption tax. Not all stores offer the refund, however, so ask first. For a list of duty-free shops, see www.akiba.or.jp.

Best Places to Eat

➡ Isegen (p153)

➡ Kanda Yabu Soba (p154)

➡ Botan (p153)

For reviews, see p153 ➡

Best Places to Drink

➡ Milonga Nueva (p154)

➡ Boo (p154)

➡ @Home Café (p154)

For reviews, see p154 ➡

Best Places to Shop

➡ Yodobashi Akiba (p155)

➡ 2k540 Aki-Oka Artisan (p154)

➡ Mandarake Complex (p154)

For reviews, see p154 ➡

AKIHABARA & AROUND

◉ SIGHTS

◉ Akihabara

AKIHABARA ELECTRIC TOWN (DENKI-GAI) NEIGHBOURHOOD

Map p298 (秋葉原電気街; 및JR Yamanote to Akihabara, Denki-gai exit) What the Tsukiji Central Fish Market is to the food trade, Akihabara is to Japan's legendary electronics industry: bustling, busy and fun to watch, and you don't have to get up early in the morning to catch the action (afternoon is prime time). Akihabara can no longer claim exclusive rights to the title of the city's electronics centre (thanks to increased competition from denser hubs such as Shinjuku and Ikebukuro), yet it is still quite the scene. Akihabara is where many items are market-tested, so even if you have no intention of shopping now, it's worth a peek to see what you may be buying two years hence.

As the electronics business has moved elsewhere (Korea, China and Taiwan), Akihabara has turned to the boom market in cartoon manga, often pornographic, to round out its fiscal activity. If you like your cheap thrills of the PG-13 variety, don't miss the opportunity to have a cup of coffee and curry rice in any of Akihabara's unique maid cafes (see p154).

TOKYO ANIME CENTER AKIBA INFO INFORMATION DESK

Map p298 (東京アニメセンターakiba info; www.animecenter.jp; 2nd fl, Akihabara UDX Bldg, 4-14-1 Soto-Kanda, Chiyoda-ku; ⊙11am-7pm Tue-Sun; 및JR Yamanote Line to Akihabara, Denki-gai exit) If you're hunting for specific anime or manga merchandise, try the English-speaking information desk here. It's part of a shop that sells a decent variety of character goods such as Astro Boy; the underwhelming Tokyo Anime Center proper is on the 4th floor of the Akihabara UDX Building. There are also computer terminals with free internet access.

AKIHABARA RADIO CENTER ELECTRONICS

Map p298 (秋葉原ラジオセンター; 1-14-2 Sotokanda, Chiyoda-ku; ⊙varies; 및JR Yamanote to Akihabara, Electric Town exit) Strictly for old-school electronics otaku, this two-storey warren of several dozen electronics stalls under the elevated railway is the original, still-beating heart of Akihabara. By old-school, we mean connectors, jacks, LEDs, switches, semiconductors and other components. It's worth a peek as a cultural study; the easiest access is the narrow entrances under the tracks on Chūō-dōri.

◉ Kanda & Around

ORIGAMI KAIKAN CRAFT

Map p298 (おりがみ会館; International Origami Centre; ☎3811-4025; www.origamikaikan.co.jp, in Japanese; 1-7-14 Yushima, Bunkyō-ku; admission free; ⊙shop 9am-6pm, gallery 10am-5.30pm Mon-Sat; 및JR Chūō or Sōbu Lines to Ochanomizu, Hijiribashi exit) Dating to 1858, this multistorey exhibition centre and

---

LOCAL KNOWLEDGE

FINDING AN ADDRESS

Finding a place from its address in Tokyo can be difficult, even for locals. The problem is twofold: first, addresses are given within a district rather than along a street (only major streets have names or numbers); and second, building numbers are not necessarily consecutive, as prior to the mid-1950s numbers were assigned by date of construction. During the US occupation after WWII, an attempt was made to impose some 'logic' upon the system, and main streets were assigned names, though the city reverted to its own system after the Americans left.

Tokyo, like most Japanese cities, is divided first into ku (wards; Tokyo has 23 of them), which in turn are divided into chō or machi (towns) and then into numbered chōme (pronounced cho-may), areas of just a few blocks. Subsequent numbers in an address refer to blocks within the chōme and buildings within each block. Addresses sometimes only have two numbers or even one.

To find an address you generally have to ask for directions. Numerous kōban (police boxes) exist largely for this purpose. If you're arriving by train or subway, be sure to also get the closest exit number from the station.

workshop is dedicated to this quintessentially Japanese art. In a shop/gallery on the 1st floor and a gallery on the 2nd, many of the works are so sculptural you'd mistake them for wood, and with patterns so intricate you'd mistake them for fabric, while on the 4th floor is a workshop where visitors can watch the process of dyeing and painting origami paper. Although admission is free, origami lessons (offered most days in Japanese) cost ¥1000 to ¥2500 for one to two hours, depending on the complexity of that day's design. First-timers would do well to try for a class with the centre's director, Kobayashi Kazuo. It's best to request a reservation by emailing admin@origamikaikan.co.jp.

KANDA MYŌJIN (KANDA SHRINE) SHRINE

Map p298 (神田明神; www.kandamyoujin.or.jp; 2-16-2 Sotokanda, Chiyoda-ku; admission free; 圓Marunouchi Line to Ochanomizu, exit 2) Hidden behind the main streets, this little known but quite splendid Shintō shrine boasts vermillion-coloured halls surrounding a stately courtyard. It traces its history back to AD 730, though its present location dates from 1616. The *kami* (gods) enshrined here are said to bring luck in business and in finding a spouse. It is the home shrine of the Kanda Matsuri (Kanda Festival; p26) in mid-May, one of the largest festivals in Tokyo.

NIKOLAI CATHEDRAL CHURCH

Map p298 (ニコライ堂; 4-1-3 Kanda-Surugadai, Chiyoda-ku; admission ¥300; ◷1-4pm Apr-Sep, 1-3.30pm Oct-Mar; 圓Chiyoda Line to Shin-Ochanomizu, exit 2) This Russian Orthodox cathedral is named for St Nikolai of Japan (1836–1912), who first arrived as chaplain of the Russian consulate in the port city of Hakodate (Hokkaidō) and through missionary work soon amassed about 30,000 faithful. The Tokyo building, complete with a distinctive onion dome, was first constructed in 1891. The original copper dome was, like parts of so many grand buildings, damaged in the 1923 earthquake, forcing the church to downsize to the (still enormous) dome that's now in place. If you're interested in attending worship services, enquire inside for times.

TOKYO WONDER SITE HONGO ART GALLERY

Map p298 (トーキョーワンダーサイト本郷; www.tokyo-ws.org; 2-4-16 Hongo, Bunkyō-ku; admission free; ◷variable; 圓JR Chūō or Sōbu Line to Ochanomizu, Ochanomizu-bashi exit) Operated by the Tokyo Metropolitan Government, Tokyo Wonder Site comprises three floors of galleries with the aim of promoting new and emerging artists. There is a regularly changing program of exhibitions, competitions and lectures in media ranging from painting to video art. Check the website before setting out.

YUSHIMA SEIDŌ (YUSHIMA SHRINE) SHRINE

Map p298 (湯島聖堂; 1-4-25 Yushima, Bunkyō-ku; admission free; ◷9.30am-5pm Apr-Sep, 9.30am-4pm Oct-Mar; 圓JR Chūō or Sōbu Lines to Ochanomizu, Hijiribashi exit) Established in 1691 and later used as a school for the sons of the powerful during the Tokugawa regime, Yushima Seidō is one of Tokyo's few Confucian shrines. There's a Ming dynasty bronze statue of Confucius in its black-lacquered main hall, which was rebuilt in 1935. The sculpture is visible only from 1 to 4 January and the fourth Sunday in April, but you can turn up at weekends and holidays to see the building's interior.

✖ EATING

✖ Kanda

BOTAN SUKIYAKI ¥¥¥

Map p298 (ぼたん; ☑3251-0577; 1-15 Kanda-Sudachō, Chiyoda-ku; set meals around ¥7000; ◷11.30am-9pm Mon-Sat; ☎; 圓Marunouchi Line to Awajichō, exit A3) Botan has been making a single, perfect dish in the same button-maker's house since the 1890s. Sit cross-legged on rattan mats as chicken *nabe* (鍋; meat cooked in broth with vegetables) simmers over a charcoal brazier next to you, allowing you to take in the scent of prewar Tokyo. Try to get a seat in the handsome upstairs dining room.

ISEGEN TRADITIONAL ¥¥

Map p298 (いせ源; ☑3251-1229; 1-11-1 Kanda-Sudachō, Chiyoda-ku; set meals from ¥3400; ◷11.30am-2pm & 5-9pm Mon-Sat, closed Sat Jun-Aug; 圓Marunouchi Line to Awajichō, exit A3) Set in a rare, 80-year-old building, this Edo-style restaurant dishes up monkfish stew in a splendid communal tatami room from early autumn to mid-spring. When monkfish is out of season, expect the same traditional surroundings and a menu offering fresh river fish.

KANDA YABU SOBA
SOBA ¥

Map p298 (神田やぶそば; ☑3251-0287; 2-10 Kanda-Awajichō, Chiyoda-ku; noodles ¥700-2000; ⏰11.30am-8.30pm; 📷; 🚇Marunouchi Line to Awajichō, exit A3) A wooden wall and a small garden enclose this venerable buckwheat noodle shop. When you walk in, staff singing out the orders is one of the first signs that you've arrived in a singular, ageless place. Raised tatami platforms and a darkly wooded dining room set the stage for show-stopping soba. There's a similar but unaffiliated restaurant in Asakusa: **Namiki Yabu Soba** (並木やぶそば; ☑3841-1340; 2-11-9 Kaminarimon, Taitō-ku; ⏰11am-7.30pm Fri-Wed; 📷; 🚇Ginza Line to Asakusa, exit A4).

🍷 DRINKING

MILONGA NUEVA
CAFE

Map p298 (ミロンガヌオーバ; 1-3 Kanda Jimbōchō, Chiyoda-ku; ⏰10.30am-10.30pm Mon-Fri, 11.30am-7pm Sat & Sun; 🚇Shinjuku Line to Jimbōchō, exit A7) Off an alley parallel to Yasukuni-dōri, this wonderfully retro Euro cafe plays old tango tunes on the sound system and serves up blends like Kilimanjaro coffee for ¥650.

BOO
CAFE

Map p298 (遊食家Boo; 5-9 Ueno, Taitō-ku; ⏰lunch & dinner daily, 11am-8pm Sat; 🚇Ginza Line to Suehirochō, exit 2) Tucked under the JR train tracks in the 2k540 Aki-Oka Artisan arcade, this quirky little place shares space with Studio Uamou and the cartoonish characters of designer Takagi Ayako. While not the most atmospheric place, Boo is an interesting spot to unwind due to its location, and has beer, teas and light pastas on the menu.

@HOME CAFÉ
CAFE

Map p298 (@ほぉ〜むカフェ; www.cafe-at home.com; 7F Mitsuwa Bldg, 1-11-4 Soto-kanda, Chiyoda-ku; mains ¥1100-1200, drinks & desserts ¥400-800, plus per person ¥700; ⏰11.30am-10pm Mon-Fri, 10.30am-10pm Sat, Sun; 🚇JR Sōbu Line to Akihabara, Electric Town exit) Do you fancy walking on the wild side of Tokyo's fetish for *kawaii* (cuteness)? You'll be welcomed as *go-shujinsama* (master)

the minute you enter this cafe. It's a little titillating, perhaps, but this is no sex joint – just (more or less) innocent fun for Akihabara's *otaku*. Dishes such as curried rice are even topped with smiley faces. Waitresses are dressed as French maids and adopt an especially fawning demeanour to customers. Customers can expect cute girls, giggles and plenty of *kawaii* love going around.

🛍 SHOPPING

TOP CHOICE 2K540 AKI-OKA ARTISAN
CRAFT

Map p298 (アキオカアルチザン; www.jrtk.jp/2k540, in Japanese; 5-9 Ueno, Taitō-ku; ⏰varies; 🚇Ginza Line to Suehirochō, exit 2) This laid-back, minimalist arcade under the JR tracks (its name refers to the distance from Tokyo Station) groups a few dozen shops focused on craftsmanship. The eclectic mix includes everything from pottery to wood products to cute aliens, a nod to Akihabara from a mall that is more akin to Kyoto than Electric Town. You can find customisable wood cases for your iPhone at **Hacoa** (ハコア), dainty kaleidoscopes at **Sōshin Kaleidoscopes** (創心万華鏡) or figurines at **Studio Uamou** (スタジオ ウアモウ), showcasing the cartoonish creations of designer Takagi Ayako. The latter shares space with **Boo** (see p154), one of a handful of quirky cafes here.

TOP CHOICE MANDARAKE COMPLEX
MANGA, ANIME

Map p298 (まんだらけコンプレックス; www.mandarake.co.jp; 3-11-2 Sotokanda, Chiyoda-ku; ⏰noon-8pm; 🚇JR Yamanote Line to Akihabara, Electric Town exit) When *otaku* dream of heaven, it probably looks a lot like this giant store. Mandarake has long been Tokyo's go-to store for manga and anime, and its Akihabara branch is the largest. Eight storeys are piled high with comic books and DVDs, action figures and cel art just for starters. The 5th floor, in all its pink splendour, is devoted to women's comics, while the 4th floor is for men. Mandarake's original branch is in **Nakano** (5-52-15 Nakano, Nakano-ku; ⏰noon-8pm). Other branches include **Shibuya** (B2 fl, Shibuya Beam Bldg, 31-2 Udagawa-chō, Shibuya-ku; ⏰noon-8pm) and one in **Ikebukuro** (Map p298; B1 fl, Lions Mansion Ikebukuro, 3-15-2 Higashi-Ikebukuro, Tōshima-ku; ⏰noon-8pm) that specialises in manga for women.

ELECTRONICS SHOPPING IN AKIHABARA

Akihabara's main and back streets clang, buzz, whir, flash and blare with big-box electronics retailers – Ishimaru Denki, Laox, Onoden, Sato Musen, Yamagiwa and Yodobashi Akiba among them – selling famous name brands. Before you buy, though, note that many items are programmed for use in Japan and may not work properly elsewhere. Some stores have departments with items intended for export; make sure the voltage and plugs match what you use at home.

AKIHABARA RADIO KAIKAN   MANGA, ANIME

Map p298 (秋葉原ラジオ会館; ☎3253-1030; 1-15-6 Sotokanda, Chiyoda-ku; ⊙11am-8pm; ⊠JR Yamanote Line to Akihabara, Electronic Town exit) Despite its name, Radio Kaikan has nothing to do with radios and everything to do with anime. There are more than a dozen shops over eight storeys, selling manga, anime, collectables like models and figurines, fanzines, costumes and gear. Shops include **Kotobukiya** (寿や; 1st & 2nd fl), **K-Books** (Kブックス; 3rd fl) and **Kayōdō Hobby Lobby** (海洋堂ホビーロビー; 4th fl).

TECHNOLOGIA   ELECTRONICS

Map p298 (テクノロジア; www.technologia.co.jp, in Japanese; 4-12-9 Sotokanda, Chiyoda-ku; ⊙11am-7pm Fri-Wed; ⊠Ginza Line to Suehirochō, exit 2) Are you on the lookout for a bipedal humanoid robot? Or would a talking Hello Kitty do the trick? Technologia is at the forefront of the home robot revolution and specialises in DIY robot kits with numerous motors and dance routines. It also carries a range of electronic components, robot combat DVDs, magazines and other robot goods.

OHYA SHOBŌ   BOOKS

Map p298 (大屋書房; www.ohya-shobo.com; 1-1 Kanda-jimbōchō, Chiyoda-ku; ⊙10am-6pm Mon-Sat; ⊠Hanzōmon Line to Jimbōchō, exit A7) You really could lose yourself for hours in this splendid, musty old bookshop that specialises in *ukiyo-e* (woodblock prints) as well as antique maps. The staff are very friendly and can help you with whatever you're looking for.

YODOBASHI AKIBA   ELECTRONICS

Map p298 (ヨドバシカメラAkiba; www.yodobashi-akiba.com, in Japanese; 1-1 Kanda-hanaokachō, Chiyoda-ku; ⊙9.30am-10pm; ⊠JR Yamanote Line to Akihabara, Shōwa-tōriguchi exit) Although this monster branch of Shinjuku's Yodobashi Camera doesn't have a duty-free section or export goods, it's where many locals shop because it has eight floors of electronics, cameras, toys, appliances and everything else, even restaurants. It's a worthwhile experience even if you're not buying.

AKIHABARA & AROUND SHOPPING

Ueno & Around

Neighbourhood Top Five

1 Persuing samurai swords, woodblock prints, kimono and paintings at the Honkan gallery of **Tokyo National Museum** (p158), the finest collection of Japanese art in the world.

2 Strolling through the cherry groves in the enormous **Ueno-kōen** (Ueno Park; p159), chock-a-block with museums, temples and a zoo.

3 Exploring the old-world lanes, temples and graves of **Yanaka** (p164), where time stands still.

4 Bargaining Shitamachi-style for candy, fruit, luggage and just about anything else in **Ameya Yokochō** (Amey-oko Arcade; p160).

5 Enjoying the hill of blooming plum trees at **Yushima Tenjin** (Yushima Shrine; p160) in February.

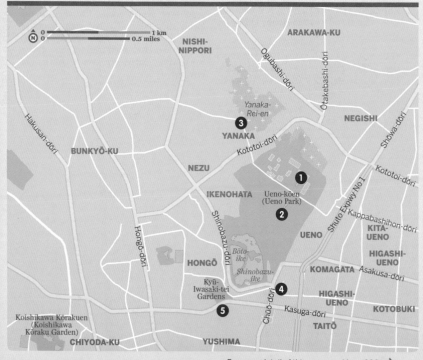

For more detail of this area, see Map p300 ➡

Explore Ueno

Ueno and the northern neighbourhoods of Yanaka, Nezu and Sendagi (aka Yanesen) form a large area that can take up the best part of a day to explore. Start at Ueno-kōen, taking the Ueno Park exit from Ueno Station. Boasting a wealth of museums and shrines, and some phenomenal cherry-blossom viewing, Ueno Park is the perfect antidote to the urban grind. Don't miss the Tokyo National Museum and the National Museum of Western Art, a short walk apart.

Ueno Hill is famous for a last-ditch defence of the Tokugawa shōgunate by an estimated 2000 loyalists in 1868. Devoted to preventing the restoration of the emperor, these adherents stationed themselves at Kanei-ji, a grand temple compound on the hill. They were duly dispatched by the imperial army, and the subsequent Meiji government decreed that Ueno Hill would become one of Tokyo's first parklands.

Although rising real estate prices and recent gentrification have erased most vestiges of the old atmosphere, Ameya Yokochō, to the south of the station, was once the site of the largest postwar black market and still holds true to its proud roots even if the goods are now legit. It's full of Japanese housewives and hawkers haggling over fish and produce, as well as foreign merchants selling everything from Turkish kebabs to Chinese-made bags.

For a far slower vibe, Yanesen, north of Ueno Park, seems stubbornly stuck in the past. This temple-thick area, famed for its stray cats and cemetery, seems more like Kyoto than Tokyo. Walking its gentle hills and lanes is a very refreshing way to spend an afternoon or morning.

Local Life

➡ **Eating** Browsing the cracker and sweet shops along Yanaka Ginza (p164) is perfect for refuelling your meanderings.

➡ **Shopping** Aside from Ameya Yokochō (p160), Ueno has large retailers like Yodobashi Camera and Matsuzakaya Department Store.

➡ **Flower-viewing** Ueno-kōen (p159) is one of the prime spots to party under cherry blossoms in spring. Finding space on the ground, though, can be challenging.

Getting There & Away

➡ **Train** The JR Yamanote Line stops at Ueno, and is the best choice for Ueno-kōen. Okachimachi, one stop south, is more convenient for Ameya Yokochō. Ueno is also a hub with Keisei Line trains to Narita Airport and *shinkansen* (ultra-fast bullet train) services to points north.

➡ **Subway** The Ginza and Hibiya Lines stop at Ueno.

Lonely Planet's Top Tip

Getting from Ueno Park to the Yanesen neighbourhoods is easiest by riding the Megurin community bus (¥100). Get on at the No 2 Tōzai Megurin (東西めぐりん) stop across from the Ueno Park exit at Ueno Station. You can get off at No 9 Yanaka Cemetery (Yanaka Rei-en Iriguchi) or No 12 Yanaka Ginza (Yanaka Ginza Yomise-dōri), which are announced on the bus.

Best Museums

➡ Tokyo National Museum (p159)
➡ National Museum of Western Art (p159)
➡ Shitamachi Museum (p160)
➡ Daimyo Clock Museum (p160)

For reviews, see p159 ➡

Best Places to Eat

➡ Izu-ei Inagi (p161)
➡ Fire House (p161)
➡ Sasa-no-Yuki (p161)

For reviews, see p161 ➡

Best Places to Shop

➡ Ameya Yokochō (p160)
➡ Isetatsu (p165)
➡ Nippori Nuno No Machi (p165)

For reviews, see p161 ➡

UENO & AROUND

TOP SIGHTS **TOKYO NATIONAL MUSEUM (TOKYO KOKURITSU HAKUBUTSUKAN)**

If you visit only one museum in Tokyo, make it this one. The Tokyo National Museum's grand buildings hold the world's largest collection of Japanese art, and you could easily spend many hours perusing the galleries here. The Gallery of Hōryū-ji Treasures presents a stunning collection of Buddhist artwork.

While the Tokyo National Museum (東京国立博物館) has been undergoing quake-resistant construction following the 11 March 2011 earthquake, don't let the renovations throw you off; it's still a very worthwhile sight and has a collection of some 90,000 artefacts. The museum also hosts excellent special exhibitions, as well as four permanent galleries, the most important of which is the **Honkan** (Main Gallery). For an introduction to Japanese art history from Jōmon to Edo in one fell swoop, head to the 2nd floor. Other galleries include ancient pottery, religious sculpture, arms and armour, exquisite lacquerware and calligraphy.

The stunningly designed **Gallery of Hōryū-ji Treasures** displays masks, scrolls and gilt Buddhas from Hōryū-ji (in Nara Prefecture, dating from 607) in a spare, elegant box of a contemporary building (1999) by Taniguchi Yoshio.

Due to reopen around 2013 following earthquake retrofitting, the three-storied **Tōyōkan (Gallery of Eastern Antiquities)** is devoted to the art and architecture of Asia, featuring Chinese Buddhas, Southeast Asian ceramics, and even some Egyptian mummies.

Open in spring and autumn, the **garden** behind the Honkan makes for a pleasant breather. It contains a picturesque pond and five vintage teahouses, as well as gravestones of the Arima samurai clan.

DON'T MISS

➡ Honkan

➡ Gallery of Hōryū-ji Treasures

➡ Tōyōkan (Gallery of Eastern Antiquities)

➡ The garden in spring

PRACTICALITIES

➡ Map p300

➡ ☎3822-1111

➡ www.tnm.jp

➡ 13-9 Ueno-kōen, Taitō-ku

➡ adult/child & senior/university student ¥600/free/¥400 (extra charges for special exhibitions)

➡ ⊙9.30am-5pm Tue-Thu year round, to 8pm Fri (Mar-Dec) & to 6pm Sat & Sun (Mar-Sep)

➡ Ⓡ JR Yamanote Line to Ueno, Ueno-kōen exit

SIGHTS

TOKYO NATIONAL MUSEUM (TOKYO KOKURITSU HAKUBUTSUKAN) MUSEUM

See p158.

UENO-KŌEN (UENO PARK) PARK

Map p300 (上野公園; ⌚5am-11pm; 🚉JR Yamanote Line to Ueno, Ueno-kōen exit) There are two entrances to Tokyo's oldest park. The main one takes you into the museum area, but for the temples, it's better to start at the southern entrance by Keisei Ueno Station – take the Ikenohata exit and turn right. Just around the corner is a flight of stairs leading up into the park.

Situated slightly to your right at the top of the stairs is a statue of **Saigō Takamori**. Fans of the film *The Last Samurai* should note that Katsumoto, the character played by Ken Watanabe, was loosely based on Takamori, a legendary Tokugawa loyalist. Today he remains an exemplar of the samurai spirit in Japan.

Continue along the way, bear to the far left and follow a wide tree-lined path until you reach **Kiyōmizu Kannon-dō**, modelled after the landmark Kiyōmizu-dera (Kiyomizu Temple) in Kyoto. During Ningyō-kuyō, those wishing to conceive a child leave a doll here for the Senjū Kannon (the 1000-armed Buddhist goddess of mercy), and the accumulated dolls are burnt ceremoniously every 25 September.

From the temple, continue down to the narrow road that follows the pond named **Shinobazu-ike**. Passing through a red *torii* (gate), located on an island in the pond, you'll find **Benten-dō**, a memorial to Benten, a patron goddess of the arts. You can hire a **small rowboat** (per hr ¥600) to take out on the water.

Make your way back to the road that follows Shinobazu-ike and turn left. Where the road begins to curve and leaves Shinobazu-ike behind, there is a stair pathway to the right. Follow this path and take the second turn to the left. This will take you into the grounds of **Tōshō-gū** (p185), devoted to the shōgun Tokugawa Ieyasu.

Inside, the shrine is all black lacquerwork and gold leaf. Miraculously, the entire structure has survived all of Tokyo's many disasters, making it one of the few surviving early Edo structures. There's a good view of the 17th-century, five-storey pagoda **Kanei-ji**, now stranded inside Ueno Zoo.

LOCAL KNOWLEDGE

THE BATTLE OF UENO

Attached to northern Ueno-kōen (Ueno Park), the modest temple of Kanei-ji shows few signs that it was once one of Japan's most important Buddhist centres. Built in the 17th century, it was the family temple for the Tokugawa shōgun; its main hall had over 30 rooms and its lands covered about twice the park's area. But when pro-imperial forces led by Saigō Takamori clashed with shōgun loyalists, nearly all of Kanei-ji's buildings burned – Tōshō-gu and a five-storied pagoda survived. The victorious imperial government was keen to turn the area into a medical school, but a Dutch surgeon convinced it that a park was a better idea.

The cherry-blossom viewing spots are impossible to miss – just look for the many revellers under the cherries along the main walkways in the park.

NATIONAL MUSEUM OF WESTERN ART (KOKURITSU SEIYŌ BIJUTSUKAN) MUSEUM

Map p300 (国立西洋美術館; www.nmwa.go.jp; 7-7 Ueno Kōen, Taitō-ku; adult/student ¥420/130, permanent collection free 2nd & 4th Sat; ⌚9.30am-5.30pm Tue-Thu, Sat & Sun, to 8pm Fri; 🚉JR Yamanote Line to Ueno, Ueno-kōen exit) This museum has its roots in French Impressionism, but runs the gamut from medieval Madonna and Child images to 20th-century abstract expressionist painting. All the big names are here, particularly Manet, Rodin, Miró and the Dutch Masters. It also hosts wildly popular temporary exhibits from such stalwarts as the Museo del Prado in Madrid. The main building was designed by Le Corbusier in the late 1950s and is now on Unesco's World Heritage list.

UENO ZOO (UENO DŌBUTSU-EN) ZOO

Map p300 (上野動物園; www.tokyo-zoo.net; 9-83 Ueno-kōen, Taitō-ku; adult/child ¥600/free; ⌚9.30am-5pm Tue-Sun; 🚉JR Yamanote Line to Ueno, Ueno-kōen exit) Japan's oldest zoo was established in 1882, and is home to lions, tigers and bears, but the biggest attractions are two giant pandas that arrived from China in 2011 – Rī Rī and Shin Shin – on a $950,000 per year lease.

Ueno Zoo is larger than you'd think, given the obvious space constraints of Tokyo. Plus, all of the big-name animals from around the globe are well represented. If you're visiting with kids, you can take a ride on the monorail to the petting zoo, where they can mingle with ducks, horses and goats.

NATIONAL SCIENCE MUSEUM (KOKURITSU KAGAKU HAKUBUTSUKAN) MUSEUM

Map p300 (国立科学博物館; www.kahaku. go.jp; 7-20 Ueno-kōen, Taitō-ku; adult/child ¥600/free; ☺9am-5pm Tue-Thu, Sat & Sun, to 8pm Fri; ℝJR Yamanote Line to Ueno, Ueno-kōen exit) This sprawling science museum is packed with delights, especially if you're travelling with children. Dinosaur and other displays are imaginatively presented, and some allowing kids to climb up, down, around and even within. And you can't miss the life-sized replica of a blue whale that soars over the entrance. There is English signage throughout, plus an English-language audio guide (¥300).

SHITAMACHI MUSEUM MUSEUM

Map p300 (下町風俗資料館; www.taitocity.net/taito/shitamachi; 2-1 Ueno-kōen, Taitō-ku; adult/child ¥300/100; ☺9.30am-4.30pm Tue-Sun; ℝJR Yamanote to Ueno, Shinobazu exit) This museum re-creates life in the plebeian quarters of Tokyo during the Meiji and Taishō periods (1868–1926) through an exhibition of typical Shitamachi buildings. Take off your shoes and look inside an old tenement house or around an old sweet shop while soaking up the atmosphere of long-gone Shitamachi. Ask for an English-language leaflet.

CLOSED FOR RENOVATION: ASAKURA CHŌSO MUSEUM

The primary work of sculptor Asakura Fumio (artist name Chōso; 1883–1964) consisted of realistic sculptures of people and cats, and this fanciful house and studio was designed by the artist himself. The building (朝倉彫塑館), along the walking-tour route in this section (p164), was closed for renovation as we went to press and was scheduled to reopen in 2013.

AMEYA YOKOCHŌ (AMEYOKO ARCADE) MARKET

Map p300 (アメヤ横町; ☺10am-8pm; ℝJR Yamanote Line to Okachimachi, north exit) This unabashed shopping street is one of the few areas in which some of the rough-and-readiness of old Shitamachi still lingers. Step into this alley paralleling the JR Yamanote Line tracks, and ritzy, glitzy Tokyo may seem like a distant memory. The gravelly *irasshai* ('Welcome') and *ikaga desu ka?* ('How about buying some?') of fishmongers, fruit and vegetable sellers and clothing vendors, and the healthy smattering of open-air markets, couldn't be further from Ginza or Aoyama.

In the **Ameyoko Center building**, Chinese, Korean and Southeast Asian merchants have set up their own shopping arcade where you'll find exotic cooking spices, fresh seafood, durians and other unusual imported items.

DAIMYO CLOCK MUSEUM (DAIMYŌ TOKEI HAKUBUTSUKAN) MUSEUM

Map p300 (大名時計博物館; 2-1-27 Yanaka, Taito-ku; adult/child ¥300/100; admission varies; ☺10am-4pm Tue-Sun, closed Jul-Sep & 25 Dec-14 Jan; ℝChiyoda Line to Nezu, exit 1) Before the 1860s, the only people who could see the wonderful clocks displayed in this one-room, ramshackle museum were samurai lords. Also known as *wadokei,* these unique timepieces told time according to variable hours named after animals of the Chinese zodiac. It's about a 10-minute walk from Nezu Station.

SCAI THE BATHHOUSE ART GALLERY

Map p300 (Shiraishi Contemporary Art Inc; www.scaithebathhouse.com; 6-1-23 Yanaka, Taito-ku; ☺noon-6pm Tue-Sat; ℝChiyoda Line to Nezu, exit 1) A converted 200-year-old bathhouse, SCAI showcases scores of Japanese and international artists, such as Lee Ufan and Yokoo Tadanori, in its austere vaulted space.

YUSHIMA TENJIN (YUSHIMA SHRINE) SHRINE

Map p300 (湯島天神; Yushima Tenmangū; 3-30-1 Yushima, Bunkyō-ku; ☺6am-8pm; ℝChiyoda Line to Yushima, exit 1) This attractive Shintō shrine traces its lineage all the way back to the 5th century. In the 14th century, the spirit of a renowned scholar was also enshrined here, which leads to its current popularity: it receives countless students in search of academic success. The best time to visit is during the *ume matsuri* (plum festival) of February and early March when dozens of plum trees erupt in white blossoms.

EATING

Holding on to its Shitamachi (low city) style, Ueno's culinary landscape pales in comparison to the bigger players inside the Yamanote (high city). Of course, after a long day of meandering along the halls of Ueno-kōen's many museums, you may want to stick around for dinner.

IZU-EI UNAGI ¥¥

Map p300 (伊豆栄; 2-12-22 Ueno, Taitō-ku; set meals ¥1785-4410; ◎11am-2pm & 5-11pm; 🍴; 🚃JR Yamanote Line to Ueno, Hirokō-ji exit) Izu-ei specialises in *unagi* (eel), which you can take in one of two ways: either in a *bentō* (boxed lunch) that includes tempura and pickled vegetables; or (as *unagi* purists would always insist upon) charcoal-grilled, sauced and then laid on a bed of steamed rice.

FIRE HOUSE HAMBURGERS ¥

off Map p300 (ファイアーハウス; 4-5-10 Hongo, Bunkyō-ku; burgers ¥950-1450; ◎11am-11pm; 🍴; 🚃Ōedo Line to Hongō-sanchōme, exit 3) Around the corner from elite Tokyo University, Fire House serves up some of the tastiest burgers in Tokyo, if not Japan. Grab a seat on some of the antique furniture and pile a fried egg, baked apple or avocado on your beef – or stick to the basics with a perfectly grilled cheeseburger. You'll never look at MOS Burger again.

HANTEI TRADITIONAL ¥¥

Map p300 (はん亭; 2-12-15 Nezu, Bunkyō-ku; set meals lunch ¥3150, set meals dinner from ¥2835; ◎noon-3pm & 5-10pm Tue-Sun; 🚃Chiyoda Line to Nezu, exit 2) In an updated Meiji-era house, delectable skewers of *kushiage* (fried meat, fish and vegetables) are counterbalanced by small, refreshing side dishes. Lunch courses are eight sticks, and dinner courses start with six. Add-on courses available from ¥1365.

SASA-NO-YUKI TOFU ¥¥

Map p300 (笹乃雪; 2-15-10 Negishi, Taitō-ku; dishes ¥350-1000, set meals ¥2600-4500; ◎11.30am-8pm Tue-Sun; 🍴; 🚃JR Yamanote Line to Uguisudani, north exit) Sasa-no-Yuki opened its doors in the Edo period, and continues to serve tofu in elegant arrangements and traditional surroundings; the best seats overlook a tiny garden with a koi pond. Set meals allow you to sample a broad range of tofu delicacies, like *hiryuzu* (tofu dumpling with vegetables), *gomadofu* (sesame tofu), and even *aisukuriimu* (ice cream). Vegetarians take note: many dishes include chicken and fish stock, if not the actual meat itself.

CHALET SWISS MINI SWISS ¥

Map p300 (シャレースイスミニ; 🕾3822-6034; 3-3-12 Nishi-Nippori, Arakawa-ku; dishes ¥350-600, fondues ¥3675-5040; ◎10am-7pm Tue, Wed & Sun, to 9pm Thu-Sat; 🍴; 🚃JR Yamanote Line to Nishi-Nippori, south exit) Nestled among the temples and shrines on a hill, this log house with small rooms upstairs serves fondue (cheese or meat), pasta, sandwich lunch sets, coffee, herbal tea and pastries. If you want chocolate fondue (per person ¥1800, minimum of two), call a few days in advance.

DRINKING

IRIYA PLUS CAFÉ CAFE

off Map p300 (イリヤプラスカフェ; 2-9-10 Iriya, Taitō-ku; set meals ¥1785-4410; ◎11.30am-8pm Tue-Sun; 🚃Hibiya Line to Iriya, exit 4) Once an old electrical-supply shop, this cosy cafe today serves up fair-trade organic coffees, pastas, soups and more. It's a typical example of the reinvigoration of Shitamachi businesses by young entrepreneurs. From the station, walk a block west and then cross the street, going down a smaller street by a Chinese restaurant with yellow-orange awnings. Look for a white cafe sign on your right.

SHOPPING

Aside from branches of Yodobashi Camera and Matsuzakaya Department Store, the main reason to shop in the Ueno Station area is Ameya Yokochō, a place that's bursting with character and a step back in time.

WILL ROBB / LONELY PLANET IMAGES ©

ANTHONY PLUMMER / LONELY PLANET IMAGES ©

1. Tokyo National Museum (p158)
Gusokku-style armour on display at Tokyo's leading historical museum.

2. Ueno-kōen (p159)
Visitors break for refreshment at a teahouse in Ueno Park.

3. Shinobazu-ike (p159)
A family takes to the water in the Shinobazu pond in Ueno-kōen.

4. Benten-dō (p159)
The main hall of Benten-dō temple in Ueno-kōen.

MIGUEL ANGEL MUÑOZ PELLICER / ALAMY ©

START SENDAGI STATION
(EXIT 2)
FINISH UENO-KŌEN
DISTANCE 2KM TO 3KM
DURATION ONE TO 1½ HOURS
(WITHOUT MUSEUM VISITS)

Neighbourhood Walk

Yanaka

This is one of the city's most rewarding strolls, featuring a colourful shopping street, a handful of small Buddhist temples, and a grand cemetery. It's mostly flat, making for a gentle excursion. The neighbourhood is full of older, low-rise residential buildings, temples and alleyways.

Exiting left from Sendagi Station, cross the street and turn right at the post office, bear left, and make a quick right onto 1 **Yanaka Ginza** (谷中ぎんざ) *shōtengai* (shopping street), where decidedly retro shops sell tea, crafts, basketry and everyday wear. Pick up street foods and rice crackers made before your eyes. Note the cat figurines on nearby roofs, and perhaps some real cats on the stairs. Climb the stairs and turn right.

This narrow street is lined with Buddhist temples (feel free to peek in), the under-renovation Asakura Chōso Museum, and 2 **Sandara Kōgei** (さんだら工芸屋), a quaint family-run shop that sells traditional baskets and crafts.

Nearby Buddhist temple 3 **Kannon-ji** (観音寺) has a comforting representation of the bodhisattva Kannon (the deity of mercy). Past it you'll find shops selling Buddhist religious objects. Bear left at the Daily Yamazaki convenience store towards the cemetery.

A stroll through historical and scenic 4 **Yanaka Rei-en** (谷中霊園) feels like old Edo. Wander through rows of ancient tombstones haunted by territorial cats. One point of interest is the family tomb of a branch of the Tokugawa shōgun family.

At the cemetery's far end, 5 **Tennō-ji** (天王寺) belongs to the important Tendai sect. The highlight here is the large Buddha image, cast in 1690, inside a modernist enclosure.

Walk back through the cemetery with Tennō-ji behind you, and bear left when you reach the street. Cross the street at Kototoi-dōri, and at the next light bear to the left. In a couple of blocks you will see the 6 **Tokyo National Museum** grounds on your left; access to Ueno Station is across the street on your right.

ISETATSU
CRAFT

Map p300 (いせ辰; 🕾3823-1453; 2-18-9 Yanaka, Taitō-ku; ⏰10am-6pm; 🚉Chiyoda Line to Sendagi, exit 1) Dating back to 1864, this venerable stationery shop specialises in *chiyogami*: gorgeous, colourful paper made using woodblocks. These decorative creations, incorporating traditional Japanese and modern motifs, are beautiful enough to be framed.

NIPPORI NUNO NO MACHI
(NIPPORI FABRIC TOWN)
FABRICS

Map p300 (日暮里布の街; Nippori Chūō-dōri, Arakawa-ku; ⏰varied; 🚉JR Yamanote Line to Nippori, south exit) If you've got a notion to sew, this stretch of shops east of Nippori Station will hit you like a proverbial bolt. Dozens of shops purvey buttons and brocade, bathrobes and blankets, and used kimono and contemporary wear.

🏃 SPORTS & ACTIVITIES

KŌDŌKAN JUDŌ INSTITUTE
MARTIAL ARTS

off Map p300 (講道館; www.kodokan.org; 1-16-30 Kasuga, Bunkyō-ku; ⏰4.30-8pm Mon-Fri; 🚉Ōedo Line to Kasuga, exits A1 & A2) Students of judō who are looking to keep up their practice while in Tokyo are welcome to stop by in the afternoons for open practice. Visitors are welcome to observe training sessions.

ROKURYU KŌSEN
BATHHOUSE

Map p300 (六龍鉱泉; 3-4-20 Ikenohata, Taitō-ku; admission ¥450; ⏰3.30-11pm Tue-Sun; 🚉Chiyoda Line to Nezu, exit 2) The bubbling amber water here contains minerals said to cure ailments. Ancient leaves that work their way up the pipes into the tub are reputed to be excellent for your skin. The bath is located down a small lane that is next to a shop with a green awning.

UENO & AROUND SPORTS & ACTIVITIES

Asakusa & Sumida River

ASAKUSA | OSHIAGE | RYŌGOKU | KIYOSUMI & FUKAGAWA

Neighbourhood Top Five

1 Entering the Thunder Gate, and walking shop-lined Nakamise-dōri to the great **Sensō-ji** (Sensō Temple; p168), grabbing an *age-manjū* (bean bun) en route.

2 Scaling the world's tallest tower at **Tokyo Sky Tree** (p170) and seeing the capital at your feet.

3 Stepping back in time in Asakusa's old-world **crafts shops** (see boxed text, p178).

4 Heading ringside to watch the big boys slap each other silly in a sumō bout at **Ryōgoku** (p170).

5 Sailing the Sumida-gawa (Sumida River) by **Tokyo Cruise ferryboat** (see boxed text, p73).

For more detail of this area, see Map p302 ➡

Explore Asakusa & Sumida River

Asakusa (ah-*saku*-sah) is where the spirit of old Edo proudly lives, but it takes some old-fashioned footwork to get to know it. Replete with charming shops and restaurants, the district is well suited for walking and can take up a leisurely half-day. The outlying sights across and along the Sumida River, such as Ryōgoku, can take the rest of the day and into the evening.

Begin your journey through the historic Shitamachi district at Asakusa Station on the Ginza Line. Follow the signs to Kaminarimon (Thunder Gate), the magnificent entrance to the Nakamise-dōri shopping arcade leading to Sensō-ji (Sensō Temple). The temple itself and neighbouring Asakusa-jinja (Asakusa Shrine) are surrounded by a web of old-world streets and shopping arcades.

After a meal at one of Asakusa's traditional restaurants, head back towards the Sumida River to catch a Tokyo Cruise ferry heading downstream to the Shimbashi area or Odaiba, or head to Tōbu Asakusa Station and cross the river on the Tōbu Isesaki Line to go to Tokyo Sky Tree. The view from its observation decks is spectacular during winter months and sunsets.

Local Life

➡ **Snacking** Asakusa brims with great bun and cracker shops, many of which make their goodies on site.

➡ **Spectacles** Tokyoites flock to Asakusa for New Year's temple visits, spring festivals and summer fireworks.

➡ **Hanami** Line the banks of the river in Asakusa-kōen park for *hanami* (cherry-blossom viewing) in April.

Getting There & Away

Asakusa

➡ **Train** The Tōbu Isesaki Line stops at Tōbu Asakusa and Tokyo Sky Tree. The Tsukuba Express stops at a different Asakusa Station, west of Sensō-ji.

➡ **Subway** The Ginza Line stops at Asakusa. The Asakusa Line also stops at a separate Asakusa Station south of Sensō-ji.

➡ **Boat** Azuma-bashi is the northern terminus of Tokyo Cruise ferries.

Ryōgoku & Sumida River

➡ **Train** The JR Sōbu Line goes to Ryōgoku.

➡ **Subway** The Ōedo Line connects the Ryōgoku, Kiyosumi and Fukagawa areas via Ryōgoku, Kiyosumi-Shirakawa and Monzen-Nakachō Stations. The Hanzōmon and Tōzai Lines also serve the last two stations, respectively.

Best Places to Eat

➡ Asakusa Imahan (p175)
➡ Daikokuya (p175)
➡ Otafuku (p175)

For reviews, see p175 ➡

Best Places to Drink

➡ Popeye (p177)
➡ Lucite Gallery (p177)
➡ Café Meursault (p177)

For reviews, see p177 ➡

Best Views

➡ Tokyo Sky Tree (p170)
➡ Lucite Gallery (p177)
➡ Tokyo Cruise ferries (p73)

ASAKUSA & SUMIDA RIVER

TOP SIGHTS
SENSŌ-JI (SENSŌ TEMPLE)

Founded over 1000 years before Tokyo got its start, Sensō-ji is the capital's oldest temple and is the spiritual home of its ancestors. Enshrining a sacred image of Kannon (the bodhisattva of compassion), this grand temple stands out for its old-world atmosphere – just metres away is a glimpse of a bygone Japan that is difficult to experience outside places like Kyoto.

DON'T MISS

➡ Nakamise-dōri treats
➡ Temple lights at sunset

PRACTICALITIES

➡ Map p302
➡ 🕿03-3842-0181
➡ www.senso-ji.jp
➡ 2-3-1 Asakusa, Taitō-ku
➡ ⏰dawn-dusk
➡ 🚊Ginza Line to Asakusa, exit 1

Nakamise

Asakusa's raison d'être, Sensō-ji (浅草寺) enshrines a golden statue of Kannon. The statue was miraculously fished out of the nearby Sumida-gawa (Sumida River) by two fishermen in AD 628. In time, a structure was built to house the image, which has remained on the spot through successive reconstructions of the temple – including a complete postwar reconstruction following aerial bombings at the end of WWII.

The temple precinct begins at the majestic **Kaminarimon** (Thunder Gate), which houses a pair of ferocious protective deities: Fūjin, the god of wind, on the right; and Raijin, the god of thunder, on the left.

Straight on through the gate is the bustling shopping street **Nakamise-dōri**. With over 80 stalls, everything is sold here from purses made with obi (kimono sash) fabric to Edo-style crafts and wigs to be worn with kimono. Also along this route are stands specialising in salty, crunchy *sembei* (flavoured rice crackers) and *age-manjū* (deep-fried *anko* – bean paste – buns).

Main Hall

Nakamise-dōri leads north to another gate, **Hōzō-mon**, with fierce guardians you must pass to reach the main temple compound. On the gate's back side, behind these guardians, are a pair of 2500kg, 4.5m-tall *waraji* (straw sandals) crafted for Sensō-ji by some 800 villagers in northern Yamagata prefecture. These are meant to symbolise the Buddha's power, and it's believed that evil spirits will be scared off by the giant footwear.

Off the courtyard stands a 53m-high **five-storey pagoda**, a 1973 reconstruction of a pagoda built by Tokugawa Iemitsu. The current structure is the second-highest pagoda in Japan.

Before the Hondō (Main Hall), smoke winds its way up from a huge incense cauldron around which supplicants stand, wafting the smoke and its scent over their bodies and heads to ensure good health. The Kannon image (a tiny 6cm) is cloistered away from view deep inside the main hall, as is common in Buddhist temples in Japan. Nonetheless, a steady stream of worshippers makes its way to the temple, where they cast coins, pray and bow in a gesture of respect. Do feel free to join in.

The main hall and its gates are **illuminated** every day from sunset until 11pm. The minutes just before the sun sinks make for some of the best pictures of this photogenic sanctuary.

Precincts

Holy though it may be, Sensō-ji and its precincts are often very busy and distinctly not Zen-like, resounding with camera clicks and voices featuring accents from across the country and around the world. To escape the fray, just south of the pagoda is **Dembō-in** (伝法院), a subtemple of Sensō-ji that adjoins the residence of the chief priest. The garden here is said to have been designed in the late 18th century after Katsura-rikyu, the sprawling imperial villa in Kyoto.

The pond in the centre of the garden is in the shape of the kanji character for 'heart', and other elements of classic temple garden design include a stone representing a dock; flowering trees that cascade over the shore; and a *horai* (island) in the far corner, which represents the place of enlightenment. Here you can almost forget that you're in Tokyo, though you'll have to ignore the boxy buildings just outside the garden's confines. Dembō-in is officially closed to the public, but visitors can phone in advance (in Japanese) to arrange a visit. Visits without a reservation are not permitted.

DROP THE NEEDLE

In Sensō-ji's western garden stands Awashimado Hall, home to an unusual ceremony: the *hari-kuyō* (the needle funeral). Annually on 8 February, dozens of kimono-clad women gather with monks to perform last rites for broken or old sewing needles. Kimono makers and seamstresses express their thanks to the needles by sticking them in a block of soft tofu. *Hari-kuyō* reflects ancient animistic Shintō beliefs, and also marks the end of New Year celebrations.

Before the main hall, try your hand at finding your *omikuji* (paper fortune). Drop ¥100 into the slots by the wooden drawers at either side of the approach to the hall; then grab a silver canister and shake it. Extract a stick and note its number (in kanji). Replace the stick, find the matching drawer and withdraw a paper fortune. Celebrate if you see the characters 大吉 (*dai-kichi*, Great Blessing); if you pull out 大凶 (*dai-kyō*, Great Curse), never fear. Just tie the paper on the nearby rack, ask the gods for better luck, and try again!

◉ SIGHTS

◉ Asakusa

SENSŌ-JI (SENSŌ TEMPLE) TEMPLE
See p168.

ASAKUSA-JINJA (ASAKUSA SHRINE) SHRINE
Map p302 (浅草神社; 2-3-1 Asakusa, Taitō-ku;
admission free; ⓇGinza Line to Asakusa, exit 1)
The proximity of this Shintō shrine, behind
Sensō-ji and to the northeast, testifies to
the coexistence of Japan's two major religions. Asakusa-jinja was built in honour of
the brothers who discovered the Kannon
statue and is renowned as a fine example
of an architectural style called *gongen-zukuri*. It's also the epicentre of one of Tokyo's most important festivals, May's Sanja
Matsuri (p26), a three-day extravaganza of
costumed parades, 100 or so lurching *mikoshi* (portable shrines), and stripped-to-the-waist *yakuza* (Japanese mafia) sporting
remarkable tattoos.

**TRADITIONAL CRAFTS MUSEUM
(EDO SHITAMACHI DENTŌ
KŌGEIKAN)** MUSEUM
Map p302 (江戸下町伝統工芸館; 2-22-13 Asakusa, Taitō-ku; Ⓣ10am-8pm; ⓇGinza Line to
Asakusa, exit 1) Gallery Takumi, as this small
hall is also known, is a great place to view
dozens of handmade crafts that still flourish in the heart of Shitamachi. The gallery
on the 2nd floor is crammed with a rotating selection of works by neighbourhood
artists: fans, lanterns, knives, brushes, gold
leaf, precision wood-working and glass,
just for starters. Craft demonstrations take
place most Saturdays and Sundays around
noon. If anything you see strikes your interest, staff can direct you to artisans or shops
selling their work.

**TAIKO DRUM MUSEUM
(TAIKO-KAN)** MUSEUM
Map p302 (太鼓館; 2-1-1 Nishi Asakusa, Taitō-ku;
adult/child ¥300/150; Ⓣ10am-5pm Wed-Sun;
ⓇGinza Line to Tawaramachi, exit 3) More than
600 drums make up this collection, gathered from around the world, though only
about 200 are available at any one time in
the splendidly interactive drum display.
You have free rein to touch or play any instrument that doesn't have a mark – those
with a blue dot should be handled carefully,
while a red dot means 'off limits'.

**KAPPABASHI-DŌRI
(KAPPABASHI STREET)** STREET
off Map p302 (合羽橋通り; ⓇGinza Line to Tawaramachi, exit 3) A 10-minute walk west of
Sensō-ji, Kappabashi-dōri is the country's
largest wholesale restaurant-supply and
kitchenware district. Gourmet accessories
include colourful, patterned *noren* (doorway curtains), pots and pans, restaurant
signage, tableware and a number of bizarre
Japanese kitchen gadgets to make you go
'Hmmm?' The drawcard for overseas visitors is the plastic models of food, such as
you see in restaurant windows throughout
Tokyo. Whether you want steak and chips,
a lurid pizza, a bowl of *rāmen* (noodles in
broth) or a plate of spaghetti bolognaise
complete with an upright fork, you'll find
it here.

◉ Oshiage

TOKYO SKY TREE TOWER
off map p302 (東京スカイツリー; www.tokyo
-skytree.jp; 1 Oshiage, Sumida-ku; admission to
350m/450m observation decks ¥2000/3000;
Ⓣ8am-10pm; ⓇHanzōmon Line to Oshiage) Even
if you don't go in for heights, Tokyo Sky Tree
is an engineering marvel. It opened in May
2012 as the world's tallest tower at 634m,
nearly twice the height of Tokyo Tower
(p82), and is a new landmark for Tokyo and
the surrounding Kantō region.

Its silvery exterior of steel mesh morphs
from a triangle at the base to a circle at
300m. We were given a preview before
Sky Tree opened, and were whisked to the
first observation deck at 350m in less than
a minute. The panorama is spectacular,
though visitors will be best rewarded with
views of Mt Fuji (p198) when it's not hazy
(go in the early mornings, at sunsets, and
in winter months). The 450m observation
deck beneath the digital broadcasting antennas features a circular glass corridor
for vertiginous thrills, while the lower deck
houses restaurants and cafes. The surrounding Sky Tree Town has more dining
options and shops, as well as an **aquarium**.

◉ Ryōgoku

RYŌGOKU KOKUGIKAN SUMŌ STADIUM
(両国国技館; ☎3623-5111; www.sumo.or.jp/
eng/index.html; 1-3-28 Yokoami, Sumida-ku; ad-

WORTH A DETOUR

SHIBAMATA

Star Wars, Harry Potter, Chucky...all of the movies in those series combined wouldn't come close to the whopping 48 films of *Otoko wa Tsurai Yo* (*It's Tough Being a Man*; 1968–95). *Otoko wa Tsurai Yo* starred Tora-san (played by Atsumi Kiyoshi and directed by Yamada Yōji), the fedora-sporting, plaid-blazer-wearing, awkward-in-love bloke who is to Japan what Archie Bunker is to America: a working-class everyman in a suburb just outside the big city. The films were set in Shibamata (柴又), at the eastern edge of Tokyo, making a visit here a must for Tora-san fans. Even if you've never heard of Tora-san, Shibamata's atmospheric streets and workaday feel make it a comfy-cosy throwback to the post-WWII period.

Shibamata's main street, **Taishakuten-sandō** (帝釈天参道), feels like a film set lined with dozens of wood-built shops specialising in *unagi* (eel), *sembei* (flavoured rice crackers) and *kusa-dango* (sweet bean-paste dumplings wrapped in leaves). The street ends at the small temple **Taishakuten** (帝釈天), which was founded in 1629 and boasts exquisite wood carvings.

At the lovely garden **Yamamoto-tei** (山本亭; 7-19-32 Katsushika Shibamata, Katsuhika-ku; admission ¥100; ⊘9am-5pm, closed 3rd Tue of month), you can take a seat inside over a bowl of powdered green tea and a sweet (¥500) and contemplate this Kyoto-style classical garden, which is ranked fourth best in Japan by the *Journal of Japanese Gardening*. Nearby is a **Tora-san Museum** (寅さん記念館; 6-22-19 Shiamata, Katsushika-ku; adult/child/senior ¥500/300/400; ⊘9am-5pm, closed 3rd Tue of the month), which serious fans will want to visit, although there isn't a lot of English signage. Finally, **Yagiri no Watashi** (矢切の渡し; Yagiri Ferryboat; one-way adult/child ¥100/50, ⊘9.30am-4.30pm mid-Mar–Nov & early Jan) has plied the Edo-gawa (Edo River; separating Tokyo and Chiba-ken) since the Edo Period. It's Tokyo's only remaining human-powered ferry.

To reach Shibamata, take the Toei Asakusa Line to Oshiage, and transfer at Keisei-Takasago to the Keisei Kanamachi Line (from Oshiage ¥180, about 20 minutes). Taishakuten-sandō begins about 100m from the station, past the statue of... guess who?

mission ¥2100-14,300; ⊘main bout ceremonies from 3.40pm, ticket office same-day sales 8am-5pm, advance sales 10am-4pm; ☒JR Sōbu Line to Ryōgoku, west exit) Tokyo's *bashō* (sumō wrestling tournaments) take place at this massive stadium in January, May and September. Together, these *bashō* decide who will be the *yokozuna* (grand champion). Unless you're aiming for a big match at a weekend you should be able to secure a ticket: *bashō* take place over 15 days. Upstairs seats are usually available and cost from ¥2100 to ¥8200. Tickets can be purchased up to a month in advance of the tournament at http://sumo.pia.jp or at FamilyMart and Lawson convenience-store ticket machines (although they're all in Japanese), or you can simply turn up on the day of the match. Tickets can also be purchased online from anywhere in the world by visiting www.buysumotickets.com.

The stadium's small **Sumō Museum** (admission free, open to ticket holders only during tournaments; ⊘10am-4.30pm Mon-Fri) displays a rotating selection of interesting artefacts of sumō history and art – mostly woodblock prints.

EDO-TOKYO MUSEUM　　　MUSEUM
(江戸東京博物館; www.edo-tokyo-museum.or.jp; 1-4-1 Yokoami, Sumida-ku; adult/child ¥600/free; ⊘9.30am-5.30pm Tue-Sun, to 7.30pm Sat; ☒JR Sōbu Line to Ryōgoku, west exit) This massive, futuristic institution is by far the best city-history museum we have ever encountered. The permanent collection on the upper floors starts with a reconstruction of half of the bridge at Nihombashi (p64), on either side of which are thorough histories of Edo and Tokyo respectively, mostly with excellent English signage. Highlights include the lodgings of the *daimyō* (domain lords), wood-block printing, the evolution of kabuki and Tokyo's headlong rush to Westernise. There are often special exhibits, but the extent of the permanent collection is usually enough to overwhelm most visitors.

1. Edo-Tokyo Museum (p171)
Traditional boats and architecture on display in Tokyo's city museum.

2. Tokyo Cruise (p73)
A ferry cruises the Sumida River, with the Tokyo Sky Tree (p170) in the background.

3. Ryōgoku Kokugikan (p170)
Sumō wrestler Asashoryu performs the *dohyo iri* (ring-entering) ceremony in Ryōgoku's sumō stadium.

KANTŌ EARTHQUAKE MEMORIAL MUSEUM MUSEUM

(東京都復興記念館; Yokoami-kōen, Sumida-ku; admission free; ⏰9am-4.30pm Tue-Sun; 🚇Ōedo Line to Ryōgoku, exit A1) This museum presents sombre exhibits about the 1923 earthquake that destroyed more than 70% of the city and killed more than 50,000 people. There is a harrowing collection of photographs and paintings of the aftermath. The museum has generalised to cover other disasters to strike Tokyo prefecture, including WWII air raids. The museum sits in **Yokoami-kōen** (Yokoami Park), with other memorial buildings and a garden dedicated to quake victims.

⊙ Kiyosumi & Fukagawa

MUSEUM OF CONTEMPORARY ART, TOKYO ART GALLERY

(東京都現代美術館; MOT; www.mot-art-museum .jp; 4-1-1 Miyoshi, Kōtō-ku; adult/child ¥500/free; ⏰10am-6pm Tue-Sun; 🚇Ōedo Line to Kiyosumi-Shirakawa, exit B2) Dedicated to showcasing postwar artists and designers from Japan and abroad, MOT also holds some 3800 pieces exhibited (on rotation) in its permanent collection gallery. These include works by the likes of David Hockney, Sam Francis and Andy Warhol, as well as Japanese artists such as Yokō Tadanori. The building's stone, steel and wood architecture by Yanagisawa Takahiko is a work of art in its own right – highlights include a sunken garden, V-shaped structural supports and a water-and-stone promenade.

The museum is in Metropolitan Kiba Park. It takes about 10 well-signposted minutes on foot from the subway station.

FUKAGAWA EDO MUSEUM MUSEUM

(深川江戸資料館; 1-3-28 Shirakawa, Kōtō-ku; adult ¥300, student ¥50-200; ⏰9.30am-5pm, closed 2nd & 4th Mon of month; 🚇Ōedo Line to Kiyosumi-Shirakawa, exit A3) This museum recreates a 17th-century Edo neighbourhood, complete with a fire lookout tower, life-sized facades and buildings you can enter. Explore the shops like the greengrocer's and rice shop, or slip off your shoes to enter the tenement homes and handle the daily utensils and children's toys. Be sure to note the Inari shrine, and the *kura* (mud-walled storehouses) where belongings were kept for protection from fire and from Edo's legendary humidity.

KIYOSUMI TEIEN (KIYOSUMI GARDEN) GARDENS

(清澄庭園; 3-3-9 Kiyosumi, Kōtō-ku; adult/child ¥150/free; ⏰9am-5pm; 🚇Ōedo Line to Kiyosumi-Shirakawa, exit A3) This marvellous garden was the first location to be designated a site of scenic beauty by the Tokyo Metropolitan Government – and it's easy to see why. The origins of Kiyosumi Teien date back to 1721 when it was a villa for a *daimyō*. Although the villa itself was destroyed in the 1923 earthquake, the property was purchased by Iwasaki Yatarō, founder of the Mitsubishi Corporation. He was able to use company ships to transport prize stones here from all over Japan – count all 50 (they're numbered). They're set around a pond ringed with Japanese black pine, hydrangeas, Taiwan cherries and other plants designed to bloom at different times of the year.

FUKAGAWA BANSHO GALLERY ART GALLERY

(深川番所ギャラリー; gallery.kawaban.net; 2nd fl, 1-1-1 Tokiwa, Kōtō-ku; ⏰noon-7pm Tue-Sun; 🚇Ōedo Line to Kiyosumi-Shirakawa, exit A1) Housed in an old printing shop, this Zen-like room often hosts mind-bending exhibitions by young Japanese artists such as Soga Takuji, Ishikawa Chisato and Sakai Yoshihito.

FUKAGAWA FUDŌ-DŌ (FUKAGAWA FUDŌ TEMPLE) TEMPLE

(深川不動尊; Fukagawa Fudō Hall; 1-17-13 Tomioka, Kōtō-ku; admission free; 🚇Ōedo Line to Monzen-Nakachō, exit 1) The history of this giant temple dates from 1703, as a subtemple of Shinshō-ji in the city of Narita (one of the head temples of Shingon Buddhism). The large wooden main image is Fudōmyō – a fierce-looking representation of Buddha's determination. Nearby is a trippy prayer corridor with 9500 miniature Fudōmyō crystal statues. The 2nd floor has a gallery depicting all 88 temples of the 1400km pilgrimage route on the island of Shikoku; it is said that offering a prayer at each alcove has the same effect as visiting each temple. One of the best times to visit is around 3pm, when priests read Sutras in a thunder of *taiko* (drums) and fire.

TOMIOKA HACHIMAN-GŪ (TOMIOKA HACHIMAN SHRINE) SHRINE

(富岡八幡宮; 1-20-3 Tomioka, Kōtō-ku; admission free; 🚇Ōedo Line to Monzen-Nakachō, exit 1) Next door to Fukagawa Fudō-dō, this large shrine dates from 1627, and is closely associated with the world of sumō. Around the back of the main building is the *yokozuna* stone, carved with the names of each of these champion wrestlers. Also of note are two treasured *mikoshi*, used in the Fukagawa Hachiman festival in mid-August. The current *mikoshi* date from 1991, and are encrusted with diamonds and rubies – look in the eyes of the phoenix and other birds on top.

A **flea market** takes place here on the 15th and 28th of most months, from around 8am to sunset.

BASHŌ MUSEUM (BASHŌ KINENKAN) MUSEUM

(芭蕉記念館; 1-6-3 Tokiwa, Kōtō-ku; admission ¥100; ⏰9.30am-5pm Tue-Sun; ❻Toei Ōedo Line to Morishita, exit A1) Fukagawa was considered a very remote area of Edo in 1680 when the revered haiku poet Matsuo Bashō arrived here. At this small, plain museum, you can see some scrolls of poetry written by Bashō and those inspired by him, as well as souvenirs of his journeys. There's no English signage, but nonetheless it's a unique opportunity to enter his world. There's a small garden out back, or walk out to the Sumida River, take a left and discover a lookout where you can view the skyscrapers while contemplating Bashō's long-lost Edo.

 EATING

Asakusa

ASAKUSA IMAHAN SHABU-SHABU ¥¥¥

Map p302 (浅草今半; ☎3841-1114; 3-1-12 Nishi-Asakusa, Taitō-ku; lunch courses ¥2100-5250, dinner courses from ¥6300; ⏰11.30am-9.30pm; ⓘ; ❻Ginza Line to Tawaramachi, exit 3) It's fitting that the original branch of Imahan, the city's most famous chain of *shabu-shabu* (sautéed beef) restaurants, is located at the edge of Shitamachi as the eating style here reflects the unpretentious nature of the neighbourhood. Sitting at low tables on the tatami, you can get happy on sake as your meat and seasonal vegetables simmer. Although it's certainly an expensive affair (prices rise with the quality of the meat ordered), a meal at Imahan is the most dignified way to enjoy this revered culinary treat.

DAIKOKUYA TEMPURA ¥

Map p302 (大黒家; 1-38-10 Asakusa, Taitō-ku; mains ¥1500-1950; ⏰11am-8.30pm Mon-Fri, to 9pm Sat; ⓘ; ❻Ginza Line to Asakusa, exit 6) The long queues around the building should give you something of a clue about this much-loved tempura place – even before you catch the unmistakable fragrance wafting from within. Sneak off to the other branch around the corner if the line seems to be putting too much distance between you and your *ebi tendon* (tempura prawns over rice).

KOMAGATA DOJŌ TRADITIONAL ¥

(駒形どぜう; ☎3842-4001; 1-7-12 Komagata, Taitō-ku; set meals ¥1500-1750; ⏰11am-9pm; ⓘ; ❻Ginza Line to Asakusa, exit A2 or A4) The sixth-generation chef running this marvellous restaurant is continuing the tradition of transforming the humble river fish called *dojō* (Japanese loach, which looks something like a miniature eel) into various incarnations: from grilled to miso-simmered, to stewed on your own private hibachi. The open seating around wide, wooden planks heightens the traditional flavour.

SOMETARŌ OKONOMIYAKI ¥

Map p302 (染太郎; 2-2-2 Nishi-Asakusa, Taitō-ku; mains ¥390-880; ⏰noon-10pm; ⓘ; ❻Ginza Line to Tawaramachi, exit 3) Sometarō is a fun and funky place to try *okonomiyaki* (savoury Japanese-style pancakes filled with meat, seafood and vegetables that you cook yourself). This historic, vine-covered house is a friendly spot where the menu includes a how-to guide for even the most culinarily challenged.

OTAFUKU TRADITIONAL ¥

off Map p302 (大多福; www.otafuku.ne.jp, in Japanese; 1-6-2 Senzoku, Taitō-ku; oden ¥150-530; ⏰dinner Tue-Sun; ❻Tsukuba Express Line to Asakusa, exit 1) Celebrating its centenary year in 2015, Otafuku feels like the Japanese grandmother you never had. It specialises in *oden*, whuch is a mixed stew of ingredients such as fish cakes, daikon radish, *konnyaku* (a tuber) and *ginnan* (ginko nuts). There's a useful picture menu, but you can also order an *oden* course (¥5250) as well as à la carte items such as *yakibuta* (grilled pork, ¥1300). Seating is mostly on tatami mats. Look for a shacklike entrance and lantern on the northern side of Kototoi-dōri.

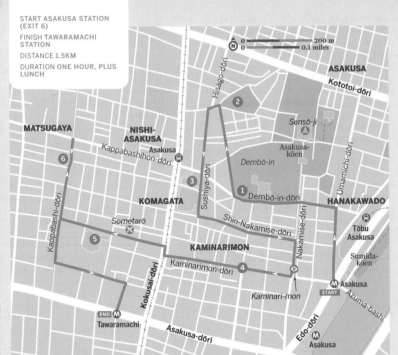

START ASAKUSA STATION (EXIT 6)

FINISH TAWARAMACHI STATION

DISTANCE 1.5KM

DURATION ONE HOUR, PLUS LUNCH

Neighbourhood Walk
Shitamachi

This walk gives you a feel for the flavour of Shitamachi (the 'Low City'), which still looks something like the settings depicted in wood-block prints produced here in Edo times.

Start at Asakusa Station and make your way to the Sensō-ji subtemple ❶ **Chingodō**, which pays tribute to *tanuki* (raccoon dogs that figure in Japanese myth as shape-shifters and pranksters). Entering the temple, notice the *jizō* (statues protecting travellers and children).

Head north to the nostalgic ❷ **Hanayashiki Amusement Park**, which opened in 1853 as a flower garden before it was turned into a freak show. A haunted house attraction allegedly housed a real ghost that still appears on the grounds.

Returning south along Sushiya-dōri, a street with more-modern architecture, you'll arrive at the centrepiece of Asakusa's old cinema district, ❸ **Asakusa Engei Hall**, where *rakugo* (performances of stand-up comedy or long tales) are still held. As

you wander through this historic area, consider that this was once the liveliest of Tokyo's entertainment districts and the preferred haunt of prostitutes, gangsters, novelists and artisans.

Walking to Nakamise-dōri, the approach to Sensō-ji, exit the Kaminarimon and turn right onto ❹ **Kaminarimon-dōri**. It's lined with traditional Japanese restaurants, any of which are perfect for a relaxing lunch break. Sometarō is handy for cheap and quick *okonomiyaki* (savoury pancakes).

To escape the tourist crowds, take time out amid the gleaming gold-leaf columns and screen paintings of the little-visited ❺ **Higashi Hongan-ji**, headquarters of some 300 temples of the Higashi Hongan-ji sect of Jōdō Buddhism.

At the end of the street, ❻ **Kappabashi-dōri** has shop upon shop selling plastic food models, bamboo cooking utensils, batik cushions and even the *aka-chōchin* (red lanterns) that light the back alleys of Tokyo.

Ryōgoku

TOMOEGATA
CHANKONABE ¥¥

(巴潟; 2-17-6 Ryōgoku, Sumida-ku; lunch courses ¥840-4725, chankonabe ¥2940; ⏰lunch & dinner; ⚊JR Sōbu Line to Ryōgoku, west exit) Given the preponderance of sumō stables in Ryōgoku, it's only natural that you'll find restaurants serving the calorie-rich *chankonabe*. Recipes vary for this hearty stew, but count on beef, chicken, pork, fish and possibly seasonal vegetables. Tomoegata has been serving it for generations – go with a group, or eat it all by yourself if you'd like to become the size of a sumō wrestler.

DRINKING & NIGHTLIFE

TOP CHOICE POPEYE
BAR

(ポパイ; www.40beersontap.com; 2-18-7 Ryōgoku, Sumida-ku; ⏰Mon-Sat; ☺; ⚊JR Sōbu Line to Ryōgoku, west exit) The list of beers that Popeye stocks takes about 20 scrolls of a mouse to get through, and manager Aoki Tatsuo boasts the largest selection of Japanese beer in the world – from Echigo Weizen to Hidatakayama Karumina. The happy hour deal (5pm to 8pm) offers select brews like Fujizakura Kōgen with free half-plates of pizza, sausages and other munchables. Popeye also has a 'hopulator' machine that can add extra hops to any beer. There's a convivial, nonsmoking atmosphere here as well as jovial staff who know their suds. From the station's west exit, take a left on the main road and pass under the tracks; take the second left and look for Popeye on the right.

LUCITE GALLERY
CAFE

off Map p302 (ルーサイトギャラリー; http://lucite-gallery.com; 1-28-8 Yanagibashi, Taitō-ku; ⏰irregular closings; ⚊JR Sōbu Line to Asakusa-bashi, east exit) Entering this unique gallery in the former Yanagibashi entertainment district is like stepping back in time. Overlooking the Sumida River, it was once the home of geisha and popular singer Ichimaru. Rotating exhibits by potters and other artists are shown in the downstairs tatami rooms, while the 2nd-floor tearoom (*matcha* – powdered green tea – sets are

¥800) opens to a veranda with views of the Tokyo Sky Tree. It's a five-minute walk east of Asakusa-bashi Station.

CAFÉ MEURSAULT
CAFE, BAR

Map p302 (カフェムルソー; http://cafe-meursault.com; 2-1-5 Kaminarimon, Taitō-ku; ⏰11am-10pm; ⚊Toei Asakusa Line to Asakusa, exit A3) With a large window open to Sumida River, this cake shop with views serves coffee (from ¥630), tea (from ¥840) and lunches such as lemon-herb chicken sandwiches (from ¥1100). You can sip beers (¥630) here at night and watch the ferry boats roll by.

ENTERTAINMENT

ASAKUSA ENGEI HALL
COMEDY

Map p302 (浅草演芸ホール; 1-43-12 Asakusa, Taitō-ku; adult/student/child ¥2500/2000/1100; ⚊Ginza Line to Tawaramachi, exit 3) Asakusa Engei Hall hosts traditional *rakugo* (performances of stand-up comedy or tall tales), all conducted in Japanese. The linguistic confusion is mitigated by lively facial expressions and traditional props (performers use only a hand towel and a folding fan), which help translate comic takes on universal human experiences.

🛍 SHOPPING

TRUNKS-YA
CLOTHING

Map p302 (とらんくすや; www.trunks-ya.com, in Japanese; 1-19-10 Asakusa, Taitō-ku; ⚊Ginza Line to Asakusa, exit 1) This unique upstairs shop in the Kannon-dōri shopping arcade overflows with boxer shorts printed with traditional Japanese motifs ranging from *maneki-neko* (lucky cats) to dragons. The shop's ebullient owner will also sing the virtues of *fundoshi* (traditional cotton loincloths for men), which are just about halfway to going commando.

YOSHITOKU
CRAFT, SOUVENIRS

(吉徳; www.yoshitoku.co.jp, in Japanese; 1-9-14 Asakusa-bashi, Taitō-ku; ⏰9.30am-6pm; ⚊JR Sōbu Line to Asakusa-bashi, east exit) Once known as doll maker to the emperor, Yoshitoku has been crafting and distributing dolls since 1711. The 1st floor is filled with miniatures that depict kabuki actors, *hina* (princess dolls displayed for the Girl's Day

ASAKUSA & SUMIDA RIVER SPORTS & ACTIVITIES

ASAKUSA TRADITIONAL PRODUCTS

Bengara (べんがら; Map p302; www.bengara.com, in Japanese; 1-35-6 Asakusa, Taitō-ku; ⊙closed 3rd Thu monthly; ⊠Ginza Line to Asakusa, exit 1) Sells *noren* (the curtains that hang in front of shop doors). Some *noren* are very artistic, with the spirit of the *mingei* (folk crafts) movement. It's one block east of Nakamise-dōri.

Fujiya (ふじ屋; Map p302; www.asakusa.gr.jp; 2-2-15 Asakusa, Taitō-ku; ⊙Fri-Wed; ⊠Ginza Line to Asakusa, exit 1) Fujiya specialises in *tenugui* (hand-dyed towels) featuring artistic Edo-period designs and humorous scenes. Many are beautiful enough to frame.

Kanesō (かね惣; Map p302; www.kanesoh.com, in Japanese; 1-18-12 Asakusa, Taitō-ku; ⊠Ginza Line to Asakusa, exit 1) This place has been selling knives since the early Meiji period. In a country where knives are serious business, this shop is known as a favourite of the pros.

Miyamoto Unosuke Shoten (宮本卯之助商店; Map p302; www.miyamoto-unosuke.co.jp; 2-1-1 Nishi Asakusa, Taitō-ku; ⊙9am-6pm Thu-Tue; ⊠Ginza Line to Tawaramachi, exit 3) If it's festival products you're after, Miyamoto is one-stop shopping, from *mikoshi* (portable shrines) to drums, clappers and festival masks. It's on the ground floor of the building and downstairs from the Taiko Drum Museum (Taiko-kan; p170).

If there are other crafts you're interested in – and there are dozens more – visit the Traditional Crafts Museum (Edo Shitamachi Dentō Kōgeikan; p170) or check www.asakusa-e.com.

holiday, 3 March), samurai (for Boy's Day, 5 May), geisha and sumō wrestlers in minute detail and exquisite dress. Figures are designed with the serious collector in mind.

KAPPABASHI-DŌRI   HOMEWARES

off Map p302 (合羽橋通り; ⊠Ginza Line to Tawaramachi, exit 3) This street is most famous for its shops selling plastic food models, but Kappabashi-dōri supplies many a Tokyo restaurant in bulk, selling matching sets of chopsticks, uniforms, woven bamboo tempura trays and tiny ceramic *shōyu* (soy sauce) dishes. This makes it the perfect street for stocking up if you're setting up an apartment or seeking small, useful souvenirs.

SPORTS & ACTIVITIES

ASAKUSA KANNON ONSEN   BATHHOUSE

Map p302 (浅草観音温泉; 2-7-26 Asakusa, Taitō-ku; admission ¥700; ⊙6.30am-6pm Fri-Wed; ⊠Tsukuba Express Line to Asakusa, exit 2) The brownish water at this traditional bathhouse is a steamy 40°C. It's near Sensō-ji, and Asakusa's historic ambience makes this a great place for a soul-soothing soak.

JAKOTSU-YU   BATHHOUSE

Map p302 (蛇骨湯; 1-11-11 Asakusa, Taitō-ku; admission ¥450; 1pm-midnight Wed-Mon; ⊠Ginza Line to Tawaramachi, exit 3) Once you've cooked in the hot indoor bath here, you're ready for the real treat: the lovely, lantern-lit, rock-framed *rotenburo* (outdoor bath) that's just outside. The sauna is an extra ¥200.

TOMOZUNA STABLE   SUMŌ

(友綱部屋; www.tomozuna-beya-fansite.biz; 3-1-9 Narihira Sumida-ku; ⊠Hanzōmon Line to Oshiage, exit A2) Established in 1757, the Tomozuna *beya* (training house) is home to former sumo wrestler Kaiō and younger wrestlers. You can watch them butting heads at morning practice; send an email in advance to overseas_visitor@tomozuna-beya.jp. Be sure to follow the conduct rules.

KYŪMEIKAN   MARTIAL ARTS

(久明館; ☎3930-4636; www.kyumeikan.info; 2-1-7 Akatsuka-Shinmachi, Itabashi-ku; per lesson ¥5000; ⊠Yūrakuchō Line to Chikatetsu-Narimasu, main exit) Kyūmeikan dojo welcomes foreign observers as well as practitioners of kendō (wooden-sword) fighting. If you're interested in taking a lesson, phone to book – you can usually reach an English speaker on the phone.

Odaiba & Tokyo Bay

Neighbourhood Top Five

1 Seeing a different side of Tokyo. From the promenades of **Odaiba Kaihin-kōen** (p181) or the terrace of a waterfront restaurant, the city appears as a glittering port rather than tightly woven, endless sprawl.

2 Soaking in the hot spring baths at **Ōedo Onsen Monogatari** (p181), Tokyo's only 'onsen theme park.'

3 Looking into the future at the **National Museum of Emerging Science & Innovation** (p181).

4 Circling the harbour on a pleasure boat, like Tokyo Cruise's **Jicoo The Floating Bar** (p183).

5 Trying out virtual-reality games at the arcade-meets-amusement park **Tokyo Joypolis** (p181).

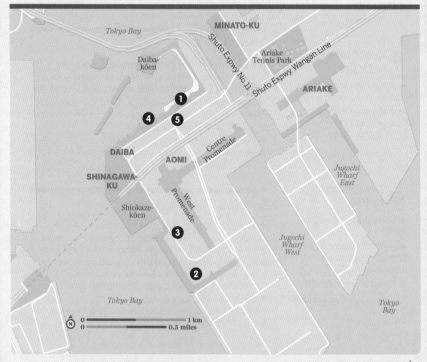

For more detail of this area, see Map p303 ➡

Lonely Planet's Top Tip

The Yurikamome Line – fully automated and run entirely on elevated rails – is an attraction itself. The best seats are right up front. Kids love it, but grown-ups do, too, especially at night. From Shimbashi Station, the train snakes through skyscrapers before crossing the Rainbow Bridge to Odaiba. The fares are a bit higher than for other city trains; unless you're just making a round trip it makes sense to get the ¥800 day pass.

Best Places to Eat

➡ TY Harbor Brewing Company (p182)
➡ Hibiki (p182)
➡ Bills (p182)

For reviews, see p182 ➡

Best Places to Drink

➡ Jicoo The Floating Bar (p183)
➡ Waterline Floating Lounge (p183)
➡ Canteen (p183)

For reviews, see p182 ➡

Best Places to Play

➡ Ōedo Onsen Monogatari (p181)
➡ National Museum of Emerging Science & Innovation (p181)
➡ Tokyo Joypolis (p181)

For reviews, see p181 ➡

Explore Odaiba & Tokyo Bay

Developed mostly in the '90s on reclaimed land, Odaiba is a bubble-era vision of urban planning, where the buildings are large, the streets are wide and the waterfront is the primary attraction. Love or hate it, you'll definitely feel as though you're in an alternative Tokyo.

Not all of the sights here will appeal to everyone, so pick and choose. For most visitors, Ōedo Onsen Monogatari and the nearby National Museum of Emerging Science & Innovation are the big attractions; both could easily take up a half-day or more. There's also interesting, contemporary architecture, notably the Fuji Television Japan Broadcast Centre and Tokyo Big Sight.

The shopping, dining and amusement centres clustered around Tokyo Teleport Station are popular with local teens. They're less interesting for foreign tourists; however, if you're travelling with kids, these all-in-one complexes can be excellent on rainy days.

With pavements and promenades, Odaiba is manageable on foot, though the walk from one end to the other is long. Alternatively, the Yurikamome Line makes a neat and easy circuit of the major sights. Note that Odaiba can get crowded on weekends and school holidays.

Even if you don't make it out here for a day, it's worth visiting in the evening for the views of the bay and the skyline. If you stick to the city centre, it's easy to forget that Tokyo started as a seaside town.

Local Life

➡ **Boat Cruises** Groups of friends and colleagues organise private parties on the bay, particularly during the summer and winter holidays (see boxed text, p183).
➡ **Photo Spot** Waterfront park Odaiba Kaihin-kōen (p181) is popular with amateur photographers working to perfect their city-by-night shot.
➡ **Dining** Weekend brunch on the terrace at TY Harbor Brewing Company (p182) is a favourite ritual for Tokyo's expat community.

Getting There & Away

➡ **Train** The Rinkai Line runs from Osaki through Odaiba to Shin-Kiba, stopping at Tennōzu Isle, Tokyo Teleport and Kokusai Tenjijō Stations. The Yurikamome Line runs from Shimbashi through Odaiba to Toyosu, including stops at Odaiba Kaihin-kōen, Daiba, Telecom Centre, Aomi, Kokusai tenjijō-Seimon and Ariake.
➡ **Boat** Tokyo Cruise (see boxed text, p73) stops at Odaiba Kaihin-kōen (Odaiba Seaside Park), Palette Town and Tokyo Big Sight (Ariake).

👁 SIGHTS

ŌEDO ONSEN MONOGATARI BATHHOUSE

Map p303 (大江戸温泉物語; Ōedo Onsen Story; www.ooedoonsen.jp/higaeri/english/index.html; 2-6-3 Aomi, Kōtō-ku; adult/child from ¥2900/1600, 6pm-2am ¥2000/1600; ⊙11am-8am; 🏛; 🚝Yurikamome Line to Telecom Centre, Rinkai Line to Tokyo Teleport with free shuttle bus) This public bathhouse bills itself as Tokyo's first and only 'onsen theme park'. Just to experience the truly Japanese phenomenon that is an amusement park centred on bathing is reason enough to visit. The baths are filled with real onsen (hot spring) water, pumped from 1400m below Tokyo Bay. There are a variety of styles, including indoor tubs and outdoor *rotenburo* (outdoor baths). Some, like the *iwashioyoku* (hot stone bath) and *tsunaburo* (hot sand bath), cost extra and require reservations.

In the centre of the complex is a lantern-lit re-creation of an old Tokyo downtown area with food stalls and games. Upon entering, visitors change their clothes for colourful *yukata* (light cotton summer kimono) to wear while they stroll around the mock-up town. This area, which also includes an outdoor foot bath, is communal, meaning mixed groups and families can hang out together. The baths and changing area are divided by gender.

There's a surcharge of ¥1700 per person between 2am and 5am. Note that last entry in the morning is 7am (the baths close from 8am to 11am) and that visitors with tattoos will be denied admission.

NATIONAL MUSEUM OF EMERGING SCIENCE & INNOVATION (MIRAIKAN) MUSEUM

Map p303 (未来館; www.miraikan.jst.go.jp; 2-3-6 Aomi, Kōtō-ku; adult/child ¥600/200; ⊙10am-5pm Wed-Mon; 🚝Yurikamome Line to Telecom Centre) *Miraikan* means 'hall of the future', and exhibits here present the science and technology that will shape the years to come. Lots of hands-on displays make this a great place for kids. There are several demonstrations, too, including one of the humanoid robot ASIMO. The popular Gaia dome theatre/planetarium has an English audio option; reserve your seats as soon as you arrive.

TOKYO JOYPOLIS AMUSEMENT PARK

Map p303 (東京ジョイポリス; http://tokyo-joypolis.com; 3rd to 5th fl Decks Tokyo Beach, 1-6-1 Daiba, Minato-ku; adult/child ¥500/300,

all-rides passport ¥3500/3100, passport after 5pm ¥2500/2100; ⊙10am-11pm; 🚝Yurikamome Line to Odaiba Kaihin-kōen) This indoor amusement park has three storeys of virtual reality attractions and action rides. Popular big-kid attractions include the Spin Bullet, an indoor spinning roller coaster, and the snowboard-like, video-enhanced Halfpipe Canyon; there are rides for little ones, too. When this book went to print, Joypolis was closed for renovation, but planed to re-open with more high-tech attractions. Separate admission and individual ride tickets (most from ¥500) are available, but if you plan to go on more than a half-dozen attractions the unlimited 'passport' makes sense.

ODAIBA KAIHIN-KŌEN (ODAIBA SEASIDE PARK) PARK

Map p303 (お台場海浜公園; Odaiba Seaside Park; 1-4-1 Daiba, Minato-ku; ⊙24hr; 🚝Yurikamome Line to Odaiba Kaihin-kōen) From the park's promenades and elevated walkways the city across the bay looks less sinister than it does downtown, pretty even – especially at night. Old-fashioned *yakatabune* (see boxed text, p183) traverse the waterways beyond the landscaped park; decorated with coloured lights at night, they're popular with photographers. There's also a small-scale **Statue of Liberty** – another popular photo-op.

RISŪPIA MUSEUM

Map p303 (リスーピア; risupia.panasonic.co.jp; Panasonic Centre Tokyo, 3-5-1 Ariake, Kōtō-ku; adult/child ¥500/free; ⊙10am-6pm Tue-Sun; 🚝Yurikamome Line to Ariake) In the back of the Panasonic showroom, this museum has hands-on exhibits illustrating maths and science principles. The 1st-floor Quest Gallery is free but the 3rd-floor Discovery Field, which charges admission, is more fun. Look out for the 'prime number' air hockey game that uses numbers instead of pucks. There are explanations throughout in English.

FREE TOYOTA MEGA WEB SHOWROOM

Map p303 (トヨタメガウェブ; www.megaweb.gr.jp; 1-3-12 Aomi, Kōtō-ku; admission free; ⊙11am-9pm; 🚝Yurikamome Line to Aomi, main exit, Rinkai Line to Tokyo Teleport, main exit) Toyota's company showroom, in the Palette Town development, draws car fans big and small. There's actually a lot to do here, including test-driving cars (international licence required) and futuristic 'personal mobility' devices, though some Japanese ability is necessary. The History Garage, showcasing cars from the Golden Age, requires no explanation. Some facilities close early. Next door, don't miss **Dai-kanransha**, one of the world's tallest Ferris wheels; it's as high as the second viewing platform of the Eiffel Tower.

EATING

Odaiba is well known for themed restaurant malls that are fun for a ramble: on the 4th floor of **Decks Tokyo Beach** (Map p303) you'll find **Daiba Ichōme Shōtengai** (台場一丁目商店街; ⓇYurikamome Line to Odaiba Kaihin-kōen), a mock up of postwar Tokyo with food stalls serving nostalgic treats like *age-pan* (sugary fried bread). There's also a '*takoyaki* museum' that serves these octopus-filled dough balls a dozen different ways. Otherwise, its mostly branches of popular Tokyo chains here, including an outpost of **Gonpachi** (Map p303; ⌨3599-4807; 4th fl, Aqua City Odaiba, 1-7-1 Daiba, Minato-ku; dishes ¥250-1350, lunch set ¥800-1050; ⓈⒷ11am-11pm; ⓇYurikamome Line to Daiba, south exit) featuring *kushiyaki* (skewers) and *soba* (buckwheat noodles), enjoyed with sweeping views.

TY HARBOR BREWING COMPANY AMERICAN ¥
(ティーワイハーバーブルワリー; ⌨5479-4555; www.tyharborbrewing.co.jp/ty-harbor; 2-1-3 Higashi Shinagawa, Minato-ku; lunch set ¥1200-1700, dinner mains from ¥1700; Ⓢlunch & dinner Mon-Fri & Sun, dinner Sat; ⊖◨; ⓇRinkai Line to Tennōzu Isle, exit B) In a former warehouse on the waterfront, TY Harbor serves up excellent burgers, steaks and crab cakes with views of canals around Tennōzu Isle. They also brew their own beer on the premises; a rare feat in central Tokyo. Call ahead to book a seat on the terrace.

HIBIKI JAPANESE ¥
Map p303 (響; 6th fl, Aqua City Odaiba, 1-7-1 Daiba, Minato-ku; lunch set ¥1000, dishes ¥750-1700; Ⓢ11am-11pm; ◨; ⓇYurikamome Line to Daiba, south exit) The menu here features seasonal dishes, hearty grilled meats and fresh tofu along with sake, *shōchū* (strong distilled alcohol often made from potatoes) and glittering views across the bay. The lunch set is a good deal and includes a small salad bar; choose your main dish from the samples out th e front.

BILLS INTERNATIONAL ¥¥
Map p303 (ビルズ; 3rd fl, Decks Tokyo Beach, 1-6-1 Daiba, Minato-ku; mains from ¥1300; Ⓢ9am-11pm; ⊖◨◨; ⓇYurikamome Line to Odaiba Kaihin-kōen) Australian chef Bill Granger has done well in Japan – this is his third restaurant. It's an inviting, spacious place and there's a terrace with bay views. The menu includes breakfast classics like ricotta hotcakes and lunch and dinner mains like *wagyu* burgers.

DRINKING & NIGHTLIFE

TOP CHOICE **AGEHA** CLUB
(アゲハ; www.ageha.com; 2-2-10 Shin-Kiba, Kōtō-ku; admission ¥4000; Ⓢ11pm-5am Thu-Sat; ⓇYūrakuchō Line to Shin-Kiba, main exit) This gigantic waterside club, the largest in To-

---

ODAIBA ARCHITECTURE

Odaiba soars from the high to the low. On one hand there is the futuristic, Tange Kenzō-designed **Fuji Television Japan Broadcast Centre** (フジテレビ日本放送センター; Map p303; observatory admission adult/child ¥500/300; Ⓢ10am-6pm), which is a lattice-shaped structure suspending a giant orb. On the other hand there is **Venus Fort** (ヴィーナスフォート; Map p303; Ⓢ10am-9pm), a squat, concrete shopping mall that stages simulated sunrises and sunsets inside its kitschy Italian Renaissance–themed interior. Then there's **Tokyo Big Sight** (東京ビッグサイト; Map p303; www.bigsight.jp/english/index.html), an exhibition hall that looks like four Egyptian pyramids that fell to earth – upside down. It's also where big annual events like the Tokyo Motor Show and Design Festa (p237) take place. None of these structures, however, have captured the hearts of Tokyoites quite like **Rainbow Bridge** (レインボーブリッジ; off Map p303), the 798m suspension bridge that spans the bay; the name was chosen by a public opinion poll.

YAKATABUNE

Those twinkling pleasure boats out on the bay are *yakatabune* and they've been a Tokyo tradition since the days of Edo. They're used for private parties, which usually include lavish meals and plenty of sake and karaoke. If you can pull together at least 15 people, you can arrange a 2½ hour feast aboard a traditional wooden boat through **Komatsuya** (☏3851-2780; www.komatuya.net/annai, in Japanese; per person from ¥10,500), but you'll need a Japanese speaker to make the arrangements.

kyo, rivals any you'd find in LA or Ibiza. Mostly international DJs appear here, with Japanese DJs filling out the mix. Free buses run to the club from the east side of Shibuya Station on Roppongi-dōri; check the website for details and bring photo ID.

JICOO THE FLOATING BAR   COCKTAIL BAR
Map p303 (ジクーフローティングバー; ☏0120-049-490; www.jicoofloatingbar.com; admission ¥2500; ◷8-10.30pm Thu-Sat; ⌘Yurikamome Line to Hinode or Odaiba Kaihin-kōen) Manga (Japanese comics) and anime artist Leiji Matsumoto designed this spaceshiplike cruise ship that doubles as a bar in the

evening. It makes half-hour runs around Odaiba, boarding on the hour at Hinode and the half-hour at Odaiba Kaihin-kōen. The evening-long 'floating pass' usually includes some sort of live music entertainment. Naturally, space is limited; make a reservation online in advance. A clubby vibe makes it popular with 20-somethings.

WATERLINE FLOATING LOUNGE   LOUNGE
(ウォーターラインラウンジ; www.tyharborbrewing.co.jp/waterline; 2-1-3 Higashi Shinagawa, Minato-ku; ◍; ⌘Rinkai Line to Tennōzu Isle, exit B) From the same folks behind the TY Harbor Brewing Company, this bar is actually a barge floating in front of the restaurant. Grab one of the cosy sofas by the glass front and sip one of TY's signature brews (¥800) while pleasure boats cruise by before your eyes.

CANTEEN   CAFE
Map p303 (ザキャンティーン; Soho, 1st fl, 2-7-4 Aomi, Kōtō-ku; ◷9am-10pm Mon-Fri, 10am-6pm Sat; ⌘◍; ⌘Yurikamome Line to Telecom Centre) On the ground floor of an office building, Canteen serves up coffee and lunch specials in a colourful setting, designed by locally famous creative firm Wonderwall. There's also a posh **bar** (◷Mon-Fri) with panoramic views hidden away on the 13th floor in the same building; ask the folks at Canteen for directions to '*za bā*' ('the bar'), if you're dressed for it.

ODAIBA & TOKYO BAY DRINKING & NIGHTLIFE

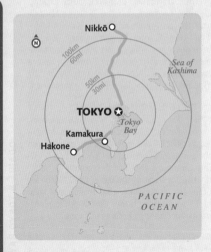

Day Trips from Tokyo

Nikkō p185
Take in the grandeur of old Edo at the spectacular shrines and temples of Nikkō, in the wooded mountains north of Tokyo.

Hakone p189
A centuries-old hot-spring resort, Hakone offers everything you could desire from the Japanese countryside: onsen (hot springs), traditional inns and even a smoking volcano.

Kamakura p193
An ancient feudal capital, seaside Kamakura has a high concentration of temples and shrines, plus the famous Kamakura Daibutsu (Big Buddha) statue.

Mt Fuji p198
Follow the pilgrim trail up Japan's most famous peak for a sunrise to beat all others; or hunt for views of the perfect snow-capped cone from below.

Shimoda p200
This port town witnessed the treaties that opened Japan in 1858. Come for the history, the beaches and the fresh seafood.

NIKKŌ 日光

Explore

Nikkō's premier attraction is its cluster of World Heritage shrines and temples, set amongst towering cedars. Among these is Tōshō-gū, an elaborate shrine rebuilt in 1634 as a memorial to the first Tokugawa shōgun. The major sights, a 30-minute walk (or a five-minute bus ride) from the train station, can be visited on foot in an afternoon; however, it's well worth budgeting more time to explore. In the hills beyond are a smattering of smaller sights, often overlooked by the crowds.

On weekends and holidays, Nikkō can become extremely packed. It's best to visit early on a weekday; alternatively, stay the night to get an early start and use the extra day to explore the mountains, marshlands and onsen (hot springs) of the sprawling Nikkō National Park.

The Best...

➡ **Sight** Tōshō-gū
➡ **Place to Eat** Gyōshintei (p188)
➡ **Hike** Senjōgahara Shizen-kenkyū-rō (p188)

Top Tip

Nikkō is most attractive – and thus most crowded – in October when the hills blaze red. During this time expect serious traffic delays on the way to Chūzen-ji Onsen.

Getting There & Away

Train From Tokyo, Tōbu-Nikkō Line trains leave from Tōbu Asakusa Station (it's well signposted from the subway). You can usually get last-minute seats on the hourly reserved *tokkyū* (limited-express) trains (¥2720, 110 minutes). *Kaisoku* (rapid) trains (¥1320, 2½ hours, hourly from 6.20am to 4.50pm) require no reservation; be sure to ride in the last two cars (some cars may separate at an intermediate stop). Note that with either train, you may need to change at Shimo-Imaichi.

Bus In front of Nikkō Station, buses leave regularly for the short trip to Shin-kyō, the bus stop for the World Heritage sites (¥190, 5 minutes).

Need to Know

➡ **Area Code** 0288
➡ **Location** 120km north of Tokyo
➡ **Tourist Office** (日光郷土センター; ☎54-2496; www.nikko-jp.org; 591 Gokō-machi; internet access per 15 min ¥50; ⏰9am-5pm)

◉ SIGHTS

Sights are open 8am to 5pm (to 4pm November to March). There's little English signage; however the Tourist Office has plenty of English-language maps and brochures.

TŌSHŌ-GŪ   SHRINE

(東照宮) It took 15,000 artisans two years to turn Tōshō-gū into a fitting memorial for the warlord Tokugawa Ieyasu, laid to rest in a mausoleum behind the shrine.

The entrance to the main shrine is through the *torii* (gate) at **Omote-mon** (表門), protected on either side by deva kings. Just inside are the **Sanjinko** (三神庫; Three Sacred Storehouses). On the upper storey of the last storehouse, look for the imaginative relief carvings of elephants by an artist who had apparently never seen the real thing. To the left of the entrance is the **Shinkyūsha** (神厩舎; Sacred Stable), adorned with allegorical relief carvings of monkeys. They include the famous 'hear no evil, see no evil, speak no evil' trio that demonstrate the three principles of Tendai Buddhism.

Pass through another *torii* and climb another flight of stairs, and on the left and right you will see a drum tower and a belfry. To the left of the drum tower is **Honji-dō** (本地堂). This hall is famous for its Nakiryū (Crying Dragon) ceiling painting. Monks demonstrate how the dragon 'roars' (a bit of a stretch) when two sticks are clapped beneath the dragon's mouth, but not elsewhere.

Next comes **Yōmei-mon** (陽明門; Sunset Gate), with gold leaf and intricate carvings of Chinese sages, dragons and other mythical creatures. Worrying that its perfection might arouse the anger and envy of the gods, the creators had the final supporting pillar on the left side placed upside down as a deliberate error intended to express humility.

Nikkō

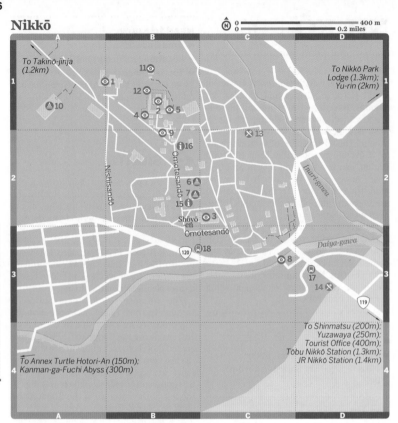

Nikkō

⊙ Sights

⊗ Eating

ⓘ Information

ⓘ Transport

To the left is **Jinyosha** (神輿車), storage the *mikoshi* (portable shrines) used during the May and October festivals. The **Honden** (本殿; Main Hall) and **Haiden** (拝殿; Hall of Worship), with its elaborate ceiling paintings, can also be seen in the enclosure.

Through Yōmei-mon and to the right is **Nemuri-neko** (眠り猫; Sleeping Cat), a small wooden sculpture of a sleeping cat that's famous throughout Japan for its life-like appearance (though admittedly the attraction is lost on some visitors). From here,

Sakashita-mon (坂下門) opens onto a path that climbs up through towering cedars to the appropriately solemn **tomb of Ieyasu** (徳川家康の墓). If you are using the combination ticket (see the boxed text), it will cost an extra ¥520 to see the cat and the tomb.

RINNŌ-JI   TEMPLE

(輪王寺) This Tendai-sect temple was founded 1200 years ago by Shōdō Shōnin, the Buddhist priest who established a hermitage in Nikkō in the 8th century. The **Sanbutsu-dō** (三仏堂; Three-Buddha Hall), constructed from some 360m of zelkova trees, is the main attraction. It's being renovated until 2020, though it's still possible to enter. Inside are three 8m gilded wooden Buddha statues. The central image is Amida Nyorai (one of the primal deities in the Mahayana Buddhist canon), flanked by Senjū (1000-armed Kannon, deity of mercy and compassion) and Batō (a horse-headed Kannon), whose special domain is the animal kingdom. Rinnō-ji's **Hōmotsu-den** (宝物殿; Treasure Hall; admission ¥300) houses some 6000 treasures associated with the temple; the separate admission ticket includes entrance to **Shōyō-en** (逍遥園) strolling garden.

SHIN-KYŌ   BRIDGE

(神橋; crossing fee ¥300) Much-photographed, this red bridge over the Daiya-gawa is located at the sacred spot where Shōdō Shōnin was said to have been carried across the river on the backs of two giant serpents. It's a reconstruction of the 17th-century original.

FUTARASAN-JINJA   SHRINE

(二荒山神社) This structures dates from 1619, making it Nikkō's oldest. It's the protector shrine of Nikkō itself, dedicated to the nearby mountain, Nantai-san (2484m), the mountain's consort, Nyotai-san, and their mountainous progeny, Tarō.

TAIYŪIN-BYŌ   TEMPLE

(大猷院廟) Ieyasu's grandson Iemitsu (1604–51) is enshrined here. Though it possesses many of the same elements as Tōshō-gū (storehouses, drum tower, Chinese-style gates etc), its smaller, more intimate scale and setting in a cryptomeria forest make it very appealing.

TAKINŌ-JINJA   SHRINE

(滝尾神社) In between Futarasan-jinja and Taiyūin-byō a stone-paved path leads to Takinō-jinja, about 25 minutes' walk away. It's rather less grand than the area's main attractions and thus is delightfully less crowded. The stone *torii*, called Unmeshi-no-torii, dates back to 1696. Before entering, it's customary to try your luck tossing three stones through the small hole near the top. Head back down to the fork in the path and take the trail to the left to pass a handful of small temples and the tomb of Shōdō Shōnin before coming out behind Rinnō-ji.

KANMAN-GA-FUCHI ABYSS   PARK

(憾満ガ淵) Another quiet alternative is the 20-minute walk to this collection of *jizō* (the Buddhist protector of travellers and children) statues set along a wooded path. It's said that if you try to count them

DAY TRIPS FROM TOKYO NIKKŌ

DISCOUNT PASSES

Transportation passes are available at the **Tōbu Sightseeing Service Centre** (☎3841-2871; www.tobu.co.jp/foreign/index.html; 7.45am-5pm) in Asakusa Station. Note that you'll have to pay a surcharge (¥1040–1120, one-way) to ride the limited-express trains.

➡ **Nikkō Combination Ticket** (¥1000, two-day validity) Covers entry to Rinnō-ji, Tōshō-gū and Futarasan-jinja; get it at the ticket booths near the sights.

➡ **World Heritage Pass** (adult/child ¥3600/1700, two-day validity) Includes roundtrip *kaisoku* (rapid) train travel between Asakusa, Nikkō and Kinugawa Onsen, buses within Nikkō, and admission to the sites covered in the combination ticket.

➡ **All Nikkō Pass** (adult/child ¥4400/2210, four-day validity) Includes the same deal on trains and buses as the World Heritage Pass, plus transportation to and from Chūzen-ji and Yumoto Onsen, but not admission to the sites.

there and back you'll end up with a different number, hence the nickname *Bake-jizō* (ghost *jizō*). Take a left after passing the Shin-kyō bridge and follow the river for about 800m, crossing another bridge en route.

YU-RIN
ONSEN

(ゆりん; www.syungyotei.com/yurin.htm; 2823 Tokorono; admission ¥800; ⊙2pm-2am) This modern onsen has both an indoor and outdoor bath. It's best at night, when the trees surrounding it are illuminated and drinks are served at the cafe-bar (¥500), though the road that approaches it is rather dark. It's in the foothills east of Tōshō-gū; follow signs to the Nikkō Chirifuri Ice Arena and keep going for another 500m.

 ## EATING

The speciality in Nikkō is *yuba*, the skin that forms when making tofu (really, it's a delicacy!). Note that many restaurants close early or irregularly in Nikkō, especially outside of the peak season.

GYŌSHINTEI
TOFU ¥¥

(尭心亭; ☎0288-53-3751; 2339-1 Sannai; sets from ¥4389; ⊙11.30am-7pm Fri-Wed; ⊜🚲🚗) Splurge here on deluxe spreads of *shōjin ryōri* (Buddist vegetarian cuisine), featur-

ing local bean curd and vegetables served half a dozen delectable ways. The elegant tatami dining room overlooks a carefully tended garden.

SHINMATSU
SHOKUDŌ ¥¥

(新松; 934-1 Chūhatsu-ishimachi; meals ¥2600; ⊙11am-3pm & 5.30pm-11pm Thu-Tue) This small, homey restaurant serves two choices of *bentō* (boxed lunch), *yuba* and *himemasu* (sockeye salmon). In the evening, Shinmatsu morphs into a cosy *izakaya* (Japanese version of a pub/eatery) with an expanded menu (including sashimi and yakitori).

HIPPARI DAKO
YAKITORI ¥

(ひっぱり凧; 1011 Kamihatsu-ishimachi; mains ¥600-850; ⊙11am-7pm Mon-Sat, to 4pm Sun; ⊜🚲🚗) Good, cheap *yakitori* (skewers of grilled chicken) and *yaki-udon* (fried noodles) have made Hippari Dako a favourite travellers' spot for years. The walls are papered with business cards and testimonies to the virtues of hot sake. The *mama-san* (woman who runs drinking, dining and entertainment venues) can also whip up veggie-friendly stir-fries and even kosher noodles (without the customary pork).

YUZAWAYA
TEAHOUSE ¥

(湯沢屋; 946 Kamihatsu-ishimachi; tea sets from ¥450; ⊙11am-5pm; ⊜🚗) This 200-year-old teahouse specialises in *manju* (bean jam buns) and other traditional sweets.

WORTH A DETOUR

CHŪZEN-JI ONSEN & YUMOTO ONSEN

This highland area 11.5km west of Nikkō offers some natural seclusion and striking views of Nantai-san from Chūzen-ji's lake, Chūzenji-ko. The big-ticket attraction is the billowing, 97m-high **Kegon-no-taki** (華厳の滝; Kegon Falls; 2479-2 Chūgūshi; adult/child ¥530/320; ⊙8am-5pm). Take the elevator to a platform to observe the full force of the plunging water. You can also soak in the milky white waters of the onsen at the **Nikkō Lakeside Hotel** (日光レークサイドホテル; 2482 Chūgūshi; admission ¥1000; ⊙12.30-6pm).

From Chūzen-ji Onsen, you can continue on to the quieter hot-springs resort of Yumoto Onsen by bus (¥840, 30 minutes) or by a three-hour hike across picturesque marshland on the **Senjōgahara Shizen-kenkyū-rō** (戦場ヶ原自然研究路; Senjō Plain Nature Study Trail). For the latter option, take a Yumoto-bound bus and get off at Ryūzu-no-taki (竜頭ノ滝), a waterfall that marks the start of the trail.

In Yumoto Onsen, towards the back of the town, the hot-spring temple **Onsen-ji** (温泉寺; adult/child ¥500/300; ⊙9am-4pm mid-Apr–Nov) has a humble bathhouse and a tatami lounge for resting weary muscles.

Buses leave twice an hour from Tōbu Nikkō Station for Chūzen-ji Onsen (¥1100, 45 minutes) and Yumoto Onsen (¥1650, 1½ hours). If the line for the bus looks long, you can try catching the same bus from the stop in front of JR Nikkō Station (100m to the east), usually the lesser-crowded of the two stations.

SLEEPING IN NIKKŌ

The nicer places to stay are in the residential or wooded fringes of town. English is spoken at all of the following.

➔ **Nikkō Park Lodge** (日光パークロッジ; ☎0288-53-1201; www.nikkoparklodge.com; 2828-5 Tokorono; dm/d from ¥2990/7980; ❀@❀) This cute, cosy guesthouse in the wooded hills east of the sights offers a choice of meals (breakfast/dinner from ¥395/650) in its spacious common area and pick-up service from Nikkō Station between 3pm and 5pm.

➔ **Annex Turtle Hotori-An** (アネックスタートルほとり庵; ☎0288-53-3663; www.turtle -nikko.com; 8-28 Takumi-chō; s/d ¥6650/12,700; ❀❀) This popular inn, with mostly tatami rooms, is west of town; ask for a river view when you reserve. The onsen bath looks out into the woods. It's a 15-minute walk along the river from the Sōgō-kaikan-mae bus stop.

➔ **Rindō-no-Ie** (りんどうの家; ☎53-0131; www3.ocn.ne.jp/~garrr; 1462 Tokorono; r per person from ¥3500; ❀@❀) This friendly *minshuku* (the Japanese equivalent of a bed and breakfast) has small but thoughtfully arranged Japanese-style rooms with shared bath, tasty meals (breakfast/dinner ¥700/1800) and a pick-up service from Nikkō Station. From Tobu Nikko Station, head right across the river and look for the sign that marks the turn towards the inn. There's also a useful map on the website.

HAKONE 箱根

Explore

Hakone is a natural wonder, with hot springs and a shimmering lake set among forested peaks. Then add a dizzying variety of transport options: the standard route takes visitors from the Hakone-Yumoto in a narrow-gauge switchback train to Gōra; it's worth stopping off at the excellent Hakone Open Air Museum one stop before. You continue by funicular and ropeway to steaming, sulphurous Ōwakudani before ending with a cruise across the lake in a kitschy pirate ship to Moto-Hakone.

During holidays, Hakone can feel busy and highly packaged. To beat the crowds, plan your trip during the week. You'll need the whole day, especially if you plan to soak in the excellent baths.

The **Hakone Freepass** (adult/child ¥5000/ 1500, valid for two days), available at Odakyū stations, covers the return express train fare from Shinjuku to Hakone-Yumoto, unlimited use of most transport around Hakone and discounts at some attractions.

The Best...

➔ **Sight** Hakone Open Air Museum (p191)
➔ **Tea Break** Amazake-chaya (p192)
➔ **Onsen** Tenzan Tōji-Kyō (p192)

Top Tip

Mt Fuji looks particularly lovely when spotted from the lake; your best chances to see it are in the winter or early in the morning.

Getting There & Away

Train The private Odakyū Line (www. odakyu.jp) runs from Shinjuku Station to Hakone-Yumoto. You can take either the convenient Romance Car (¥2020, 85 minutes) or the *kyūkō* (express) service (¥1150, two hours), although the latter may require a transfer in Odawara. From Hakone-Yumoto, the Hakone-Tōzan line (¥390, 40 minutes) continues on to Gōra.

Bus Hakone Tōzan (which is included in the Hakone Freepass) and Izu Hakone buses run between Hakone-Yumoto, Gōra, Hakone-machi and Moto-Hakone, stopping at all the major attractions in between.

Need to Know

➔ **Area Code** 0460
➔ **Location** 92km southwest of Tokyo
➔ **Tourist Office** (観光案内所; ☎85-8911; www.hakonenavi.jp; 706-35 Yumoto, Hakone-machi; ☺9.30am-5.30pm).

Hakone Region

N

0 ——— 5 km
0 ——— 3 miles

To Odawara
Station (1km)

Odawara-Atsugi
Toll Rd

To Atami
(20km)

Tōkaidō Line

Nebukawa

135

Iriuda

Hakone-
Yumoto

Hakone-Yumoto

6

Tōnozawa

14

Hayu-kawa

Odakyū Line

Tōkaidō Shinkansen Line

Miyanoshita

Ōhiradai

Miyanoshita

Hakone-Tōzan Line

1

7

Hakone Turnpike

Chōkoku-no-Mori

13

Kowakidani

Sengen-yama
(800m)

Fuji-Hakone-Izu
National Park

Old Hakone Hwy

Hakone Shindō Toll Rd

732

Hatajuku

Hatsujuku

Gōra

Gōra

Cable Car

10

Ashi-no-yu

Shukumo-
gawa

Sōun-zan

1

12

5

9

Kami Futago-san
(1090m)

Fuji-Hakone-Izu
National Park

138

Hayu-kawa

Sōun-zan
(1153m)

8

11

Suginamiki
(Cryptomeria Ave)

Moto-Hakone

4

Hakone-machi

Owakudani

3

Komaga-take
(1357m)

Hakone-en

Ashi-no-ko

Ubako

Owakudani-Kojiri
Nature Trail

Kami-yama
(1438m)

Kōmaga-take
Ropeway

Togendai

Trail

Skyline Toll Rd

Ashino-ko

Hakone Region

◎ SIGHTS

HAKONE OPEN-AIR MUSEUM   MUSEUM
(箱根彫刻の森美術館; www.hakone-oam.or.jp;
1121 Ni-no-taira; adult/student/child ¥1600/400/
free; ⊘9am-5pm) This 70,000-sq-metre outdoor sculpture park has an impressive collection of 19th- and 20th-century Japanese
and Western sculptures (including many
works by Henry Moore). The outdoor bronz-
es are particularly lovely in the winter under a light blanket of snow. The museum is
a short walk from Chōkoku-no-Mori Station
on the Hakone-Tōzan Line; Hakone Freepass holders get a ¥200 discount.

ŌWAKUDANI   NATURE RESERVE
(大湧谷) The apocalyptic landscape at
Ōwakudani, which means 'Great Boiling Valley', was formed during a volcanic
eruption roughly 3000 years ago. The
Ōwakudani-Kojiri Nature Trail (大涌谷湖
尻自然探勝歩道; Ōwakudani Kojiri Shizen
Tanshō Hodō) passes by some of the boiling
pits. Here you can buy *onsen tamago* (eggs
boiled in the blackened sulphurous waters).
The cable car from Sōun-zan (included in
the Hakone Freepass) stops midway at
Ōwakudani.

ASHI-NO-KO   LAKE
(芦ノ湖) This lake is touted as the primary
attraction of the Hakone region; however,
it is Mt Fuji, with its snow-clad slopes reflected on the water, that lends the lake its
true poetry. **Hakone Sightseeing Cruise**
(¥970 or use Hakone Freepass, 30 min) ships
traverse the lake from the cable-car terminus in Tōgendai to either Hakone-Machi or
Moto-Hakone.

HAKONE MUSEUM OF ART   MUSEUM
(箱根美術館; www.moaart.or.jp/english/hakone/
index.html; 1300 Gora; adult/child ¥900/free;
⊘9am-4.30pm Fri-Wed Apr-Nov, 9am-4pm Dec-
Mar) Set in a velvety moss garden, this small
museum has a collection of Japanese pottery dating as far back as the Jōmon period
(5000 years ago).

HAKONE SEKISHO   MUSEUM
(箱根関所; Hakone Checkpoint Museum; www.
hakonesekisyo.jp/english/; 1 Hakone-machi;
adult/child ¥500/250; ⊘9am-5pm) This is
a recent reconstruction of the feudal-era
checkpoint, used by the Tokugawa regime
as a means of controlling the movement
of people and ideas in and out of Edo. It's
free to walk through, but you need to buy a
ticket to see the exhibitions.

HAKONE-JINJA   SHRINE
(箱根神社; ⊘9am-4pm) A pleasant stroll
around the lake follows a cedar line path to
this shrine set in a wooded grove, in Moto-
Hakone. Its signature red *torii* (gate) rises
from the lake.

OLD HAKONE HIGHWAY   HIKING
(箱根旧街道) Just up the hill from the lakeside Moto-Hakone bus stop is the entrance
to the stone-paved Old Hakone Highway,
which is part of the Edo-era Tokkaidō
Highway that connected the shōgun's
capital with Kyoto. You can walk back to
Hakone-Yumoto via the trail through the
woods, which will take about 3½ hours.
Along the way you'll pass Amazake-chaya
(see p192) and the small village of **Hatajuku**
(畑宿), where *yosegi* (a local woodcraft) is
produced.

SLEEPING IN HAKONE

Staying at one of Hakone's (often pricey) lodgings is one of the main reasons for visiting. Here are our top choices in different price ranges, all with onsen baths.

➡ **Fuji-Hakone Guest House** (富士箱根ゲストハウス; ☎0460-84-6577; www.fujihakone.com; 912 Sengokuhara; r per person from ¥5400; ➔@＠🖨) Run by a friendly English-speaking family, this popular guesthouse has cosy tatami rooms with shared bath and a wealth of information on area hikes. It's north of the sights, accessible by bus from Hakone-Yumoto or Odawara.

➡ **Fukuzumirō** (福住楼; ☎85-5301; www.fukuzumi-ro.com; fax 85-5911; 74 Tōnozawa; r per person with 2 meals from ¥18,000) No two rooms are alike at this 100-year-old inn, though all have exquisite original woodwork and river or garden views. Note that there are no private facilities.

➡ **Fujiya Hotel** (富士屋ホテル; ☎0460-82-2211; www.fujiyahotel.jp; 359 Miyanoshita; d from ¥19,830) Famous as one of the first Western-style hotels in the country, Fujiya Hotel (1878) shows its age, but that's part of the charm. Foreign travellers should enquire about the weekday special of roughly US$135 for a twin room (you pay the equivalent in yen).

ONSEN

Hakone has seven distinct onsen towns, all with bathing options galore. Ask at the Tourist Information Centre for a list of onsen hotels and ryokan that allow day visitors (typical admission fee is ¥1000)

TENZAN TŌJI-KYŌ   MODERN ONSEN

(天山; 208 Yumoto-Chaya; admission ¥1200; ⊙9am-10pm) Hakone's best upmarket bathing complex has indoor and outdoor baths of varying temperatures and designs. Take the B Course shuttle bus from Hakone-Yumoto Station (¥100); otherwise, it's a 20-minute walk along the river. It can get crowded on holidays and weekends.

YUNESSUN   MODERN ONSEN

(ユネッサン; www.yunessun.com; 1297 Ni-no-taira; adult weekday/weekend ¥1800/2600, child ¥1300; ⊙9am-7pm) More like an onsen amusement park, Yunessun has baths with roman columns, a red wine *rotenburo* (outdoor bath) and water slides among its attractions. It's family-friendly mixed bathing here and swimsuits are required.

KAPPA TENGOKU   ROTENBURO

(かっぱ天国; 777 Yumoto; admission ¥750; ⊙10am-10pm) This bath is little more than a stone pool with a wooden roof, perched precariously on the hill above the Hakone-Yumoto train station. It's a little seedy, though some would argue that that's part of the appeal. Follow the *chōchin* (lanterns) up the rickety staircase.

EATING & DRINKING

🔝 AMAZAKE-CHAYA   TEAHOUSE ¥

(甘酒茶屋; 395-1 Futoko-yama; drinks & snacks from ¥400; ⊙7am-5.30pm; 🖫) This wonderful thatched-roofed teahouse has been serving naturally sweet *amazake* (warm, fermented rice milk) and seasoned *mochi* (pounded rice) cakes for more than 360 years. If you happen to visit in winter, you can warm yourself around the *irori* (traditional fireplace). Amazake-chaya is about 550m up the Old Tōkaidō Hwy from Moto-Hakone, or take a Hakone-Yumoto bound bus from Moto-Hakone and get off at the Amazake-chaya stop.

GYŌZA CENTER   GYŌZA ¥

(餃子センター; www.gyozacenter.com, in Japanese; 1300 Gōra; mains from ¥735; ⊙lunch & dinner Fri-Wed; ➔🖫) The humble *gyōza* (dumpling) is the undoubted star attraction here. Dumplings play a dozen different roles, from plain pan-fried (*nōmaru*) to boiled in soup with kimchi (kimchi *sui-gyōza*). Gyōza Center is between Gōra and Chōkoku-no-Mori Stations, with an English sign.

MIYAFUJI   SUSHI ¥

(鮨みやふじ; 310 Miyanoshita; meals from ¥1575; ⊙lunch & dinner Wed-Mon; ➔🖋🖫) This friendly sushi shop, a short walk up the hill from the Fujiya Hotel, is known for its *aji-don* (horse mackerel over rice). There are also a variety of sushi rolls on the menu, including vegie options.

KAMAKURA
鎌倉

Explore

Kamakura has dozens of temples and shrines – a legacy of its glory days as the country's first feudal capital (1192–1333). Fortunately for visitors, several of the more important ones form a neat path from Kita-Kamakura Station to Kamakura Stationand are easily visited on foot. The Daibutsu (Big Buddha) and Hase-dera, Kamakura's most famous attractions, lie to the west in Hase, reachable by a short ride on the old-fashioned Enoden Line or a hike through the hills along the Daibutsu Hiking Course (see p195). Get an early start if you plan to do the hike.

For souvenir shopping, head to narrow Komachi-dōri, to the left of Kamakura Station's east exit. Kamakura's beach, Yuigahama, is a sandy stretch with a smattering of eateries and bars frequented by the hippies and surfers who call Kamakura home.

The Best...

→ **Sight** Daibutsu
→ **Place to Eat** Magokoro (p198)
→ **Hike** Daibutsu Hiking Course (p195)

Top Tip

Bikes are perfect for touring Kamakura's temples; get wheels at **Rent-a-Cycle Kurarin** (per hr/day ¥600/1600 ⊘8.30-5pm), outside the station's east exit.

Getting There & Away

Train JR Yokosuka line trains run to Kamakura from Tokyo (¥890, 56 minutes), via Shinagawa (¥690, 46 minutes). The Shōnan Shinjuku line runs from the west side of Tokyo (Shibuya, Shinjuku and Ikebukuro, all ¥890) in about an hour, though some trains require a transfer at Ofuna. The Enoden (Enoshima Dentetsu) Line runs past Hase, where the Daibutsu is, along the coast to Enoshima. The **JR Kamakura-Enoshima Excursion Ticket** (from Tokyo/Yokohama ¥1970/1130) is valid for two days and covers the trip to Kamakura from Tokyo or Yokohama, as well as trains around Kamakura including the Enoshima Enoden Line.

Need to Know

→ **Area Code** 0467
→ **Location** 65km south of Tokyo
→ **Tourist Office** (観光案内所; ☑22-3350; www.city.kamakura.kanagawa.jp/english/index.html; 1-1-1 Komachi; ⊘9am-5.30pm Apr-Sep, to 5pm Oct-Mar)

◉ SIGHTS

DAIBUTSU   MONUMENT

(鎌倉大仏; Great Buddha; Kōtoku-in, 4-2-28 Hase; adult/child ¥200/100; ⊘8am-5.30pm Apr-Sep, 8am-5pm Oct-Mar) Kamakura's most iconic sight is an 11.4m bronze statue of Amida Buddha ('amitābha' in Sanskrit). Completed in 1252, it's said to have been commissioned by Japan's first shōgun Minamoto no Yoritomo, who set up his capital in Kamakura, after a visit to an even taller Daibutsu in Nara. Once housed in a huge hall, today the statue sits in the open, the hall having been washed away by a tsunami in 1495. For an extra ¥20, you can duck inside the statue to see how the sculptors pieced the 850-tonne statue together. Take the Enoden Enoshima line to Hase Station and walk north for about five minutes, or take the Daibutsu Hiking Course (see p195).

DAY TRIPS FROM TOKYO KAMAKURA

ZEN BUDDHISM

Kamakura's glory days coincided with the spread of Zen Buddhism and many of the temples here belong to Zen sects. Of course their original purpose was training, not sightseeing, and many are still active today. Experience Zen for yourself, with an hour of *zazen* (seated meditation). Kenchō-ji (see p195) has beginner-friendly, public sessions on Friday and Saturday evenings from 5pm to 6pm, though you'll need to enter before the temple closes at 4.30pm and arrive at the hall by 4.45pm. Instruction is in Japanese but you can easily manage by watching and following everyone else.

Kamakura

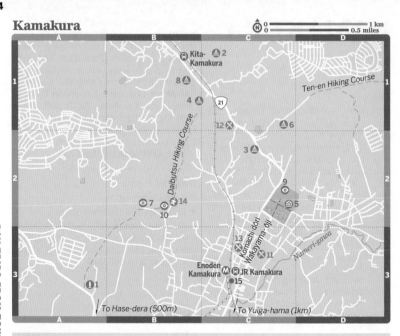

Kamakura

◎ Sights
1 Daibutsu	A3
2 Engaku-ji	C1
3 Ennō-ji	C2
4 Jōchi-ji	B1
5 Kamakura Museum	C2
6 Kenchō-ji	C1
7 Sasuke-inari-jinja	B2
8 Tōkei-ji	B1
9 Tsurugaoka Hachiman-gū	C2
10 Zeniarai-benten	B2

⊗ Eating
11 Bowls Donburi Café	C3
12 Chaya-kado	C1
13 Milk Hall	C3

⊕ Sports & Activities
14 Daibutsu Hiking Course	B2

⊕ Transport
15 Rent-a-Cycle Kurarin	C3

HASE-DERA   TEMPLE

(長谷寺; 3-11-2 Hase; adult/child ¥300/100; ⊘8.30am-5pm Mar-Sep, 8am-4.30pm Oct-Feb) About a 10-minute walk southfrom the Daibutsu, Hase-dera (Jōdo sect) is one of the most popular temples in the Kantō region. The main attraction here is a 9m-high carved wooden *jūichimen* (11-faced) Kannon statue. Kannon (which means 'avalokiteshvara' in Sanskrit) is the bodhisattva of infinite compassion and, along with Jizō, is one of Japan's most popular Buddhist deities. According to legend, the statue washed up on the shore near Kamakura in 736, and the temple was subsequently built to house it.

TSURUGAOKA HACHIMAN-GŪ   SHRINE

(鶴岡八幡宮; 2-1-31 Yukinoshita; exhibition hall ¥200; ⊘9am-4pm) Kamakura's most important shrine is dedicated to Hachiman, the god of war. Japan's first shōgun Minamoto no Yoritomo, who set up his capital in Kamakura, ordered its construction in 1191 and designed the pine-flanked central promenade that leads to the coast. The sprawling grounds are ripe with historical symbolism: the Gempei Pond, bisected by bridges, is said to depict the rift between the Minamoto (Genji) and Taira (Heike) clans.

Behind the pond is the **Kamakura Museum** (鎌倉国宝館; Kamakura Kokuhōkan; 2-1-1 Yukinoshita; admission ¥300; ⊘9am-4.30pm

Tue-Sun), housing remarkable Buddhist sculptures from the 12th to 16th centuries.

ENGAKU-JI   TEMPLE

(円覚寺; 453 Yamanouchi; adult/child ¥300/100; ☻8am-5pm Apr-Oct, 8am-4pm Nov-Mar) One of the five major Rinzai Zen temples in Kamakura, Engaku-ji was founded in 1282, as a place where Zen monks might pray for soldiers who lost their lives defending Japan against Kublai Khan. Engaku-ji remains an important temple, and a number of notable priests have trained here. All of the temple structures have been rebuilt over the centuries. The Shariden, a Song-style reliquary, is the oldest structure, last rebuilt in the 16th century; it's said to enshrine one of the Buddha's teeth, though it's off-limits to the public.

KENCHŌ-JI   TEMPLE

(建長寺; 8 Yamanouchi; adult/child ¥300/100; ☻8.30am-4.30pm) Dating from 1253, Kenchō-ji is Japan's oldest Zen monastery. The central Butsuden (Buddha hall) was brought piece by piece from Tokyo in 1647. Its Jizō Bosatsu statue, unusual for a Zen temple, reflects the valley's ancient function as an execution ground (Jizō consoles lost souls). There's also a bell cast in 1253 and the juniper grove, believed to have sprouted from seeds brought from China by Kenchō-ji's founder some seven centuries ago.

TŌKEI-JI   TEMPLE

(東慶寺; 1367 Yamanouchi; admission ¥100; ☻8.30am-5pm Mar-Oct, 8.30am-4pm Nov-Feb) For 600 years Tōkei-ji was known as the Divorce Temple, the only place in Japan where abused wives could seek refuge from unhappy marriages. A woman could be officially recognised as divorced after three years as a nun in the temple precincts. Today, there are no nuns; the grave of the last abbess can

be found in the **cemetery**, shrouded by cypress trees. The main object of worship here is a statue of Shaka Nyorai (the Enlightened Buddha), which, according to temple records, dates back the 14th century.

ENNŌ-JI   TEMPLE

(円応寺; 1543 Yamanouchi; admission ¥200; ☻9am-4pm Mar-Nov, 9am-3.30pm Dec-Feb) Ennō-ji is distinguished by its statues depicting the judges of hell holding court inside this small temple. According to the Juo concept of Taoism, which was introduced to Japan from China during the Heian period (794–1185), these 10 judges decide the fate of souls, who, being neither truly good nor truly evil, must be assigned to spend eternity in either heaven or hell. Presiding over them is Emma (Yama), a Hindu deity known as the gruesome king of the infernal regions.

DAIBUTSU HIKING COURSE   HIKING

This 3km wooded trail connects Kita-Kamakura with the Daibutsu in Hase (allow about 1½ hours). The path begins at the steps just up the lane from pretty **Jōchi-ji** (浄智寺; 1402 Yamanouchi; adult/child ¥200/100; ☻9am-4.30pm), a few minutes from Tōkei-ji. Along the course you'll pass **Zeniarai-benten** (銭洗弁天; admission free; ☻8am-5pm), one of Kamakura's most alluring Shintō shrines. A cave-like entrance leads to a clearing where visitors come to bathe their money in natural springs in the name of financial success. From here, continue down the paved road, turning right at the first intersection; walk along a path lined with cryptomeria (cypress) that passes through a succession of *torii* to **Sasuke-inari-jinja** (佐助稲荷神社; admission free; ☻24hr). From here, pick up the path that continues to the Daibutsu. To hike in the opposite direction, follow the road beyond Daibutsu and the trail entrance is on the right, just before a tunnel.

WORTH A DETOUR

ENOSHIMA

A short ride on the Enoden Line from Enoden Kamakura will take you to beachside Enoshima where rocky Enoshima Island is the main attraction. Cross the bridge that begins on the beach and head up the narrow cobblestone lane (or the escalator if you prefer) to **Enoshima-jinja** (江島神社; ☻9am-4pm), a shrine to the sea goddess Benzaiten. The island is a popular date spot, and cliffside restaurants offer sunset views along with local specialties like *sazae* (turban shell). There's a park and some caves, too. During the summer, Enoshima's black sand beach transforms into a sort of Shibuya-by-the-sea, as super-tan teens crowd the sand.

1. Mt Fuji (p198)
The iconic mountain, with the Chureito pagoda in the foreground.

2. Tōshō-gū (p185)
Stone lanterns sit in front of a temple building within this Nikkō shrine.

3. Daibutsu (p193)
The 11.4m bronze Buddha statue in the grounds of Kōtoku-in.

✕ EATING

Vegetarians can eat well in Kamakura: pick up the free, bilingual *Vegetarian Culture Map* at the tourist office. Snackers will love Komachi-dōri, with its vendors and ice cream stands.

🍽 MAGOKORO   VEGETARIAN ¥

(麻心; 2nd fl, 2-8-11 Hase; meals from ¥1000; ⊙lunch & dinner Tue-Sun; 🖉🗐) With eclectic fare like hemp-seed curry and additive-free sake, this organic vegetarian joint is a favourite with the local green crowd. From Hase, walk to the beach and turn left onto the coastal road; you'll see the 2nd-floor picture windows on your left after a few minutes.

BOWLS DONBURI CAFÉ   DONBURI ¥

(鎌倉どんぶりカフェbowls; 2-14-7 Komachi; lunch/dinner from ¥880/1280; ⊙11am-10pm; ⊜@🗐🏠) The humble *donburi* (rice bowl) gets a hip, healthy remake here, with toppings such as seared tuna and avocado. You get a discount if you discover the word *atari* at the bottom of your bowl.

CHAYA-KADO   SOBA ¥

(茶屋かど; 1518 Yamanouchi; mains from ¥900; ⊙10am-5pm) Serving up hot, hearty soup, this humble soba spot is conveniently located on the route from Kita-Kamakura to Kamakura, just before you reach Kenchō-ji. The restaurant may close without notice, and during the low season, may only open for lunch.

MILK HALL   CAFE, BAR ¥

(ミルクホール; 2-3-8 Komachi; dishes from ¥600; ⊙11.30am-10.30pm) This local cafe-scene landmark is also an antiques shop and, by evening, a moody bar. From Kamakura Station, go down Komachi-dōri for two blocks, then take a left and another left down the first alley.

Mt Fuji 富士山

Explore

If you're thinking of climbing Japan's most famous peak (3776m), you're not alone – roughly 300,000 people climb it every year. Even with the crowds, the view from the top at dawn is truly spectacular. Many climbers opt to hike the whole thing at night (*dangan-tozan*; literally 'bullet climb') to arrive at the summit for sunrise; however, you'll find a less-crowded mountain if you start out during the day, stay overnight in a mountain hut and continue early in the morning. You do not want to arrive on the top too long before dawn, as it's likely to be very cold and windy. The official climbing season is from 1 July to 31 August; weekdays see far fewer climbers.

The Best...

→ **Sight** Mt Fuji
→ **Place to Eat** Kosaku (p200)
→ **Challenge** Old Yoshidaguchi Trail (p198)

Top Tip

Weather can make or break your climb (and cloud your view from the top); check the conditions (www.snow-forecast.com/resorts/Mount-Fuji/6day/top) before setting out.

Getting There & Away

Bus From 1 July to 31 August, **Keiō Dentetsu Bus** (☏03-5376-2222; www.highwaybus.com, in Japanese) runs direct buses (¥2600, 2½ hours; reservations necessary) from the Shinjuku Highway Bus Terminal (map p294) to Mt Fuji Fifth Station. The same company runs buses

---

SLEEPING AT MT FUJI

→ **K's House Mt Fuji** (☏83-5556; http://kshouse.jp; 6713-108 Funatsu; dm/d from ¥2500/7800; ⊜@🏠) This clean, modern hostel in Kawaguchi-ko has dorm beds and private Japanese-style rooms, spacious lounge and kitchen facilities and helpful English-speaking staff. Rooms fill up fast during the climbing season.

→ **Fujisan Hotel** (富士山ホテル; ☏22-0237; www.fujisanhotel.com; per person with/without meals from ¥7900/5700) Located at the eighth station on the Yoshida Trail, this mountain hut is popular with foreign climbers and usually has an English speaker on hand.

MT FUJI: KNOW BEFORE YOU GO

Although children and grandparents regularly reach the summit of Fuji-san, this is a serious mountain. It's high enough for altitude sickness, and as on any mountain, the weather can be volatile. You can count on it being close to freezing in the morning, even in summer.

At a minimum, bring clothing appropriate for cold and wet weather, including a hat and gloves. If you're climbing at night, bring a torch (flashlight) or headlamp and spare batteries. Descending the mountain is much harder on the knees than ascending; hiking poles can really help.

From the fifth stations and up, dozens of mountain huts offer hikers simple hot meals and a place to sleep. Though much maligned for their spartan conditions (a blanket on the floor sandwiched between other climbers), they can fill up fast – reservations are recommended (and are essential on weekends). Most huts allow you to rest inside as long as you order something. Camping is not permitted on the mountain.

Authorities strongly caution against climbing outside the regular season, when the weather is highly unpredictable and first-aid stations on the mountain are closed. Many mountain huts on the Yoshida Trail do stay open through mid-September, when conditions may still be good for climbing; none open before late June, when snow still blankets the upper stations.

Outside of the climbing season, check weather conditions carefully before setting out (see www.snow-forecast.com/resorts/Mount-Fuji/6day/top), bring appropriate equipment, do not climb alone, and be prepared to retreat at any time. Once snow or ice is on the mountain, Fuji becomes a very serious and dangerous undertaking and should only be attempted by those with winter mountaineering equipment and plenty of experience. Off-season climbers must register with the local police department; download the form from the Fuji-Yoshida City website and fax it in (www.city.fuji yoshida.yamanashi.jp/div/english/html/index.html; fax 055-224-1180). The website also has an up to date list of mountain huts and contact information.

The Shobunsha Yama-to-kōgen Mt Fuji Map (山と高原地図・富士山; in Japanese), available at major book stores, is the most comprehensive map of the area.

year-round to Kawaguchi-ko (¥1700, 1¾ hours; reservations necessary), also leaving from the Shinjuku Highway Bus Terminal. From roughly mid-April to early December, buses run between Kawaguchi-ko and Mt Fuji Fifth Station (one way/return ¥1500/2000, 50 minutes). The schedule is highly seasonal; call **Fujikyū Yamanashi bus** (☏0555-72-6877) for details. At the height of the climbing season there are buses until 9.15pm – ideal for climbers intending to make an overnight ascent.

Need to Know

➡ **Area Code** 0555

➡ **Location** 110km west of Tokyo

➡ **Tourist Office** (☏24-1236; www. city.fujiyoshida.yamanashi.jp/div/english/ html/index.html; 1842 Shimo-Yoshida, Fujiyoshida-shi; ⊗8.30am-5.15pm Mon-Fri)

 SIGHTS

MT FUJI   HIKING

The mountain is divided into 10 'stations' from base (first station) to summit (10th), but most climbers start from one of the four fifth stations, reachable by road. Climbers coming from Tokyo usually take the **Yoshida Trail** from the Mt Fuji Fifth Station (2305m), because of its direct access from Shinjuku Station. From the fifth stations, allow five to six hours to reach the top and about three hours to descend, plus 1½ hours for circling the crater at the top.

Trails below the fifth stations are now used mainly as short hiking routes, but you might consider the challenging but rewarding 19km hike from base to summit on the historic **Old Yoshidaguchi Trail**, which starts at Fuji Sengen-jinja in the town of Fuji-Yoshida. You can start from the station or take a bus part of the way to Umagaeshi (¥490).

The *Climbing Mt Fuji* brochure, available at the tourist centres at both Mt Fuji and Kawaguchi-ko Stations, is useful.

MT FUJI FIFTH STATION   HIKING

The road to the fifth station from Kawaguchi-ko, on the Fuji Subaru Line, stays open as long as the weather permits (from roughly mid-April to early December). Even when summiting is off-limits, it's still possible to take the bus here just to stand in awesome proximity to the snow-capped peak.

From roughly mid-May to late October, you can hike the flat **Ochūdō** (御中道) trail that hugs the mountain at the tree line; it stretches 4km to **Okuniwa** (奥庭), where you'll have to double back. At either end of the climbing season, check conditions before setting out.

EATING

KOSAKU   NOODLES ¥

(小作; 1638-1 Funatsu; www.kosaku.co.jp, in Japanese; hōtō from ¥1100; ⏰11am-9pm; 📶🚭) Thick, hearty hōtō noodles are Kawaguchi-ko's speciality and this popular barn of a restaurant serves them in cast-iron bowls with a variety of toppings, like pumpkin and wild boar. It's about 1.2km from Kawaguchi-ko station; turn left at the 7-Eleven and then right at the next traffic light, walk down to the second light and make a left, and the restaurant will be on your left.

HŌTŌ FUDŌ   NOODLES ¥

(ほうとう不動; 3631-2 Funatsu, Kawaguchi-ko-machi; hōtō from ¥1050; ⏰11am-7pm) This branch of Hōtō Fudo, another noodle shop, is in front of Kawaguchi-ko Station; it keeps irregular hours and may only be open for lunch.

SHIMODA
伊豆半島

Explore

Considering Shimoda's crucial role in history – it's where the famous Black Ships first landed – it's surprising that the town remains what it was then, a quiet port town. The main sights, a handful of temples and museums, are all within walking distance south of the station.

A neat loop takes you down Mai Mai-dōri, the main drag, to Perry Rd, a narrow lane with picturesque old buildings. From here you can wind back up on the road that hugs the harbor. Pick up an English map at the tourist centre, near the train station.

While the sights can be explored in half a day, you'll likely want more time to visit the beguiling white sand beaches, just a short bus ride either north or south of the city.

The Best...

➡ **Sight** Ryōsen-ji
➡ **Place to Eat** Gorosaya (p202)
➡ **Place to Drink** Tosaya (p202)

ONSEN & BEACHES

The western coast of Izu is rugged and less visited. In **Dōgashima** (30km northwest of Shimoda) you'll find stunning sea views and a teeny tiny cliff-side onsen, the **Sawada Kōen Rotemburo** (沢田公園露天風呂; admission ¥500; ⏰9am-6pm Wed-Mon). Buses to Dōgashima leave from platform 5 in front of Shimoda Station (¥1360, one hour). There's a tourist centre at the Dōgashima bus stop that can give you a map to the onsen; bring your own soap and towel.

If you prefer sand, the beaches in Kisami, just south of Shimoda, are among the best in Japan. **Ōhama** (大浜) has the largest stretch of sand and **Tatado** (多々戸) is popular with surfers. Irōzaki-bound buses (buses 3 and 4; ¥340, 10 minutes) stop at Kisami, from where it's a 10-minute walk to the coast. North of Shimoda, **Shirahama** (白浜; bus 9; ¥320, 10 minutes) isn't bad either – its name means 'white-sand beach'. For young Kantō area surfers it's a popular place to spend the summer (yes, it gets packed). Board and wetsuit rentals are available at Tatado and Shira-hama for about ¥4000 per day.

SLEEPING IN SHIMODA

The tourist office can assist in booking rooms.

➜ **Ōizu Ryokan** (大伊豆旅館; ☏22-0123; 3-3-25 Shimoda; r per person ¥3500) Popular with international travellers, Ōizu has plain but comfy Japanese-style rooms and a two-seater onsen. It's two blocks north of Perry Rd; phone ahead as it sometimes closes on weekdays.

➜ **Yamane Ryokan** (やまね旅館; ☏22-0482; 1-19-15 Shimoda; r per person from ¥4630) Tidy, well-maintained Japanese-style rooms, shared onsen bath and a central location. The owners are very friendly but speak little English. Breakfast is available for ¥1000.

➜ **Ernest House** (アーネストハウス; ☏22-5880; www.ernest-house.com; 1893-1 Kisami; tw from ¥12,600; ♨@☎) A minute's walk from Kisami Ōhama beach, this pension has Western-style rooms, a restaurant (dinner ¥2625) and a youthful vibe. Reservations are recommended and note that rates can double at peak times.

Top Tip

Shimoda is famous for its *kinmedai* (golden eye sea bream); it's available all year, but most prized during the winter months when the fat content is highest.

Getting There & Away

Train Limited express Odoriko *tokkyū* trains leave from Tokyo Station (¥6090, 2¾ hours). You can also take the JR Tokkaidō line to Atami from Tokyo (¥1890, 2 hours) or Shinagawa (¥1890, 1¾ hours) and transfer to a regular Izukyūkō train for Shimoda (¥1890, 1½ hours). Try to catch Izukyū's Resort 21 train, with sideways-facing seats for full-on sea views.

Need to Know

➜ **Area Code** 0558
➜ **Location** 170km south of Tokyo
➜ **Tourist Office** (観光案内所; ☏22-1531; http://shimoda-city.info; 1-1 Sotogaoka; ☺10am-5pm)

◉ SIGHTS

RYŌSEN-JI & CHŌRAKU-JI TEMPLE

(了仙寺・長楽寺) Ryōsen-ji, off of Perry Rd, was the site of the treaty that opened Shimoda, signed by Commodore Perry and representatives of the Tokugawa shōgunate. The temple's **Black Ship Art Gallery** (了仙寺宝物館; Hōmotsukan; 3-12-12 Shimoda; adult/child ¥500/150; ☺8.30am-5pm) displays artefacts relating to Perry, the Black Ships, and Japan as seen through foreign eyes and vice versa. Behind and up the steps from Ryōsen-ji is Chōraku-ji, where a Russo-Japanese treaty was signed in 1854; look for the cemetery and *namako-kabe* (black-and-white lattice patterned) walls.

HŌFUKU-JI TEMPLE

(宝福寺; 1-18-26 Shimoda; admission ¥300; ☺9am-5pm) This temple is chiefly a museum memorialising the life of Okichi, maid (and possibly more) to Townsend Harris, the first American consul in Shimoda. The museum is filled with scenes and artefacts from the various movie adaptations of her life on stage and screen. Okichi's grave is also here, in the far corner of the back garden, next to a faded copper statue. The temple is about halfway down Mai Mai-dōri, on the right.

IZU CRUISE CRUISE

(伊豆クルーズ; 19 Sotogaoka; adult/child ¥1000/500; ☺9am-3.30pm) Replica *kurofune* (Black Ships) run a 20-minute loop around the bay, departing from a dock on the east edge of town approximately every 30 minutes.

SHIMODA ROPEWAY ROPEWAY

(下田ロープウェイ; 1-3-1 Higashi Hongō; return fare adult/child ¥1000/500; ☺9am-5pm) This ropeway skirts up Nesugata-yama (200m), from where there are excellent views of the bay and beyond to the Izu Islands. It's from this position that lookouts kept a wary eye on the approaching Black Ships of US Commodore Matthew Perry.

✖ EATING & DRINKING

TOP
CHOICE GOROSAYA   SEAFOOD ¥

(ごろさや; 1-5-25 Shimoda; sets from ¥1575;
⏰lunch & dinner Fri-Wed; 📷) The seafood here
is fantastic, and comes at a surprisingly
reasonable price. The simmered fish of the
day, usually *kinmedai*, is particularly delicious. All sets come with the restaurant's
signature *isōjiru* soup, made from a dozen
varieties of shellfish; it looks like a tide
pool in a bowl. Take the second left after
the tourist centre and you'll soon see the
entrance, marked by a wooden fish hanging
over the door.

SUSHI TAKE   SUSHI ¥

(寿司竹; 2-4-6 Shimoda; sets ¥1200-2400;
⏰lunch daily, dinner Fri-Wed) This friendly
spot near Perry Rd has good sets of locally
caught fish (*jizakana sushi setto;* ¥1500).
It's two blocks east of Yamane Ryokan;
there's a picture menu and a green-and-
white sign outside.

MUSASHI   UDON ¥

(むさし; 1-13-1 Shimoda; mains from ¥630; ⏰lunch
Wed-Mon) In business since 1915, Musashi
serves hearty comfort food like *kamo na-
beyaki* udon (duck hotpot; ¥1000). Take the
first right after passing the tourist centre
and look for the big badger on your left.

TOSAYA   BAR

(土佐屋; 3-14-30 Shimoda; drinks & snacks from
¥600; 📷📶) One of the oddest mash-ups
we've seen: a traditional residence from the
era of the Black Ships that is now a soul-
music bar. It's actually wicked fun; look
for the lattice-pattern walls and twinkling
lights on Perry Rd.

Sleeping

Tokyo has thousands of places to sleep, and not all of them will cost you an arm and a leg. If you've come here on a budget, you have plenty of options, especially near Asakusa. For more luxurious digs, central neighbourhoods like Ginza, Shinjuku and Akasaka are ideal. Ryokan (traditional Japanese inns) are highly recommended.

Accommodation Styles

BUSINESS HOTELS

A common form of midrange accommodation is the so-called 'business hotel' – usually functional and economical. Geared to the lone traveller on business, it will have pay TV (often used with prepaid cards) a tiny bathroom, and cost from ¥7000 to ¥12,000. Some of the nicer business hotels have large shared baths and saunas. Most accept credit cards.

BOUTIQUE HOTELS

As Tokyo's accommodation becomes more international, boutique hotels are cropping up. Emphasising architecture and design, they usually have fewer than 100 rooms.

CAPSULE HOTELS

Of course they're small, but they're roomy enough to recline in, and each capsule has a bed, reading light, TV and alarm clock. Most are men-only, while others are segregated. Despite the room's size, prices still range from ¥3500 to ¥5000; capsules are also cash only. Many have a well-appointed bath area.

HOSTELS

The good news for budget travellers is that more hostels are opening in Asakusa and elsewhere along the Sumida River. They are usually clean and well managed, and have a mixture of dorms and private rooms. Expect to pay about ¥3200; check their websites.

GAIJIN HOUSES

If you're a budget traveller planning to settle in Tokyo, you might consider landing first at a *gaijin* (foreigner) house while getting your bearings. These are private dwellings that have been partitioned into rooms or apartments and rented out to *gaijin*. See p207.

LUXURY HOTELS

In the top-end bracket, you can expect to find the amenities of deluxe hotels anywhere in the world: satellite TV, high-speed internet access and enough space to properly unwind. The staff speak English, the rooms are spotless and the service is impeccable. In addition, most of Tokyo's luxury hotels have several good restaurants and bars, many of which offer outstanding city views.

RYOKAN

For those travellers who crave a really traditional Japanese experience with tatami (woven-mat floor) rooms and futon (traditional quilt-like mattress) instead of beds, ryokan can certainly provide it. Although the more exclusive establishments can charge upwards of ¥25,000, there are a number of relatively inexpensive ryokan in Tokyo.

Some ryokan offer rooms with private baths, but the communal ones are often designed with 'natural' pools or a window looking onto a garden. Bathing is communal, but sexes are segregated. Make sure you can differentiate between the bathroom signs for men and women.

At traditional ryokan, dinner is usually eaten in the room. Standard dishes include miso soup, *tsukemono* (pickles), *zensai* (hors d'oeuvres), sashimi and perhaps tempura and a stew. Although some ryokan will allow you to pay by credit card, you should always inquire at check-in if you hope to do so.

SLEEPING

NEED TO KNOW

Price Range
Prices reflect the price for one night's accommodation for one person:

➡ ¥¥¥   over ¥16,000
➡ ¥¥   ¥6500 to ¥16,000
➡ ¥   under ¥6500

Tax
A 5% tax applies to room rates in nearly all categories. At high-end places a 3% tax is added to the 10–15% service charge. There's also a per-person tax on rooms over ¥10,000: ¥100 for rooms up to ¥14,999 and ¥200 for rooms ¥15,000+.

Discounts
Rack rates are quoted here, but prices can vary drastically. Most business and high-end hotels offer discounts for reservations made in advance via phone or internet.

Reservations
Book your hotel in advance if possible. For more reviews and recommendations check out our online booking service at hotels.lonelyplanet.com.

Websites
➡ **Jalan** (www.jalan.net) Japan-based site has nationwide listings and English pages.
➡ **JAPANiCAN** (www.japanican.com) Accommodation site run by the JTB group, Japan's largest travel agency.
➡ **Hostelworld** (www.hostelworld.com) Budget-oriented site lists nearly 90 properties for Tokyo.

Lonely Planet's Top Choices

Sawanoya Ryokan (p214) Impeccable service and a budget gem in quiet Yanaka.

Claska (p209) A dream of design, this boutique hotel is one of the city's most stylish.

Ritz-Carlton Tokyo (p207) A gorgeously wrought perch over Roppongi with stunning views.

Park Hyatt Tokyo (p210) Nothing is Lost in Translation at this palatial Shinjuku high-rise.

Hōmeikan (p214) This government-designated cultural gem is an old-fashioned inn of wood, tatami and hospitality.

Best Ryokan

Sukeroku No Yado Sadachiyo (p215)

Ryokan Shigetsu (p215)

Tokyo Ryokan (p215)

Andon Ryokan (p215)

Best Luxury hotels

Mandarin Oriental Tokyo (p206)

ANA Intercontinental Tokyo (p208)

Shangri-La Hotel (p206)

Imperial Hotel (p206)

Best Midrange

Shibuya Granbell Hotel (p209)

Hotel Villa Fontaine Roppongi Annex (p207)

Andon Ryokan (p215)

Ginza Nikkō Hotel (p206)

Best Views

Conrad Hotel (p206)

Cerulean Tower Tōkyū Hotel (p209)

Hotel New Otani (p208)

Best Budget Sleeps

Toco (p214)

Sakura Hotel Jimbōchō (p213)

Anne Hostel (p215)

K's House (p216)

Best Capsule Hotels

Capsule & Sauna Century (p210)

Ladies 501 (p212)

Green Plaza Shinjuku (p212)

Where to Stay

Neighbourhood	For	Against
Marunouchi (Tokyo Station)	Ultra-convenient for all sights and trips to Kyoto (or anywhere in Japan)	Area is mostly businesspeople, non-residential, sky-high prices and very quiet on weekends
Ginza & Tsukiji	Very handy for Ginza's shops and restaurants, as well as early morning visits to the fish market	Congested and few inexpensive options compared to other districts
Roppongi	A wealth of good eating and drinking options, as well as sights	Roppongi can be noisy at night, plus there's an elevated expressway
Ebisu, Meguro & Around	Right on the handy JR Yamanote Line, close to hubs Shibuya and Shinjuku	Not as close to Tokyo's major sights, but within reach of Roppongi
Shibuya & Around	Uberhip kids and street energy, convenient transport links	Youth-centric area has no real adult vibe; extremely crowded; sensory overload
Shinjuku & West Tokyo	Superb transport links for all of Tokyo's big sights, a wealth of food and nightlife options	Very crowded around station area; bureaucrat-centred Nishi-Shinjuku empties on nights and weekends
Iidabashi & Northwest Tokyo	Very central; some quiet options away from noise & traffic, good budget options in Ikebukuro	Ikebukuro has little charm, huge crowds, and is far from major sights
Akihabara & Around	Kanda options are central to big sights and surrounded by easy transport links	Area is mostly for businesspeople and has little charm
Ueno & Around	Ryokans abound; lots of greenery in Ueno Park, a wealth of top museums and other sights	The good ryokan here tend to be isolated and somewhat remote
Asakusa & Sumida River	Atmospheric Shitamachi (low city) neighbourhood, close to Sensō-ji; good budget options	Asakusa is very quiet at night, and is a good 20-minute subway ride from more central areas

SLEEPING

205

🛏 Marunouchi (Tokyo Station)

SHANGRI-LA HOTEL   LUXURY HOTEL ¥¥¥
Map p286 (シャングリ・ラ ホテル東京; ☎6739-7888; www.shangri-la.com; 1-8-3 Marunouchi, Chiyoda-ku; r from ¥53,330;🈂@🈳; 🚋JR Yamanote Line to Tokyo, Yaesu exit) Nestled in the Marunouchi Trust Tower beside Tokyo Station, the beautifully designed 202 rooms of the Shangri-La offer outstanding views of the Nihombashi district, a range of pillow options, rain showers and deep, luxurious bedding. Decor is understated but luxurious and the staff offer impeccable service. The delightful CHI spa is themed on a Tibetan oasis in the sky. You won't want to come back down to earth.

PENINSULA HOTEL   LUXURY HOTEL ¥¥¥
Map p286 (ザ・ペニンシュラ東京; ☎6270-2288; http://tokyo.peninsula.com; 1-8-1 Yūrakuchō, Chiyoda-ku; r from ¥69,300; 🈂@🈳; 🚋JR Yamanote Line to Yūrakuchō, Hibiya exit) One almost gets a feeling of guilty extravagance when sprawling out in the Peninsula's vast rooms (starting at 51 sq metres), which overlook the Imperial Palace and Hibiya Moat and have floor-to-ceiling windows. Latticed caramel woodwork, sumptuous marble bathrooms and a dark central atrium unite in a delicious symphony of design.

MANDARIN ORIENTAL TOKYO   LUXURY HOTEL ¥¥¥
Map p286 (マンダリン オリエンタル 東京; ☎3270-8800; www.mandarinoriental.com/tokyo; 2-1-1 Nihonbashi-muromachi, Chūō-ku; r/ste from ¥73,500/141,750; 🈂@🈳; 🚋Ginza Line to Mitsukoshimae, exit A7) The Mandarin boasts cavernous, exquisitely decorated suites, two Michelin-starred restaurants and a lofty spa from which you can sometimes poke Mt Fuji with your toes. Rooms incorporate kimono weaving designs and glass-walled baths. The highlight here is the atrium lobby and breathtaking views.

MARUNOUCHI HOTEL   LUXURY HOTEL ¥¥¥
Map p286 (丸の内ホテル; ☎3215-2151; www.marunouchi-hotel.co.jp; Oazo Bldg, 1-6-3 Marunouchi, Chiyoda-ku; s/d from ¥23,300/31,385; 🈂@; 🚋JR Yamanote Line to Tokyo, Marunouchi north exit) In the Oazo Building, this swanky hotel deftly synthesises modern conveniences with Japanese style. Rooms have vaulted ceilings and views of Tokyo Station.

YAESU TERMINAL HOTEL   BUSINESS HOTEL ¥¥
Map p286 (八重洲ターミナルホテル; ☎3281-3771; www.yth.jp; 1-5-14 Yaesu, Chūō-ku; s/d ¥11,340/16,590; @; 🚋JR Yamanote Line to Tokyo, Yaesu north exit) This sleek little business hotel on cherry-tree-lined Sakura-dōri has contemporary lines and a minimalist look. Though room sizes are most definitely on the microscopic side, they're decently priced for this neighbourhood and very modern.

🛏 Ginza & Tsukiji

IMPERIAL HOTEL   LUXURY HOTEL ¥¥¥
Map p286 (帝国ホテル; ☎3504-1111; www.imperialhotel.co.jp; 1-1-1 Uchisaiwaichō, Chiyoda-ku; s/d from ¥32,000/37,000; 🈂@; 🚋Hibiya Line to Hibiya, exit A13) The legendary Imperial Hotel's present building is the successor to Frank Lloyd Wright's 1923 masterpiece, and small tributes to Wright can be found in the lobby and elsewhere. Large rooms on the newest Imperial floor have been updated with features such as large-screen plasma TVs and high-speed internet. Service at the Imperial is virtually peerless.

HOTEL SEIYŌ GINZA   LUXURY HOTEL ¥¥¥
Map p286 (ホテル西洋 銀座; ☎3535-1111; www.seiyo-ginza.com; 1-11-2 Ginza, Chūō-ku; r ¥63,525-219,450; 🈂🈸; 🚋Yūrakuchō Line to Ginza-itchōme, exit 7) The Hotel Seiyō Ginza, part of the Leading Hotels of the World, resembles a rambling but homey mansion. Each of the rooms here has a personal butler (with 20 on staff altogether). The rooms are cavernous, though the decor could use an update. For those requiring rarefied isolation, the Seiyō can be a secret hideaway.

GINZA NIKKŌ HOTEL   BUSINESS HOTEL ¥¥
Map p286 (銀座日航ホテル; ☎3571-4911; www.ginza-nikko-hotel.com; 8-4-21 Ginza, Chūō-ku; s/d from ¥8000/11,000; 🈂@; 🚋JR Yamanote Line to Shimbashi) Though this Ginza hotel has been around for some 50 years, it's looking fine and bright after a thorough renovation. The decor is a cut above business-hotel generic, with commodious beds and full bathtubs. Check the website for discounts on late check-ins.

CONRAD HOTEL   LUXURY HOTEL ¥¥¥
Map p286 (コンラッド東京ホテル; ☎6388-8000; www.conradtokyo.co.jp; 1-9-1 Higashi-Shimbashi, Minato-ku; s/d from ¥37,000/76,000; 🈂🈸@🈸; 🚋Ōedo Line to Shiodome) One of the

gigantic, glittery gems of the Shiodome development adjacent to Hama Rikyū Onshiteien, the Conrad Hotel is definitely a new contender for the attention of upmarket travellers looking for that central, super-sophisticated base in Tokyo. The garden or city views are equally spectacular, as are the varnished hardwood interiors and floor-to-ceiling glassed bathrooms.

HOTEL VILLA FONTAINE
SHIODOME   BUSINESS HOTEL ¥¥
Map p286 (ホテルヴィラフォンテーヌ汐留; ☑3569-2220; www.hvf.jp/eng; 1-9-2 Higashi-Shimbashi, Minato-ku; s/d from ¥13,115/14,000; @; ⓇŌedo Line to Shiodome) Cone-shaped lanterns light the high-ceilinged black marble lobby. Sculptural red blobs and flame-themed art on the walls lead to upmarket rooms with internet, TV and partial views of Hama Rikyū Onshi-teien. With breakfast thrown in, this is an excellent deal in one of Tokyo's newest neighbourhoods.

MERCURE HOTEL GINZA
TOKYO   BOUTIQUE HOTEL ¥¥¥
Map p286 (メルキュールホテル銀座; ☑4335-1111; www.mercure.com; 2-9-4 Ginza, Chūo-ku; s/d from ¥18,375/24,150; @; ⓇYūrakuchō Line to Ginza-itchōme, exit 11) This refreshingly designed boutique hotel has chinoiserie prints, floral decor, snazzy red doors and leather chairs. It's a short walk from the department stores.

HOTEL COM'S GINZA   BUSINESS HOTEL ¥¥
Map p286 (ホテルコムズ銀座; ☑3572-4131; www.granvista.co.jp; 8-6-15 Ginza, Chūo-ku; s/d from ¥14,500/25,000; @; ⓇJR Yamanote Line to Shimbashi, Ginza exit) Recently relaunched, the Hotel Com's rooms are presented in mahogany and caramel tones, with special 'Audrey' rooms featuring amenities for women. Restaurants here serve udon noodles, Chinese fare and healthy breakfasts.

🛏 Roppongi

TOP
CHOICE / RITZ-CARLTON
TOKYO   LUXURY HOTEL ¥¥¥
Map p288 (ザ・リッツ・カールトン東京; ☑3423-8000; www.ritzcarlton.com; Tokyo Midtown, 9-7-1 Akasaka, Minato-ku; s/ste from ¥73,500/126,500; ⊖🍴@; ⓇHibiya Line to Roppongi, exit 8) Crowning Tokyo Midtown, the Ritz-Carlton literally begins where other hotels leave off. The lobby – with giant paintings by Sam

LONGER-TERM RENTALS

Renting an apartment in Tokyo can be challenging – expect a big deposit and an unwillingness to rent to foreign tenants. If you plan on staying in Japan for more than a year, it's worth paying the larger deposit to get a bigger place with lower rent. If you're in Tokyo for more than a week or a month, serviced apartments can be more comfortable and affordable than a hotel. Try the following websites:

➡ Tokyo Apartments
(www.tokyoapartments.jp)

➡ Kimi Information Center
(www.kimiwillbe.com)

➡ Sakura House
(www.sakura-house.com)

➡ Oakwood Worldwide
(www.oakwood.com)

Francis and views clear to the Imperial Palace – is on the 45th floor, and capacious rooms go up from there. Concierges can do just about anything, blackout curtains open at the touch of a button, and if you send your shoes for a complimentary shine they return in a lovely wooden box.

GRAND HYATT TOKYO   LUXURY HOTEL ¥¥¥
Map p288 (グランド ハイアット 東京; ☑4333-1234; www.grandhyatttokyo.com; 6-10-3 Roppongi, Minato-ku; s/d from ¥57,750/63,525; @🍴; ⓇHibiya Line to Roppongi, exits 1C & 3) Architecturally open and bright despite its somewhat labyrinthine layout, the Grand Hyatt is warmly and gorgeously chic. Smooth mahogany and natural fabrics give an organic flavour to the rooms, while its Roppongi Hills location imbues it with vibrant energy. Even the bathrooms feature rainshower fixtures and rough-cut stone, continuing a nature-in-architecture motif.

VILLA FONTAINE ROPPONGI
ANNEX   BUSINESS HOTEL ¥¥
Map p288 (ホテルヴィラフォンテーヌ六本木アネックス; ☑3560-5550; www.hvf.jp/eng/roppongi_annex.php; 3-2-7 Roppongi, Minato-ku; s/d from ¥9500/11,000; ⓇNamboku Line to Roppongi-itchōme, exit 1, Hibiya or Toei Ōedo Line to Roppongi, exit 5) Stylish, modern and reasonably priced, the new Roppongi Annex offers 140cm-wide beds, a complimentary buffet breakfast and free LAN access

ALTERNATIVES TO SLEEPING

If you've missed the last train back to your hotel, that ¥3000 in your pocket might be better spent staying out all night than on a taxi ride home. Happily, there's often a nearby manga (comic book) cafe. For around ¥1500 for a 'night pack', you can while away the wee hours watching DVDs, reading manga, surfing the internet or napping in your lounge chair.

Gera Gera (まんが喫茶グラグラ; Map p294; ☎3204-8532; www.geragera.co.jp, in Japanese; 3rd fl, Chūdai Bldg, 1-27-9 Kabukichō, Shinjuku-ku; ◷24hr; ⊞JR Yamanote Line to Shinjuku, east exit)

Gran Cyber Cafe Bagus (バグース; Map p288; ☎5786-2280; www.gcc-bagus.jp, in Japanese; 12th fl, Roi Bldg, 5-5-1 Roppongi, Minato-ku; ◷24hr; ⊞Hibiya Line to Roppongi, exit 3)

Manga Hiroba (まんが広場; Map p292; ☎3770-7747; www.mangahiroba.com, in Japanese; Dōgenzaka Hidenaga Bldg, 2-28-5 Dōgenzaka, Shibuya-ku; ◷24hr; ⊞JR Yamanote Line to Shibuya, Hachikō exit)

if you're lugging a laptop. It's close enough to Roppongi's centre to experience its madness, but far enough away for a quiet sleep.

HOTEL ŌKURA
LUXURY HOTEL ¥¥¥

Map p288 (ホテルオークラ東京; ☎3582-0111; www.okura.com/tokyo; 2-10-4 Toranomon, Minato-ku; s/d from ¥36,750/42,000; @; ⊞Ginza Line to Toranomon, exit 3) The Ōkura is an old-fashioned, elegant standby and the meeting place of Japan's political and business elite. Lovely and lived-in, the 1960s decor and low-lying architecture are matched by personable staff. The beautiful Japanese garden and top-notch restaurants complete the picture.

HOTEL NEW ŌTANI
LUXURY HOTEL ¥¥¥

Map p288 (ホテルニューオータニ; ☎3265-1111; www.newotani.co.jp; 4-1 Kioi-chō, Chiyoda-ku; s/d from ¥31,500/37,800; @🖂; ⊞Ginza Line to Akasaka-mitsuke, exit D) There's a whiff of pretension about the New Ōtani, but it's justified, loaded as it is with large, luxurious rooms, upmarket restaurants, boutiques and gift shops. This landmark has its own art museum and an immaculate 400-year-old garden (p83).

ANA INTERCONTINENTAL TOKYO
LUXURY HOTEL ¥¥¥

Map p288 (ANAインターコンチネンタルホテル東京; ☎3505-1111; www.anaintercontinental-tokyo.jp/e; 1-12-33 Akasaka, Minato-ku; s/d from ¥26,200/36,750; @🖂; ⊞Ginza Line to Tameike-sannō, exit 13) A short walk from Roppongi, the plush 37-storey ANA Intercontinental has large, gorgeously designed rooms with LCD screens and fantastic night views. With an outdoor pool, a small gym and an excellent business centre, this remains a sleek and sophisticated choice. Renovated club floors feature bathroom windows and evening cocktails.

B ROPPONGI
BUSINESS HOTEL ¥¥¥

Map p288 (ザ・ビー六本木; ☎5412-0451; www.theb-hotels.com/the-b-roppongi/en/index.html; 3-9-8 Roppongi, Minato-ku; s/d from ¥18,000/22,000; @; ⊞Hibiya Line to Roppongi, exit 5) The b roppongi has slick, white-brown rooms ranging in size from 10 to 31 sq metres, albeit with small, prefab bathrooms. Atmosphere is business-casual and the location is perfect for Roppongi's nocturnal attractions. A light breakfast is included.

HOTEL AVANSHELL AKASAKA
BUSINESS HOTEL ¥¥

Map p288 (ホテル アバンシェル赤坂; ☎3568-3456; www.avanshell.com, in Japanese; 2-14-14 Akasaka, Minato-ku; s/d from ¥15,750/19,950; ⊜@; ⊞Chiyoda Line to Akasaka, exit 2) The rooms in this beautifully designed 2004 high-rise are laid out under themes such as 'primo', and have zippy decor ranging from black leather couches and puffy white bedspreads to cool green tatami spaces. It's a visually appealing cut above most business hotels.

HOTEL IBIS
BUSINESS HOTEL ¥¥

Map p288 (ホテルアイビス六本木; ☎3403-4411; www.ibis-hotel.com; 7-14-4 Roppongi, Minato-ku; s/d from ¥13,382/16,285; ⊜@; ⊞Hibiya Line to Roppongi, exit 4A) The decor here is uninspiring and utilitarian, but the Ibis is just steps from Roppongi's bars and restaurants. The singles are somewhat cramped, so go for the semidoubles. Light sleepers should request a quiet room not facing the back.

ASIA CENTER OF JAPAN   BUSINESS HOTEL ¥¥
Map p288 (ホテル　アジア会館; ☎3402-6111; www.asiacenter.or.jp; 8-10-32 Akasaka, Minato-ku; s/d from ¥7980/11,130; @; ⓡGinza Line to Aoyama-itchōme, exit 4) The Asia Center covers the basics of a business hotel – the decor is generic and forgettable but the rooms are decently sized and staff are old hands at helping foreign visitors.

🛏 Ebisu, Meguro & Around

TOP CHOICE **CLASKA**   BOUTIQUE HOTEL ¥¥
(クラスカ; ☎3719-8121; www.claska.com/en/hotel; 1-3-18 Chūō-chō, Meguro-ku; s/d from ¥12,600/19,950, weekly per night s from ¥7875; @; ⓡJR Yamanote Line to Meguro, west exit) The Claska is hands-down Tokyo's most stylish hotel, though you might not know it from the retro business-hotel facade. Inside, however, different designers have taken over the direction of the rooms. Some have tatami and floor cushions; others have spacious terraces and glass-walled bathrooms. The new DIY rooms have quirky touches. There is also a restaurant in the lobby, which serves an excellent traditional breakfast, and a rooftop terrace. The hotel is located on Meguro-dōri, 2km west of the station, alongside many interior design stores (see MISC p95). It's well off the beaten path, which is the main drawback; the easiest way to get here is by taxi from Meguro Station (about ¥1000, 10 min). Book early.

HOTEL EXCELLENT EBISU   BUSINESS HOTEL ¥¥
Map p291 (ホテルエクセレント恵比寿; ☎5458-0087; www.soeikikaku.co.jp/english/index.html; 1-9-5 Ebisu-nishi, Shibuya-ku; s/d from ¥9150/11,550; @@; ⓡJR Yamanote Line to Ebisu, west exit) This reasonably-priced hotel is located a minute's walk from Ebisu Station. Rooms here are small and basic; their proximity to the neighbourhood's excellent restaurants and bars is the real draw. The beds in the double rooms are on the small side for two; the beds in the single and twin rooms are roomy for one.

RYOKAN SANSUISŌ   RYOKAN ¥
(旅館山水荘; ☎3441-7475; www.sansuiso.net; 2-9-5 Higashi-Gotanda, Shinagawa-ku; s/d ¥5000/8600; @@; ⓡJR Yamanote Line to Gotanda, east exit) This 10-room inn, run by a friendly older couple, is one of the few tatami options on the west side of town. The rooms are cosy and well-kept; if you're staying two to a room it's worth 'splurging' for a room with a private bath (an extra ¥400). It's just 500m walk from here to Gotanda Station, one stop past Meguro on the Yamanote Line; note that it gets a bit of rail noise from the JR tracks nearby. From the east exit, follow the tracks south until you reach the river and a towering apartment complex – the inn is behind it.

WESTIN HOTEL TOKYO   LUXURY HOTEL ¥¥¥
Map p291 (ウェスティンホテル東京; ☎5423-7000; www.westin-tokyo.co.jp; 1-4-1 Mita, Meguro-ku; r from ¥65,100; @@@; ⓡJR Yamanote Line to Ebisu, east exit) Rooms here are on the opulent side but tasteful, with a laid-back European panache. The hotel is located at the far end of Yebisu Garden Place, which gives it a more secluded feel than other luxury hotels in the centre of the city.

🛏 Shibuya & Around

SHIBUYA GRANBELL HOTEL   BOUTIQUE HOTEL ¥¥
Map p292 (渋谷グランベルホテル; ☎5457-2681; www.granbellhotel.jp; 15-17 Sakuragaoka-chō, Shibuya-ku; s/d from ¥13,000/22,000; @@@; ⓡJR Yamanote Line to Shibuya, south exit) One of the city's few boutique hotels, the Granbell is a step up from your average business hotel, though it's priced about the same. Rooms have glass-enclosed bathrooms, Simmons beds and pop-art curtains; those in the newer annex are brighter than the ones in the main building. The hotel is on the other, quieter side of Shibuya, towards Daikanyama and away from the bars and clubs. Still, it's only a few minutes' walk from here to the station. Try to book early.

CERULEAN TOWER TŌKYŪ HOTEL   LUXURY HOTEL ¥¥¥
Map p292 (セルリアンタワー東急ホテル; ☎3476-3000; www.ceruleantower-hotel.com/en; 26-1 Sakuragaoka-chō, Shibuya-ku; s/d from ¥33,000/43,500; @@@; ⓡJR Yamanote Line to Shibuya, south exit) Sprawl out on the huge beds and drink deeply of the big views, because there's room to breathe in these enormous rooms. Prices rise according to the floor number, as the views get better the higher you go; lavish suites at the top have amazing city views from the bathtub. Bar Bello Visto (p110) is on the 40th floor.

EXCEL HOTEL TŌKYŪ
HOTEL ¥¥¥

Map p292 (エクセルホテル東急; ☑5457-0109; www.tokyuhotelsjapan.com/en; 1-12-2 Dōgenzaka, Shibuya-ku; s/d from ¥22,500/29,000; ❀@; ᴙJR Yamanote Line to Shibuya, Shibuya Mark City exit) This tower, connected to Shibuya Station, boasts excellent night views from the upper floors. Rooms are spacious though ordinary, but at least you're right on top of the action. A breakfast buffet (¥2310) is served in the 25th-floor restaurant, along with terrific skyline panoramas.

HOTEL FUKUDAYA
RYOKAN ¥

(ホテル福田屋; ☑3467-5833; www2.gol. com/users/ryokan-fukudaya/index.html; 4-5-9 Aobadai, Meguro-ku; s/d from ¥6300/10,500; ❀@☎; ᴙJR Yamanote Line to Shibuya, south exit) A rare ryokan near Shibuya, Hotel Fukudaya has recently renovated tatami rooms with and without private baths. It's pretty classy for a budget accommodation too. The inn is located in a residential stretch near the upscale neighbourhoods of Daikanyama and Ikejiri-Ōhashi. While Shibuya is technically the closest station, it's still a 20-minute walk. Head west on route 246 past three traffic lights then make a right on the first small street; alternatively, a taxi ride should cost less than ¥1000.

SHIBUYA CITY HOTEL
BUSINESS HOTEL ¥¥

Map p292 (渋谷シティホテル; ☑5489-1010; www.shibuya-city-hotel.com, in Japanese; 1-1 Maruyama-chō, Shibuya-ku; s/d from ¥9800/17,900; ❀@; ᴙJR Yamanote Line to Shibuya, Hachikō exit) Shibuya City Hotel is in the Love Hotel district, famous for by-the-hour hotels; however, this isn't one of them. Surprisingly, it's not seedy at all. Rooms are simple but big enough to move around in and the location is superb: a short downhill roll from loads of good live-music venues and clubs. There's a wheelchair-friendly room (¥19,640), too.

CAPSULE & SAUNA CENTURY
CAPSULE HOTEL ¥

Map p292 (カプセル＆サウナセンチュリー; ☑3464-1777; 1-19-14 Dōgenzaka, Shibuya-ku; capsules from ¥3700; ❀; ᴙJR Yamanote Line to Shibuya, Hachikō exit) This men-only capsule hotel perched atop Dōgenzaka hill was recently redone. Extras include large shared bathrooms, massage chairs, coin laundry machines and free coffee in the morning. It's a clean, well-run place, and major credit cards are accepted. Note that last check-in is midnight, so you can't just roll up here after missing the last train.

HOTEL METS SHIBUYA
BUSINESS HOTEL ¥¥

Map p292 (ホテルメッツ渋谷; ☑3409-0011; www.hotelmets.jp/shibuya; 3-29-17 Shibuya, Shibuya-ku; s/d from ¥13,500/22,000, wheelchair-accessible r ¥22,000; ❀@; ᴙJR Yamanote Line to Shibuya, new south exit) Super convenient and comfortable, the Hotel Mets is inside Shibuya Station's quiet south exit. It's worth laying out the extra ¥500 for a roomier deluxe single. Rates include free broadband internet and the rarity of a free buffet breakfast.

SHIBUYA TŌKYŪ INN
BUSINESS HOTEL ¥¥

Map p292 (渋谷東急イン; ☑3498-0109; www. tokyuhotels.co.jp/en; 1-24-10 Shibuya, Shibuya-ku; s/tw from ¥15,600/24,500; ❀@; ᴙJR Yamanote Line to Shibuya, east exit) This chain hotel has some style thanks to a recent renovation, with clean lines and sliding window screens in primary shades. Singles are relatively spacious and come with a modern work desk and a flat-screen TV.

🛏 Harajuku & Aoyama

NATIONAL CHILDREN'S CASTLE HOTEL
BUSINESS HOTEL ¥¥

Map p293 (こどもの城ホテル; Kodomo-no-Shiro Hotel; ☑3797-5677; www.kodomono-shiro. com/english/hotel; 5-53-1 Jingūmae, Shibuya-ku; s/d ¥7455/11,340, Japanese-style r per person ¥7875; ❀@ⓗ; ᴙGinza Line to Omote-sandō, exit B2) It's not technically a castle, but with neat and clean rooms within walking distance of Shibuya, Harajuku and Aoyama, it doesn't need to be. The hotel, though itself rather bland, is located within a kids' play complex (National Children's Castle). Naturally it caters to families, though travellers without kids are welcome too. Note that it books out early on weekends and during the summer holidays.

🛏 Shinjuku & West Tokyo

ᴛᴏᴘ ᴄʜᴏɪᴄᴇ PARK HYATT TOKYO
LUXURY HOTEL ¥¥¥

Map p294 (パークハイアット東京; ☑5322-1234; http://tokyo.park.hyatt.com; 3-7-1-2 Nishi-Shinjuku, Shinjuku-ku; r from ¥70,455; ❀@☎✉; ᴙŌedo Line to Tochōmae, exit A4) Tokyo's most famous hotel has 177 rooms spread out over a dozen floors of a Tange Kenzō–designed skyscraper in west Shinjuku. They're really more like apartments, and painfully hip ones at that (see the Fellini storyboard sketches on the walls). The service here is gracious and above all accommodating; perks for guests include complimentary mobile phone rentals (you pay for outgoing calls only). The hotel only starts on the 41st floor, meaning even the entry-level rooms have otherworldly views. The **New York Grill** (p135) is on the dazzling 52nd floor.

YADOYA GUEST HOUSE HOSTEL ¥

(やどやゲストハウス; ☑3868-2772; http://cheap-hostel-tokyo.com; 2-18-6 Nakano, Nakano-ku; dm/tw ¥2200/5000; ⊜@🛜; ☑JR Chūō Line to Nakano, south exit) Handmade bunks and art sketched on the wall give this new hostel a DIY vibe. Note that the dorm rooms are tiny, but there's a cosy common area with a kitchen. In residential Nakano, you won't wake up with the sights at your door; however, many of the staff here are local and can give you the scoop on where to hang out in the neighbourhood. Yadoya also manages some long-stay guesthouses nearby for those planning to stay at least a month. From Nakano Station, head south on the main road and turn left at the second traffic light; the hostel is on the left across the street from a convenience store.

HOTEL CENTURY SOUTHERN TOWER LUXURY HOTEL ¥¥¥

Map p294 (ホテルセンチュリーサザンタワー; ☑5354-0111; www.southerntower.co.jp/english; 2-2-1 Yoyogi, Shibuya-ku; s/d from ¥16,000/24,000; ⊜@🛜; ☑JR Yamanote Line to Shinjuku, south exit) This is one of the best deals for accommodation in Shinjuku, considering the central location, just a couple minutes' walk from Shinjuku Station. Rooms are comfortable but not splashy, with winter views of Mt Fuji possible from one side and the green space of Shinjuku-gyoen on the other.

KADOYA HOTEL BUSINESS HOTEL ¥¥

Map p294 (かどやホテル; ☑3346-2561; www.kadoya-hotel.co.jp; 1-23-1 Nishi-Shinjuku, Shinjuku-ku; s/d from ¥7560/13,650; ⊜@; ☑JR Yamanote Line to Shinjuku, west exit) A steal for its Nishi-Shinjuku address, the Kadoya has simple, clean rooms with flat screen TVs and free LAN access. The newer 'comfort' rooms

have Simmons beds and the best decor. There's also a coin laundry in the building and an *izakaya* (Japanese version of a pub/eatery) with an English menu downstairs.

CITADINES APARTMENT HOTEL ¥¥¥

(シタディーン; ☑5379-7208; www.citadines.com; 1-28-13 Shinjuku, Shinjuku-ku; r from ¥21,000; ⊜@🛜; ☑Marunouchi Line to Shinjuku-gyoenmae, exit 2) This new hotel has bright and modern, if not compact, rooms that include a small kitchenette. It's a bit far from the Shinjuku action, though travellers staying for more than a few days will likely come to appreciate the relative quiet. There's a fitness room and laundrette too.

HILTON TOKYO LUXURY HOTEL ¥¥¥

Map p294 (ヒルトン東京; ☑3344-5111; www.hilton.com; 6-6-2 Nishi-Shinjuku, Shinjuku-ku; s/d from ¥27,900/35,900; @⊛; ☑Marunouchi Line to Nishi-Shinjuku, exit C8) The Hilton caters mainly to a business clientele. The *shōji* (sliding rice-paper screens) on the windows were designed to remind disoriented jetsetters that they're in Tokyo. The rooms, renovated in 2009, are naturally attractive and spacious. The lounge and fitness centre are open 24 hours.

SHINJUKU PRINCE HOTEL LUXURY HOTEL ¥¥¥

Map p294 (新宿プリンスホテル; ☑3205-1111; www.princehotels.com/en/shinjuku; 1-30-1 Kabukichō, Shinjuku-ku; s/d from ¥19,00/21,000; ⊜@; ☑JR Yamanote Line to Shinjuku, east exit) Beside Shinjuku Station and the Kabukichō nightlife, this towering wedge has an attractive location and some of the best views in town. Rooms, though recently renovated, are on the small side and low on glam; however, the sparkling neon should make up for it. Be sure to ask for an upper-floor room and try not to let the faded lobby throw you.

CITY HOTEL LONESTAR BUSINESS HOTEL ¥¥

Map p294 (シティホテルロンスター; ☑3356-6511; www.thehotel.co.jp/en/lonestar/index.html; 2-12-12 Shinjuku, Shinjuku-ku; s/d from ¥7350/12,075; ⊜@🛜; ☑Marunouchi to Shinjuku-sanchōme, exit C8) This is a friendly place to bunk with rooms that are small but cheery. Though it's located in Shinjuku-nichōme, Tokyo's gay district, much of its clientele seem to be out-of-town Japanese for whom 'nichōme' has little meaning. A basic continental breakfast is laid out free of charge.

TOKYO BUSINESS HOTEL BUSINESS HOTEL ¥

Map p294 (東京ビジネスホテル; ☎3356-4605; 6-3-2 Shinjuku, Shinjuku-ku; s/d from ¥3700/8800; ❄@; ⓡMarunouchi Line to Shinjuku-gyoenmae, exit 1) This no-frills hotel off Meiji-dōri is an older building and very simple in terms of decor and amenities. However, the service is friendly, the *o-furo* (traditional Japanese bath) is large and some rooms have views of the skyscrapers in west Shinjuku. The cheaper singles have shared bath; the larger 'type A' singles (¥5200) have their own small bath. There's a buffet breakfast for ¥735; internet hook up is in the lobby only.

IBIS TOKYO SHINJUKU BUSINESS HOTEL ¥¥

Map p294 (イビス東京新宿; ☎3361-1111; www.accorhotels.com; 7-10-5 Shinjuku, Shinjuku-ku; s/d ¥12,000/14,000; ❄@; ⓡJR Yamanote Line to Shinjuku, west exit) The old Star Hotel was recently acquired by an international hotel group, which promised to give the dowdy old rooms here a facelift. They'll still be small, but you're really paying for convenience here; the hotel is just a couple minutes' walk from Shinjuku Station. Note that when renovations are completed (sometime in 2012), prices may rise slightly.

KEIŌ PLAZA HOTEL LUXURY HOTEL ¥¥¥

Map p294 (京王プラザホテル; ☎3344-0111; www.keioplaza.com; 2-2-1 Nishi-Shinjuku, Shinjuku-ku; s/d from ¥25,000/28,000; ❄@❄; ⓡŌedo Line to Tochōmae, exit B1) The 47-storey Keiō Plaza has a whopping 1440 rooms, and while all have excellent city views, be sure to ask for one that has been recently renovated. Note that the pool is outdoor and only open during the summer.

LADIES 501 CAPSULE HOTEL ¥

(レディース501; ☎3200-1945; www.capsule510.jp/ladies510, in Japanese; 2-40-1 Kabukichō, Shinjuku-ku; capsule ¥4500; ⓡJR Yamanote Line to Shinjuku, east exit) This is the rare capsule hotel just for women. It's not exactly classy, but it's clean enough. Park your stuff in the narrow locker on arrival and switch to the pyjamas provided; towels, hairbrushes and skin creams are also included. There's a shared bath, sauna and cafe too. It's a small place and books up early on weekends.

GREEN PLAZA SHINJUKU CAPSULE HOTEL ¥

Map p294 (グリーンプラザ新宿; ☎3207-4923; www.hgpshinjuku.jp/hotel, in Japanese; 1-29-2 Kabukichō, Shinjuku-ku; capsules from ¥4300; @;

ⓡJR Yamanote Line to Shinjuku, east exit) Smack in the middle of sleazy Kabukichō, Green Plaza Shinjuku offers 630 standard and 'upgrade' capsules for men only. However, the ladies' sauna on the 9th floor, with a communal lounge area, allows women to check in for the night (¥3400).

HOTEL METS KŌENJI BUSINESS HOTEL ¥¥

(ホテルメッツ高円寺; ☎5327-0011; www.hotel-mets.jp/koenji; 2-5-1 Kōenji-kita, Suginami-ku; s/d from ¥9500/15,000; ❄❄; ⓡJR Chūō Line to Kōenji, north exit) The solid Mets chain (see p210) has a new branch conveniently located inside Kōenji Station (make a quick left from the north exit and you'll soon see the entrance). It's cheaper than rooms at the Shibuya branch and laidback Kōenji is a nice place to base yourself for a longer stay.

⌂ Iidabashi & Northwest Tokyo

KIMI RYOKAN RYOKAN ¥

Map p296 (貴美旅館; ☎3971-3766; www.kimi-ryokan.jp; 2-36-8 Ikebukuro, Toshima-ku; s ¥4000, d ¥5800-6700; ❄; ⓡJR Yamanote Line to Ikebukuro, west exit) Easily one of the best budget ryokan in Tokyo, this convivial inn provides a welcoming base for travellers discovering the city. Fragrant tatami rooms are small but not cramped, and the large, wood-floored lounge area is a comfortable place to meet fellow travellers over green tea. Clean showers and toilets are shared, and there's a lovely Japanese cypress bath. Book well in advance.

FOUR SEASONS HOTEL CHINZAN-SŌ LUXURY HOTEL ¥¥¥

(フォーシーズンズホテル椿山荘; ☎3943-2222; www.fourseasons.com/tokyo; 2-10-8 Sekiguchi, Bunkyō-ku; r from ¥43,000; ❄❄; ⓡYūrakuchō Line to Edogawabashi, exit 1a) Tastefully opulent with Japanese antiques and a European feel, the Four Seasons Hotel Chinzan-sō is about 2km east of Takadanobaba Station on the grounds of a Meiji-era ornamental garden. It abuts the Kanda-gawa canal, which is very pleasant during cherry-blossom season. From exit 1a, cross the Edogawabashi bridge over the Kanda-gawa canal and then turn left into the park along the canal. Walk west along the path. In about 500m you'll see the entrance to the hotel garden on the right.

TOKYO CENTRAL YOUTH HOSTEL   HOSTEL ¥

Map p299　(東京セントラルユースホステル;
☑3235-1107; www.jyh.gr.jp/tcyh; 18th fl, 1-1
Kagurakashi, Shinjuku-ku; dm adult/student
¥3960/3360; 🛜; 📮JR Sōbu Line to Iidabashi,
west exit) These clean, well-managed dorm
rooms have some of the best sunset and
night views in all of Tokyo, looking west
over the old outer moat of Edo Castle. The
design is rather institutional (there's even
a conference room), but this is a superbly
run hostel outfitted with a cafeteria (serving breakfast and dinner), laundry and internet access.

HOTEL METROPOLITAN   LUXURY HOTEL ¥¥¥

Map p296　(ホテルメトロポリタン; ☑3980-1111;
www.metropolitan.jp, in Japanese; 1-6-1 Nishi-Ikebukuro, Toshima-ku; s/d from ¥18,000/24,000;
🍴🛜; 📮JR Yamanote Line to Ikebukuro, west exit)
The commodious rooms here have been
updated with boutique patterns, flatscreen
TVs and deluxe wooden panelling. Mt Fuji
is sometimes visible, and some superior
rooms have unique round beds.

SAKURA HOTEL IKEBUKURO   HOSTEL ¥

Map p296　(サクラホテル池袋; ☑3971-2237;
www.sakura-hotel-ikebukuro.com; 2-40-7 Ikebukuro, Toshima-ku; dm ¥3200, s/d from ¥6800/
9000; 🛜@; 📮JR Yamanote Line to Ikebukuro,
west exit) The Sakura Hotel is divided into
two buildings, both a six-minute walk from
the station. This large facility also has family and Japanese-style rooms, several shared
kitchens and a 24-hour terrace cafe-restau-
rant. Check the website for deals.

HOTEL STRIX TOKYO   BUSINESS HOTEL ¥¥

Map p296　(ホテルストリックス東京; ☑5396-
0111; www.strix.jp; 2-3-1 Ikebukuro, Toshima-ku;
s/d from ¥15,000/20,000; @; 📮JR Yamanote
Line to Ikebukuro, west exit, Yūrakuchō, Fukutoshin or Marunouchi Line to Ikebukuro, exit C6)
The renovated Strix has some very appealing, modern rooms with wide beds, cosy
couches and spacious bathrooms. High-
speed internet is available in all rooms.
Navigate towards its teal-coloured roof; it's
just steps from the C6 subway station exit of
Ikebukuro Station.

HOUSE IKEBUKURO   HOSTEL ¥

Map p296　(池袋之家; ☑3984-3399; www.house-
jp.com.tw; 2-20-1 Ikebukuro, Toshima-ku; r ¥4000-
12,000; 🍴🛜; 📮JR Yamanote Line to Ikebukuro,
west exit) Spotless tatami rooms are the rule
at House Ikebukuro, a rather institutional,

but very clean, place run by Taiwanese and
catering mainly to Asian backpackers. It's
a busy, well-run establishment that's often
fully booked. All singles share bathrooms,
but some doubles have private ones.

TAMA RYOKAN   RYOKAN ¥

Map p296　(多摩旅館; ☑3209-8062; www.tama-
ryokan.com; 1-25-33 Takadanobaba, Shinjuku-ku;
s/d ¥4500/8000; 📮JR Yamanote Line to Takadanobaba, Waseda-dōri exit) Four traditional
tatami rooms fill out the 2nd floor of this
aging private home, kept by a sweet couple.
The ryokan is up a small alley – look for
the Starbucks to the right of it on the road.
While it lacks a traditional bath, there's a
local *sentō* (public bath) nearby.

🛌 Akihabara & Around

HOTEL MY STAYS
OCHANOMIZU   BUSINESS HOTEL ¥¥

Map p298　(ホテルマイステイズ御茶ノ水;
☑5289-3939; www.mystays.jp; 2-10-6 Kanda
Awajichō, Chiyoda-ku; s/d from ¥10,000/13,000;
@; 📮JR Chūō Line to Ochanomizu, Hijiribashi exit)
Reopened in 2007, this stylish business hotel stands out for its bold brown-and-white
colour scheme, good prices and extras such
as large Simmons beds.

SAKURA HOTEL JIMBŌCHŌ   HOSTEL ¥

Map p298　(サクラホテル神保町; ☑3261-3939;
www.sakura-hotel.co.jp; 2-21-4 Kanda-Jimbōchō,
Chiyoda-ku; dm/s/d from ¥3150/6090/8200;
🍴@; 📮Marunouchi Line to Jimbōchō, exit A6)
The Sakura Hotel is a great budget option
with a sociable atmosphere. Staff are bilingual and helpful, and the rooms, though
basic, are comfortable and clean. There's a
24-hour cafe, a laundry and internet access.

PRESSO INN KANDA   BUSINESS HOTEL ¥¥

Map p298　(プレッソイン神田; ☑3252-0202;
www.presso-inn.com; 2-8 Kanda-Tachō, Chiyoda-
ku; s/d ¥7770/13,650; @; 📮JR Yamanote Line to
Kanda, west exit) The Presso Inn chain is very
much a businessperson's hotel, with purely
functional decor and few frills – rooms
are cramped and institutional but fine
for crashing in. There is a complimentary
breakfast of croissants baked on site.

NEW CENTRAL HOTEL   BUSINESS HOTEL ¥¥

Map p298　(ニューセントラルホテル; ☑3256-
2171; www.pelican.co.jp/newcentralhotel; 2-7-2
Kanda-Tachō, Chiyoda-ku; s/d ¥6200/7700; 🍴@;

R JR Yamanote Line to Kanda, west exit) The New Central may be as generic as its salaryman clientele, but the homey shared bath facilities (separate for men and women) make it stand out. The location, on a quiet side street, makes this a worthwhile base.

🛏 Ueno & Around

TOP CHOICE HŌMEIKAN
RYOKAN ¥¥

Map p300 (鳳明館; ☑3811-1181; www.homeikan. com; 5-10-5 Hongō, Bunkyō-ku; r from ¥11,600; 🐶; 🚇Ōedo Line to Kasuga, exit A6) Atop a slope in a quiet residential neighbourhood, the venerable Hōmeikan is a beautifully crafted wooden ryokan, with its main Honkan wing from the Meiji era registered as an important cultural property. The Daimachi Bekkan wing is equally inviting, with 31 tatami rooms and a large downstairs communal bath. This old-world oasis in the middle of Tokyo is a real treasure. It's close to the sprawling campus of the University of Tokyo, as well as **Fire House** (p161), one of the city's best burger joints.

TOP CHOICE SAWANOYA RYOKAN
RYOKAN ¥

Map p300 (旅館澤の屋; ☑3822-2251; www. sawanoya.com; 2-3-11 Yanaka, Taitō-ku; s/d from ¥5040/10,080; 🖳; 🚇Chiyoda Line to Nezu, exit 1) The Sawanoya is a budget gem in quiet Yanaka, with very friendly staff and all the traditional hospitality you would expect of a ryokan – even origami paper cranes perched on your futon pillow. The shared cypress and earthenware bathrooms are the perfect balm after a long day of walking. The lobby overflows with information about travel options in Japan and bicycles are available for rent; biking the quiet temple lanes of the Yanaka area is highly recommended.

TOCO
HOSTEL ¥

off Map p300 (トコ; ☑6458-1686; http://back packersjapan.co.jp; 2-13-21 Shitaya, Taitō-ku; dm/r from ¥2600/6000; 🖳🐶; 🚇Hibiya Line to Iriya, exit 4) This delightful hostel nestles in a venerable wooden building (which geisha once frequented) dating to 1920; a charming garden and temple outside form a small oasis in this corner of Shitamachi. There's a tatami room that can sleep three, as well as a funky bar-lounge for chatting. The equally groovy Iriya Plus Café (p161) is nearby.

HOTEL PARKSIDE
BUSINESS HOTEL ¥¥

Map p300 (上野 ホテル パークサイド; ☑3836-5711; www.parkside.co.jp; 2-11-18 Ueno, Taitō-ku; s/d from ¥7300/12,500, Japanese-style r from ¥16,000; 🖳; 🚇Yamanote Line to Ueno, Shinobazu exit) This has some of the best midrange accommodation in Ueno, as well as views of the giant lily pads on Shinobazu Pond. Pick either a Western or Japanese room, but ensure it's above the 4th floor for great views.

SUIGETSU HOTEL ŌGAISŌ
BUSINESS HOTEL ¥¥

Map p300 (水月ホテル鴎外荘; ☑3822-4611; www.ohgai.co.jp, in Japanese; 3-3-21 Ikenohata, Taitō-ku; s/d from ¥6400/9600, Japanese-style r from ¥11,500; 🖳; 🚇Chiyoda Line to Nezu, exit 2) Japanese literary great Mori Ōgai lived here in the late 1880s, and part of his lovely tiled wooden home still fronts the peaceful interior garden. Skip the cramped standard singles and go for the deluxe version instead, or sprawl out on tatami. The cypress baths are open to visitors for ¥1500.

SUTTON PLACE HOTEL UENO
BOUTIQUE HOTEL ¥¥

Map p300 (上野サットンプレイスホテル; ☑3842-2411; www.thehotel.co.jp; 7-8-23 Ueno, Taitō-ku; s/d from ¥7800/11,000; 🖳; 🚇Yamanote Line to Ueno, Iriya exit) This snazzy little joint by Ueno Station hits all the right notes, with chocolate-coloured wood and black leather in designer rooms. There are large tiled bathrooms, rare four-person rooms for families and complimentary light breakfasts.

ANNEX KATSUTARŌ RYOKAN
RYOKAN ¥

Map p300 (アネックス勝太郎旅館; ☑3828-2500; www.katsutaro.com; 3-8-4 Yanaka, Taitō-ku; s/d ¥6300/10,500; 🖳; 🚇Chiyoda Line to Sendagi, exit 2) Opened in 2001, this spotless, efficient establishment seems more modern hotel than traditional ryokan. Though far from Ueno Station, it's ideal for exploring the old Yanaka district. The 17 tatami rooms, while rather small, have attached Western bathrooms.

RYOKAN KATSUTARŌ
RYOKAN ¥

Map p300 (旅館勝太郎; ☑3821-9808; www. katsutaro.com; 4-16-8 Ikenohata, Taitō-ku; s/d ¥5200/8400; 🐶; 🚇Chiyoda Line to Nezu, exit 2) This older, more homey sister inn to Annex Katsutarō Ryokan has a quiet and family-like atmosphere, with very affable managers. Though the building may be aged, the seven tatami rooms here have been renovated without ruining the inn's character.

🛏 Asakusa & Sumida River

SUKEROKU NO YADO SADACHIYO   RYOKAN ¥¥

Map p302 (助六の宿　貞千代; ☎3842-6431; www.sadachiyo.co.jp; 2-20-1 Asakusa, Taitō-ku; s/d ¥14,000/19,000; @; 🚇Ginza Line to Asakusa, exit 1) This stunning ryokan virtually transports its guests to old Edo. Gorgeously maintained tatami rooms are spacious for two people, and all come with modern, Western-style bathrooms. Splurge on an exquisite meal here, and make time for the *o-furo*, one made of fragrant Japanese cypress and the other of black granite. Look for the rickshaw parked outside.

RYOKAN SHIGETSU   RYOKAN ¥¥

Map p302 (旅館指月; ☎3843-2345; www.shigetsu.com; 1-31-11 Asakusa, Taitō-ku; Western-style r ¥6700, Japanese-style s/d ¥8400/14,700; @; 🚇Ginza Line to Asakusa, exit 1) South of Sensō-ji, this spotless and atmospheric ryokan has mostly Japanese-style rooms. The entire inn is immaculate, with carpeted entrance halls and *shōji*-screened doors and windows. It's absolutely a requirement to take at least one bath here.

ANDON RYOKAN   RYOKAN ¥¥

off Map p300 (行燈旅館; ☎3873-8611; www.andon.co.jp; 2-34-10 Nihonzutsumi, Taitō-ku; r per person ¥8190; 🛜; 🚇Hibiya Line to Minowa, exit 3) About 2km north of Asakusa in the Sanya area, the minimalist and modern Andon Ryokan is fabulously designed in form and function. It has tiny but immaculate tatami rooms and a spectacular upper-floor bath. Other pluses include free internet access, DVD players, cheap breakfast and laundry facilities.

ANNE HOSTEL   HOSTEL ¥

(浅草橋旅荘　庵; ☎5829-9090; http://j-hostel.com; 2-21-14 Yanagibashi, Taitō-ku; dm/tw from ¥1900/5400; @; 🚇JR Sōbu Line to Asakusabashi, east exit) Located in a former corporate space, laid-back Anne has standard wooden bunk beds, modern toilets and showers, and a homey, cosy atmosphere. To find it, look for the traditional wooden lantern on the street outside. From the east exit, cross the street, turn left and walk two blocks until the Chinese restaurant with red signs. Turn right just before the restaurant, and then left at the second corner. Turn right at the first corner, and look for Anne Hostel on the left.

TOKYO RYOKAN   RYOKAN ¥¥

Map p302 (東京旅館; ☎090-8879-3599; www.tokyoryokan.com; 2-4-8 Nishi-Asakusa, Taitō-ku; r from ¥7000; ⊗@; 🚇Ginza Line to Tawaramachi, exit 3) This tidy inn has only three tatami rooms and no en suite bathrooms but tonnes of charm. There are touches of calligraphy, attractive woodwork and sliding screens. This is an authentic ryokan experience on the cheap.

CHEAP SLEEPS IN SANYA

Sanya is an old neighbourhood north of Asakusa notorious for its down-and-out day labourers, but it also has a wealth of cheap places to bunk. Rooms can be very small, though discounts are available for stays of a week or more. See websites for directions.

Hotel New Kōyō (ホテルニュー紅陽; ☎3873-0343; www.newkoyo.com; 2-26-13 Nihonzutsumi, Taitō-ku; r ¥2300-4000; @; 🚇Hibiya Line to Minowa, exit 3) Very friendly, and featuring some of Tokyo's cheapest rooms, the New Koyo has rooms such as the golden, minute Samurai Suite (about the size of two tatami mats) and a large shared bathroom.

Juyoh Hotel (ホテル寿陽; ☎3875-5362; www.juyoh.co.jp; 2-15-3 Kiyokawa, Taitō-ku; s/d ¥2900/5400; @; 🚇Hibiya Line to Minami-senju, south exit) The three tiny doubles and numerous three-tatami-mat singles fill up fast at this hospitable little spot. For reservations, check the excellent website.

Tokyo Backpackers (東京バックパッカーズ; ☎3871-2789; www.tokyo-backpackers.com; 2-2-2 Nihonzutsumi, Taitō-ku; d ¥2100; @; 🚇Hibiya Line to Minami-senju, south exit) Tokyo Backpackers' clean, modern dorm rooms have six wooden bunk beds, and there is free internet and a women-only floor. The entire place shuts from 11am to 4pm daily for cleaning.

KHAOSAN TOKYO GUESTHOUSE HOSTEL ¥

Map p302 (カオサン東京ゲストハウス; ☎3842-8286; www.khaosan-tokyo.com; 2-1-5 Kaminarimon, Taitō-ku; dm/tw ¥2000/5000; @; ℝGinza Line to Asakusa, exits 4 & A2b) If you are visiting Tokyo during the summer fireworks season in late July, this comfy hostel's rooftop terrace offers a front-row seat for the popular river spectacle. But you'll get a warm welcome at all times of the year here, and it's also one of the cheapest spots in central Tokyo.

ASAKUSA VIEW HOTEL LUXURY HOTEL ¥¥¥

Map p302 (浅草ビューホテル; ☎3847-1111; www.viewhotels.co.jp/asakusa/english; 3-17-1 Nishi-Asakusa, Taitō-ku; s/d from ¥15,750/23,100; @≋; ℝTsukuba Express Line to Asakusa, hotel exit) If you're not into ryokan, the Asakusa View is the ritziest Western-style hotel around. From the lacquer-patterned elevator walls to the cypress and granite baths, the hotel is lavishly designed. While the spacious rooms aren't striking, large windows overlook Sensō-ji.

SAKURA HOSTEL HOSTEL ¥

Map p302 (サクラホステル; ☎3847-8111; www.sakura-hostel.co.jp; 2-24-2 Asakusa, Taitō-ku; dm/tw ¥2940/8295; @; ℝTsukuba Express Line to Asakusa, exit A1) Billed as the largest in Tokyo, this new hostel in a modern, comfortable building has helpful staff and a great location near Sensō-ji. Rooms with wooden bunks overlook the aged Hanayashiki amusement park. There's no curfew, breakfast is only ¥315 and major credit cards are accepted. Check out the old-time shopping arcade behind it.

K'S HOUSE HOSTEL ¥

(ケイズハウス; ☎5833-0555; http://kshouse.jp; 3-20-10 Kuramae, Taitō-ku; dm/d ¥2800/3400; @; ℝŌedo Line to Kuramae, exit A6) This homey, modern hostel is quickly becoming a backpacker fave. Just steps from the Sumida-gawa and Sensō-ji, K's feels more like someone's apartment, with comfy sofas in the living room and a tatami common space. Another branch – the family-oriented K's House Tokyo Oasis – recently opened closer to Sensō-ji; see the website for details. From exit A6, walk northwest along Asakusa-dōri and turn left at the first corner. K's House will be at the end of the block, across the street.

KHAOSAN TOKYO NINJA HOSTEL ¥

(カオサン東京忍者; ☎6905-9205; www.khaosan-tokyo.com; 2-5-1 Nihonbashi-Bakurochō, Chūō-ku; dm/tw from ¥2200/3000; @; ℝJR Sōbu Line to Asakusabashi, east exit) There's no mistaking the black-and-white pattern of flying stars on the exterior of this hip, young hostel, which features capsule-like wooden sleeping berths and a funky living room that plays host to DJ events and performances of traditional culture. From the east exit, turn right and walk south along Edo-dōri and cross the Asakusabashi bridge. Then take a right at the second corner and walk one block. You will see the hostel on the right.

CAPSULE HOTEL RIVERSIDE CAPSULE HOTEL ¥

Map p302 (カプセルホテル浅草リバーサイド; ☎3844-5117; 2-20-4 Kaminarimon, Taitō-ku; capsules ¥3000; ℝGinza Line to Asakusa, exit 4) The spotless Riverside sells an encapsulated night's sleep by the river. Unlike most capsule hotels, it accepts both women and men, with the 8th floor reserved for women only.

Understand Tokyo

Tokyo Today

After being sideswiped by the magnitude-9.0 earthquake that devastated northern Japan in 2011, Tokyo shrugged off power shortages and slight damage, pulled itself together, and worked to help victims. It returned its conservative mayor to office, refurbished the historic Tokyo Station in 2011, and in 2012 unveiled the world's tallest tower, Tokyo Sky Tree. For a city at the heart of the largest metropolitan area on Earth, destruction and innovation are a constant part of life. That's how Tokyo survives.

Best on Film

Tokyo Story (1953) An aging couple's devastating visit to Tokyo.

Godzilla (1954) The monster masterpiece that spawned an industry.

When a Woman Ascends the Stairs (1960) The confessions of a Ginza bar hostess.

Train Man (2005) A shy *otaku* (geek) falls for a woman, and attempts to date her.

Best in Print

A Strange Tale from East of the River (Nagai Kafu; 1937) The story of an unlicensed prostitute in prewar Tokyo.

Coin Locker Babies (Murakami Ryu; 1980) The tale of two boys left to die in coin lockers.

Snakes and Earrings (Kanehara Hitomi; 2003) The fall of a 'Barbie girl' spellbound by a tattoo artist.

1Q84 (Murakami Haruki; 2009–10) An assassin enters an alternate reality in Shibuya.

The Great Wave of Tōhoku

When the quake and tsunamis struck the Tōhoku region of northeast Japan on 11 March 2011, train and subway services were disrupted, stranding millions of commuters in Tokyo. Thousands began a long walk home to suburbs, marching for hours until they could catch a bus or taxi. Of course, the disruptions to life in Tokyo, including damage to its port and Tokyo Disneyland, were nothing compared to the devastation in the north: nearly 20,000 dead and over 125,000 buildings damaged or destroyed. It was the worst crisis to hit Japan since WWII, and its effects continued for months. Power rationing by Tokyo Electric Power Company (TEPCO), operator of the crippled Fukushima Daiichi nuclear plant, seriously affected manufacturing and other businesses. Leaking radiation was detected in minute quantities in Tokyo, but fears of contamination slammed Japanese exports, and travellers stayed away. Tokyoites, however, invoked the age-old mantra of *ganbaru* (to do one's utmost) and donated their time, money and goods to help their compatriots up north. They diligently observed *setsuden* power-saving campaigns, and the electricity squeeze gradually eased. The government has moved to nationalise TEPCO, and the cost of the disaster is still being counted.

While earthquakes have and will always be a possibility in Tokyo, fears about radiation have subsided significantly one year after the disaster. Background radiation in Tokyo is no higher (and in some cases is less) than that of other world cities.

Olympic Dreams

As it has done so often in the past, after fires, earthquakes and the US air raids of WWII, Tokyo carried on with its day-to-day business after the disaster. In 2011, despite calling the Tōhoku quake 'divine punishment' for greed, and mounting a costly but failed attempt to win the 2016 Summer Olympics, Tokyo Governor Ishihara Shintarō was returned to office. The octogenarian has since renewed his determination for Tokyo to host the games and said he plans to get the 2020 Olympics 'at any cost'. Many remember the 1964 Tokyo Olympics as Japan's coming out after the war, an event that was part of a golden age of economic growth. Similarly, the 2020 competition could prove a much-needed stimulus for the moribund national economy.

Tokyo has meanwhile continued with a raft of building projects that belie its economic health. New redevelopment zones have transformed neighbourhoods like Marunouchi, Roppongi and Shiodome into chic new centres of entertainment, business and media. The new Fukutoshin subway line is funnelling people between Ikebukuro and Shibuya, and a new high-speed rail link that cuts travel time between central Tokyo and Narita Airport to 36 minutes has begun services. Grand schemes, such as returning Tokyo Station to its original 1914 glory, are also changing the urban landscape.

Schoolgirl Sensations

When a band of teenage girls rakes in more than US$215 million in a single year (2011), you have to sit up and take notice. AKB48, Japan's answer to the Spice Girls, is not only Japan's largest pop band, but it's also probably the biggest earner. Founded in 2005 by entrepreneur Akimoto Yasushi, AKB48's sexy, bubble-gum pop has appealed to *otaku* (geeks) who frequent Akihabara electronics district, where the band has a permanent concert hall, cafe and cinema. The girls are divided into teams and make frequent appearances in Japanese media and in product advertisements. They broke new ground in 2012 when they were featured on Japan Post stamps (which sold out). AKB48 continues to titillate *otaku* with its racy videos, and shows no sign of slowing down.

Culinary Flourishing

Even if you don't use Michelin guides, its awarding of 32 three-star rankings to Japan (of which 17 are in the Tokyo area) compared to the 25 for its home country of France reflects a renewed emphasis on superb food and drink here. The government has considered recommending to Unesco that Japanese cuisine be recognised as an intangible cultural heritage. Yet Tokyoites, while maintaining a massive appetite for high-end gastronomy are singing the praises of humble foods such as *yaki-soba* (soba noodle stir-fry) and curry rice. Workaday noodles may well knock sushi off its global culinary throne, but Tokyo is also enjoying a drinking transformation. As Japanese whisky turns heads on the global stage, cocktails are back in vogue and craft beer bars are opening throughout the capital. Now more than ever is a perfect time to eat, drink and be merry in Tokyo.

if Tokyo were 100 people

12 would be 0-14
68 would be 15-64
20 would be 65 years and over

TOKYO TODAY

ethnicity
(% of population)

97 Japanese
1 Korean
1 Chinese
1 Other

population per sq km

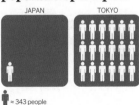

JAPAN   TOKYO

≈ 343 people

History

One of the world's great cities, Tokyo has led a fascinating but precarious life as samurai stronghold, imperial capital and modern metropolis, repeatedly menaced by destruction but continuing to thrive regardless. Its enormous construction projects and ever-changing galaxy of restaurants, shops and high-rise buildings reflect the fact that Tokyo is never in a state of completion. Indeed, its latest identity as a city of the future – reflected in portrayals in manga (Japanese comics) and anime (Japanese animation) – as well as a new culinary mecca, crystallises its protean character. Tokyo has, in fact, always reinvented itself.

IT CAME FROM THE SWAMP!

The monstrous metropolis that is Tokyo, population 13 million, has come a long way from its origins as a collection of tidal pools at the mouth of the Sumida-gawa (Sumida River). Its first permanent inhabitants were part of a pottery-producing culture who settled here during the late Neolithic Jōmon period (Jōmon means 'rope marks' for the design on pottery fragments discovered from this time) around 10,000 BC. These early Tokyoites lived as fishers, hunters and food gatherers.

Some 4000 years later, during the Yayoi period (400 BC to AD 250), wet-rice farming techniques were introduced from Korea, and the Shintō religion also began to develop. By AD 300 Japan was basically a unified nation, with its cultural base in the Osaka area. While the Roman Empire rose and fell, Edo (the old name for Tokyo) continued as a sleepy fishing village for another thousand years.

Meanwhile, the proto-Japanese nation came under the control of the Yamato clan (forerunners of the current imperial family), who claimed descent from the sun goddess Amaterasu and introduced the title of *tennō* (emperor) around the 5th century.

But the most important event in Japan's early history was the arrival of Buddhism in the 6th century. Buddhism introduced a highly evolved system of metaphysics, codes of law and the Chinese writing system, a conduit for the principles of Confucian statecraft.

TIMELINE	10,000 BC	AD 710	794
	Tokyo area inhabited by pottery-making people during late Neolithic Jōmon period. The Kantō region around Tokyo is among the most densely settled in this era.	Japan's first permanent capital established at Nara, ending the practice of moving the capital following an emperor's death. The city is modelled on Chang'an, capital of Tang dynasty China.	Imperial capital moved to Heian-kyō, renamed Kyoto in the 11th century. It is laid out in a grid in accordance with Chinese geomancy principles.

LIVE BY THE SWORD, DIE BY THE SWORD

Few would have guessed it, but Edo was to play a central role in Japan's life as a warrior state. By the end of the 8th century, the Buddhist clerical bureaucracy had become vast, threatening the authority of the imperial administration. The emperor responded by relocating the capital to Heian-kyō (modern day Kyoto). From that point on, Kyoto generally served as the capital until the Meiji Restoration in 1868, when Tokyo became the new chief city.

From Kyoto's early days, a samurai class in the employ of the *daimyō* (feudal lords) emerged. The relationship was one of absolute service; samurai were sworn to do anything for the sake of their clan and lord, and were always prepared to die (see box p222). Much of Japan's subsequent history revolved around bloody struggles for power among the *daimyō* while the emperor mostly watched impotently from the sidelines in Kyoto.

Near the mid-15th century, a *waka* (31-syllable poem) poet named Ōta Dōkan constructed the first castle at Edo on the site of an old fortress above Hibiya Cove. By 1467, when the disastrous Ōnin civil war was devastating the capital in Kyoto, many aristocrats and monks had fled the capital to become supplicants in Dōkan's secure eastern hold. This was a foretaste of Edo's explosive growth, but despite Dōkan's contribution to establishing the city, his overlord ordered his assassination.

BATTLE FOR SUPREMACY

By the time Portuguese traders and missionaries arrived in 1543, feudal lords had carved Japan into a patchwork of fiefdoms. One of the most powerful *daimyō*, Oda Nobunaga of the Chūbu region, near present-day Nagoya, was quick to see how the Portuguese could support his ambitious plans. He viewed their Christianity as a potential weapon against the power of the Buddhist clergy and made ample use of the firearms they introduced. By the time he was assassinated in 1581, Oda had united much of central Japan. Toyotomi Hideyoshi took over the job of consolidating power, but looked less favourably on the growing Christian movement, subjecting it to systematic persecution.

Toyotomi's power was briefly contested by Tokugawa Ieyasu, son of a minor lord allied to Oda. After a brief struggle for power, Tokugawa agreed to a truce with Toyotomi; in return, Toyotomi granted him eight provinces in eastern Japan, including all of the Kantō region and Edo. While Toyotomi intended this to weaken Tokugawa by separating him from his ancestral homeland Chūbu, the upstart looked upon the gift as an opportunity to strengthen his power. He set about turning Edo into a real city.

1457	1600
Ōta Dōkan orders construction of first Edo Castle. Later developed by shōgun Tokugawa Ieyasu in the 17th century, it became the largest fortress the world has seen.	Tokugawa Ieyasu, victor in the Battle of Sekigahara, establishes his capital in Edo, beginning two-and-a-half centuries of peace under Tokugawa rule, known as the Edo period.

Statue of Tokugawa Ieyasu, Tōshō-gū (p185), Nikkō

SAMURAI: THOSE WHO SERVE

The prime duty of a samurai, a member of the warrior class, was to give faithful service to his *daimyō* (feudal lord). In fact, the origin of the term 'samurai' is closely linked to a word meaning 'to serve'. Over the centuries, the samurai established a code of conduct that came to be known as *bushidō* (the way of the warrior), drawn from Confucianism, Shintō and Buddhism.

Confucianism required a samurai to show absolute loyalty to his lord. Towards the oppressed, a samurai was expected to show benevolence and exercise justice. Subterfuge was to be despised, as were all commercial and financial transactions. A real samurai had endless endurance and total self-control, spoke only the truth and displayed no emotion. Since his honour was his life, disgrace and shame were to be avoided above all else, and all insults were to be avenged.

From Buddhism, the samurai learnt the lesson that life is impermanent – a handy reason to face death with serenity. Shintō provided the samurai with patriotic beliefs in the divine status both of the emperor and of Japan – the abode of the gods.

Seppuku (ritual suicide), also known as hara-kiri, was a practice to which Japanese Buddhism conveniently turned a blind eye and was an accepted means of avoiding dishonour. Seppuku required the samurai to ritually disembowel himself, watched by an aide, who then drew his own sword and lopped off the samurai's head. One reason for this ritual was the requirement that a samurai should never surrender but always go down fighting.

The samurai's standard battle dress or armour (*yoroi* in Japanese, usually made of leather or maybe lacquered steel) consisted of a breastplate, a similar covering for his back, a steel helmet with a visor, and more body armour for his shoulders and lower body. Samurai weaponry – his pride and joy – included a bow and arrows (in a quiver), swords and a dagger.

Not all samurai were capable of adhering to their code of conduct – samurai indulging in double-crossing or subterfuge, or displaying outright cowardice, were popular themes in Japanese theatre.

Though the samurai are long gone, there are echoes of *bushidō* in the salaryman corporate warriors of today's Japan. Under the once-prevalent lifetime employment system, employees were expected to show complete obedience to their company, and could not question its decisions if, for example, they were transferred to distant Akita-ken.

The salaryman system has greatly changed in the past two decades with growth in part-time employees and corporate restructuring, but you can still see hordes of blue-suited warriors rushing to their duties every morning in train stations. Instead of swords, they wield business cards.

Next time you see a salaryman who has had one too many, spare a thought for these overworked drivers of the Japanese economy. Like the samurai of old, they are the bedrock of the social order.

1638	1657	1707	1721
Sakoku national isolation policy; Japan cuts off all contact with the outside world save limited trade with Dutch and Chinese off Nagasaki. The policy remains until the 1850s.	Great Meireki Fire devastates Edo, killing over 100,000 and destroying two-thirds of the city. Reconstruction plans include the widening of streets to prevent further conflagrations.	Mt. Fuji erupts, spewing ash over the streets of Edo 100km to the northeast. The stratovolcano is currently considered to be active but with a low risk of eruption.	Edo's population grows to 1.1 million as people move in from rural areas, making it the world's largest city. London's population at the time was roughly 650,000.

When Toyotomi Hideyoshi died in 1598, power passed to his son, Toyotomi Hideyori. However, Tokugawa Ieyasu had been busily scheming to secure the shōgunate for himself and soon went to war against those loyal to Hideyori. Tokugawa's forces finally defeated Hideyori and his supporters at the legendary Battle of Sekigahara in 1600, moving him into a position of supreme power. He chose Edo as his permanent base and began two-and-a-half centuries of Tokugawa rule.

BOOMTOWN EDO

In securing a lasting peace nationwide and ruling from Edo, Tokugawa Ieyasu laid the foundation for Tokyo's ascendancy as one of the world's great cities. In 1603 the emperor appointed him shōgun (military administrator), and the Tokugawa family ruled from Edo Castle (Edo-jō), on the grounds of the current Imperial Palace. It built up into the largest fortress the world had ever seen, with elaborate rituals shaping the lives of its many courtiers, courtesans, samurai and attendants. Edo would also grow to become the world's largest city, topping one million in the early 1700s and dwarfing much older London and Paris, as people from all over Japan flocked here to serve the growing military class.

This was the result of a canny move by the Tokugawa that ensured their hegemony. They implemented the *sankin kōtai* system that demanded that all *daimyō* in Japan spend at least one year out of two in Edo. Their wives and children remained in Edo while the *daimyō* returned to their home provinces. This dislocating policy made it hard for ambitious *daimyō* to usurp the Tokugawas. The high costs of travelling back and forth with a large retinue also eroded their financial power.

Society was made rigidly hierarchical, comprising (in descending order of importance) the nobility, who had nominal power; the *daimyō* and their samurai; the farmers; and finally the artisans and merchants. Class dress, living quarters and even manner of speech were all strictly codified, and interclass movement was prohibited.

The caste-like society imposed by Tokugawa rule divided Edo into a high city (Yamanote) and a low city (Shitamachi). The higher Yamanote (literally 'hand of the mountains') was home to the *daimyō* and their samurai, while the merchants, craftsmen and lower orders of Edo society were forced into the low-lying Shitamachi (literally 'downtown').

One distinguishing feature of those days was the pleasure quarters, where samurai would come to indulge in activities forbidden in the Yamanote: wine, women and song and not necessarily in that order. The most legendary of these districts was the Yoshiwara, to the northeast of present-day Asakusa.

NINJA

Besides loyal samurai, Tokugawa Ieyasu stocked his capital with ninja. Their commander was Hattori Hanzō, renowned for his cunning, deadly tactics that helped Ieyasu at key moments in his career. The ninja master's legacy was enshrined in Hanzōmon, a gate that still exists today at the Imperial Palace.

1853	1868	1871	1872
Black ships of the US navy arrive in Japan under the command of Commodore Matthew Perry, who succeeds in forcing Japan open to US trade at Hakodate and Shimoda.	Meiji Restoration; Tokugawa shōgunate loyalists are defeated in civil war. The imperial residence moves to Edo, which is renamed Tokyo.	Samurai domain system abolished, and Tokyo Prefecture (Tokyo-fu) established out of the former Musashi Province. Tokyo is initially divided into 15 wards, later expanding to 35.	Japan's first train line connects Shimbashi in Tokyo with Yokohama to the southwest; Osaka–Kōbe services are launched in 1874 and Osaka–Kyoto services in 1877.

Otherwise the typical residential neighbourhood of the Shitamachi featured squalid conditions, usually comprising flimsy wooden structures with earthen floors. These shanty towns were often swept by great conflagrations, which locals referred to as *Edo-no-hana,* or flowers of Edo; the expression's bravura sums up the spirit of Shitamachi. Under great privation, Shitamachi subsequently produced a flourishing culture that thumbed its nose at social hardships and the strictures of the shōgunate, patronising both the kabuki theatre and sumō wrestling, and generally enjoying a *joie de vivre* that the dour lords of Edo castle frowned upon. Today, the best glimpses we have into that time come from *ukiyo-e* (wood-block prints; see p239).

Edo was divided into *machi* (towns) according to profession. It's still possible to stumble across small enclaves that specialise in particular wares. Most famous are Jimbōchō, the bookshop area; Kappabashi, with its plastic food and kitchen supplies; and Akihabara, which now specialises in electronics and manga (comics).

THE 'EASTERN CAPITAL' IS BORN

Edo's transformation from a grand medieval city into a world-class capital required an outside nudge, or *gaiatsu* (external pressure). This came in the form of a fleet of black ships, under the command of US Navy Commodore Matthew Perry, that sailed into Edo-wan (now Tokyo Bay) in 1853. Perry's expedition demanded that Japan open itself to foreign trade after centuries of isolation. The coming of Westerners heralded a far-reaching social revolution against which the antiquated Tokugawa regime was powerless. In 1867–68, faced with widespread antigovernment feeling and accusations that the regime had failed to prepare Japan for this threat, the last Tokugawa shōgun resigned and power reverted to Emperor Meiji. In 1868 Meiji moved the seat of imperial power from Kyoto to Edo Castle, renaming the city Tokyo (Eastern Capital). This was known as the Meiji Restoration, and signified that power was restored to the emperor, and the imperial and political capitals were once again unified.

The word Meiji means 'enlightenment' and Japan's new rulers pushed the nation into a crash course in industrialisation and militarisation. In 1872 the first railroad opened, connecting Tokyo with the new port of Yokohama, south along Tokyo Bay, and by 1889 the country had a Western-style constitution.

In a remarkably short time, Japan achieved military victories over China (1894–95) and Russia (1904–05) and embarked on modern, Western-style empire building, with the annexation of Taiwan (1895), then Korea (1910) and Micronesia (1914).

Nationalists were also busy transforming Shintō into a jingoistic state religion. Seen as a corrupting foreign influence, Buddhism suffered badly – many valuable artefacts and temples were destroyed, and the common people were urged to place their faith in the pure religion of State Shintō.

EDO TOWNS

1889
Constitution of the Empire of Japan declared. Based on a Prussian model of constitutional monarchy, the emperor shares power with an elected parliament.

1914
Tokyo Station opens. Designed by Tatsuno Kingo, it begins operations with four platforms. Greatly expanded over the past 100 years, it now serves over 3000 trains per day.

MIXA / GETTY IMAGES ©

Tokyo Station, Nihonbashi exit (p61)

During the Meiji period, and the following Taishō period, changes that were taking place all over Japan could be seen most prominently in the country's new capital city. Tokyo's rapid industrialisation, uniting around the nascent *zaibatsu* (huge industrial and trading conglomerates), drew job seekers from around Japan, causing the population to grow rapidly. In the 1880s electric lighting was introduced. Western-style brick buildings began to spring up in fashionable areas such as Ginza. If the Meiji Restoration sounded the death knell for old Edo, there were two more events to come that were to erase most traces of the old city.

A CATFISH JUMPS – THE GREAT KANTŌ EARTHQUAKE

Japanese have traditionally believed that a giant catfish living underground causes earthquakes when it stirs. At noon on 1 September 1923 the catfish really jumped – the Great Kantō Earthquake caused unimaginable devastation in Tokyo. More than the quake itself, it was the subsequent fires, lasting some 40 hours, that laid waste to the city, including some 300,000 houses. A quarter of the quake's 142,000 fatalities occurred in one savage firestorm in a clothing depot. (There are some sombre reminders of the earthquake exhibited at the Kantō Earthquake Memorial Museum; see p174).

In true Edo style, reconstruction began almost immediately. The spirit of this rebuilding is perhaps best summed up by author Edward Seidensticker (see the sidebar Tokyo Tomes): popular wisdom had it that any business which did not resume trading within three days of being burnt out did not have a future. Opportunities were lost in reconstructing the city – streets might have been widened and the capital transformed into something more of a showcase.

THE BEGINNING OF SHŌWA & WWII

From the accession of Emperor Hirohito (*Shōwa tennō* to the Japanese) and the initiation of the Shōwa period in 1926, Japanese society was marked by a quickening tide of nationalist fervour. In 1931 the Japanese invaded Manchuria, and in 1937 embarked on full-scale hostilities with China. By 1940 a tripartite pact with Germany and Italy had been signed and a new order for all of Asia formulated: the Greater East Asia Co-Prosperity Sphere. On 7 December 1941 the Japanese attacked Pearl Harbor, bringing the US, Japan's principal rival in the Asia-Pacific region, into the war.

In 1904 Mitsukoshi became Japan's first Western-style department store, and its annex in Nihombashi (1914) was called the grandest building east of the Suez Canal. The retailer remains one of the most prestigious shops in Tokyo.

Tokyo Tomes

Edo, the City that Became Tokyo (Akira Naito)

Low City, High City (Edward Seidensticker)

Tokyo: Exploring the City of the Shogun (Sumiko Enbutsu)

1923	1923	1926	1936
Great Kantō Earthquake kills over 140,000. An estimated 300,000 houses are destroyed; a reconstruction plan is only partly realised due to money shortages.	Yamanote Line completed. One of Japan's busiest lines, the 34.5km loop around the heart of Tokyo now has 29 stations. It takes trains about an hour to circle the city.	Hirohito ascends the throne to become the Shōwa emperor. Presiding over Japan's military expansion across East Asia and atrocities, he is spared trial by Allied forces after WWII.	February 26 Incident. Over 1000 Imperial Japanese Army troops stage a coup d'etat, killing political leaders and occupying the centre of Tokyo before surrendering to government loyalists.

Despite initial successes, the war was disastrous for Japan. On 18 April 1942, B-25 bombers carried out the first bombing and strafing raid on Tokyo, with 364 casualties. Much worse was to come. Incendiary bombing commenced in March 1944, notably on the nights of the 9th and 10th, when some two-fifths of the city, mainly in the Shitamachi area, went up in smoke and 70,000 to 80,000 lives were lost. The same raids destroyed Asakusa's Sensō-ji (p168), and later raids destroyed Meiji-jingū (p116). By the time Emperor Hirohito made his famous capitulation address to the Japanese people on 15 August 1945, much of Tokyo had been decimated – sections of it were almost completely depopulated, like the charred remains of Hiroshima and Nagasaki after they were devastated by atomic bombs. Food and daily necessities were scarce, the population was exhausted by the war effort and fears of marauding US military overlords were high.

Based on the price paid for the most expensive real estate in the late 1980s, the land value of Tokyo exceeded that of the entire US. Japanese companies went on a purchasing spree of international icons including Pebble Beach Golf Course, the Rockefeller Center and Columbia Pictures movie studio.

THE POSTWAR MIRACLE

Tokyo's phoenixlike rise from the ashes of WWII and its emergence as a major global city is something of a miracle. Once again, Tokyoites did not take the devastation as an opportunity to redesign their city (as did Nagoya, for example), but rebuilt where the old had once stood.

During the US occupation in the early postwar years, Tokyo was something of a honky-tonk town. Now-respectable areas such as Yūrakuchō were the haunt of the so-called *pan-pan* girls (prostitutes), and areas such as Ikebukuro and Ueno had thriving black-market zones. The remains of Ueno's black market can be seen in Ameyoko Arcade (p160), which is still a lively market.

In 1947 Japan adopted its postwar constitution, with the now-famous Article 9, which barred the use of military force in settling international disputes and maintaining a military for warfare (although the nation does maintain a self-defence force).

By 1951, with a boom in Japanese profits arising from the Korean War, Tokyo rebuilt rapidly, especially the central business district, and the subway began to take on its present form. The once-bombed-out city has never looked back from this miraculous economic growth.

During the 1960s and '70s, Tokyo re-emerged as one of the centres of growing Asian nationalism (the first phase was in the 1910s and '20s). Increasing numbers of Asian students came to Tokyo, taking home with them new ideas about Asia's role in the postwar world.

One of Tokyo's proudest moments came when it hosted the 1964 summer Olympics. In preparation the city embarked on a frenzy of construction unequalled in its history. Many Japanese see this time as a

1944-45	1947	1948	1951
US drops two atomic bombs on Hiroshima and Nagasaki; US occupation begins. American rulers embark on a successful program of demilitarisation and democratisation.	New constitution adopted, including Article 9 in which Japan renounces war and the possession of armed forces. But Japan's Self-Defense Forces are built into a formidable military arsenal.	Tokyo War Crimes Tribunal concludes, resulting in the execution of six wartime Japanese leaders. In 1978, they are secretly enshrined at Yasukuni-jinja.	Japan signs San Francisco Peace Treaty, officially ending WWII, renouncing Japan's claims to overseas colonies, and outlining compensation to be paid to Allied territories.

turning point in the nation's history, the moment when Japan finally recovered from the devastation of WWII to emerge as a fully fledged member of the modern world economy.

Construction and modernisation continued at a breakneck pace through the '70s, with the interruption of two Middle East oil crises, to reach a peak in the late '80s, when wildly inflated real-estate prices and stock speculation fuelled what is now known as the 'bubble economy'. When the bubble burst in 1989 with the crash of the stock market, the economy went into a protracted slump that was to last more than 20 years.

There were other, more disturbing, troubles in Japanese society. In March 1995 members of the Aum Shinrikyō doomsday cult released sarin nerve gas on crowded Tokyo subways, killing 12 and injuring more than 5000. This, together with the devastating Kōbe earthquake of the same year, which killed over 6000 people, signalled the end of Japan's feeling of omnipotence, born of the unlimited successes of the '80s.

Even after decades of economic stagnation, Tokyo remains a business powerhouse. It hosts 47 of the Fortune Global 500 companies, outranking New York and London and every other city on the list.

CITY OF THE FUTURE

Tokyo has weathered a long hangover since the heady days of the bubble economy. The doldrums have finally given way to lacklustre growth and unemployment that flirts with record 5% highs, but the government maintains the economy is still on a recovery path.

The declining birth rate and population pose major problems for Tokyo and Japan – the birth rate for the capital is below 1% (even lower than the national average of 1.24%), while Japan's elderly continue to make up an ever-larger share of the population. Nobody really knows how the system will manage to support the 30% of the population that is projected to be over the age of 65 in the next 25 years. The workforce is shrinking, but there are few signs that Japan is ready to embrace Western-style immigration, recently making all foreign visitors to the country subject to fingerprinting and facial photography upon entry as part of its security policy.

The government may fear deception and fraud, but domestic headlines are rife with corporate malfeasance scandals, from revelations that buildings in Tokyo have been constructed with forged quake-resistance data to news that Japanese paper companies have been passing off unused paper as recycled material.

Japan is also struggling with its international role, particularly the leeway allowed by its 'Peace Constitution'; former Prime Minister Koizumi Junichirō's decision to deploy Self-Defense Force (SDF) troops to aid allies in the war in Iraq was met with massive protests. The Defense Agency was promoted to a fully fledged ministry and Japanese military cooperation with the US has escalated.

MEGA-WEALTH

1952	1955	1958	1964
US occupation ends; Japan enters a period of high economic growth. The Korean War provides an incentive for Japanese manufacturers, who supply US forces.	Liberal Democratic Party (LDP) founded; it has a virtually uninterrupted hold on power into the 21st century despite recurring corruption scandals and deep-seated factionalism.	Tokyo Tower (333m) completed. Designed for broadcasts and inspired by the Eiffel Tower, it became a tourist magnet and symbol of Japan's high growth in the 1960s.	Tokyo Olympic Games held, marking Japan's postwar reintegration into the international community and the first time the Games are hosted by a non-Western country.

A GRAND OLD LADY GETS A MAKEOVER

If you pass through Tokyo Station before 2013, it will still be undergoing a historic transformation. The capital's titulary train hub has pride of place before the Imperial Palace and the prestigious Marunouchi business district, and is also the city's main intercity rail link. Designed by Tatsuno Kingo and built in 1914, it survived the 1923 Great Kanto Earthquake, WWII bombing and a postwar fire. It was also the site of a political assassination (of Prime Minister Hara Takashi in 1921) and the launch of the first *shinkansen* (bullet train). Meanwhile, it has handled 1.75 million passengers a day in recent years. Tokyo Station is finally getting the facelift it deserves – just in time for its centenary.

For one, the elegant red brick building on the Marunouchi side, originally three stories tall until it was bombed in 1945, will be restored to its former height and glory with its rooftop domes rebuilt. It will house the Tokyo Station Hotel, which will be expanded and reopened as the premiere JR Group hotel. Within the ticket gates, the Ekinaka GranSta shopping complex will connect the Marunouchi and Yaesu sides of the station. The whole structure will be made quake resistant.

To give Tokyo Station a 21st-century backdrop, skyscrapers housing shopping, dining and office space will stand on the ends of the Shinkansen areas and Yaesu side. The GranTokyo North and South towers, 43 and 42 stories respectively, will be linked by the 240m-long, sail-like GranRoof pedestrian deck, due to be completed in spring 2013. The Sapia Tower near the Nihonbashi exit will house another hotel, offices and university campuses.

The entire nine-year, ¥200 billion redevelopment project is akin to building a city within a city, and, naturally, it's been named Tokyo Station City. Goto Shinpei, a railway bureaucrat who a century ago called for a station design that would 'surprise the rest of the world,' would surely be proud.

Japan's international image has suffered due to its so-called 'scientific' whaling program and a perceived lack of repentance over its wartime atrocities. The government has turned to Japanese pop culture products such as anime and manga as a foreign policy tool in the hopes that popular cartoon heroes will convince people to embrace 'cool Japan'.

Meanwhile, mainstays of Japanese society have buckled under social and economic pressures. The conservative Liberal Democratic Party (LDP) lost its 54-year lock on political power in late 2009 to the opposition Democratic Party of Japan (DPJ), which elected Yukio Hatoyama prime minister. The LDP had only been out of power once since 1955 – an 11-month period in 1993–94 – so the change shocked many Japanese.

1968-69	1972	1989
Tokyo University students take over administrative buildings to protest the Vietnam War. No one is allowed to graduate in 1969 and entrance exams are cancelled.	Okinawa, captured and held by US forces in WWII, is returned to Japan. High concentration of lingering US military bases on the islands has angered locals ever since.	Death of Emperor Hirohito; Heisei era begins as Hirohito's son Akihito ascends the throne; stock market decline begins, initiating a decade-long economic slump in Japan.

Emperor Akihito and family

JEREMY SUTTON-HIBBERT / ALAMY ©

A far greater shock, however, was the magnitude-9.0 earthquake and subsequent tsunamis that struck northeast Japan off Sendai 11 March 2011. One of the strongest quakes in recorded history, the tremor and its effects killed nearly 20,000 people and sparked a meltdown at the Daiichi nuclear plant in Fukushima-ken. Tokyo sustained minor damage and was able to receive thousands of refugees from the northern coastal areas. The Fukushima nuclear crisis, meanwhile, continued through December 2011 (when a state of 'cold shutdown' was declared at the plant), causing electricity shortages and prompting the cancellation of many public events. The cost of rebuilding the devastated areas has been estimated at ¥10 trillion (US$122 billion). The disaster was the greatest catastrophe to hit Japan since WWII, but the people of Tōhoku and Tokyo, who volunteered in droves in the quake zone, have weathered it just as their forebears in Edo times and WWII dealt with terrifying destruction: by quietly aiding one another, working together and rebuilding their lives.

> The 2011 earthquake that devastated northeast Japan reignited proposals to move the capital, or at least core government functions, from Tokyo to mitigate risks in disasters. Proposed sites include Osaka and Tochigi, north of Tokyo.

1995	2009	2011	2012
Doomsday cult Aum Shinrikyō releases sarin gas on the Tokyo subway, killing 12 and injuring more than 5000. Guru Shōkō Asahara is sentenced to death for Aum-related crimes in 2004.	LDP loses control of the House of Representatives to the opposition Democratic Party of Japan (DPJ), ending the LDP's virtually unbroken rule of Japan since 1955.	Magnitude 9.0 earthquake strikes off Sendai in Tōhoku, unleashing tsunami waves, killing nearly 20,000, and crippling the Fukushima Da-ichi nuclear plant.	Tokyo Sky Tree opens as a digital broadcasting tower. At 634 metres, it is the tallest tower in the world, nearly twice as high as Tokyo Tower.

Tokyo Pop

Giant robots, gothic Lolita schoolgirls and martial-arts superheroes. That's fun for kids of all ages in Japan, where the gravitational force of manga (comics) and anime (Japanese animation) is overwhelming.

Manga & Anime

Walk into any convenience store in Tokyo and pick up a phone directory-sized weekly manga anthology. You'll find about 25 tales of heady pulp fiction: comic narratives spanning everything from gangster sagas and bicycle racing to *shōgi* (Japanese chess), often with generous helpings of sex and violence. Anime can be even wilder: legions of saucer-eyed schoolgirls, cute fluorescent monsters and mechatronic superheroes go light years beyond Disney and Pixar. This onslaught of fantasy has also achieved critical mass overseas.

In 2004 manga accounted for 37% of all publications sold in Japan, though sales have declined 20% over the past decade due to the low birth rate, proliferation of electronic diversions like mobile phones and the availability of material through secondhand shops, libraries and cafes.

Anime has fared better. Japan's most revered animator Miyazaki Hayao enjoyed international acclaim by winning the 2003 Oscar for Best Animated Feature for *Spirited Away* – the most successful Japanese movie of all time in Japan. Fans will want to visit the Ghibli Museum (p130) for a behind-the-scenes look at the art of this unique Japanese genre. However, overseas sales have been struggling largely due to the proliferation of file-sharing internet sites.

There are hundreds of anime/manga shops throughout Tokyo. One district to explore is Nakano, where many secondhand collectors' shops have sprouted. A major chain is Mandarake (p154), with a superstore in Nakano that can steal many hours of your time, and a major outlet in Akihabara, Tokyo's electronics mecca.

Comiket (www.comiket.co.jp; short for 'Comic Market') and the Tokyo International Animation Fair (www.tokyoanime.jp) are held yearly in Tokyo Big Sight (p182). Comiket, the more frenzied event of the two, is a massive gathering of fan-produced amateur manga known as *dōjinshi*. To the untrained eye, *dōjinshi* looks like 'official' manga, but most are parodies of famous manga characters. Complete subgenres exist here, from gag-strips to sexual reimaginings of popular titles.

ALL-TIME BEST ANIME

- *Ghost in the Shell* (1995) Oshii Mamoru
- *Spirited Away* (2001) Miyazaki Hayao
- *My Neighbor Totoro* (1988) Miyazaki Hayao
- *Grave of the Fireflies* (1988) Takahata Isao
- *Neon Genesis Evangelion* (1995–96) Anno Hideaki
- *Millennium Actress* (2001) Kon Satoshi

Clockwise from top left
1. Hatsune Miku character and *cosplay* (costume play) girl, Akihabara 2. Manga for sale

Hyperfashion

You don't have to go far to see the far-out in Tokyo. Get off the train at JR Harajuku Station on a Saturday and you'll likely encounter a patchwork of subcultures if you walk to Yoyogi-kōen, but the most striking are the *gosurori* (gothic Lolita) kids posing like vampires at noon on Jingū-bashi (Jingū Bridge). Think Halloween meets neo-Victorian with the odd glam-rock accent and you'll get the idea.

But whatever subgenre you find and wherever you go, visitors to Tokyo are often in awe of this city's incredible sense of style. From the cosplay (costume play) get-up worn by Harajuku girls (and boys) to the sleek black shoes that click along the avenues in Ebisu, people here think carefully about design, trends and beauty.

Since the late 19th century, the Japanese have been eager adopters of Western fashions but have maintained their traditional dress for special occasions – it's common to see Japanese wearing kimono at weddings, and *yukata* (light summer kimono) for fireworks shows. Japanese workaday wear ranges from the standard-issue salaryman suit (overwhelmingly dark blue or black) to ubiquitous uniforms like frumpy 'office lady' vests, to the skirts over jeans and thigh-high hosiery favoured by Tokyo girls. In the last couple of decades, Tokyo's fashion scene has been loosely organised around the work of Issey Miyake (p125), Yohji Yamamoto (p125) and, more recently, Rei Kawakubo of Comme des Garçons (p125), who show internationally in addition to maintaining their presence in Tokyo. Other designers include Koshino Hiroko and Utsugi Eri. Visionaries like Fujiwara Hiroshi, the renowned streetwear fashion arbiter, have a huge impact on what Japanese youth wear.

Young designers have initiated an antifashion movement in Japan, designing clothes meant to be worn with comfort inside and outside of the house. Sneaker and streetwear preachers A Bathing Ape (aka BAPE; p126), the creation of designer and Teriyaki Boyz DJ Nigo, has sold

GREG ELMS / LONELY PLANET IMAGES ©

Clockwise from top left

1. Fashionable young women, Harajuku 2. Window display, Jingūmae 3. Clothing shop, Jingūmae

ANTHONY PLUMMER / LONELY PLANET IMAGES ©

GREG ELMS / LONELY PLANET IMAGES ©

premium urban footwear at slick outlets that feel like shrines to j-hop (Japanese hip hop). Even casual wear may not be inexpensive compared to your home; Tokyo's parasite singles have money. Hot casual brand GDC, which groups labels like Ugly and Ventura, sells fab T-shirts for a cool ¥10,000. Districts in which to see the newest and most fashionable wares are Omote-sandō and Aoyama, Daikanyama and Shimo-kitazawa; see p50 for more details.

Super Future Tech

It may be the 30 buttons on your state-of-the-art Japanese toilet or a USB memory drive that looks exactly like a piece of sushi, or a new smartphone that picks up live TV shows and also checks for bad breath – Japanese are inimitable in their flair for tricking out ordinary gadgets with primo engineering and lots of fun, hot looks. It's all driven by an insatiable desire for novelty.

CATWALKING

Two of the many high-profile fashion events in the capital are Tokyo Fashion Week (http://tokyo-mbfashionweek.com/en/), which recently partnered with Mercedes-Benz and features prominent designers such as Sakabe Mikio, and the massively popular Tokyo Girls Collection (TGC; http://tgc.st), which draws tens of thousands to stadium-sized venues and features concerts, celebrity hosts and affordable, everyday clothing.

Finally, an amateur and informal but nonetheless fascinating event is Harajuku Fashion Walk. Dozens of young Japanese who are into colourful, unusual dress assemble in the Harajuku area and parade down Omote-sandō. Styles range from princesses to *gosurori* (Gothic lolita) but pink is usually in abundance. It's a great opportunity for photos. Check online magazine Tokyo Fashion (http://tokyofashion.com) for news about upcoming walks.

234

The humble photo booth, for instance, has evolved beyond recognition in the *purikura* (print club), a mini graphics studio that can spit out extensively user-designed photo stickers and has enough room for you to change into your favourite superhero costume.

In addition to ranking your vocalist skills, karaoke music players count the number of calories burned per song. Inescapable vending machines (p147) dispense a cornucopia of consumer goods from underwear to steaming *rāmen* (noodles in broth).

Japan has long been an export powerhouse for cameras, stereos and cars, and now it's pinning its hopes on 'partner robots' to take up the slack as the workforce shrinks.

Robot exhibitions are big in Tokyo, as are do-it-yourself kits that can be assembled into little soccer-playing humanoids (see Technologia, p155). Only in Tokyo would millions gather to witness an 18m replica of a robot from the animated *Gundam* sci-fi series erected in a park in Odaiba in 2009.

Design Power

Tokyo brims with innovative Japanese designs – be it futuristic buildings, patterned handkerchiefs or sexy novelties like an electronic candlestick. Recent recipients of the state-sponsored Good Design Award include KDDI's G11 smartphones, Nissin cup noodles and Series N700 *shinkansen* (bullet trains). Fuelled by public hunger for new products, uniquely Japanese design is ubiquitous in Tokyo.

Clothing retailers for the masses like Muji (p77) and Uniqlo (p76) have inspired, practical clothes that are simple without being bland; the former's amazing selection of no-name, generic umbrellas, batteries, toasters and even chocolates are a refreshing tonic to brand-saturated modern culture.

Electronics junkies already know about Akihabara and its 3D-TV screens, mobile-

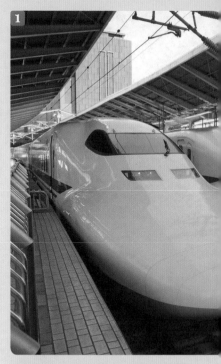

AHUWLEN.N / JAPAN STOCK PHOTOGRAPHY / ALAMY ©

Clockwise from top left
1. *Shinkansen* (bullet train), Tokyo Station (p61)
2. Casual wear on display at Uniqlo (p76)
3. ASIMO (p81), a robot created by Honda

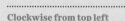

phone accessories and robot stores. Trade shows like Tokyo Designer's Week and 100% Design Tokyo draw the brightest designers and manufacturers from around Japan, as well as massive public attendance.

But the best places to find cool designs in Tokyo are the unexpected: an ergonomic, multifunction rice cooker that looks like a mini spaceship; an origami crane expertly poised on a ryokan pillow in welcome; or a tilting, three-wheeled moped for delivering pizza.

Like kata, the progressive steps to learning a traditional art (such as karate or ikebana), design is a fundamental part of life in Tokyo, an everyday expression of the highly prized qualities of beauty and functionality.

ULTRAPOP: AKB48

Heard of Morning Musume, the eight-girl J-pop idol group that was big in the early 2000s? AKB48 carries the manufactured idol supergroup concept to an almost Guinness World Record level – it consists of over 90 fresh-faced young girls from all over Japan, including one who is entirely computer generated. Divided into three teams, the AKB48 girls have their own TV show and their own concert hall, coffee shop and theatre in Akihabara. Fans, mostly grown men, line up daily to see these young idols on stage. A recent fan election to decide which girls get to record the latest single drew over a million votes.

But it's not just an *otaku* (geek) obsession: AKB48 has become so popular with mainstream Japanese that even stodgy Japan Post began issuing stamps with the girls on them. When it announced the stamp sheets, its website drew so many hits that it promptly crashed.

Arts

Tokyo's density has a sheer visual quality that sometimes makes it seem like a lurid anime or video-game backdrop. In its better moments it may resemble an *ukiyo-e* (wood-block print), such as when snow blanches the roof of Sensō-ji in Asakusa. Yet art occurs in the most unassuming places: museums exist atop office buildings, theatres reside in train stations and galleries lurk inside hair salons and drab apartment buildings.

PERFORMING ARTS

Traditional Drama & Storytelling

Tokyo, when it was Edo (1600–1868), had a rich theatre culture. Above all, there was kabuki, captivating, occasionally outrageous and beloved by the townspeople. *Rakugo* (comic monologue) too was a thoroughly common diversion and remains even more so today; while kabuki tickets now fetch a handsome price and carry an air of sophistication, *rakugo* draws working men and women happy to sit on a space on the floor. Then, like now, highly symbolic *nō* (stylised Japanese dance-drama) was performed for more rarefied circles.

Kabuki

Originally from Kyoto, kabuki came into its own in Edo. There, it developed hand in hand with the increasingly affluent merchant class, whose decadent tastes translated into the breathtaking costumes, dramatic music and elaborate stagecraft that have come to characterise kabuki.

A charismatic shrine priestess in Kyoto is credited with creating kabuki, around the year 1600. She led a troupe of female performers in a new type of dance people dubbed 'kabuki', a slang expression that meant 'cool' or 'in vogue'.

The dancing – rather ribald and performed on a dry riverbed for gathering crowds – was also a gateway to prostitution, which eventually led the Tokugawa establishment to ban the female performers. Adolescent men took their place, though they too attracted amorous admirers (who engaged in the occasional brawl with competing suitors). Finally, in 1653, the authorities mandated that only adult men with shorn forelocks could perform kabuki, which gave rise to one of kabuki's most fascinating elements, the *onnagata* (an actor who specialises in portraying women).

Over several centuries, kabuki has developed a repertoire of popular themes, such as famous historical accounts and stories of love-suicide. It has also borrowing copiously from other art forms like bunraku (puppet theatre), which was popular at the same time though particularly so in Osaka.

More than plot, however, kabuki is driven by its actors, who train for the profession from childhood. The leading families of modern kabuki go back many generations, as sons follow their fathers into the *yago* (kabuki acting house) in order to perpetuate an ancestor's name on stage. Thus the generations of certain families (eg Bando and Ichikawa) run into the double digits. The Japanese audience takes great interest in watching how different generations of one family perform the same part. Actors today enjoy great social prestige, and their activities on and off the stage attract as much interest as those of film and TV stars.

A unique aspect of kabuki is the *kakegoe*, enthusiastic fans who shout out the name of the *yago* of their favourite actors at pivotal moments such as well-known lines of dialogue or *mie* (dramatic poses held for a pause). Actors note they miss this reinforcement when performing overseas.

Nō

Kabuki was seen as too unrefined for the military classes (though they may have secretly enjoyed it). *Nō*, a dramatisation of the aesthetic quality *yūgen* (subtle, elusive beauty), was considered a better match.

Nō has its roots in indigenous Shintō rituals and developed in Kyoto between 1350 and 1450. Rather than a drama in the usual sense, *nō* seeks to express a poetic moment by symbolic and almost abstract means: glorious movements, grand and exaggerated costumes and hairstyles, sonorous chorus and music, and subtle expression. Actors frequently wear masks while they perform before a spare, unchanging set, which features a painting of a large pine tree.

Most plays centre around two principal characters: the *shite,* who is sometimes a living person but more often a demon or a ghost whose soul cannot rest; and the *waki,* who leads the main character towards the play's climactic moment. The elegant language used is that of the court of the 14th century.

Some visitors find *nō* rapturous and captivating; others (including many Japanese) find its subtlety all too subtle. It's a good idea to familiarise yourself with the story and characters beforehand. The intermissions of *nō* performances are punctuated by *kyōgen* (short, lively comic farces).

Rakugo

Comedic *rakugo* (literally 'dropped word') was popularised in the Edo period. The performer, usually in kimono, sits on a square cushion on a stage. Props are limited to a fan and hand towel. The monologue begins with a *makura* (prologue), which is followed by the story itself and, finally, the *ochi* (punch line or 'drop', which is another pronunciation of the Chinese character for *raku* in *rakugo*). Many of the monologues in the traditional *rakugo* repertoire date back to the Edo and Meiji periods, and while well known, reflect a social milieu unknown to modern listeners. Accordingly, many performers today also write new monologues addressing issues relevant to contemporary life. A number of famous comedians, including movie director Kitano Takeshi, have studied *rakugo* as part of their development.

ARTS EVENTS

February
The year's top animation, manga and digital installations go on display at the **Japan Media Arts Festival**, held at the National Art Center.

March
Performances and larger-than-life installations take over the streets of Roppongi for **Roppongi Art Night**.

April
Art fair **Geisai** gives young artists a chance to present their work. Also the more high-brow **Art Fair Tokyo**.

May
Weekend-long **Design Festa**, at Tokyo Big Sight, is the largest art event in Asia.

July
The **International Gay & Lesbian Film Festival** screens dozens of films from Japan and around the world. Also music festivals like **Fuji Rock**.

September
The **Tokyo Jazz Festival** has three days of shows by international and local stars.

October
Tokyo International Film Festival and **FILMeX** screen works by Japanese directors with English subtitles.

November
Tokyo Designer's Week attracts the international design world with a large exhibition at Meiji-Gaien. Also this month: round two for **Design Festa**.

Contemporary Movements

Theatre in Tokyo doesn't play the same influential role that it did in the days of Edo or as it does in major Western cities – much to the lament of those involved. Commercially successful theatre tends to fall into two categories: mainstream Western imports (especially musicals) and performances starring celebrities. Still, in wealthy and intellectual residential pockets of the city, public and underground theatres play to full houses.

Shōgeki

Theatre the world over spent the 1960s redefining itself, and it was certainly no different in Tokyo. The *shōgekijo* (small theatre) movement, also called *angura* (underground), has given Japan many of its leading playwrights, directors and actors. Like their counterparts in the Western world, these productions took place in any space available – in small theatres, tents, basements, ope n spaces and on street corners.

Today's *shōgeki* takes on realistic themes, including socially and politically critical works (such as those by Kaneshita Tatsuo and Sakate Yōji), psychological dramas (eg those by Iwamatsu Ryō, Suzue Toshirō and Hirata Oriza) and satirical portrayals of modern society (eg those by Nagai Ai and Makino Nozomi).

Among the next generation, Okada Toshiki and his troupe Chelfitsch earned critical acclaim for *Five Days in March* (*Sangatsu no Itsukukan*; 2004), a hyper-real portrayal of two *freeters* (part-time workers) holed up in a Shibuya love hotel at the start of the Iraq War.

Butō

Butō is Japan's unique and fascinating contribution to contemporary dance. It was born out of a rejection of the excessive formalisation that characterises traditional forms of Japanese dance and of an intention to return to more ancient roots. Hijikata Tatsumi (1928–86) is credited with giving the first *butō* performance in 1959; Ōno Kazuo (1906–2010) was also a key figure.

Butō performances are best likened to performance art rather than traditional dance. During a performance, one or more dancers use their naked or seminaked bodies to express the most elemental and intense human emotions. Nothing is forbidden in *butō* and performances often deal with taboo topics such as sexuality and death. For this reason, critics often describe *butō* as scandalous, and *butō* dancers delight in pushing the boundaries of what can be considered beautiful in artistic performance.

Takarazuka

Popular but quirky, the all-female Takarazuka troupe offers a musical experience that is unlike any other. Founded in 1913, partly as an inversion of the all-male kabuki theatre and partly as a form of entertainment for a growing male middle class with money to burn, Takarazuka combines traditional Japanese elements with Western musical styles.

Interestingly, in light of its history, its most devoted admirers now comprise young women who swoon with romantic abandon over the troupe's beautiful drag kings. Takarazuka adopted its present revue format in the late 1920s, and except for the WWII years – during which the troupe proved an ideal propaganda tool – has continued to perform musicals and revues set in exotic locations.

VISUAL ARTS

Tokyo's contemporary art scene is broad, dynamic and scattered – much like the city itself. The opening of the first wave of influential commercial galleries in the '90s was a small revolution; until then, artists themselves paid to rent exhibition space. Among those still around are Gallery Koyanagi, in Ginza, and Tomio Koyama Gallery, east of the Sumida-gawa. Through there are now dozens of galleries, the city has no cohesive arts district; small, younger galleries are constantly on the move, chasing cheap rent.

The opening of the Mori Art Museum (p80) in 2003 was then something of a watershed moment, giving contemporary art a central, highly visible home. The museum's once-every-three-years exhibition of up-and-coming artists, called Roppongi Crossing (next up in 2013), has emerged as an important barometer of current trends.

While Tokyo is not much of a production centre for crafts, there are many fine museums in the city specialising in the ceramics, lacquerware and tea utensils that shaped the Japanese aesthetic.

Ukiyo-e

Far from the classical landscapes and religious-themed paintings, *ukiyo-e* (woodblock prints, but literally 'pictures of the floating world') were for the common people, used in advertising or in much the same way posters are used today. The subjects of these wood-block prints were images of everyday life, characters in kabuki plays and scenes from the 'floating world', a term derived from a Buddhist metaphor for life's fleeting joys.

Edo's particular floating world revolved around pleasure districts such as the Yoshiwara. In this topsy-turvy kingdom, an inversion of the usual social hierarchies imposed by the Tokugawa shōgunate, money meant more than rank, actors and artists were the arbiters of style, and prostitutes elevated their art to such a level that their accomplishments matched those of the women of noble families.

The vivid colours, novel composition and flowing lines of *ukiyo-e* caused great excitement when they finally arrived in the West; the French came to dub it 'Japonisme'. *Ukiyo-e* was a key influence on Impressionists and post-Impressionists (eg Toulouse-Lautrec, Manet and Degas). Yet among the Japanese, the prints were hardly given more than passing consideration – millions were produced annually in Edo, often thrown away or used as wrapping paper for pottery. For years, the Japanese were perplexed by the keen interest foreigners took in this art form.

Nihonga

Japan has a rich history of painting, though it owes its origins to China. Traditionally, paintings consisted of ink on *washi* (Japanese paper) or silk, sometimes

JAPANESE CINEMA

1930s
Directors hone their styles. **Watch** Ozu Yasujirō's *I Was Born, But...* (*Umarete wa mita keredo*; 1929); Mizoguchi Kenji's *Osaka Elegy* (*Naniwa Ereji*; 1936).

1940s
Censors demand nationalist themes. **Watch** Mizoguchi's classic vendetta story *The 47 Rōnin* (*Chūshingura*; 1941).

1950s
The golden age of Japanese film. **Watch** Kurosawa Akira's *Rashōmon* (1950); Mizoguchi's *Ugetsu Monogatari* (1953).

1960s
Colour and prosperity arrive. **Watch** Ozu's *An Autumn Afternoon* (*Sanma no Aji*; 1962).

1970s
Ōshima Nagisa brings new-wave visual techniques and raw sex. **Watch** *In the Realm of the Senses* (*Ai no Korīda*; 1976).

1980s
Imamura Shōhei and Itami Jūzō earn critical success. **Watch** Imamura's *The Ballad of Naruyama* (*Naruyama Bushiko*; 1983); Itami's *Tampopo* (1986).

1990s
Actor Takeshi Kitano emerges as a successful director. **Watch** *Fireworks* (*Hana-bi*; 1997).

2000s
Anime and horror flicks boom. **Watch** Miyazaki Hayao's *Spirited Away* (*Sen to Chihiro no Kamikakushi*; 2001).

IKEBANA

What sets Japanese ikebana (literally 'living flowers') apart from Western forms of flower arranging is the suggestion of space and the symbolism inherent in the choice and placement of the flowers and, in some cases, bare branches. It's not as esoteric as it sounds. Get a hands-on introduction to Japanese aesthetics at one of Tokyo's ikebana schools.

Ohara School of Ikebana (小原流いけばな; ☑5774-5097; www.ohararyu.or.jp; 5-7-17 Minami-Aoyama, Minato-ku; ℝGinza Line to Omote-sandō, exits B1 & B3) The Ohara school dates back to the late 19th-century and was the first to incorporate Western flowers; today it's taught all over the world. One-timers and short-term visitors are welcome, as are those who'd just like to watch (observation fee ¥800). English classes are Wednesdays and Thursdays; a trial lesson costs ¥4000.

Sōgetsu Kaikan This avant-garde school was founded in the 1920s. Trial lessons in English are held on Mondays from 10am to noon and cost ¥3800; reservation required. See p83.

MURAL

Okamoto Taro's mural *Asu no Shinwa* (Myth of Tomorrow; 1967) was commissioned by a Mexican luxury hotel but went missing two years later. It finally turned up in 2003, and in 2008 the haunting 30-metre-long work, which depicts the bomb exploding over Hiroshima, was installed on a wall inside Shibuya Station.

in monochrome and sometimes in highly pigmented colours and gold leaf. These works adorned folding screens, sliding doors and hanging scrolls; never behind glass, they were a part of daily life. Throughout the Edo period, the nobility patronised artists such as those by the Kanō school, who depicted Confucianism subjects, mythical Chinese creatures or scenes from nature.

With the Meiji Restoration (1868) – when artists and ideas were sent back and forth between Europe and Japan – painting necessarily became either a rejection or an embracement of Western influence. Two terms were coined: *yōga* for Western-style works and *nihonga* for Japanese-style works, though in reality, many *nihonga* artists incorporate shading and perspective into their works while using techniques from all the major traditional Japanese painting schools.

Superflat & Beyond

The '90s was a big decade for Japanese contemporary art: love him or hate him, Murakami Takashi brought Japan back into an international spotlight it hadn't enjoyed since 19th-century collectors went wild for *ukiyo-e*. His work makes fantastic use of the flat planes, clear lines and decorative techniques associated with traditional painting, while lifting motifs from the lowbrow subculture of manga (Japanese comics). As much an artist as a clever theorist, Murakami proclaimed in his 'Superflat' manifesto that his work picked up where Japanese artists left off during after Meiji Restoration – and might just be the future of painting, given that most of us now view the world through the portals of our two-dimensional computer screens.

Murakami inspired a whole generation of artists who worked in his 'factory' Kaikai Kiki and presented their works at his Geisai art fairs. The artist Yoshitomo Nara also made it big in the 90s with his paintings, again with manga-like styling, of punkish tots of unsettling depth.

Naturally, younger artists have had trouble defining themselves in the wake of 'Tokyo Pop' – as the highly exportable art of the '90s came to be known. There are a handful of artists gaining recognition for works that could be described as neo-*nihonga*; among them are Tenmyouya Hisashi, Yamaguchi Akira and Konoike Tomoko, all represented by Mizuma Art Gallery. Other names to look out for are those of sculptors Nawa Kohei and Motohiko Odani and the collection of irreverent pranksters known as ChimPom.

LITERATURE

Most of Japan's national literature since the Edo period has been penned by authors writing in Tokyo; consequently no other city in Japan has a greater hold on the national imagination – and as more and more Japanese works are translated – the global one.

Haiku

While Japanese traditional poetry, such as the 17-syllable haiku or the 31-syllable *waka*, is most closely associated with the ancient capital of Kyoto, it has a history in Tokyo as well. Japan's most famous poet of all time, Matsuo Bashō (1644–1694), led a literary society here and began his journey to write his renowned work *Oku no Hosomichi* on the banks of the Sumida-gawa. Haiku remains popular: it's not uncommon to see large busloads of retirees setting off on haiku composition trips, often to inspired locations such as the stops on Bashō's journey. Its five-seven-five syllable structure is also used in the media to construct ad slogans.

20th-Century Modernism

The most important writer of the modern era, Sōseki Natsume (1867–1916) was born in Tokyo in the last year that it could be called Edo. One of the first generation of scholars to be sent abroad, Sōseki studied English literature in London. His ability to convey Japanese subtlety and wit through the lines of the then newly imported Western-style novel, while taking a critical look at modernising Japan and its morals, has endeared him to generations of Japanese readers.

Nobel Prize winner Kawabata Yasunari (1899–1972) may not have been born in the capital, but he made up for it during his 20s, which he spent living in Asakusa – then Tokyo's equivalent of Montmartre. In works like *Snow Country*, Kawabata draws tense, bittersweet lines between the capital and the provinces. Japan's other Nobel Laureate, Ōe Kenzaburo (b 1935), confronts modern Japan head-on, using the individual as a stand-in for society in disturbing works like *A Personal Matter*. Ōe grew up in rural Shikoku but made the capital his home where, as a vocal pacifist, he can still be found speaking at rallies and symposiums.

Japan's most controversial literary figure, Mishima Yukio (1925–1970) grew up in central Tokyo, attending the elite Gakushūin (the school attended by the aristocracy). A prolific writer, Mishima wrote essays and *nō* plays in addition to dense, psychological novels. His growing obsession with *bushidō* (the samurai code) eventually led to a bizarre, failed takeover of the Tokyo headquarters of the Japanese Self Defence Forces that ended with Mishima committing *seppuku* (ritual suicide).

TEA CEREMONY

Sadō (the way of tea) is a celebration of the aesthetic principle of *wabi-sabi*, reached when naturalness, spontaneity and humility come together. Many Japanese art forms, including pottery, ikebana, calligraphy and garden design, developed in tandem with the tea ceremony. A few of Tokyo's most prestigious hotels have tearooms where ceremonies are performed in English. These include the **Imperial Hotel** (Map p286; ☎3504-1111; ⊗10am-4pm Mon-Sat; ¥1500), **Hotel Ōkura** (Map p288; ☎3582-0111; ⊗11am-4pm; ¥1050) and **Hotel New Ōtani** (off Map p288; ☎3265-1111; ⊗11am-4pm Thu-Sat; ¥1050); reservations are necessary.

Contemporary Writers

Among contemporary novelists, Murakami Haruki (1949–) is the biggest star, both at home and internationally. His latest work, *1Q84* (published as a trilogy in 2009–10), was an instant bestseller – and this at time when bestseller lists are dominated by genre works and cookbooks. Of all of his books, the one most Japanese are likely to mention as their favourite is the one that launched his career, *Norwegian Wood* (1987). Before becoming a writer, Murakami ran a jazz cafe in Kokubunji on the Chūō Line and many young writers hoping to follow in his footsteps are drawn to the neighbourhood.

Proving that literature is not, entirely, a boys' club, is Banana Yoshimoto (1964–). Her popular novel *Kitchen* (1988) was an international hit; more recently, in 2011, her novel *The Lake* (2005) was short-listed for the Man Asian Literary Prize.

More signs that the literary world is opening up: in 2004 the Akutagawa Prize – one of the nation's most prestigious – was awarded to the two youngest Japanese writers to have ever received it. Both of them are women: 19-year-old Kanehara Hitomi and Wataya Risa, aged 20.

Beyond Books

The latest trend (although arguably they are not literature at all) are self-published novels typed out on mobile phones. These melodramatic stories written in the abbreviated languages of text messages are uploaded by teens, usually female and often anonymous, to social networking sites. Some popular *keitai shōsetsu* (mobile novels) have been picked up by publishers and gone on to sell millions. Critics have called it the death of the novel; defenders have drawn parallels between *keitai shōsetsu* and the serialised depictions of court life in Japan's most famous work of literature, the Heian era *Tale of the Genji*, also written by a woman. More interestingly perhaps, is that these stories are often composed in public space – meaning you could be sitting next to an author at work on the subway.

TOKYO IN FICTION

➡ *Sanshirō* (1908) by Sōseki Natsume – Fresh off the train from provincial Kyūshū, a Tokyo University student is confronted by the perils of academia, women and a rapidly changing Japan.

➡ *Scarlet Gang of Asakusa* (*Asakusa Kurenaidan*; 1930) by Kawabata Yasunari – Kawabata based this lively chronicle of a gang of street urchins in Asakusa on his own days spent in the colourful neighbourhood.

➡ *A Strange Tale from East of the River* (*Bokutō Kidan*; 1937) by Nagai Kafu – An unapologetically elegiac tale of an encounter with an unlicensed prostitute in Tamanoi and a Tokyo swept up in modernisation.

➡ *Coin Locker Babies* (*Koinrokkā Beibīzu*; 1980) by Murakami Ryu – A coming-of-age tale of two boys left to die in coin lockers by their mothers. Both survive; though the Tokyo that they live to face is literally toxic.

➡ *Snakes and Earrings* (*Hebi ni Piasu*; 2003) by Kanehara Hitomi – This Akutagawa Prize winner traces the downward spiral of a Shibuya 'Barbie girl' spellbound by a mysterious tattoo artist.

➡ *1Q84* (2009–10) by Murakami Haruki – A nod to George Orwell's classic dystopia, this serialised tale follows an assassin who finds herself in an alternate-reality Shibuya.

TOKYO ON FILM

➡ *Stray Dog* (*Nora Inu;* 1949) – Kurosawa Akira's noir thriller concerns a rookie detective and a lost gun in sweltering, occupied Tokyo.

➡ *Tokyo Story* (*Tōkyō Monogatari;* 1953) – Ōzu Yasujirō's story of an older couple who come to Tokyo to visit their children only to find themselves treated with disrespect and indifference.

➡ *When a Woman Ascends the Stairs* (*Onna ga Kaidan wo Agaru Toki;* 1960) – Mikio Naruse's sympathetic portrayal of Ginza hostesses opens the doors to an otherwise exclusive world.

➡ *Lost in Translation* (2003) – Tokyo takes on a muted gleam in Sofia Coppola's Oscar winner about two hotel guests sharing a moment away from loveless marriages.

➡ *Train Man* (*Densha Otoko;* 2005) – After a shy *otaku* (geek) falls for a woman he defended from a drunkard on the train, he turns to online pals for help. This hit from director Masanori Murakami brought Akihabara culture into the mainstream.

➡ *Tokyo!* (2008) – This surrealistic romp by foreign directors Michel Gondry, Leos Carax and Bong Joon-ho is actually three stories, taking in sewer-dwellers, shut-ins and the challenge of finding good housing.

MUSIC

Tokyo has a huge, shape-shifting music scene supported by a local market of audiophiles willing to try almost anything. Classical music is revered – and performed by several outstanding local orchestras; jazz has a huge following, as does rock, house and electronica.

Traditional Legacy

When Tokyo was Edo, you could walk through the east side of town and hear the music of the *shamisen* – a three-stringed, banjo-like instrument – coming from the teahouses. This was the instrument played by the geisha, who spent the afternoon hours practising, and also one that was used in kabuki and bunraku. Japan has many traditional instruments, but it's the *shamisen* that best lends itself to modern settings.

Walking through the older parts of town in Tokyo today, you're more likely to overhear *enka*, a music style derived from old folk songs that came into vogue during the postwar years. Its lyrics emphasise themes of longing and tears, and musically its languid pace and scale borrows from traditional Japanese music. It's popular among the older generation, who belt out their favourite songs at karaoke bars after work.

Current Trends

While a whole generation of Western hipsters were turned on to Japan through the *Shibuya-kei* (Shibuya-style) music scene in the '90s, which included bands like Flipper's Guitar and Pizzicato Five, the country's current output is often written off as overly commercial. Most of the biggest acts today are young *aidoru* (idol) singers who owe their popularity to cute looks, powerful talent agencies and a flood of media appearances.

One exception is the music produced for anime (Japanese animation) and the game industry. It's not unusual to hear teenagers say their favourite music style is *anison* (short for 'anime song'). Soundtracks from TV series and from video game music (as it becomes increasingly more sophisticated) can become huge hits. Faceless composers and vocal artists have inspired loyal followings for the soundscapes they add to the popular narratives of shows and games. Sheet-music books also sell well, inspiring a whole new generation to pick up instruments.

Show & Exhibition Listings

Tokyo Art Beat (www.tokyoart beat.com)

Real Tokyo (www.realtokyo.co.jp)

Metropolis (metropolis.co.jp/listings)

Architecture

Tokyo's awesome built environment looks part Legoland, part sci-fi video game backdrop and part heaving neon anarchy. Disasters and lax planning laws have obliterated most heritage buildings and modern ones are scrapped and rebuilt every 20 years or so, giving the cityscape an inspired heterogeneous character similar to an immense Escher print. Unlike Kyoto, Tokyo evolved concentrically around Edo Castle, and its medieval design has a strong labyrinthine dimension. The resulting cityscape is a fantastic mishmash of impermanent structures grafted onto ancient patterns, so old and new are always right before your eyes.

Tokyo's oldest buildings

Tōshō-gu (1651)

Bank of Japan (1896)

Kyū Iwasaki-tei (1896)

Akasaka Palace (1909)

Tokyo Station (1914)

Harajuku Station (1924)

National Diet Building (1936)

FOREIGN INFLUENCES

Until the end of the Edo period, the city's houses and shops were almost entirely constructed of wood, paper and tile, and early photos show a remarkable visual harmony in the old skyline. Japan first opened its doors to Western architecture with the Meiji Restoration (1868). Japanese architects immediately responded to these new influences, but some 20 years later, a nationalistic push against the influence of the West saw a resurgence in the popularity of traditional Japanese building styles.

This ambivalence towards Western architecture continued until after WWI, when foreign architects, such as Frank Lloyd Wright, came to build the Imperial Hotel in Tokyo (since demolished for safety reasons, although the facade can be seen at Meiji Mura, a culture-history park near Nagoya, two hours from Tokyo on the bullet train). Wright introduced the International Style, characterised by sleek lines, cubic forms and materials such as glass, steel and brick. Other pre-WWII monoliths still stand in Marunouchi and Yūrakuchō opposite the east side of Hibiya Park; American bombers spared them and they were used for postwar command facilities.

After WWII the aggressively sculptural stone and concrete work of French architect Le Corbusier exerted strong influence on Japanese architects, and by the mid-1960s Japanese architects were beginning to attract attention on the world stage for their unique style.

TEMPLE OR SHRINE?

They may seem the same, but Buddhist temples and Shintō shrines are two different beasts. The quickest way to distinguish them is by checking their entrances. The main entrance of a shrine is a *torii* (gate), usually composed of two upright pillars, joined at the top by two horizontal crossbars, the upper of which is normally slightly curved. *Torii* are often painted a bright vermilion. In contrast, the *mon* (main entrance gate) of a temple is often a much more substantial affair, constructed of several pillars or casements, joined at the top by a multitiered roof. Temple gates often contain guardian figures, usually *Niō* (deva kings). Keep in mind, though, that shrines and temples sometimes share the same precincts (often a small shrine can be found on temple grounds), and it is not always easy to tell where one begins and the other ends. This reflects the flexible attitude Japanese people often take toward religion.

EARLY STYLE ICONS

The best known of Japan's 20th-century builders was Tange Kenzō (1913–2005). The influence of Le Corbusier combined with traditional Japanese forms can be seen in Tange's buildings, including the National Gymnasium (1964; p117) in Yoyogi-kōen and Sōgetsu Kaikan (1977; p83). His skyscraping Tokyo Metropolitan Government Offices (1991; p129) was modelled after the great European cathedrals – look up from the plaza below and see if it doesn't remind you of Notre Dame in Paris. Also look out for the Fuji Television Japan Broadcast Centre (1996; p182) in Odaiba; its latticelike frame suspends a giant orb that looms like the Death Star over Tokyo Bay.

In the 1960s architects such as Shinohara Kazuo, Kurokawa Kishō, Maki Fumihiko and Kikutake Kiyonori began a movement known as Metabolism, which promoted flexible spaces and functions at the expense of fixed forms in building. Kurokawa's **Nakagin Capsule Tower** (1972; 16-10 Ginza, Chūō-ku; Ōedo Line to Tsukijishijō) is a seminal work, designed as pods that could be removed whole from a central core and replaced elsewhere. His last great work, the National Art Center in Roppongi (2006; p81), weaves undulating vertical forms into a strikingly latticed, organic structure.

Shinohara finally came to design in a style he called Modern Next, incorporating both modern and postmodern design ideas combined with Japanese influences. This style can be seen in his Centennial Hall (1987) at the Tokyo Institute of Technology, an elegant and uplifting synthesis of clashing forms in shiny metal cladding. Maki, the master of minimalism, pursued design in a modernist style while still emphasising elements of nature – such as the roof of his Tokyo Metropolitan Gymnasium (1990; p126), which takes on the form of a sleek metal insect. Another Maki design, the Spiral Building (1985; p114) is a favourite with Tokyo residents for its user-friendly design, gallery space, cafe and shops.

Isozaki Arata, who originally worked under Tange, also promoted the Metabolist style before becoming interested in geometry and postmodernism. His work includes the Cultural Centre (1990) in Mito, about an hour from Tokyo, which contains a striking geometric, snake-like tower clad in different metals, and the Museum of Contemporary Art in Los Angeles.

Kikutake, meanwhile, went on to design the Edo-Tokyo Museum (1992; p171). This enormous structure encompasses almost 50,000 sq metres of built space and reaches 62.2m (the height of Edo Castle) at its peak.

Another Tokyo architect to break into the international scene recently is Taniguchi Yoshio. He had some important commissions in Japan – including the Gallery of Hōryū-ji Treasures (1999;p159) at Tokyo Kokuritsu Hakubutsukan (Tokyo National Museum) – but his first overseas project was as big as they get: the 2004 renovation and expansion of the Museum of Modern Art (MoMA) in New York.

NEXT GENERATION BUILDERS

In the 1980s a second generation of Japanese architects began to gain recognition within the international architecture scene, including Itō Toyō, Hasegawa Itsuko and Andō Tadao. This younger group has continued to explore both modernism and postmodernism, while incorporating the renewed interest in Japan's architectural heritage. One of Ito's most striking recent designs, built in 2004, **TOD's Omotesandō Building** (Map p293; 5-1-15 Jingūmae, Shibuya-ku) looks as if it was

QUAKE-PROOF

When the 2011 earthquake struck, the Tokyo Sky Tree suffered almost no damage. At its centre is ancient construction technology from Japanese pagodas: a *shimbashira* column of reinforced concrete that is structurally separate from the exterior truss. It acts as a counterweight when the tower sways, cutting vibrations by 50%.

CONTEMPORARY BUILDINGS

Asahi Flame (1989; Map p302) Famously capped by a representation of a golden flame come to be known as the 'golden turd', Philippe Starck's late Bubble-Era design is one of Tokyo's most recognisable modern structures.

Tokyo Metropolitan Government Offices (1991; p129) Tange Kenzō's city hall has both heft and airiness; great, free observatories mean it's popular, too.

Fuji Television Japan Broadcast Center (1994; p182) The signature building of Odaiba; a fantasy in geometry.

Museum of Contemporary Art, Tokyo (1995; p174) Yanagisawa Takahiko's wild design feels like an experiment in outrageous geometry. Steel and concrete blend harmoniously into the surrounding urban park.

Tokyo International Forum (1996; p61) This wonder of glass in Yūrakuchō looks like the hull of a ship.

Prada Aoyama Building (2003; p119) Jacques Herzog and Pierre de Meuron's creation is a marvel of white-on-white interiors, encased in a network of bubbled glass.

Roppongi Hills (2003; p80) Jon Jerde created a phenomenon of East meets West, ancient meets future and stark beauty meets crass commercialism.

National Art Center, Tokyo (2006; p81) Kurokawa Kishō's last great work is an undulating meshwork embracing seven large exhibition halls unsupported by columns.

Tokyo Sky Tree (2012; p170) This 634m-tall broadcasting tower is the world's tallest tower. Views are especially spectacular at sunset and in winter.

wrapped in surgical tape. Andō's architecture utilises materials such as concrete to create strong geometric patterns that have so regularly appeared in Japan's traditional architecture. Two of his landmarks are around Omote-sandō: **Collezione** (6-1-3 Minami-Aoyama, Minato-ku) and **Omote-sandō Hills** (Map p293; 4-12 Jingūmae, Shibuya-ku). See also p119.

Across the street from Omote-sandō Hills is the new **Christian Dior store** (5-9-11 Jingūmae, Shibuya-ku) by a young protégée of Ito's, Sejima Kazuyo, together with her partner Nishizawa Ryūe in the firm SANAA. They and others like them are quietly becoming the next generation of great Japanese architects; projects include museums in Spain, in New York and in Toledo, Ohio.

Sejima and Nishizawa picked up the prestigious Pritzker Architecture Prize for 2010. Judges praised their design simplicity, saying, 'SANAA's architecture stands in direct contrast with the bombastic.'

Tokyo's latest architectural triumph is of course the Tokyo Sky Tree (p170), 634m high and the tallest tower in the world. Tokyoites from miles around watched it grow taller and taller until it opened with great fanfare in May 2012. Built by Ōbayashi Corporation, it's now a new landmark, tourist magnet and source of pride for a city and nation battered by the 2011 earthquake and tsunamis.

Onsen

Getting naked with total strangers may not be your typical weekend pursuit, but don't be shy. The Japanese perceive bathing as a great social leveller and revel in the anonymity that nudity allows. The blissful relaxation that follows a good long soak can turn a sceptic into a convert, and may even make you an onsen fanatic.

Many Japanese would argue that you couldn't possibly understand their culture without visiting an onsen. There are literally thousands of hot springs scattered all over the archipelago. As long as there have been people here, you can bet that they've been soaking in onsen.

ONSEN EXCURSIONS

You don't have to travel far outside the city to discover onsen with a rustic charm that adds multiple layers to the experience. Picture yourself sitting in an open-air pool on a snow-flecked riverside. With express train and bus services, it's possible to get there and back in a day, though staying in an *onsen ryokan* (traditional inn with its own baths) is certainly a treat. In addition to having longer use of the baths, a stay includes a full-course dinner of seasonal delicacies and a traditional breakfast. Many *onsen ryokan* open their baths to day trippers in the afternoon; ask at the tourist information centre which places offer *higaeri onsen* (bathing without accommodation).

Konyoku (mixed bathing) was the norm in Japan until the Meiji Restoration, when the country sought to align itself with more 'civilised' Western ideas and outlawed the practice. It remains illegal in Tokyo, but out in the countryside (where baths may be no more than a pool in a riverbed blocked off with stones) *konyoku* is common.

Hakone

This is Tokyo's favorite onsen getaway, a centuries-old resort town with several distinct hot springs set among forested peaks. See p189 for detailed coverage of inns and day spas in the area.

Izu

Round out a trip to Shimoda (see p200) with a detour to the tiny, but excellent cliffside Sawada Kōen Rotemburo in Dōgashima (see p200).

Nikko

In the mountains above Nikkō, an hour away by bus, resort towns Chūzenji Onsen and Yumoto Onsen (p188) offer some sulphurous options for day trippers.

TOKYO ONSEN

Yes, even beneath the concrete tangle that is Tokyo there is pure hot-spring water. In the city centre, the modern La Qua (p149) has several floors of upmarket baths. Ōedo Onsen Monogatari (p181), in Odaiba, bills itself as an onsen 'theme park' and includes a recreation of an old-Edo downtown, along with multiple indoor and outdoor tubs.

Onsen

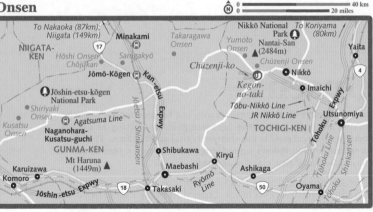

Kusatsu

Tucked away in the mountains of Gunma prefecture, northwest of Tokyo, **Kusatsu Onsen** (草津温泉; www.kusatsu-onsen.ne.jp/foreign) has been voted Japan's favourite onsen town year after year since the Edo period – even warlord Tokugawa Ieyasu was a fan of the sulphuric waters here.

There are several baths that are open to the public, including the excellent **Ōtakinoyu**, the giant *rotenburo* (outdoor bath) **Sai-no-kawara** and a dozen tiny 'secret' baths that locals don't want you to know about. Highway buses run directly from Shinjuku Station to Kusatsu in four hours; otherwise it's a 30-minute bus ride from Naganohara Kusatsu-guchi Station.

From the train station, it's also possible to get a bus (35 minutes) to nearby **Shiriyaki Onsen** (尻焼温泉). The name literally means 'arse burning' and the onsen bubbles right into a river that has been dammed to form a bathing pool, though don't go in spring when the snowmelt chills the water.

Minakami

Minakami is a sprawling onsen town – also in Gunma prefecture – that includes idyllic **Takaragawa Onsen** (宝川温泉; www.takaragawa.com/english.html). The four open-air baths here are large. Spread out along both sides of a river, they are connected by a footbridge. All of the bathing pools, save one just for women, are mixed bathing. No swimsuits are allowed, although women are permitted to wrap themselves in a 'modesty towel'. Takaragawa is particularly popular in autumn when the maples overhanging the baths become a blaze of red. There are hourly buses from Minakami Station to Takaragawa Onsen.

On the other side of town, the ryokan **Hōshi Onsen Chōjukan** (法師温泉長寿館; www.houshi-onsen.jp) has a gorgeous wooden bathhouse, with rows of individual bathing pools, that dates back to 1896. It's mixed bathing here too, with an additional modern facility just for women. The baths are open to day-trippers from 10am to 1.30pm; however, you might want to consider staying a night at the rustic, highly photogenic inn. To get here, take a bus from Jōmō-Kōgen Station to Sarugakyō, where you can transfer to a bus for Hōshi Onsen Chōjukan.

In print

The Japanese Spa: A Guide to Japan's Finest Ryokan and Onsen *(Akihiko Seki & Elizabeth Heilman Brooke; 2005) is a lush coffee table book with full colour photos of the country's most luxurious baths.*

Japan's Hidden Hot Springs *(Robert Neff; 1995) is a little out of date but still offers up some classic gems.*

SENTŌ

Prior to Japan's post-WWII economic revolution, most private homes in Japan did not have baths, so every evening people gathered their toiletries into a bowl and headed off to the local neighbourhood *sentō* (public bath). More than just a place to wash oneself, the *sentō* served as a kind of community meeting hall, where news and gossip were traded and social ties strengthened.

Unfortunately, the number of sentō in Japan is rapidly declining. In 1968, the peak of their popularity, Tokyo had 2687; now there are around 1000. Still, most neighbourhoods have one. Some look as though they haven't changed in decades. Others have evolved with the times, adding novelties like saunas, jet baths and *denki-buro* (literally an 'electric bath' that's spiked with an electric current; it feels as unsettling as it sounds).

A soak in a *sentō* is not just a cultural experience, but also an ideal way to recover from a day of sightseeing. Bathhouses can be identified by their distinctive *noren* (half-length curtains over the doorway), which usually bear the hiragana (ゆ; yu) for hot water (occasionally, it may be written in kanji: 湯). *Sentō* usually cost between ¥300 and ¥500. If you've forgotten any of your toiletries or a towel, you can buy them here for a small price; most stay open from around 3pm to midnight. Asakusa (p178) is particularly good for ambient old-fashioned soaks.

Online

1010 (www.1010.
or.jp/index.php,
in Japanese) is
a searchable
database of sentō
in Tokyo.

Onsen Blog
(http://japanport.
weblogs.jp/onsen)
is the travelogue
of a die-hard
Japanese onsen
fan.

ONSEN SENTŌ

BATHING ETIQUETTE

Bathing isn't just a pastime, it's a ritual – one so embedded in Japanese culture that everyone knows exactly what to do. This can be intimidating to the novice, but really all you need to know to avoid causing alarm is to wash yourself before getting into the bath. It's also a good idea to remember the characters for men (男) and women (女), which will be marked on the *noren* hanging in front of the respective baths.

MIGUEL MICHÁN / GETTY IMAGES ©

Open-air hot springs, Takaragawa Onsen

HEALING WATERS

What sets an onsen apart from an ordinary *sentō* (public bath) is the nature of the water. Onsen water comes unadulterated from natural hot springs and often contains a number of minerals; *sentō* water comes from the tap. Most Japanese will tell you that onsen water makes one's skin *sube-sube* (smooth). Particular waters are also believed to help cure such ailments as high blood pressure, poor circulation and even infertility.

Sento Murals

Designed to enhance the feeling of relaxation, and more often than not an idyllic rendition of Mt Fuji, this art is as endangered as the sentō itself. Only two penki-e (painters) remain who are qualified to paint the murals, which have adorned bathhouses for a century.

Upon entering an onsen or *sentō*, the first thing you'll encounter is a row of lockers for your shoes. After you pay your admission and head to the correct changing room, you'll find either more lockers or baskets for your clothes. Take everything off here, entering the bathing room with only the small towel.

That little towel performs a variety of functions: you can use it to wash (but make sure to give it a good rinse afterwards) or to cover yourself as you walk around. It is not supposed to touch the water though, so leave it on the side of the bath or – as the locals do – folded on top of your head.

Park yourself on a stool in front of one of the taps and give yourself a thorough wash. Make sure you rinse off all the suds. When you're done, it's polite to rinse off the stool for the next person. At more humble bathhouses you might have little more than a ladle to work with; in that case, crouch low and use it to scoop out water from the bath and pour over your body – taking care not to splash water into the tub – and scrub a bit with the towel.

In the baths, keep splashing to a minimum and your head above the water. Before heading back to the changing room, wipe yourself down with the towel to avoid dripping on the floor.

Many bathhouses refuse entry to persons with tattoos because of their association with the *yakuza* (Japanese mafia). If your tattoo is on the smaller side, you might get away with covering it up with medical tape.

Survival Guide

Transport

GETTING TO TOKYO

Most travellers arrive in the Tokyo area by air. The capital's two main passenger airports are Narita International Airport, Japan's main gateway to the world, and Haneda Airport, which is now taking on more of an international role after decades of mainly serving domestic flights. Both airports require train or bus rides to get to the capital's downtown area.

Most transpacific flights take at least nine hours from North America's west coast, or 12 to 13 hours from the east coast. If you're flying from Australia, expect a nine- to 10-hour journey. Flights from western Europe can take 12 hours to Tokyo. Note that non-Japanese visitors are fingerprinted and photographed on arrival. A neat appearance will speed your passage through passport control and customs.

Tokyo is also readily accessible by high-speed train, which is convenient if you're travelling around Japan on a JR Rail Pass. In many cases, flying is faster and not significantly more expensive than riding the *shinkansen* (bullet train) to some of the country's most far-flung destinations, such as Hokkaido and Kyūshū. *Shinkansen* services from Nagoya, Kyoto and Osaka, meanwhile, can get you to Tokyo Station in under three hours.

Flights, tours and rail tickets can be booked online at lonelyplanet.com/bookings.

Narita Airport

The excellent, modern **Narita Airport** (☑ flight information 0476-34-5000, general information 0476-32-2802; www.narita-airport.jp/en), 66km east of Tokyo, is in an inconvenient location but has a plethora of services. It's divided into two terminals, which are connected by a free shuttle-bus service; from Terminal 1 board the bus at stop 6, and from Terminal 2 board at stops 8 and 18. The airport website lists which airlines use which terminal. If you are going to Narita Airport by land, note that passports are inspected for everyone entering Narita Airport, even if they're not travelling; keep yours handy.

The airport **Tourist Information Centres** (TIC; ☑ 0476-34-6251; ⊗ 9am-8pm) are a key stop if you haven't yet booked any accommodation. There's a TIC on the 1st floor in each terminal. Narita Airport also has JR offices in each terminal, where you can make bookings and exchange your Japan Rail Pass (p256) voucher for a pass, if you're planning to start travelling straight away.

Rail

Both the Japan Railways (JR East) and the independent Keisei Line connect Narita Airport and Tokyo.

CLIMATE CHANGE & TRAVEL

Every form of transport that relies on carbon-based fuel generates CO_2, the main cause of human-induced climate change. Modern travel is dependent on aeroplanes, which might use less fuel per kilometre per person than most cars but travel much greater distances. The altitude at which aircraft emit gases (including CO_2) and particles also contributes to their climate change impact. Many websites offer 'carbon calculators' that allow people to estimate the carbon emissions generated by their journey and, for those who wish to do so, to offset the impact of the greenhouse gases emitted with contributions to portfolios of climate-friendly initiatives throughout the world. Lonely Planet offsets the carbon footprint of all staff and author travel.

Keisei Line (☎0476-32-8501; www.keisei.co.jp) The fastest service between Narita Airport and Tokyo is the comfortable Skyliner, which runs nonstop to Nippori on the JR Yamanote Line (¥2400, 36 minutes) and Ueno (¥2400, 41 minutes) stations (Map p300); Keisei runs several slower services as well.

Japan Railways (JR East; ☎in English 050-2016-1603; www.jreast.co.jp) Narita Express (N'EX; ¥2940, 53 minutes) and JR *kaisoku* (rapid express; ¥1280, 85 minutes) services run to Tokyo Station (Map p286), from where you can change for almost anywhere. N'EX is swift, smooth and comfortable, but it doesn't operate as frequently as the Keisei Line. N'EX trains depart Narita approximately every half-hour between 7am and 10pm for Tokyo Station, and they also run less frequently into Shinagawa (¥3110, 65 minutes), Shibuya (Map p292; ¥3110, 73 minutes), Shinjuku (Map p294; ¥3110, 80 minutes) and Ikebukuro (Map p296; ¥3110, 86 minutes). Japan Rail and JR East Passes (p256) are valid on N'EX trains, but you must obtain a seat reservation (no extra charge) from a JR ticket office. JR *kaisoku* service is part of the local transit network and so stops at many local stations. This service is the slowest and cheapest into Tokyo Station, leaving about once an hour.

Bus

Friendly Airport Limousine (☎3665-7220; www.limousinebus.co.jp/en; 1-way fare ¥3000) Operates scheduled, direct, all-reserved buses between Narita Airport and major hotels and train stations in Tokyo. The journey takes 1½ to two hours depending on traffic and other stops.

Taxi

In case you're wondering, a taxi to Narita Airport from Tokyo will set you back approximately ¥30,000 and, battling traffic all the way, will usually take longer than the train.

Haneda Airport

Closer to central Tokyo **Haneda Airport** (☎information 6428-0888; www.tokyo-airport-bldg.co.jp/en) has two domestic terminals and one international terminal, which opened in 2010. It is usually used for domestic flights, but with the completion of a new runway, it has greatly expanded its international flights to serve South Korea, Singapore, China, Taiwan, Malaysia, the United States, as well as Germany, the United Kingdom and France. However, noise laws restrict long-haul flights to the hours between 11pm and 6am, during which trains, buses and the monorail to central Tokyo may not be running. Be sure to check your transport before you leave or you may face a long wait unless you want to pay for a taxi.

There's a **Tourist Information Centre** (☎5.30am-1am) on the 2nd floor of the arrivals lobby of Haneda's international terminal.

Monorail

Tokyo Monorail (www.tokyo-monorail.co.jp/english; ¥470, 15 minutes) This service gets you to Hamamatsuchō Station on the JR Yamanote Line from Haneda. Trains depart every 10 minutes.

Rail

Keikyū (☎5789-8686; www.haneda-tokyo-access.com/en/) Operates trains from Haneda's international terminal to Shinagawa (¥400, 22 minutes) on the JR Yamanote Line (airport *kyūkō* services are

BAGGAGE SHIPMENT

Baggage couriers provide next-day delivery of your large luggage from Narita and Haneda Airports to any address in Tokyo (around ¥2000 per large bag). This fabulous service can also deliver luggage to points beyond Tokyo so you don't have to haul it through trains and stations all over the countryside.

ANA Sky Porter (☎toll free 0120-007-952)

JAL ABC (☎toll free 0120-919-120, in Tokyo 03-3545-2800; www.jalabc.com)

the fastest). From Shinagawa, most trains become part of the Asakusa Line subway, serving Higashi-Ginza, Nihombashi and Asakusa stations.

Bus

Friendly Airport Limousine Buses connect Haneda with hotels around central Tokyo; buses to Shinjuku cost ¥1200 (¥2000 between midnight and 5am) and take about one hour, while the fare to Shibuya is ¥1000 (¥2000 at night).

Haneda Airport Express (http://hnd-bus.com) Buses operated by Keikyū link Haneda with Tokyo and the surrounding region. Stops include Shibuya Station (¥1000, one hour) and Tokyo Station (¥900, 55 minutes), both on the JR Yamanote Line.

Taxi

Taxis to central Tokyo will set you back around ¥7000.

GETTING AROUND TOKYO

Get yourself a Suica or Pasmo store-value card at a vending machine (see p256) and moving around in Tokyo is a snap. Hyperefficient, sparkling clean and virtually crime-free, the capital's public transport system is the envy of the world. It is reasonably priced and frequent (generally five minutes at most between trains on major lines), and many stations have conveniences such as baggage lockers. There are also handy bus services – although using these can be challenging since there is less English signage.

PASSES & COMBINATION TICKETS

Here are some options to reduce your travel costs into and around Tokyo:

Available at Train Stations

Tokyo Metro One-Day Open Ticket (¥710) Unlimited rides on Tokyo Metro subway lines only. Purchase at Tokyo Metro stations.

Common One-Day Ticket for Tokyo Metro and Toei subway lines (¥1000) Valid on all 13 lines operating underground in Tokyo. Purchase at Tokyo Metro or Toei stations.

Tokyo Combination Ticket (*Tokyo Furii Kippu*; ¥1580) Unlimited same-day rides on Tokyo Metro, Toei and JR Lines operating in Tokyo. Purchase at *midori-no-madoguchi* (service counters with green signs, aka JR Ticket Offices) at JR stations.

For Passengers Coming from Narita Airport

Limousine & Metro Pass (one/two days ¥3100/6000) One-way ticket for Friendly Airport Limousine (p253) and one-day pass on Tokyo Metro subway lines. Purchase at Airport Limousine counters or at Tokyo Metro pass outlets.

N'EX & Suica (¥3500) One-way ride on Narita Express into the city, plus a Suica (p256) worth ¥2000 (¥1500 in value, plus deposit). Round-trip also available.

Skyliner & Metro Pass (one/two days ¥2100/2480) Covers one-way ticket on Keisei Skyliner (p252) from Narita Airport plus a one- or two-day pass on Tokyo Metro subway lines. Available at Keisei counters at Narita Airport.

Tokyo Metro One- or Two-Day Open Ticket (¥600/980) Unlimited rides on Tokyo Metro subway lines. Purchase at Narita Airport Railway/Bus Ticket Counter (Terminal 1) or Entertainment Ticket/Cell Phone Counter (Terminal 2).

JR Kantō Area Pass (¥8000) Three days of unlimited rides on all JR East lines including limited expresses and *shinkansen* (but not the Tōkaidō *shinkansen*) for ¥8000. Available at Narita and Haneda airports.

Train

Tokyo's trains are a wonder. Although the train map looks like a bowl of *rāmen*, inside it's about the most orderly bowl of *rāmen* you'll ever see. Trains arrive and depart precisely on time, and even a minute's delay elicits apologies from conductors. Passengers, meanwhile, queue up at indicated points, and the trains stop right there.

Navigating

Station names are clearly marked in both Japanese and English on platform signs and/or posts, and electronic signs inside most trains show the next station. Listen for announcements. Some stations have many exits, which are numbered. When getting directions, always ask which exit to use. Individual listings in this book give this information.

Services

Outside central Tokyo, the fastest regular trains (ie slower than the shinkansen) are the tokkyū (特急; limited express services) and the kyūkō (急行; ordinary express). Local trains, which stop at all stations, are called futsū (普通).

Female carriages

Tokyo's train system is remarkably crime-free, but groping male hands have long been a problem for women when trains are packed. Tokyo train lines now reserve women-only carriages at peak times. The carriages are marked with signs (usually pink) in Japanese and English.

Japan Railways (JR) Lines

The Japan Railways (JR East; in English 050-2016-1603; www.jreast.co.jp) lines are mostly above-ground trains and are integrated with train lines, including the

TRAIN TICKETS

Unlike on many other train systems throughout the world, Japanese trains require you to swipe your ticket or store-value card upon both entering and leaving the train system. Keep your ticket in a safe place during your journey! If you've purchased a single-journey ticket, it will be collected when you exit.

shinkansen, to pretty much anywhere else in Japan. Here are some useful JR trains within the city.

YAMANOTE LINE

The most important train line in Tokyo, both in usefulness and cultural significance, the Yamanote Line makes a 35km loop around central Tokyo. It's named for the 'high city' that once functioned within. A ride on the Yamanote Line makes a great introduction to the city. Buy the cheapest fare (¥130), grab a seat, and an hour later you'll disembark at the same station where you started with a solid overview of Tokyo's main areas of interest. JR Yamanote Line trains are silver with a green stripe.

CHŪŌ & SŌBU LINES

The JR Chūō Line cuts its way across the centre of the JR Yamanote Line between Shinjuku and Tokyo Stations in about 13 minutes. Trains on this line are coloured orange. This line is contiguous with the JR Sōbu Line until Ochanomizu Station where the lines split – the Chūō heading down to Tokyo Station and the Sōbu heading out to the eastern suburbs. Chūō Line trains typically run express, while the Sōbu Line runs local. Sōbu Line cars have a yellow stripe.

OTHER LINES

The JR Yokosuka Line runs south to Kamakura (see p193) from Tokyo Station via Shimbashi and Shinagawa Stations. The JR Tōkaidō Line travels in the same direction from Tokyo Station, providing access to Atami or Shinagawa, where you can transfer for Shimoda (p200).

Subway

Ferrying millions of passengers around daily, Tokyo's subway system is indispensable for moving about. The city is home to 13 subway lines, of which nine are operated by **Tokyo Metro** (www.tokyometro.jp/en) and four by **Toei** (www.kotsu.metro.tokyo.jp/eng/services/subway.html).

Tickets

If you buy a refundable Pasmo store-value card (see p256), you can easily ride the two companies' lines just by waving the card over the sensors at the ticket gates, which will tell you how much money you have left. Buying paper tickets for each ride is also possible, but transferring from Toei to Tokyo Metro or vice versa requires a special transfer ticket. Most subway fares within central Tokyo cost between ¥160 and ¥210.

Navigating

Colour-coding and regular English signposting make the system easy to use. The Ginza Line is orange, for instance. Each station also has a an alphanumeric code to aid travellers, but you may find names easier to remember. Hubs include Nihombashi, Ōtemachi and Ginza.

Private Lines

The Yurikamome Line, which services Odaiba (Map p303), is a driverless, elevated train that departs from Shimbashi, just south of Ginza. Most

other private lines service suburban areas outside Tokyo. The ones you are most likely to use are Shibuya's Tōkyū Tōyoko Line, which runs south to Yokohama; the Keiō Inokashira Line from Shibuya to Kichijōji via Shimo-Kitazawa; Shinjuku's Odakyū Line, which runs southwest out to Hakone (p189); and Asakusa's Tōbu Nikkō Line, which goes north to Nikkō (p185).

Tickets & Passes

VENDING MACHINES
If you're willing to go through the potential headache of using paper tickets instead of a store-value card, look for the fare map above station vending machines. Unfortunately, the names are often in kanji (script) only. One solution is to buy the lowest fare (¥130 on JR, ¥160 to ¥170 on subway lines) and settle the difference on arrival (see p255). If the machine has a touch screen, there will be an option to switch the language to English. Credit cards are not accepted for local transit tickets.

JR TICKET COUNTERS
Larger JR stations have service counters called midori-no-madoguchi (緑の窓口; green window, aka JR Ticket Counters). Here you can buy bullet-train tickets, make reservations and buy special passes. Credit cards are usually accepted here.

FARE ADJUSTMENT
If the exit gate tells you to pay more, you have two options. Simply hand your ticket to an attendant, who will collect what you owe. A fare-adjustment machine, usually near the exit turnstiles, is just as simple. Insert your ticket, and the screen will tell you how much to put in, then spit out your change (if any) and a new ticket. Insert this ticket into the exit turnstiles, and off you go. These machines usually have English instructions.

SUBWAY LOGIC

Riding the rails in Tokyo is a fantastic cultural study. See if you notice your fellow passengers doing the following:

⇒ **Texting** – by far the most popular pastime.

⇒ **Reading** – manga-mania is alive and well in Tokyo's trains.

⇒ **Sleeping** – don't be surprised to find some salary-man's head on your shoulder. Amazingly, Tokyoites never seem to sleep through their stop.

⇒ **Talking** – actually, this is something you probably won't encounter much of. On most trains you can hear a pin drop. Mobile phone conversations are definitely frowned upon. See Sleeping, above.

⇒ **Eating** – again, notable for its absence on subways. Perhaps that's how the cars stay so clean. By contrast, on inter-city trains, eating is practically a commandment.

STORE-VALUE CARDS

Even if you won't spend long in Tokyo, you should strongly consider getting either a Suica (sold at JR stations) or a Pasmo (sold at subway stations) smart card. They will make moving around infinitely simpler. Either card works on virtually all trains and buses within Tokyo, and Suica is also valid on JR lines in other regions of Japan. Either card has an initial purchase price of ¥2000/1000 (Suica/Pasmo, including a ¥500 deposit). Wave the card over the turn-stiles and your fare is automatically deducted at the end of a journey. You can replenish the value of the card as needed at stations. You can even use it to pay for items in stores, vending machines and baggage lockers in stations. When you return your Suica or Pasmo card at a station office, you'll be refunded the ¥500 deposit, minus a ¥210 service fee.

JR PASSES

Many visitors to Japan purchase a **Japan Rail Pass** (www.japanrailpass.net) for travel on JR trains throughout the nation. A seven-day pass costs ¥28,300 and must be purchased *before* arriving in Japan; 14-day and 21-day passes are also available.

The regional JR company, **JR East** (www.jreast.co.jp), also offers the JR East Pass for unlimited travel on its trains in eastern Honshu and into the Japan Alps, costing from ¥20,000 for either five consecutive days or four days of your choosing with a 30-day period; the JR East Pass can be purchased in Japan. JR East also offers the new JR Kantō Area pass, with which you can get three days of unlimited rides on all JR East lines including limited expresses and *shinkansen* (but not the Tōkaidō *shinkansen*) for ¥8000.

Stations

Navigating your way around train stations in Tokyo can be confusing, particularly at complex stations such as Shinjuku Station. Most stations have adequate English signposting, with large yellow signs on the platforms posting exit numbers. Street maps of the area are usually posted near each exit.

EXITS

Since each station will usually have several different exits, you should get your bearings and decide where to exit while still on the platform. When possible, find out which exit to use when you get directions to a destination. If you have your destination written down, you can go to an attended gate and ask the station attendant to direct you to the correct exit.

LOCKERS & TOILETS

Most stations have luggage lockers, which can hold medium-sized bags. These lockers often come in several sizes and cost from ¥200 to ¥600. Storage is good for 24 hours, after which your bags will be removed and taken to the station office.

All train stations have toilets, almost all of which are free of charge. Bring pocket tissues, though, as toilet paper is not always provided. It's also a good idea to pick up a handkerchief at a ¥100 shop.

Bus

Tokyo has an extensive and convenient bus network, operated by **Toei** (www.kotsu.metro.tokyo.jp/eng/services/bus.html). Bus fares are ¥200/100 per adult/child for Tokyo Metropolitan (Toei) buses; you can pick up a copy of the Toei Bus Route Guide, including a route map and timetable, at any Toei subway station. Use your Pasmo or Suica store-value card, or deposit your fare into the box as you enter the bus; you can get change for ¥1000 notes and coins. A recording announces the name of each stop as it is reached, so listen carefully and press the button next to your seat when yours is announced.

The one-day Tokyo Combination Ticket (see p254) can be used on Toei buses as well as the subway and JR railway lines.

Boat

Tokyo Cruise river ferries are one of the most dramatic ways to take in the city. For more information on cruises down Sumida-gawa, see p73.

Taxi

Fares

Taxis in Tokyo feature white-gloved drivers, seats covered with lace doilies and doors that magically open and close. Fares start at ¥710, which buys you 2km (after 11pm it's 1.5km), then the meter rises by ¥80 every 275m (every 220m or so after 11pm). You also click up about ¥80 every two minutes while you relax in traffic jams.

Riding

It's generally quite simple to hail a taxi, and hotels and train stations usually have orderly queues. Taxi vacancy is indicated by a red light in the corner of the front window; a green light means there's a night-time surcharge; and a yellow light means that the cab is on call.

Tokyo taxi drivers rarely speak any English – it's a good idea to have your destination written down in Japanese or better yet a map (most hotels and businesses have one).

Streetcar

The last streetcar service in central Tokyo, the **Toden Arakawa Line** (p146), plies the northern part of the city between Minowabashi and Waseda (one way ¥160; day pass ¥400), taking passengers through some quaint residential neighbourhoods.

Bicycle

Despite the tangled traffic and often narrow roads, bicycles are still one of the most common forms of transport in Tokyo. Some ryokan (traditional Japanese inns) and hotels rent bicycles to their guests or you can hire one from **Tokyo Rent a Bike** (www.tokyorentabike. com; 8F, 3-5-11 Naka-Meguro, Meguro-ku).

Theft does happen, especially of cheap bicycles, so use your lock. Heed all no-parking signs for bicycles. Yours could get impounded by municipal enforcers. Getting it back again typically costs ¥3000, as well as a trip to the pound.

Car & Motorcycle

Driving

Driving in Tokyo isn't recommended. Parking is limited and expensive, traffic moves in slow-mo, traffic lights are virtually every 50m, and unless you've lived here for a while, expect to get lost. Trust us: you're much better off taking advantage of Tokyo's excellent public transport.

However, if you intend to drive in Japan, pick up the useful *Rules of the Road* (¥1000) available from the **Japan Automobile Federation** (www.jaf.or.jp/e/index. htm). You will need an International Driving Permit, which must be arranged in your own country before you go.

Hire

Car-hire agencies in Tokyo will rent you one of their vehicles upon presentation of an International Driving Permit. Small cars average ¥8000 per day. Some rental agencies that usually have English-speaking staff on hand are:

Nippon Rent-a-Car (☑3485-7196)

Toyota Rent-a-Car (☑5954-8020)

TOURS

Bus

Gray Line (☑3595-5948; www.jgl.co.jp/inbound/index. htm; tours ¥4000-9700) Buses chug along to places such as the Imperial Palace, Asakusa, Sensō-ji and the National Diet buildings. Tours run for either a morning, afternoon or full day and some include meals.

Hato Bus Tours (☑3435-6081; www.hatobus.com; tours ¥3500-14,000) Offers half-day, full-day and night-time tours of the city. It hits Sensō-ji and Tsukiji Central Fish Market, as well as some less visited spots like Akihabara.

JTB (☑5796-5759; www. japanican.com; Tokyo tours ¥4000-14,500) Boasts an extensive roster of day trips and tours in other parts of Japan. Some are return trips from Tokyo, while others originate in other big Japanese cities.

Boat

Symphony (www.symphony-cruise.co.jp; tours adult ¥1500-3800, child ¥750-1900) Offers two-hour day and evening cruises around Tokyo Bay, departing from Hinode Pier. If you lunch or dine on board, you'll pay from ¥5000 to ¥21,000 (including passage) depending on the type of meal you choose.

Vingt-et-un (www.vantean.co. jp; lunch/sunset/dinner cruises from ¥5100/7100/10,200) Departing from Takeshiba Pier, lunch, sunset and dinnertime cruises come with French meals. The route covers the Tokyo waterfront, Rainbow Bridge and Odaiba. and heads downriver toward Haneda Airport before returning.

Helicopter

Excel Air (www.excel-air. com; Urayasu Heliport; flights adult/child from ¥8500/4250) Offers 15- and 20-minute flights: a dramatic way to take in the skyline of Ginza, the Imperial Palace or Akihabara. Helicopters fly up to eight people. Flights depart from Urayasu city, east of Tokyo in Chiba Prefecture.

Directory A–Z

Business Hours

Standard opening hours are listed below. Reviews list hours only when they differ.

Banks Monday to Friday from 9am to 3pm (some to 5pm).

Shops and supermarkets From 10am to 8pm daily.

Museums Open at 9am or 10am and close at 5pm, with the last entry between 4pm and 4.30pm; the most common closing day for museums is Monday.

Restaurants Lunch 11.30am to 2.30pm; dinner 6pm to 10pm, with last orders taken about half an hour before closing.

Bars Open around 5pm until the wee hours.

Customs Regulations

Japanese penalties for violating customs laws can be very severe. You will be given a customs card when landing at Narita that stipulates what is allowed.

Alcohol 3 bottles (760ml bottle)

Tobacco 400 cigarettes or 100 cigars or 500 grams of other tobacco products

Perfume 56 grams (2 ounces)

Other goods ¥200,000 (total of overseas market value)

Discount Cards

GRUTT Pass (www.museum.or.jp/grutto; pass ¥2000) This pass allows free or discounted admission to some 70 attractions around town within two months, and it can be excellent value. The website lists points of purchase, including many convenience stores.

Electricity

Japanese plugs are the type with two flat pins, which are identical to two-pin North American plugs. The Japanese electric supply is 100V AC, an odd voltage found almost nowhere else in the world (appliances with a two-pin plug made for use in North America will work without an adaptor, but may be a bit sluggish). Tokyo and eastern Japan are on 50Hz, western Japan is on 60Hz. Transformers are easy to find at one of Japan's plentiful electronics shops.

100V/50Hz/60Hz

Emergencies

Although most emergency operators you'll reach in Tokyo don't speak English, the operators will immediately refer you to someone who does. Japan Helpline is a service that provides assistance to foreigners living in Japan.

Ambulance (⌨119)

Fire (⌨119)

A MEDLEY OF MUSEUMS

There are some 240 museums in Tokyo, and if you're planning on visiting any of them, here are some tips to keep in mind:

➡ Museum hours are generally 9am to 5pm, and nearly all museums are closed on Mondays. Hours in this book refer to closing times, not to last admission times (usually 30 minutes to one hour prior to closure). If museums are open on Mondays due to holidays, they are usually closed Tuesdays.

➡ Student discounts are commonly by school type (university, high school etc), and for the youngest visitors admission is usually free. Seniors discounts are less frequent. You may be required to show ID for any discount.

Japan Helpline (☎0120-46-1997)

Police (☎110, English-language line ☎3501-0110)

Gay & Lesbian Travellers

With the possible exception of Thailand, Japan is Asia's most enlightened nation with regard to the sexual orientation of foreigners. Tokyo in particular is a tolerant city where the bars and clubs host folks of all predilections. Tokyo has an active gay scene and a small but very lively gay quarter (Shinjuku-nichōme; see p136). Same-sex couples probably won't encounter many problems travelling in Tokyo, although some travellers have reported being turned away or grossly overcharged when checking into love hotels with a partner of the same sex. Outside Tokyo, you'll find it difficult to break into the local scene unless you spend considerable time in a place or have local contacts; Japanese would tell you much the same of their experiences in a new city.

Apart from this, it's unlikely that you'll run into difficulties. There are no legal restraints on same-sex sexual activities in Japan apart from the usual age restric-

tions. One note: Japanese of any sort do not typically engage in public displays of affection.

Cineastes visiting in summer should check the local listings for screenings of the annual **Tokyo International Lesbian & Gay Film & Video Festival** (☎6475-0388; www.tokyo-lgff.org). Another useful website to peruse when planning your travel is **Utopia Asia** (www.utopia-asia.com).

Health

Tokyo enjoys an excellent standard of medical care. Air pollution is one health issue, but this is unlikely to affect most travellers, apart from those with chronic lung conditions.

Insurance

When seeking medical care, be sure to bring proof of your travel or health insurance that clearly indicates that you're covered for any treatment you receive. If you arrive without insurance, it's possible to see a doctor at either a hospital or a clinic, but you will be expected to pay in full at the time of service.

If your health insurance doesn't cover you for all medical expenses incurred abroad, you should consider

purchasing supplemental travel insurance before leaving home. Evacuations in an emergency can cost well over US$100,000.

Medications

Some medications cannot be taken into Japan; prohibited drugs include products that contain the stimulants pseudoephedrine and codeine. If you take any regular medication, you should check with your local Japanese embassy whether there is any restriction on taking it into the country.

Internet Access

No surprise that Tokyo is a very wired city. In this book, the internet symbol (@) in lodging listings indicates internet access of some kind, either from a shared computer in a lobby or business centre, or from your own room. The wi-fi symbol (☎) indicates wi-fi is available.

In all but the most budget accommodation, internet access with your own laptop is possible from your room, and usually it is included in room rates. Wi-fi is getting more common in modern hotels. Rather, internet access is typically via LAN cable operating over a DSL or ADSL system. Most hotels supply LAN cables for free. If yours does not and if the hotel cannot rent or sell you one, electronics shops carry them for about ¥500.

Free wi-fi access is not as common as you'd expect in Tokyo. Check the **Freespot access map** (www.freespot.com/users/map_e.html), a limited free wi-fi service, for locations broken down by *ku* (wards) within Tokyo.

If you haven't brought your own laptop, you'll find an abundance of internet cafes in every major neighbourhood in Tokyo. Rates vary, usually ranging from ¥200 to ¥500 per hour, and most connections are fast DSL or ADSL.

Legal Matters

Japanese police have extraordinary powers compared with their Western counterparts. For starters, Japanese police have the right to detain a suspect without charging them for up to three days, after which a prosecutor can decide to extend this period for another 20 days. Police also have the authority to choose whether to allow a suspect to phone their embassy or lawyer or not, although, if you do find yourself in police custody, you should insist that you will not cooperate in any way until allowed to make such a call. Your embassy is the first place you should call if given the chance.

Police will speak almost no English; insist that a *tsuyakusha* (interpreter) be summoned; police are legally bound to provide one before proceeding with any questioning. Even if you are able to speak Japanese, it is best to deny it and stay with your native language.

For legal counselling in English and some other languages, seek out these resources:

Human Rights Counseling Center for Foreigners (☑5689-0518; ☉1-4.30pm Tue & Thu) Free consultation and English-Japanese translation on problems regarding human rights.

Tokyo English Life Line (TELL; ☑5774-0992; ☉9am-11pm) Free, anonymous telephone counselling.

Tokyo Foreign Residents Advisory Center (☑5320-7744; ☉9.30am-noon & 1-5pm Mon-Fri)

Medical Services

Most hospitals and clinics do not have doctors and nurses who speak English, but we've listed a few good ones that do:

Clinics

National Center for Global Health and Medicine (☑3202-7181; www.ncgm.go.jp, in Japanese; 1-21-1 Toyama, Shinjuku-ku; ☒Ōedo Line to Wakamatsu-kawada, Kawada exit) Though the website's in Japanese, operators on the phone speak English.

National Medical Clinic (☑3473-2057; www.nmclinic.net; Suite 202, 5-16-11 Minami-Azabu, Minato-ku; ☒Hibiya Line to Hiro-o, exits 1 & 2) English-speaking physicians practise general medicine here, and there are also a few specialised services.

Tokyo British Clinic (Map p291; ☑5458-6099; www.tokyobritishclinic.com; 2nd fl, Daikanyama Y Bldg, 2-13-7 Ebisu-Nishi, Shibuya-ku; ☉emergency service 24hr; ☒JR Yamanote Line to Ebisu, west exit) Founded and run by a British physician, this clinic also offers paediatric, obstetric/gynaecological and STD services.

Tokyo Medical & Surgical Clinic (Map p288; ☑3436-3028, emergency 3432-6134; www.tmsc.jp; 2nd fl, Mori Bldg, 32, 3-4-30 Shiba-kōen, Minato-ku; ☉emergency service 24hr; ☒Hibiya Line to Kamiyachō, main exit) This well-equipped clinic is staffed with English-speaking Japanese and foreign physicians.

Emergency Rooms

Japanese Red Cross Medical Centre (Map p288; ☑3400-1311; www.med.jrc.or.jp; 4-1-22 Hiro-o, Shibuya-ku; ☉24hr; ☒Hibiya Line to Hiro-o, exits 1 & 2)

Seibo International Catholic Hospital (☑3951-1111; www.seibokai.or.jp, in Japanese; 2-5-1 Nakaochiai, Shinjuku-ku; ☒JR Yamanote Line to Mejiro, main exit)

St Luke's International Hospital (Map p286; ☑3541-5151; www.luke.or.jp; 9-1 Akashichō, Chūō-ku; ☉24hr; ☒Hibiya Line to Tsukiji, exits 3 & 4)

Pharmacies

Pharmacies are located throughout Tokyo, although a bit of Japanese helps in getting the medication or item you need, as most pharmacists only speak basic (if any) English. Although Japanese law prohibits pharmacists from selling medications from other countries, they will generally be able to help you find a Japanese medication that is either identical or similar to the one you take at home.

Money

ATMs

Most Japanese ATMs do not accept foreign-issued cards. Even if they display Visa and MasterCard logos, most accept only Japan-issued versions of these cards. Also, 24-hour ATMs are exceedingly rare.

Fortunately, Citibank operates 24-hour international ATMs in major areas including Roppongi, Harajuku, Omote-sandō and Shinjuku. Better still, ATMs at Japanese post offices are linked to the international Cirrus and Plus cash networks (and some credit-card networks), making life a breeze for travellers to Tokyo. Most larger **post offices** (☉9am-5pm Mon-Fri, 9am-noon Sat) have postal ATMs. Press the handy button marked 'English Guidance' for English instructions. 7-Eleven convenience stores also have ATMs that accept overseas cards.

Cash

Although quite modern in most ways, cash is still king in Tokyo. One should always keep at least several thousand yen on hand for local transport, inexpensive restaurants and shops, and even some moderately priced restaurants and shops.

The currency in Japan is the yen (¥), and banknotes and coins are easily distinguishable. There are ¥1, ¥5, ¥10, ¥50, ¥100 and ¥500 coins; and ¥1000, ¥2000, ¥5000 and ¥10,000 banknotes (the ¥2000 note is very rarely seen). The ¥1 coin is a lightweight aluminium coin; the bronze-coloured ¥5 and silver-coloured ¥50 coins both have a hole punched in the middle. Prices may be listed using the kanji for yen (円). In most cases, prices are in Arabic numerals, but occasionally they are in traditional kanji.

Changing Money

In theory, banks and post offices will change all major currencies. In practice, some banks refuse to exchange anything but US-dollar cash and travellers cheques. Note also that the currencies of neighbouring Taiwan (New Taiwan dollar) and South Korea (won) are not easy to change, so you should change these into yen or US dollars before arriving in Japan.

With a passport, you can change cash or travellers cheques at any Authorised Foreign Exchange Bank (signs are displayed in English), major post offices, some large hotels and most big department stores. Note that you receive a better exchange rate when withdrawing cash from ATMs than when exchanging cash or travellers cheques in Tokyo. Be aware that many banks place a limit on the amount of cash you can withdraw in one day (often around US$300).

Credit Cards

For businesses that do take credit cards, Visa is the most widely accepted, followed by MasterCard, American Express and Diners Club. Getting a cash advance using your foreign-issued credit card is nearly impossible, but Sumitomo Mitsui banks (SMBC) give cash advances if you bring your passport with you. The main credit-card companies all have offices in Tokyo.

American Express (☏0120-02-0120; ⊘24hr)

MasterCard (☏5728-5200; ⊘9am-5pm Mon-Fri)

Visa (☏00531-44-0022; ⊘24hr)

Tipping & Bargaining

Despite the high quality of customer service in Japan, it is not customary to tip, even in the most expensive restaurants and bars. Bargaining is not customary either, with the exception of outdoor markets, such as Ameya Yokochō in Ueno (see p160). In higher-end restaurants and hotels, a 10% service fee is added to the bill.

Public Holidays

Japan has 15 national public holidays, and the days after or in between often become days off as well. You can expect travel and lodgings to be fully booked during Shōgatsu (New Year; 29 December to 3 January, which many extend until 6 January), Golden Week (29 April to 5 May) and the O-Bon festival in mid-August.

Japan's national public holidays are as follows:

Ganjitsu (New Year's Day) 1 January

Seijin-no-hi (Coming-of-Age Day) Second Monday in January

Kenkoku Kinen-bi (National Foundation Day) 11 February

Shumbun-no-hi (Spring Equinox) 20 or 21 March

Midori-no-hi (Green Day) 29 April

Kempō Kinem-bi (Constitution Day) 3 May

Kokumin-no-Saijitsu (Adjoining Holiday Between Two Holidays) 4 May

Kodomo-no-hi (Children's Day) 5 May

Umi-no-hi (Marine Day) Third Monday in July

Keirō-no-hi (Respect-for-the-Aged Day) Third Monday in September

Shūbun-no-hi (Autumn Equinox) 23 or 24 September

Taiiku-no-hi (Health & Sports Day) Second Monday in October

Bunka-no-hi (Culture Day) 3 November

Kinrō Kansha-no-hi (Labour Thanksgiving Day) 23 November

Tennō-no-Tanjōbi (Emperor's Birthday) 23 December

Taxes & Refunds

Japan's consumption tax is 5%, which is figured into the price of items. Often pre-tax prices are shown in parentheses next to the full prices. At some shops, visitors from overseas may be entitled to purchase items tax free, provided the item costs over ¥10,000 and they have their passports with them. Since the tax is not charged at point of sale, there is no need to collect a refund when leaving the country.

Telephone

The country code for Japan is 81: Tokyo's area code is 03, although some outer suburbs have different area codes (for listings in this book, the area code is 03 unless otherwise noted). Following the area code, 03 numbers consist of eight digits. The area code is not used if dialling within the same area code from a landline.

If you're calling Tokyo from elsewhere in Japan, dial 03 and then the eight-digit number. When dialling Tokyo from abroad, do not dial the first 0; rather, dial the international access code of the country from which you are calling, then 81-3.

The area code for mobile phones anywhere in Japan is 090 or 080, plus an eight-digit number. Calls to mobile phones are significantly more expensive than local calls. If calling from overseas, dial, for example, 81-90 and then the number. If dialling from a mobile phone, you must dial all digits including area codes.

Toll-free numbers begin with 0120, 0070, 0077, 0088 and 0800. For local directory assistance, dial 104 (cost ¥105). For international directory assistance in English, dial 0057.

Mobile Phones

For an extended stay in Japan, a mobile (cell) phone is vital. The Japanese spend every waking hour of the day texting their friends from their phones, and it's virtually impossible to stay connected to people if you don't have one.

Japan operates on the 3-G network, so overseas phones with 3-G technology will work in Tokyo, often better than they do at home. If your phone does not have 3-G technology, it will not work in Japan, and SIM cards are not widely available. Check with your telephone carrier as to whether your phone will work in Japan and how much you will be charged.

Several telecommunications companies in Japan specialise in short-term mobile-phone rental, which includes delivery and return of the phone within Japan. These include:

Mobile Phone Japan (☑090-4284-7176; www. mobilephonejp.com) Mobile phone rentals start at ¥2900

per week. Outgoing calls use SoftBank prepaid cards, which work out to about ¥90 per minute.

Rentafone Japan (☑090-9621-7318, toll free within Japan 0120-746-487; www. rentafonejapan.com) Rentals start at ¥3900 per week. Domestic calls (¥35 per minute) are less expensive than Mobile Phone Japan's, but require that you dial a code before each call.

You may even find that it costs less to purchase a prepaid phone than to rent one. Mobile-phone shops dot virtually every street in Tokyo, and larger mobile-phone shops like the Omote-Sandō location of **SoftBank** (☑03-6406-0711; http://mb.softbank.jp/en/prepaid_service; 1-13-9 Jingumae, Shibuya-ku; ☺10am-10pm) usually have English-speaking staff, or at least English-language pamphlets, explaining the options.

Public Phones

Although public phones have dwindled in recent years amid mobile phone growth, the Japanese public telephone system is very well developed; there are public phones in most public places and they work almost 100% of the time. If you are going to be making a significant number of calls, it's worth purchasing a *terehon kādo* (telephone card). These stored-value cards are available from vending machines, station kiosks and convenience stores in ¥1000 denominations and can be used in grey or green pay phones; phones display the remaining value of your card when it is inserted. They come in a myriad of designs and – this being Tokyo – people even collect them.

International Calls

If you don't have access to Skype or some other online phone application, interna-

tional calls are best made using a prepaid international phonecard. You can also call abroad on grey international ISDN phones, usually found in phone booths marked 'International & Domestic Card/Coin Phone'.

Calls are charged by six-second units, so if you don't have much to say, you can make a quick call home for the minimum charge of ¥100. If you find a public phone that allows international calls, it's more convenient to use a phone-card rather than coins. Reverse-charge (collect) international calls can be made from any pay phone by dialling ☑106.

You can save money by dialling late at night. Economy rates apply from 11pm to 8am throughout the year; these discounts also apply to domestic calls.

To place an international call through the operator, dial ☑0051 (KDDI operator; most international operators speak English). To make the call yourself, dial ☑001 010 (KDDI), ☑0041 010 (SoftBank Telecom) or ☑0033 010 (NTT), followed by the country code, area code and local number. Although these companies compete for overseas service from Japan, there's very little difference in their rates.

Prepaid international calling cards like KDDI Superworld Card, NTT Communications World Card and SoftBank Telecom Comica Card are available at convenience stores and can be used at regular pay phones.

Time

Tokyo local time is nine hours ahead of Greenwich Mean Time (GMT). When it's noon in Tokyo, it's 7pm (the day before) in Los Angeles, 10pm in Montreal and New York, 3am (the same day) in London, 4am in Frankfurt, Paris and Rome, 11am in Hong Kong, 3pm in Melbourne and

JAPANESE YEARS

In addition to the typical western calendar, Japan also counts years in terms of the reigns of its emperors – Meiji, Shōwa, et al. The current era is called Heisei (pronounced hay-say) after the ceremonial name bestowed on the current emperor, Akihito, by the Imperial Household Agency. He ascended to the throne in 1989 (Heisei 1); thus 2012 is Heisei 24, 2013 is Heisei 25, and so on.

5pm in Wellington. Japan does not observe daylight-savings time, so remember to subtract one hour when working out the time difference with a country using daylight-savings time.

Toilets

Toilets in Tokyo run the gamut from heated-seat thrones that wash and dry your most intimate of areas at the touch of a button (in fancy hotels), to humble porcelain squat toilets in the floor (typically in public places like train stations).

Deciphering the Japanese instructions on the techie loos can be a bit of a challenge; sit down before you begin pressing buttons, or you run the risk of having an inadvertent shower!

For using squat toilets, the correct position is facing the hood, away from the door; take care that the contents of your pockets don't spill out. If you just can't bear a squat toilet, look for the characters 洋式 (yō-shiki, Western style) on the stall door, and handicapped washrooms are always Western style. The most common words for toilet in Japanese are トイレ (pronounced 'toire') and お手洗い ('o-tearai'); 女 (female) and 男 (male) will probably also come in helpful!

Toilet paper isn't always provided in public washrooms, so always graciously accept those small packets of tissue handed out on the street, a common form of advertising. These same toilets will probably not have paper towels or hand-driers either, so Japanese carry a handkerchief for use after washing their hands.

In many bathrooms in homes and restaurants where you take off your shoes at the entrance, separate toilet slippers are typically provided just inside the toilet door. These are for use in the toilet only, so remember to shuffle out of them when you leave.

Tourist Information

Japan's tourist information services (観光案内所, kankō annai-sho) are first rate, and the Tokyo branch of the **Japan National Tourism Organization** (JNTO; www.jnto.go.jp) is the best of the bunch.

JNTO operates two main TICs in Tokyo:

Narita (☑0476-34-6251; 1st fl, Terminals 1 & 2, Narita Airport, Chiba; ◷9am-8pm)

Tokyo (Map p286; ☑3201-3331; 1st fl, Shin-Tōkyō Bldg, 3-3-1 Marunouchi, Chiyoda-ku; ◷9am-5pm; ®Yūrakuchō Line to Yūrakuchō, exit D3 or D5)

TIC staff cannot make transport bookings; they can, however, direct you to agencies that can, such as the **Japan Travel Bureau** (JTB; Map p294; ☑5321-3077; 1st fl, Tokyo Metropolitan Government Bldg No 1; ◷9.30am-6.30pm, closed year-end & New Year period).

Other helpful places about town include the following:

Japan Guide Association (☑3213-2706; www.jga21c.or.jp) Can put you in contact with licensed, professional guides.

Tokyo Tourist Information Center Keisei Ueno Station (TIC; Map p300; ☑3836-3471; Keisei Ueno Station)

Tokyo Tourist Information Center Tochō (TIC; Map p294; ☑5321-3077; Tokyo Metropolitan Government Offices, North Tower, 1st fl, 2-8-1 Nishi-Shinjuku, Shinjuku-ku; ®Ōedo Line to Tochōmae, exit A4)

Travellers with Disabilities

Many new buildings in Tokyo have access ramps, traffic lights have speakers playing melodies when it is safe to cross, train platforms have raised dots and lines to provide guidance and some ticket machines have Braille. Some attractions also offer free entry to travellers with disabilities and their companion. A fair number of hotels, from the higher end of midrange and above, offer a 'barrier-free' room or two. Still, Tokyo can be rather difficult for travellers with disabilities to negotiate, especially visitors in wheelchairs who are often forced to make a choice between negotiating stairs or rerouting.

For more information, check the following websites:

Accessible Japan (www.tesco-premium.co.jp/aj/index.htm) Details the accessibility of hundreds of sites in Tokyo, including hotels, sights and department stores, as well as general information about getting around Japan.

Japanese Red Cross Language Service Volunteers (☑3438-1311;

http://accessible.jp.org/tokyo/en/index.html; 1-1-3 Shiba Daimon, Minato-ku, Tokyo 105-8521) Has loads of useful information, and also produces an excellent guide, *Accessible Tokyo*, which can be requested by email, mail or telephone – or found on its website.

Visas

Generally, visitors who are not planning to engage in income-producing activities while in Japan are exempt from obtaining visas and will be issued a *tanki-taizai* (temporary visitor visa) on arrival.

Countries whose citizens are eligible for visa-free stays in Japan of up to roughly three months include the United States, Canada, Australia, New Zealand, Singapore, Spain, France and Italy, among others. Citizens of the United Kingdom, Germany, Mexico, Switzerland and Ireland can stay in Japan without a visa for up to six months. To find out if you are eligible for a temporary visitor visa contact the nearest Japanese embassy or consulate in your country, or visit the website of the **Japan Ministry of Foreign Affairs** (www.mofa.go.jp), where you can check out the Guide to Japanese Visas, read about working-holiday visas and find details on the Japan Exchange and Teaching (JET) program, which sponsors native English speakers to teach in the Japanese public-school system. You can also contact the **Immigration Information Center** (外国人在留総合インフォメーションセンター; Tokyo Regional Immigration Bureau; ☑5796-7112; 5-5-30 Kōnan, Minato-ku; ◷9am-noon & 1-4pm Mon-Fri; ℝTokyo Monorail or Rinkai Line to Tennozu Isle).

Alien Registration Card

Anyone – and this includes tourists – who stays for more than 90 days is required to obtain a *gaikokujin torokushō* (Alien Registration Card). This card can be obtained at the municipal office of the city, town or ward in which you're living. Moving to another area requires that you re-register within 14 days.

You must carry your Alien Registration Card at all times as the police can stop you and ask to see the card. If you don't have it, you could be hauled off to the police station to wait until someone fetches it for you – providing you have one.

Visa Extensions

With the exception of those nationals whose countries have reciprocal visa exemptions and can stay for six months, the limit for most nationalities is 90 days. To extend a temporary visitor visa beyond the standard limit, apply at the Immigration Information Center (Tokyo Regional Immigration Bureau).

Work Visas

Ever-increasing demand has prompted much stricter work-visa requirements than previously. Arriving in Japan and looking for a job is quite a tough proposition these days, though people still do it and occasionally succeed in finding sponsorship. With that said, there are legal employment categories for foreigners that specify standards of experience and qualifications.

Once you find an employer in Japan who is willing to sponsor you, it is necessary to obtain a Certificate of Eligibility from your nearest Japanese immigration office. The same office can then issue your work visa, which is valid for either one or three years. This procedure can take two to three months.

Working-Holiday Visas

Citizens of Australia, Canada, Denmark, France, Germany, Ireland, Korea, New Zealand and the UK and residents of Taiwan and Hong Kong can apply for a working-holiday visa if they're between 18 and 30. The visa is designed to enable young people to travel extensively during their stay; thus, employment is supposed to be part-time or temporary. In practice, many people work full-time. The working-holiday visa must be obtained from a Japanese embassy or consulate abroad.

Language

Japanese is spoken by more than 125 million people. While it bears some resemblance to Altaic languages such as Mongolian and Turkish and has grammatical similarities to Korean, its origins are unclear. Chinese is responsible for the existence of many Sino-Japanese words in Japanese, and for the originally Chinese kanji characters which the Japanese use in combination with the homegrown hiragana and katakana scripts.

Japanese pronunciation is easy to master for English speakers, as most of its sounds are also found in English. If you read our coloured pronunciation guides as if they were English, you'll be understood. In Japanese, it's important to make the distinction between short and long vowels, as vowel length can change the meaning of a word. The long vowels, shown in our pronunciation guides with a horizontal line on top of them (ā, ē, ī, ō, ū), should be held twice as long as the short ones. It's also important to make the distinction between single and double consonants, as this can produce a difference in meaning. Pronounce the double consonants with a slight pause between them, eg sak·ka (writer).

Note also that the vowel sound ai is pronounced as in 'aisle', air as in 'pair' and ow as in 'how'. As for the consonants, ts is pronounced as in 'hats', f sounds almost like 'fw' (with rounded lips), and r is halfway between 'r' and 'l'. All syllables in a word are pronounced fairly evenly in Japanese.

WANT MORE?

For in-depth language information and handy phrases, check out Lonely Planet's *Japanese Phrasebook*. You'll find it at **shop.lonelyplanet.com**, or you can buy Lonely Planet's iPhone phrasebooks at the Apple App Store.

BASICS

Japanese uses an array of registers of speech to reflect social and contextual hierarchy, but these can be simplified to the form most appropriate for the situation, which is what we've done in this language guide too.

Hello.	こんにちは。	kon·ni·chi·wa
Goodbye.	さようなら。	sa·yō·na·ra
Yes.	はい。	hai
No.	いいえ。	ī·e
Please. (when asking)	ください。	ku·da·sai
Please. (when offering)	どうぞ。	dō·zo
Thank you.	ありがとう。	a·ri·ga·tō
Excuse me. (to get attention)	すみません。	su·mi·ma·sen
Sorry.	ごめんなさい。	go·men·na·sai

You're welcome.
どういたしまして。　　dō i·ta·shi·mash·te

How are you?
お元気ですか?　　o·gen·ki des ka

Fine. And you?
はい、元気です。　　hai, gen·ki des
あなたは?　　a·na·ta wa

What's your name?
お名前は何ですか?　　o·na·ma·e wa nan des ka

My name is ...
私の名前は　　wa·ta·shi no na·ma·e wa
…です。　　... des

Do you speak English?
英語が話せますか?　　ē·go ga ha·na·se·mas ka

I don't understand.
わかりません。　　wa·ka·ri·ma·sen

Does anyone speak English?
どなたか英語を　　do·na·ta ka ē·go o
話せますか?　　ha·na·se·mas ka

ACCOMMODATION

Where's a ...?	…が ありますか?	... ga a·ri·mas ka
campsite	キャンプ場	kyam·pu·jō
guesthouse	民宿	min·shu·ku
hotel	ホテル	ho·te·ru
inn	旅館	ryo·kan
youth hostel	ユース ホステル	yū·su· ho·su·te·ru

Do you have a ... room?	…ルームは ありますか?	...rū·mu wa a·ri·mas ka
single	シングル	shin·gu·ru
double	ダブル	da·bu·ru

How much is it per ...?	…いくら ですか?	... i·ku·ra des ka
night	1泊	ip·pa·ku
person	1人	hi·to·ri

air-con	エアコン	air·kon
bathroom	風呂場	fu·ro·ba
window	窓	ma·do

DIRECTIONS

Where's the ...?
…はどこですか? ... wa do·ko des ka

Can you show me (on the map)?
(地図で)教えて (chi·zu de) o·shi·e·te
くれませんか? ku·re·ma·sen ka

What's the address?
住所は何ですか? jū·sho wa nan des ka

Could you please write it down?
書いてくれませんか? kai·te ku·re·ma·sen ka

behind ...	…の後ろ	... no u·shi·ro
in front of ...	…の前	... no ma·e
near ...	…の近く	... no chi·ka·ku
next to ...	…のとなり	... no to·na·ri
opposite ...	…の 向かい側	... no mu·kai·ga·wa
straight ahead	この先	ko·no sa·ki

Turn ...	…まがって ください。	... ma·gat·te ku·da·sai
at the corner	その角を	so·no ka·do o
at the traffic lights	その信号を	so·no shin·gō o
left	左へ	hi·da·ri e
right	右へ	mi·gi e

KEY PATTERNS

To get by in Japanese, mix and match these simple patterns with words of your choice:

When's (the next bus)?
(次のバスは) (tsu·gi no bas wa)
何時ですか? nan·ji des ka

Where's (the station)?
(駅は)どこですか? (e·ki wa) do·ko des ka

Do you have (a map)?
(地図) (chi·zu)
がありますか? ga a·ri·mas ka

Is there (a toilet)?
(トイレ) (toy·re)
がありますか? ga a·ri·mas ka

I'd like (the menu).
(メニュー) (me·nyū)
をお願いします。 o o·ne·gai shi·mas

Can I (sit here)?
(ここに座って) (ko·ko ni su·wat·te)
もいいですか? mo ī des ka

I need (a can opener).
(缶切り) (kan·ki·ri)
が必要です。 ga hi·tsu·yō des

Do I need (a visa)?
(ビザ) (bi·za)
が必要ですか? ga hi·tsu·yō des ka

I have (a reservation).
(予約)があります。 (yo·ya·ku) ga a·ri·mas

I'm (a teacher).
私は(教師) wa·ta·shi wa (kyō·shi)
です。 des

EATING & DRINKING

I'd like to reserve a table for (two people).
(2人)の予約を (fu·ta·ri) no yo·ya·ku o
お願いします。 o·ne·gai shi·mas

What would you recommend?
なにが na·ni ga
おすすめですか? o·su·su·me des ka

What's in that dish?
あの料理に何 a·no ryō·ri ni na·ni
が入っていますか? ga hait·te i·mas ka

Do you have any vegetarian dishes?
ベジタリアン料理 be·ji·ta·ri·an ryō·ri
がありますか? ga a·ri·mas ka

I'm a vegetarian.
私は wa·ta·shi wa
ベジタリアンです。 be·ji·ta·ri·an des

I'm a vegan.
私は厳格な wa·ta·shi wa gen·ka·ku na
菜食主義者 sai·sho·ku·shu·gi·sha
です。 des

I don't eat ...	…は 食べません。	… wa ta·be·ma·sen
dairy products	乳製品	nyū·sē·hin
(red) meat	(赤身の) 肉	(a·ka·mi no) ni·ku
meat or dairy products	肉や 乳製品は	ni·ku ya nyū·sē·hin
pork	豚肉	bu·ta·ni·ku
seafood	シーフード 海産物	shī·fū·do/ kai·sam·bu·tsu

Is it cooked with pork lard or chicken stock?

| これはラードか鶏 だしを使って いますか? | ko·re wa rā·do ka to·ri no da·shi o tsu·kat·te i·mas ka |

I'm allergic to (peanuts).

| 私は (ピーナッツ)に アレルギーが あります。 | wa·ta·shi wa (pī·nat·tsu) ni a·re·ru·gī ga a·ri·mas |

That was delicious!

| おいしかった。 | oy·shi·kat·ta |

Cheers!

| 乾杯! | kam·pai |

Please bring the bill.

| お勘定をください。 | o·kan·jō o ku·da·sai |

Key Words

appetisers	前菜	zen·sai
bottle	ビン	bin
bowl	ボール	bō·ru
breakfast	朝食	chō·sho·ku
cold	冷たい	tsu·me·ta·i
dinner	夕食	yū·sho·ku
fork	フォーク	fō·ku
glass	グラス	gu·ra·su

Signs	
入口	**Entrance**
出口	**Exit**
営業中/開館	**Open**
閉店/閉館	**Closed**
インフォメーション	**Information**
危険	**Danger**
トイレ	**Toilets**
男	**Men**
女	**Women**

grocery	食料品	sho·ku·ryō·hin
hot (warm)	熱い	a·tsu·i
knife	ナイフ	nai·fu
lunch	昼食	chū·sho·ku
market	市場	i·chi·ba
menu	メニュー	me·nyū
plate	皿	sa·ra
spicy	スパイシー	spai·shī
spoon	スプーン	spūn
vegetarian	ベジタリアン	be·ji·ta·ri·an
with	いっしょに	is·sho ni
without	なしで	na·shi de

LANGUAGE EATING & DRINKING

Meat & Fish

beef	牛肉	gyū·ni·ku
chicken	鶏肉	to·ri·ni·ku
duck	アヒル	a·hi·ru
eel	うなぎ	u·na·gi
fish	魚	sa·ka·na
lamb	子羊	ko·hi·tsu·ji
lobster	ロブスター	ro·bus·tā
meat	肉	ni·ku
pork	豚肉	bu·ta·ni·ku
prawn	エビ	e·bi
salmon	サケ	sa·ke
seafood	シーフード 海産物	shī·fū·do/ kai·sam·bu·tsu
shrimp	小エビ	ko·e·bi
tuna	マグロ	ma·gu·ro
turkey	七面鳥	shi·chi·men·chō
veal	子牛	ko·u·shi

Fruit & Vegetables

apple	りんご	rin·go
banana	バナナ	ba·na·na
beans	豆	ma·me
capsicum	ピーマン	pī·man
carrot	ニンジン	nin·jin
cherry	さくらんぼ	sa·ku·ram·bo
cucumber	キュウリ	kyū·ri
fruit	果物	ku·da·mo·no
grapes	ブドウ	bu·dō
lettuce	レタス	re·tas
nut	ナッツ	nat·tsu
orange	オレンジ	o·ren·ji
peach	桃	mo·mo

peas	豆	ma·me
pineapple	パイナップル	pai·nap·pu·ru
potato	ジャガイモ	ja·ga·i·mo
pumpkin	カボチャ	ka·bo·cha
spinach	ホウレンソウ	hō·ren·sō
strawberry	イチゴ	i·chi·go
tomato	トマト	to·ma·to
vegetables	野菜	ya·sai
watermelon	スイカ	su·i·ka

Other

bread	パン	pan
butter	バター	ba·tā
cheese	チーズ	chī·zu
chilli	唐辛子	tō·ga·ra·shi
egg	卵	ta·ma·go
honey	蜂蜜	ha·chi·mi·tsu
horseradish	わさび	wa·sa·bi
jam	ジャム	ja·mu
noodles	麺	men
pepper	コショウ	koshō
rice (cooked)	ごはん	go·han
salt	塩	shi·o
seaweed	のり	no·ri
soy sauce	しょう油	shō·yu
sugar	砂糖	sa·tō

Drinks

beer	ビール	bī·ru
coffee	コーヒー	kō·hī
(orange) juice	(オレンジ) ジュース	(o·ren·ji·) jū·su
lemonade	レモネード	re·mo·nē·do
milk	ミルク	mi·ru·ku
mineral water	ミネラル ウォーター	mi·ne·ra·ru· wō·tā

Question Words

How?	どのように?	do·no yō ni
What?	なに?	na·ni
When?	いつ?	i·tsu
Where?	どこ?	do·ko
Which?	どちら?	do·chi·ra
Who?	だれ?	da·re
Why?	なぜ?	na·ze

red wine	赤ワイン	a·ka wain
sake	酒	sa·ke
tea	紅茶	kō·cha
water	水	mi·zu
white wine	白ワイン	shi·ro wain
yogurt	ヨーグルト	yō·gu·ru·to

EMERGENCIES

Help!
たすけて! — tas·ke·te

Go away!
離れろ! — ha·na·re·ro

I'm lost.
迷いました。 — ma·yoy·mash·ta

Call the police.
警察を呼んで。 — kē·sa·tsu o yon·de

Call a doctor.
医者を呼んで。 — i·sha o yon·de

Where are the toilets?
トイレはどこですか? — toy·re wa do·ko des ka

I'm ill.
私は病気です。 — wa·ta·shi wa byō·ki des

It hurts here.
ここが痛いです。 — ko·ko ga i·tai des

I'm allergic to ...
私は… アレルギーです。 — wa·ta·shi wa ... a·re·ru·gī des

SHOPPING & SERVICES

I'd like to buy ...
…をください。 — ... o ku·da·sai

I'm just looking.
見ているだけです。 — mi·te i·ru da·ke des

Can I look at it?
それを見ても いいですか? — so·re o mi·te mo ī des ka

How much is it?
いくらですか? — i·ku·ra des ka

That's too expensive.
高すぎます。 — ta·ka·su·gi·mas

Can you give me a discount?
ディスカウント できますか? — dis·kown·to de·ki·mas ka

There's a mistake in the bill.
請求書に間違いが あります。 — sē·kyū·sho ni ma·chi·gai ga a·ri·mas

ATM	ATM	ē·tī·e·mu
credit card	クレジット カード	ku·re·jit·to· kā·do
post office	郵便局	yū·bin·kyo·ku
public phone	公衆電話	kō·shū·den·wa
tourist office	観光案内所	kan·kō·an·nai·jo

TIME & DATES

What time is it?
何時ですか？　　　　nan·ji des ka

It's (10) o'clock.
(10)時です。　　　　(jū)·ji des

Half past (10).
(10)時半です。　　　(jū)·ji han des

am	午前	go·zen
pm	午後	go·go
Monday	月曜日	ge·tsu·yō·bi
Tuesday	火曜日	ka·yō·bi
Wednesday	水曜日	su·i·yō·bi
Thursday	木曜日	mo·ku·yō·bi
Friday	金曜日	kin·yō·bi
Saturday	土曜日	do·yō·bi
Sunday	日曜日	ni·chi·yō·bi
January	1月	i·chi·ga·tsu
February	2月	ni·ga·tsu
March	3月	san·ga·tsu
April	4月	shi·ga·tsu
May	5月	go·ga·tsu
June	6月	ro·ku·ga·tsu
July	7月	shi·chi·ga·tsu
August	8月	ha·chi·ga·tsu
September	9月	ku·ga·tsu
October	10月	jū·ga·tsu
November	11月	jū·i·chi·ga·tsu
December	12月	jū·ni·ga·tsu

TRANSPORT

boat	船	fu·ne
bus	バス	bas
metro	地下鉄	chi·ka·te·tsu
plane	飛行機	hi·kō·ki
train	電車	den·sha
tram	市電	shi·den

What time does it leave?
これは何時に　　　　ko·re wa nan·ji ni
出ますか？　　　　　de·mas ka

Does it stop at (...)?
(…)に　　　　　　　(...) ni
停まりますか？　　　to·ma·ri·mas ka

Please tell me when we get to (...).
(…)に着いたら　　　(...) ni tsu·i·ta·ra
教えてください。　　o·shi·e·te ku·da·sai

Numbers

1	一	i·chi
2	二	ni
3	三	san
4	四	shi/yon
5	五	go
6	六	ro·ku
7	七	shi·chi/na·na
8	八	ha·chi
9	九	ku/kyū
10	十	jū
20	二十	ni·jū
30	三十	san·jū
40	四十	yon·jū
50	五十	go·jū
60	六十	ro·ku·jū
70	七十	na·na·jū
80	八十	ha·chi·jū
90	九十	kyū·jū
100	百	hya·ku
1000	千	sen

A one-way/return ticket (to ...).
(... 行きの)　　　　(...·yu·ki no)
片道/往復　　　　　ka·ta·mi·chi/ō·fu·ku
切符。　　　　　　　kip·pu

first	始発の	shi·ha·tsu no
last	最終の	sai·shū no
next	次の	tsu·gi no
aisle	通路側	tsū·ro·ga·wa
bus stop	バス停	bas·tē
cancelled	キャンセル	kyan·se·ru
delayed	遅れ	o·ku·re
ticket window	窓口	ma·do·gu·chi
timetable	時刻表	ji·ko·ku·hyō
train station	駅	e·ki
window	窓側	ma·do·ga·wa

I'd like to　…を借りたい　　... o ka·ri·tai
hire a ...　　のですが。　　　no des ga

bicycle	自転車	ji·ten·sha
car	自動車	ji·dō·sha
motorbike	オートバイ	ō·to·bai

GLOSSARY

Amida Nyorai – Buddha of the Western Paradise

ANA – All Nippon Airways

-bashi – bridge (also *hashi*)

bashō – *sumō* tournament

bentō – boxed lunch or dinner, usually containing rice, vegetables and fish or meat

bosatsu – a bodhisattva, or Buddha attendant, who assists others to attain enlightenment

bugaku – dance pieces played by court orchestras in ancient Japan

bunraku – classical puppet theatre that uses life-size puppets to enact dramas similar to those of *kabuki*

chō – city area (for large cities) sized between a *ku* and *chōme*

chōme – city area of a few blocks

Daibutsu – Great Buddha

daimyō – domain lords under the *shōgun*

dōri – street

fugu – poisonous pufferfish, elevated to haute cuisine

futon – cushion-like mattress that is rolled up and stored away during the day

futsū – local train; literally 'ordinary'

gagaku – music of the imperial court

gaijin – foreigner; the contracted form of gaikokujin (literally, 'outside country person')

-gawa – river (also *kawa*)

geisha – a woman versed in the arts and other cultivated pursuits who entertains guests

-gū – shrine

haiden – hall of worship in a shrine

haiku – 17-syllable poem

hakubutsukan – museum

hanami – cherry-blossom viewing

hashi – bridge (also -*bashi*); chopsticks

higashi – east

hiragana – phonetic syllabary used to write Japanese words

honden – main building of a shrine

hondō – main building of a temple (also *kondō*)

ikebana – art of flower arrangement

irori – open hearth found in traditional Japanese homes

izakaya – Japanese pub/eatery

-ji – temple (also *tera* or *dera*)

-jingū – shrine (also *jinja* or -*gū*)

jinja – shrine (also -*gū*)

jizō – bodhisattva who watches over children

JNTO – Japan National Tourist Organization

-jō – castle (also *shiro*)

JR – Japan Railways

kabuki – form of Japanese theatre that draws on popular tales and is characterised by elaborate costumes, stylised acting and the use of male actors for all roles

kaiseki – Buddhist-inspired, Japanese haute cuisine; called *cha-kaiseki* when served as part of a tea ceremony

kaisoku – rapid train

kaiten-sushi – conveyor-belt sushi

kamikaze – literally, 'wind of the gods'; originally the typhoon that sank Kublai Khan's 13th-century invasion fleet and the name adopted by Japanese suicide bombers in the waning days of WWII

kampai – cheers, as in a drinking toast

kanji – literally, 'Chinese writing'; Chinese ideographic script used for writing Japanese

Kannon – Buddhist goddess of mercy

karaoke – a now famous export where revellers sing along to recorded music, minus the vocals

kawa – river

-ken – prefecture, eg Shiga-ken

kimono – traditional outer garment that is similar to a robe

kita – north

-ko – lake

kōban – local police box

kōen – park

ku – ward

kyōgen – drama performed as comic relief between *nō* plays, or as separate events

kyūkō – ordinary express train (faster than a *futsū*, only stopping at certain stations)

live house – a small concert hall where live music is performed

machi – city area (for large cities) sized between a *ku* and *chōme*

mama-san – older women who run drinking, dining and entertainment venues

maneki-neko – beckoning or welcoming cat figure frequently seen in restaurants and bars; it's supposed to attract customers and trade

matcha – powdered green tea served in tea ceremonies

matsuri – festival

midori-no-madoguchi – ticket counter in large Japan Rail stations, where you can make more complicated bookings (look for the green band across the glass)

mikoshi – portable shrine carried during festivals

minami – south

minshuku – Japanese equivalent of a B&B

mon – temple gate

mura – village

N'EX – Narita Express

Nihon – Japanese word for Japan; literally, 'source of the sun' (also known as *Nippon*)

Nippon – see *Nihon*

nishi – west

nō – classical Japanese drama performed on a bare stage

noren – door curtain for restaurants, usually labelled with the name of the establishment

NTT – Nippon Telegraph & Telephone Corporation

o- prefix used as a sign of respect (usually applied to objects)

obi – sash or belt worn with *kimono*

O-bon – mid-August festivals and ceremonies for deceased ancestors

o-furo – traditional Japanese bath

onsen – mineral hot spring with bathing areas and accommodation

o-shibori – hot towels given in restaurants

pachinko – vertical pinball game that is a Japanese craze

Raijin – god of thunder

ryokan – traditional Japanese inn

ryōri – cooking; cuisine

ryōtei – traditional-style, high-class restaurant; *kaiseki* is typical fare

sabi – a poetic ideal of finding beauty and pleasure in imperfection; often used in conjunction with *wabi*

sakura – cherry trees

salaryman – male employee of a large firm

-sama – a suffix even more respectful than *san*

samurai – Japan's traditional warrior class

-san – a respectful suffix applied to personal names, similar to Mr, Mrs or Ms but more widely used

sentō – public bath

setto – set meal; see also *teishoku*

Shaka Nyorai – Historical Buddha

shakkei – borrowed scenery; technique where features outside a garden are incorporated into its design

shamisen – three-stringed, banjo-like instrument

-shi – city (to distinguish cities with prefectures of the same name)

shinkansen – bullet train (literally, 'new trunk line')

Shintō – indigenous Japanese religion

Shitamachi – traditionally the low-lying, less affluent parts of Tokyo

shōgun – military ruler of pre-Meiji Japan

shōjin ryōri – Buddhist vegetarian cuisine

shokudō – Japanese-style cafeteria/cheap restaurant

soba – thin brown buckwheat noodles

tatami – tightly woven floor matting on which shoes should not be worn

teishoku – set meal in a restaurant

tokkyū – limited express train

torii – entrance gate to a *Shintō* shrine

tsukemono – Japanese pickles

udon – thick, white, wheat noodles

ukiyo-e – woodblock prints; literally, 'pictures of the floating world'

wabi – a Zen-inspired aesthetic of rustic simplicity

wasabi – spicy Japanese horseradish

washi – Japanese paper

yakuza – Japanese mafia

Zen – a form of Buddhism

MENU DECODER

Rice Dishes

katsu-don (かつ丼) – rice topped with a fried pork cutlet

niku-don (牛丼) – rice topped with thin slices of cooked beef

oyako-don (親子丼) – rice topped with egg and chicken

ten-don (天丼) – rice topped with tempura shrimp and vegetables

Izakaya Fare

agedashi-dōfu (揚げだし豆腐) – deep-fried tofu in a dashi broth

jaga-batā (ジャガバター) – baked potatoes with butter

niku-jaga (肉ジャガ) – beef and potato stew

shio-yaki-zakana (塩焼魚) – a whole fish grilled with salt

poteto furai (ポテトフライ) – French fries

chiizu-age (チーズ揚げ) – deep-fried cheese

hiya-yakko (冷奴) – cold tofu with soy sauce and spring onions

tsuna sarada (ツナサラダ) – tuna salad over cabbage

Sushi & Sashimi

ama-ebi (甘海老) – shrimp

awabi (あわび) – abalone

hamachi (はまち) – yellowtail

ika (いか) – squid

ikura (イクラ) – salmon roe

kai-bashira (貝柱) – scallop

kani (かに) – crab

katsuo (かつお) – bonito

sashimi mori-awase (刺身盛り合わせ) – a selection of sliced sashimi

tai (鯛) – sea bream

toro (とろ) – the choicest cut of fatty tuna belly

uni (うに) – sea urchin roe

Yakitori

yakitori (焼き鳥) – plain, grilled white meat

hasami/negima (はさみ/ねぎま) – pieces of white meat alternating with leek

sasami (ささみ) – skinless chicken-breast pieces

kawa (皮) – chicken skin

tsukune (つくね) – chicken meatballs

gyū-niku (牛肉) – pieces of beef

tebasaki (手羽先) – chicken wings

shiitake (しいたけ) – Japanese mushrooms

piiman (ピーマン) – small green peppers

tama-negi (玉ねぎ) – round white onions

yaki-onigiri (焼きおにぎり) – a triangle of rice grilled with *yakitori* sauce

Rāmen

rāmen (ラーメン) – soup and noodles with a sprinkling of meat and vegetables

chāshū-men (チャーシュー麺) – *rāmen* topped with slices of roasted pork

wantan-men (ワンタン麺) – *rāmen* with meat dumplings

miso-rāmen (みそラーメン) – *rāmen* with miso-flavoured broth

chānpon-men (ちゃんぽん麺) – Nagasaki-style *rāmen*

Soba & Udon

soba (そば) – thin brown buckwheat noodles

udon (うどん) – thick white wheat noodles

kake soba/udon (かけそば/うどん) – *soba/udon* noodles in broth

kata yaki-soba (固焼きそば) – crispy noodles with meat and vegetables

kitsune soba/udon (きつねそば/うどん) – *soba/udon* noodles with fried tofu

tempura soba/udon (天ぷらそば/うどん) – *soba/udon* noodles with tempura shrimp

tsukimi soba/udon (月見そば/うどん) – *soba/udon* noodles with raw egg on top

yaki-soba (焼きそば) – fried noodles with meat and vegetables

zaru soba (ざるそば) – cold noodles with seaweed strips served on a bamboo tray

Tempura

tempura moriawase (天ぷら盛り合わせ) – a selection of tempura

shōjin age (精進揚げ) – vegetarian tempura

kaki age (かき揚げ) – tempura with shredded vegetables or fish

Kushiage & Kushikatsu

ika (いか) – squid

renkon (れんこん) – lotus root

tama-negi (玉ねぎ) – white onion

gyū-niku (牛肉) – beef pieces

shiitake (しいたけ) – Japanese mushrooms

ginnan (銀杏) – ginkgo nuts

imo (いも) – potato

Konomiyaki

mikkusu (ミックスお好み焼き) – mixed fillings of seafood, meat and vegetables

modan-yaki (モダン焼き) – *okonomiyaki* with *yaki-soba* and a fried egg

ika okonomiyaki (いかお好み焼き) – squid *okonomiyaki*

gyū okonomiyaki (牛お好み焼き) – beef *okonomiyaki*

negi okonomiyaki (ネギお好み焼き) – thin *okonomiyaki* with spring onions

Kaiseki

bentō (弁当) – boxed lunch

ume (梅) – regular course

take (竹) – special course

matsu (松) – extra-special course

Unagi

kabayaki (蒲焼き) – skewers of grilled eel without rice

unagi teishoku (うなぎ定食) – full-set *unagi* meal with rice, grilled eel, eel-liver soup and pickles

una-don (うな丼) – grilled eel over a bowl of rice

unajū (うな重) – grilled eel over a flat tray of rice

Alcoholic Drinks

nama biiru (生ビール) – draught beer

shōchū (焼酎) – distilled grain liquor

oyu-wari (お湯割り) – *shōchū* with hot water

chūhai (チューハイ) – *shōchū* with soda and lemon

whisky (ウィスキー) – whisky

mizu-wari (水割り) – whisky, ice and water

Coffee & Tea

kōhii (コーヒー) – regular coffee

burendo kōhii (ブレンドコーヒー) – blended coffee, fairly strong

american kōhii (アメリカンコーヒー) – weak coffee

kōcha (紅茶) – black, British-style tea

kafe ōre (カフェオレ) – *café au lait*, hot or cold

Japanese Tea

o-cha (お茶) – green tea

sencha (煎茶) – medium-grade green tea

matcha (抹茶) – powdered green tea used in the tea ceremony

bancha (番茶) – ordinary-grade green tea, brownish in colour

mugicha (麦茶) – roasted barley tea

Behind the Scenes

SEND US YOUR FEEDBACK

We love to hear from travellers – your comments keep us on our toes and help make our books better. Our well-travelled team reads every word on what you loved or loathed about this book. Although we cannot reply individually to postal submissions, we always guarantee that your feedback goes straight to the appropriate authors, in time for the next edition. Each person who sends us information is thanked in the next edition – and the most useful submissions are rewarded with a selection of digital PDF chapters.

Visit **lonelyplanet.com/contact** to submit your updates and suggestions or to ask for help. Our award-winning website also features inspirational travel stories, news and discussions.

Note: We may edit, reproduce and incorporate your comments in Lonely Planet products such as guidebooks, websites and digital products, so let us know if you don't want your comments reproduced or your name acknowledged. For a copy of our privacy policy visit lonelyplanet.com/privacy.

OUR READERS

Many thanks to the travellers who used the last edition and wrote to us with helpful hints, useful advice and interesting anecdotes:
Rebecca Honda, Allan Richards, Ross Underwood

AUTHOR THANKS
Timothy Hornyak

A vast *dōmo arigatō* to all who helped, especially Taira Ari. My thanks also to Takemaru Maiko, Suji Park, Nicholas Coldicott, Chris Bunting, Robert Michael Poole, Charles Spreckley, Yanagibashi goddesses Yoneyama Akiko and Terasawa Haruko, as well as Nacio Cronin and Takahashi Ayumi of JNTO. Thank you especially to my colleagues Rebecca Milner, Chris Rowthorn and Emily Wolman, and my family for their unflagging support and my mother's cooking. And Jeremy Brett's immortal Sherlock Holmes for entertainment during the write-up.

Rebecca Milner

Thank you to Julian for accompanying me to bars and shows both good and bad, and out to the countryside. To Chikara for his support and willingness to eat at 'just one more' restaurant. Also: Jun, Emi, Ivan, Jon, Kanna, Eri, Yukiko, Will, Shinji, Tom, Hiroshi, Kaz, Sydnie, Micah, Paul, Patrick, Robin and the TLR team. Thank you to Tim and everyone at Lonely Planet for their help and to Emily for the opportunity to fall in love with Tokyo again.

ACKNOWLEDGMENTS

Climate map data adapted from Peel MC, Finlayson BL & McMahon TA (2007) 'Updated World Map of the Köppen-Geiger Climate Classification', *Hydrology and Earth System Sciences*, 11, 163344.

Cover photograph: Aerial view of Tokyo Tower, Michiaki Omori/amanaimagesRF/Getty Images.

Many of the images in this guide are available for licensing from Lonely Planet Images: www.lonelyplanetimages.com.

THIS BOOK

This 9th edition of Tokyo was researched and written by Timothy Hornyak and Rebecca Milner. This guidebook was commissioned in Lonely Planet's Oakland office, and produced by the following:

Commissioning Editor
Emily K Wolman

Coordinating Editors Pete Cruttenden, Sophie Splatt

Coordinating Cartographers Corey Hutchison, Jolyon Philcox

Coordinating Layout Designer Frank Deim

Managing Editors Barbara Delissen, Angela Tinson

Senior Editor Andi Jones

Managing Cartographers Amanda Sierp, David Connolly

Managing Layout Designer Chris Girdler

Assisting Editors Joanne Newell, Charlotte Orr, Sam Trafford

Assisting Cartographer Valentina Kremenchutskaya

Cover Research Naomi Parker

Internal Image Research Rebecca Skinner

Language Content Branislava Vladisavljevic

Thanks to Naoko Akamatsu, Janine Eberle, Ryan Evans, Fayette Fox, Jane Hart, Liz Heynes, Laura Jane, David Kemp, Shawn Low, Annelies Mertens, Wayne Murphy, Trent Paton, Anrthony Phelan, Piers Pickard, Lachlan Ross, Michael Ruff, Julie Sheridan, Laura Stansfeld, John Taufa, Gerard Walker, Clifton Wilkinson

Index

🏃 SPORTS & ACTIVITIES

🛏 SLEEPING

Tokyo Maps

Map Legend

Sights
- Beach
- Buddhist
- Castle
- Christian
- Hindu
- Islamic
- Jewish
- Monument
- Museum/Gallery
- Ruin
- Winery/Vineyard
- Zoo
- Other Sight

Eating
- Eating

Drinking & Nightlife
- Drinking & Nightlife
- Cafe

Entertainment
- Entertainment

Shopping
- Shopping

Sleeping
- Sleeping
- Camping

Sports & Activities
- Diving/Snorkelling
- Canoeing/Kayaking
- Skiing
- Surfing
- Swimming/Pool
- Walking
- Windsurfing
- Other Sports & Activities

Information
- Post Office
- Tourist Information

Transport
- Airport
- Border Crossing
- Bus
- Cable Car/Funicular
- Cycling
- Ferry
- Metro
- Monorail
- Parking
- S-Bahn
- Taxi
- Train/Railway
- Tram
- Tube Station
- U-Bahn
- Other Transport

Routes
- Tollway
- Freeway
- Primary
- Secondary
- Tertiary
- Lane
- Unsealed Road
- Plaza/Mall
- Steps
- Tunnel
- Pedestrian Overpass
- Walking Tour
- Walking Tour Detour
- Path

Boundaries
- International
- State/Province
- Disputed
- Regional/Suburb
- Marine Park
- Cliff
- Wall

Geographic
- Hut/Shelter
- Lighthouse
- Lookout
- Mountain/Volcano
- Oasis
- Park
- Pass
- Picnic Area
- Waterfall

Hydrography
- River/Creek
- Intermittent River
- Swamp/Mangrove
- Reef
- Canal
- Water
- Dry/Salt/Intermittent Lake
- Glacier

Areas
- Beach/Desert
- Cemetery (Christian)
- Cemetery (Other)
- Park/Forest
- Sportsground
- Sight (Building)
- Top Sight (Building)

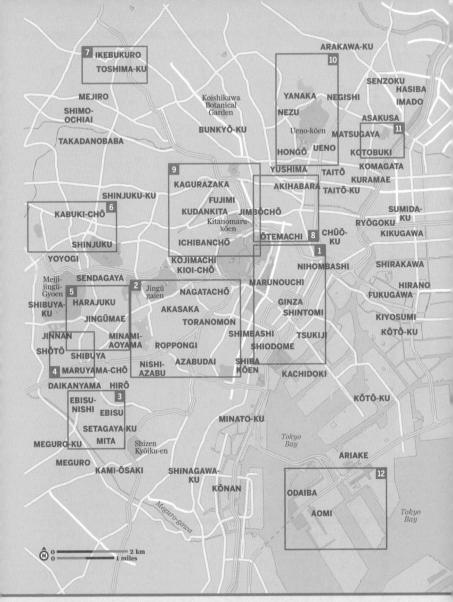

MARUNOUCHI & GINZA

400 m
0.2 miles

MARUNOUCHI & GINZA

Key on p290

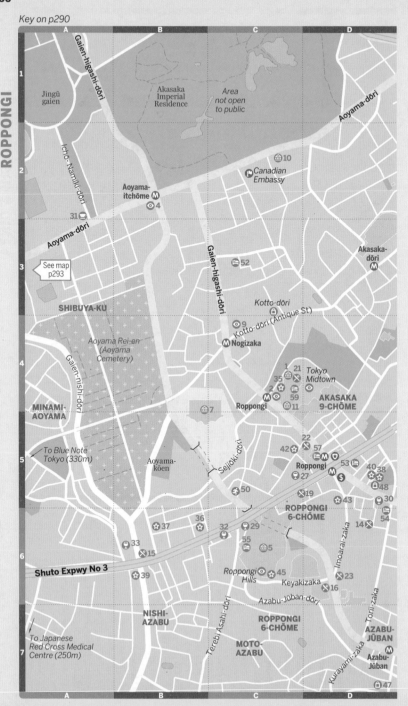

Jingū gaien

Akasaka Imperial Residence

Area not open to public

Aoyama-dōri

Gaien-higashi-dōri

Ichō-Namiki-dōri

Aoyama-itchōme Ⓜ 4

31 🖩

Aoyama-dōri

See map p293

SHIBUYA-KŪ

Aoyama Rei-en (Aoyama Cemetery)

Gaien-nishi-dōri

MINAMI-AOYAMA

To Blue Note Tokyo (330m)

Aoyama-kōen

Gaien-higashi-dōri

🖩 10

Canadian Embassy

Akasaka-dōri Ⓜ

🚌 52

Kotto-dōri

9 Kotto-dōri (Antique St)

Ⓜ Nogizaka

1 21
35
2 59 Tokyo Midtown
Ⓜ Roppongi 🖩 11

AKASAKA 9-CHŌME

🖩 7

22
42 ☆ 57
Roppongi Ⓜ Ⓥ 53 🚌 40 38
27 $ 48
19 30
☆ 43 54
ROPPONGI 6-CHŌME 14

50

37 36 32 29
33 55 5
15
39 Roppongi ⓞ 45 Keyakizaka 16 23

Shuto Expwy No 3

Sejjōki-dōri

Imoarai-zaka

Azabu-Jūban-dōri

NISHI-AZABU

Terebi-Asahi-dōri

ROPPONGI 6-CHŌME

MOTO-AZABU

AZABU-JŪBAN Ⓜ

Azabu-Jūban

Kurayami-zaka

Torii-zaka

To Japanese Red Cross Medical Centre (250m)

🔒 47

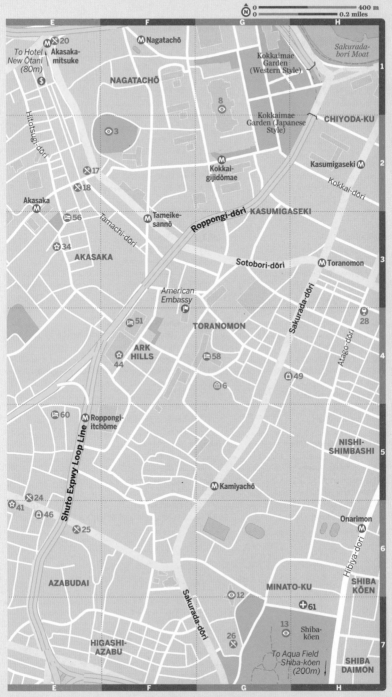

Sakurada-bori Moat

ROPPONGI

To Hotel New Ōtani (80m)

M 20 Akasaka-mitsuke

M Nagatachō

Kokkaimae Garden (Western Style)

1

NAGATACHŌ

8

Kokkaimae Garden (Japanese Style)

CHIYODA-KU

3

Kasumigaseki **M**

2

17

M Kokkai-gijidōmae

Kokkai-dōri

18

Akasaka **M**

56

Tamachi-dōri

M Tameike-sannō

Roppongi-dōri

KASUMIGASEKI

34

Sotobori-dōri

M Toranomon

3

AKASAKA

Sakurada-dōri

Atago-dōri

28

51

American Embassy

TORANOMON

ARK HILLS

44

58

49

4

6

NISHI-SHIMBASHI

5

60

M Roppongi-itchōme

Shuto Expwy Loop Line

M Kamiyachō

24

41

46

Onarimon

25

Hibiya-dōri

SHIBA KŌEN

6

AZABUDAI

Sakurada-dōri

12

MINATO-KU

61

13

Shiba-kōen

SHIBA DAIMON

HIGASHI-AZABU

26

To Aqua Field Shiba-kōen (200m)

7

N 0 ———— 400 m
0 ———— 0.2 miles

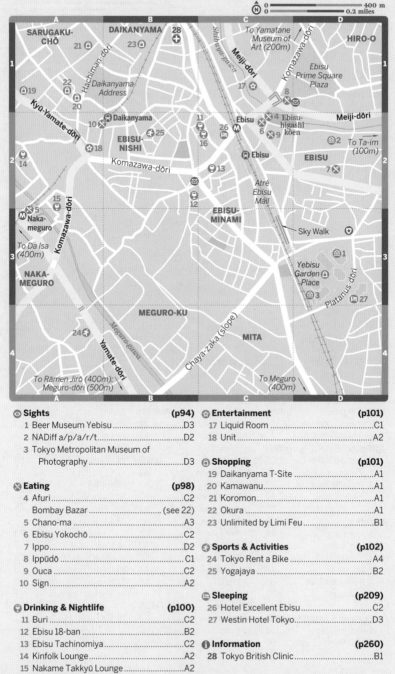

Sights	(p94)
1 Beer Museum Yebisu	D3
2 NADiff a/p/a/r/t	D2
3 Tokyo Metropolitan Museum of Photography	D3

Eating	(p98)
4 Afuri	C2
Bombay Bazar	(see 22)
5 Chano-ma	A3
6 Ebisu Yokochō	C2
7 Ippo	D2
8 Ippūdō	C1
9 Ouca	C2
10 Sign	A2

Drinking & Nightlife	(p100)
11 Buri	C2
12 Ebisu 18-ban	B2
13 Ebisu Tachinomiya	C2
14 Kinfolk Lounge	A2
15 Nakame Takkyū Lounge	A2
16 What the Dickens!	C2

Entertainment	(p101)
17 Liquid Room	C1
18 Unit	A2

Shopping	(p101)
19 Daikanyama T-Site	A1
20 Kamawanu	A1
21 Koromon	A1
22 Okura	A1
23 Unlimited by Limi Feu	B1

Sports & Activities	(p102)
24 Tokyo Rent a Bike	A4
25 Yogajaya	B2

Sleeping	(p209)
26 Hotel Excellent Ebisu	C2
27 Westin Hotel Tokyo	D3

Information	(p260)
28 Tokyo British Clinic	B1

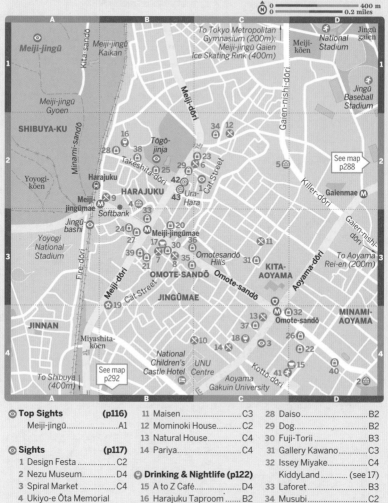

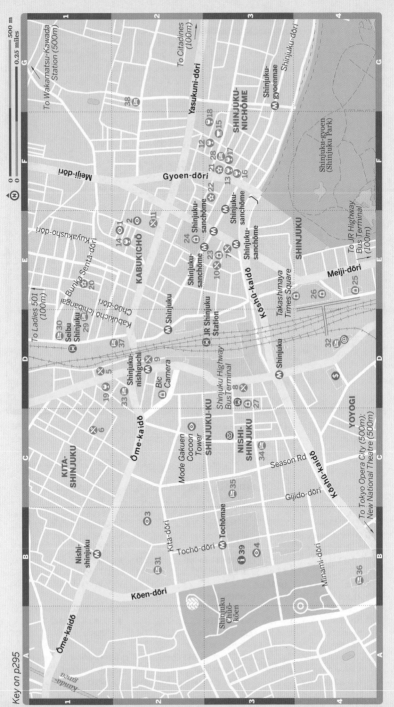

SHINJUKU

Key on p295

500 m
0.25 miles

To Wakamatsu-Kawada
Station (500m)

To Citadines
(100m)

Yasukuni-dōri

SHINJUKU-
NICHŌME

Shinjuku-
gyoemmae

Meiji-dōri

Gyoen-dōri

Shinjuku-gyoen
(Shinjuku Park)

Kuyakusho-dōri

KABUKICHŌ

Shinjuku-
sanchōme

Shinjuku-
sanchōme

Shinjuku-
sanchōme

SHINJUKU

Meiji-dōri

To JR Highway
Bus Terminal
(100m)

Bunka Senta-dōri

Chuo-dōri

Kabukicho Ichibangai

To Ladies 501
(100m)

Seibu
Shinjuku

Shinjuku

Shinjuku

Kōshū-kaidō

Takashimaya
Times Square

JR Shinjuku
Station

Shinjuku-
nishiguchi

Bic
Camera

Shinjuku Highway
Bus Terminal

Shinjuku

YOYOGI

Ōme-kaidō

Mode
Gakuen
Cocoon
Tower

SHINJUKU-KU

NISHI-
SHINJUKU

Season Rd

Kōshū-kaidō

To Tokyo Opera City (500m);
New National Theatre (500m)

KITA-
SHINJUKU

Nishi-
shinjuku

Gijido-dōri

Kita-dōri

Tochō-dōri

Tochōmae

Kōen-dōri

Shinjuku
Chūō-
kōen

Minami-dōri

Ōme-kaidō

Kanda-
gawa

SHINJUKU *Map on p294*

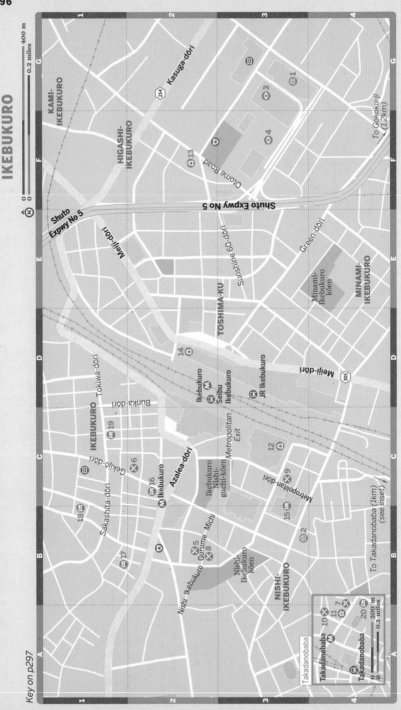

IKEBUKURO

IKEBUKURO Map on p296

AKIHABARA

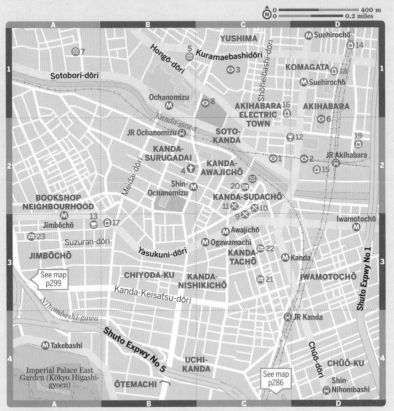

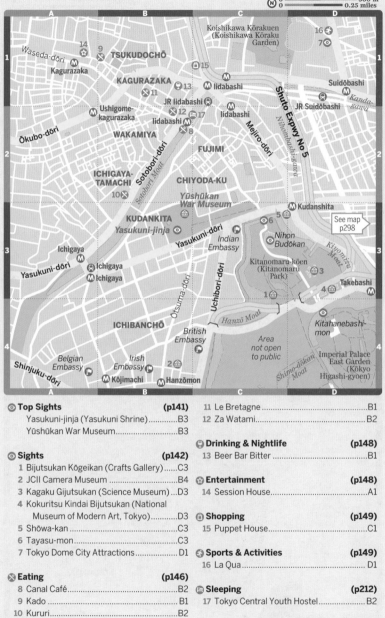

IIDABASHI & AROUND

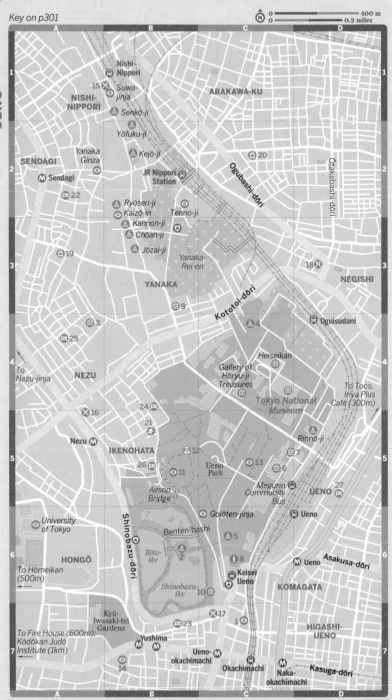

Key on p301

400 m
0.2 miles

A **B** **C** **D**

Nishi-
Nippori

15 Suwa-
jinja

NISHI-
NIPPORI

Senkō-ji

Yōfuku-ji

Yanaka
Ginza

Kejō-ji

SENDAGI

Sendagi

JR Nippori
Station

22

Ryūsen-ji

Kaizō-in

Kannon-ji

Chōan-ji

Jōzai-ji

19

YANAKA

ARAKAWA-KU

20

Tenno-ji

Yanaka-
Rei-en

Kototoi-dōri

18

NEGISHI

9

3

25

4

16

NEZU

Nezu

IKENOHATA

24

21

26

11

Aesop
Bridge

University
of Tokyo

HONGŌ

To Hōmeikan
(500m)

Shinobazu-dōri

Benten-bashi

Bōto-
ike

2

Shinobazu-
ike

Kyū-
Iwasaki-tei
Gardens

To Fire House (600m);
Kōdōkan Judō
Institute (1km)

14

Yushima

12

Ueno
Park

13

6

Gallery of
Hōryū-ji
Treasures

Heiseikan

Tokyo National
Museum

To Toco,
Iriya Plus
Café (300m)

Rinnō-ji

Uguisudani

4

Gojōten-jinja

5

8

Keisei
Ueno

10

23

17

1

Megurin
Community
Bus

Ueno

UENO

27

Ueno

Asakusa-dōri

KOMAGATA

Yushima

Ueno-
okachimachi

Okachimachi

HIGASHI-
UENO

Naka-
okachimachi

Kasuga-dōri

Ōgubashi-dōri

Ōtakebashi-dōri

To
Nezu-jinja

UENO

ASAKUSA

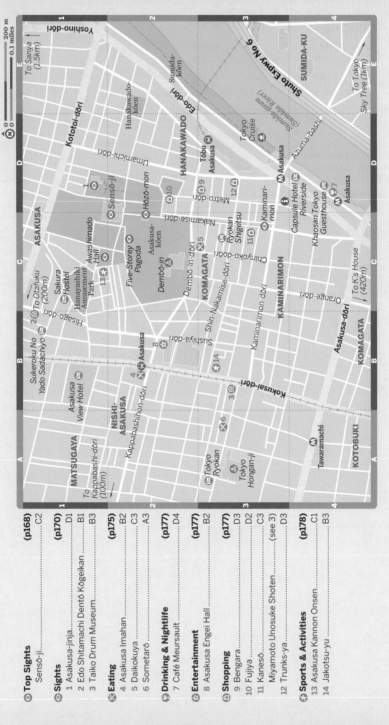

N
0 — 200 m
0 — 0.1 miles

◎ **Top Sights** (p168)
Sensō-ji..................................C2

◎ **Sights** (p170)
1 Asakusa-jinja.........................D1
2 Edo Shitamachi Dentō Kōgeikan...B1
3 Taiko Drum Museum................B3

✖ **Eating** (p175)
4 Asakusa Imahan......................B2
5 Daikokuya.............................C3
6 Sometarō..............................A3

◉ **Drinking & Nightlife** (p177)
7 Café Meursault.......................D4

✦ **Entertainment** (p177)
8 Asakusa Engei Hall..................B2

🛍 **Shopping** (p177)
9 Bengara................................D3
10 Fujiya.................................D2
11 Kanesō...............................C3
Miyamoto Unosuke Shoten......(see 3)
12 Trunks-ya...........................D3

✦ **Sports & Activities** (p178)
13 Asakusa Kannon Onsen..........C1
14 Jakotsu-yu...........................B3

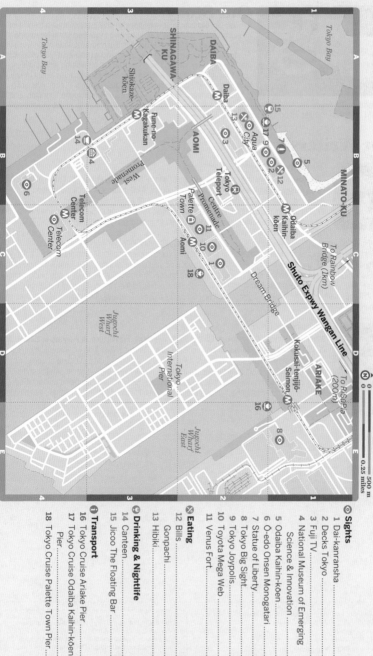

500 m
0.25 miles

Our Story

A beat-up old car, a few dollars in the pocket and a sense of adventure. In 1972 that's all Tony and Maureen Wheeler needed for the trip of a lifetime – across Europe and Asia overland to Australia. It took several months, and at the end – broke but inspired – they sat at their kitchen table writing and stapling together their first travel guide, *Across Asia on the Cheap*. Within a week they'd sold 1500 copies. Lonely Planet was born.

Today, Lonely Planet has offices in Melbourne, London and Oakland, with more than 600 staff and writers. We share Tony's belief that 'a great guidebook should do three things: inform, educate and amuse'.

Our Writers

Timothy Hornyak

Coordinating author, Marunouchi (Tokyo Station), Ginza & Tsukiji, Roppongi, Iidabashi & Northwest Tokyo, Akihabara & Around, Ueno & Around, Asakusa & Sumida River A native of Montreal, Tim moved to Japan in 1999 after watching Kurosawa's *Ran* too many times. Since then, he has written on Japanese culture, technology and history for titles including CNET News, *Scientific American* and the *New York Times*. He has played bass in a rock band in Tokyo, spoken about Japanese robots at the Kennedy Center in Washington, and travelled to the heart of Hokkaidō to find the remains of a forgotten theme park called Canadian World. As the author of *Loving the Machine: The Art and Science of Japanese Robots*, his favourite robot is Astro Boy, but he firmly believes that the greatest Japanese invention of all time is the onsen (hot springs). Tim also wrote the Welcome to Tokyo, Top Itineraries, If You Like, Tokyo Pop, Drinking & Nightlife, Entertainment, Tokyo Today, History, Architecture, Sleeping, Transport and Directory A–Z sections.

Rebecca Milner

Ebisu, Meguro & Around, Shibuya & Around, Harajuku & Aoyama, Shinjuku & West Tokyo, Odaiba & Tokyo Bay, Day Trips from Tokyo Rebecca came to Tokyo from California for 'just one year' that turned into 10. She studied at Keio University and now works as a freelance writer, covering Japan for overseas publications and interpreting American culture for Japanese publications. Rebecca also wrote the What's New, Need to Know, Month by Month, With Kids, Like a Local, For Free, Eating, Shopping, Arts and Onsen sections.

Read more about Rebecca at:
lonelyplanet.com/members/rebeccamilner

Published by Lonely Planet Publications Pty Ltd
ABN 36 005 607 983
9th edition – August 2012
ISBN 978 1 74220 040 8
© Lonely Planet 2012   Photographs © as indicated 2012
10 9 8 7 6 5
Printed in China